Founded in 1972, the Institute for Research on Public Policy is an independent, national, non-profit organization.

IRPP seeks to improve public policy in Canada by generating research, providing insight and sparking debate that will contribute to the public policy decision-making process and strengthen the quality of the public decisions made by Canadian governments, citizens, institutions and organizations.

IRPP's independence is assured by an endowment fund, to which federal and provincial governments and the private sector have contributed.

Fondé en 1972, l'Institut de recherche en politiques publiques (IRPP) est un organisme canadien, indépedent et sans but lucratif.

L'IRPP cherche à améliorer les politiques publiques canadiennes en encourageant la recherche, en menant de l'acance de nouvelles perspectives et en suscitant des débats qui contribueront au processus décisionnel en matière de politques publiques et qui rehausseront la qualité des décisions que prennent les gouvernements les citoyens. les institutions et les organismes canadiens.

L'indépendance de l'IRPP est assurée par les revenus d'un fonds de dotation auquel ont souscrit les gouvernements fédéral et provinciaux, ainsi que le secteur privé.

IRPP

Institute for
Research on
Public Policy

Institut de
recherche
en politiques
publiques

the conditions of diversity in multinational democracies

EDITED BY ALAIN-G. GAGNON, MONTSERRAT GUIBERNAU AND FRANÇOIS ROCHER

Printed in Canada
Dépôt légal 2003

Bibliothèque nationale du Québec

National Library of Canada
Cataloguing in Publication Data

The conditions of diversity in multinational democracies
edited by Alain-G. Gagnon, Montserrat Guiberneau, François Rocher.

Includes bibliographical references.
ISBN 0-88645-202-3

1. Pluralism (Social sciences). 2. Nationalism.
3. Ethnicity -- Political aspects. I. Gagnon, Alain-G. (Alain-Gustave), 1954-
II. Guiberneau, Montserrat III. Rocher, François
IV. Institute for Research on Public Policy.

JC423.C668 2003   320.54   C2003-904614-1

Suzanne Ostiguy McIntyre
Vice-president, operations

Editorial Assistant
Francesca Worrall

Copy Editing
Lesley Barry

Proofreading
Jane Broderick

Design and Production
Studio Duotone inc.

Cover Illustration
Michael Berson

Published by
The Institute for Research on Public Policy (IRPP)
L'Institut de recherche en politiques publiques
1470 Peel Street, Suite 200
Montreal, Quebec H3A 1T1

contents

part III: diversity under stress

acknowledgements

The preparation of this book was made possible by the contributions of several people. The continued support of our contributors during the many steps that went into preparing a volume of this magnitude needs to be underscored. Our thanks go to Stéphan Gervais (Quebec Studies Programme, McGill University), who assisted with the organization of the symposium entitled "The Institutional Accommodation of Diversity," which was held just after the tragic events of September 11 and gathered together most of the authors of the current volume in Saint-Marc-sur-le-Richelieu. Thanks also to Francesca Worrall (Institute for Research on Public Policy), who provided essential support with the editing of the volume.

We wish also to take this opportunity to thank Linda Cardinal, Jan Erk, Raffaele Iacovino, Daniel Latouche, Jean Le Clair, Pierre Noreau, Aristide Zolberg, Christine Straehle and James Tully, who contributed in different capacities to make the symposium a success. Along with the authors of this book, they have made diversity a notion of political value.

Finally, we would like to thank the International Quebec Studies Association (AIEQ), the Quebec government's Fonds québécois de la recherche sur la société et la culture, and the Social Sciences and Humanities Research Council of Canada for their support of the activities of UQÀM's Research Group on Multinational Societies, as well as the Institute for Research on Public Policy and its director, Hugh Segal, who believed in this project.

managing cultural differences in multinational democracies

Kenneth McRoberts

The central concept of this volume, multinational democracies, points to an important phenomenon that has yet to be fully understood by social scientists, let alone the general public. Within many established states, there continue to be entities that can credibly claim to be nations. Their roots lie not in political institutions but in social conditions such as culture, language and communication structures. Drawing upon these conditions, nationalist leaderships have fashioned conceptions of the nation that command the loyalties of large numbers of people.

"Internal Nations" versus the Nation-State

These "internal nations" stand in direct contradiction to the idea of nation that the central states have themselves articulated and which underlie their claim to be "nation-states." This nation of the nation-state is coterminous with the state and finds its clearest expression there. Indeed, it is the historical creation of the state.

Many people reject the use of "nation" to refer to internal nations within the state. They find the word provocative, even seditious. Of course, this is especially true of the leaders of central states, who tend to see the internal nations as threats to their own authority and to deny the legitimacy of such claims to nationhood. The only nation, they will argue, is the common nation to which all citizens belong, the nation of the nation-state.

There are important ambiguities surrounding the concept of internal nations. In particular, what are the boundaries? With the nation of the nation-state, the citizenship laws of the state provide clear answers as to who is a member of the nation and who is not. The internal nation may not have a central institution to perform this task. There may even be disagreement over this question among the leaders of the internal nation, with some proffering an "ethnic" definition that defines membership in terms of historical descent and others extending membership to all newcomers. Indeed, some nationalists may seek to include within the nation individuals who do not see themselves as members.

Be that as it may, the terms "multinationalism" and "internal nation" point to a reality that can be just as powerful as that of the nation-state. Few states have been able to meet the challenge posed by this reality. Rather than seeking to come to terms with their underlying multinationalism, most states simply deny its existence. In some extreme cases, states have sought to *end* the existence of their internal nations, whether through assimilation, forced emigration or outright suppression. Few of these efforts have succeeded. The Franco regime's systematic effort to eliminate the Catalan nation ended in failure. So did the British deportation of the Acadians, and the United Canada plan for securing the assimilation of French Canadians.

Nonetheless, despite the seditious overtones, these internal nations need not threaten the nation-state. At least, they may not place in question the *existence* of the nation-state or their presence within it. Within most internal nations, there is little support for secession. In many cases, simple practicality precludes any serious consideration of the idea. But even in cases where secession is practical, there may be no compelling reason to pursue it. The mere possibility of secession need not constitute a reason to seek it. Typically, the members of internal nations bear multiple identities. They have an affective or primary attachment to their nation, but they also have a sense of membership or citizenship in the larger state.

Yet, the absence of strong secessionist movements does not end the matter. Popular attachment to internal nations remains as strong ever. Nationalist leaderships are constantly seeking recognition of their existence and the creation or expansion of autonomous political structures. Still, many state leaders tend to assume that they can handle multinationalism simply by ensuring that secession appears not to be viable. Perhaps with reason, they fear that recognition or accommodation of internal nations would simply reinforce national sentiments to the point that secession is seriously considered.

As a result, in many multinational democracies political life remains hobbled by the mutual frustration of the central state and its internal nations. The frustration of the leaders of internal nations, as they vainly seek to secure recognition and structural accommodation by the state, is equalled by the frustration of central state leaders that their own idea of nation is not embraced. All manner of issues become coloured by the "national question," from social policy to immigration policy to the definition and protection of human rights. The leaders of internal nations may even contrive threats of secession in an effort to secure concessions from the state, but such threats just infuriate state leaders and the other citizenry. The challenge to multinational democracies is to find strategies and approaches that will move them beyond this sterile politics of mutual negation.

Understanding Internal Nations

Even if one limits the focus to the democracies closest at hand, in Europe and North America, a wide variety of internal nations come to mind. In Europe there are Scotland, Wales, Flanders, the Basque Country, Catalonia, Brittany and so on. In Canada there is Quebec, to be sure, but also the Acadian nation. Moreover, in Canada the compass of "internal nation" has been broadened even further with increasing reference to Aboriginal peoples as "First Nations."

It is no simple task to explain the continued strength of people's attachment to these various internal nations. For instance, one might try to root it in language. Following upon the example of Quebec, one might argue that national attachment is based on the fact that only within the national language can people fully express themselves. The same argument might also be applied to Flanders in Belgium. Indeed, each of the nations I mentioned previously does claim to possess a "national" language. Yet, in most instances, only a small minority of members of the nation actually know and can use the national language. Even where most people do speak the national language, they may be equally at ease in the language of the nation-state as a whole. For instance, Catalan and Spanish are sufficiently similar that Catalans can switch quite readily between the two. The other internal nations all feature major movements to restore the national language, but this concern with language seems to be the result of national sentiment, rather than its cause.

Another approach would be to root the persistence of these internal nations in conditions of economic deprivation and subordination. Thus, a well-known study of Welsh nationalism uses the concept of the "internal colony" to construct a general theory of nationalism.[1] Yet, however well this approach might explain the case of Wales, or Brittany for that matter, it can hardly account for Catalonia and the Basque Country, which, historically, have been the dynamic centres of the Spanish economy. There, national sentiment would have to be explained in terms of resentment over ways in which the central state can prevent the internal nations from fully capitalizing on their economic superiority. The fact that national sentiment can be strong under so widely disparate economic conditions suggests that the explanation must lie elsewhere than in economic structures.

Another approach would be to root the continuing power of internal nations in distinct national histories. Yet, what makes historical experience distinct? In large part, it is the idea of nation and the uses to which it is put by nationalist leaderships that produce a distinctive understanding of history. It is as if national sentiment creates history, rather than the opposite.

If we cannot readily explain the continuing dynamic of national sentiment in terms of any single factor, we can at least identify themes that are common to the demands that internal nations make on the central states. First and foremost, they are seeking recognition of their very existence. There can be no more important form of recognition than the central state's acknowledgement that it houses nations within. Recognition may be a matter of political discourse. After all, British politicians routinely refer to the Welsh and Scottish "nations"; Canadian politicians now talk of Aboriginal "First Nations." But it may also entail formal constitutional recognition, as with the Meech Lake Accord's recognition of Quebec as a "distinct society." The importance of this need for recognition can be seen in the reaction of Quebec francophones to the failure of the Accord. Resentment and anger produced a surge of support for Quebec independence so strong that the Quebec government almost secured a mandate for sovereignty in its 1995 referendum. At the same time, the Spanish constitution demonstrates the apprehension that, rightly or wrongly, state elites have about granting such recognition. Despite the demand of the three historic nations, the Basque Country, Catalonia and Galicia, that they be referred to as nations, the constitution dubs them "nationalities" and, for good measure, declares that the Spanish state is indissoluble.

Institutional Accommodation of Internal Nations

Almost always, the demands of internal nations on the central state go beyond mere recognition, however essential that may be. If only for protection against the hostile actions of other citizens, or the central state itself, these nations will also look for political arrangements that give them some form of autonomy. Devising such arrangements is the greatest challenge facing multinational democracies.

The literature of political science is replete with methods and techniques by which the central state may accommodate the demands of groups. Yet, few methods are adequate to the task of accommodating internal nations' demands for both recognition and autonomy.

These days, the most commonly espoused formula for accommodating cultural difference is "multiculturalism." At heart, multiculturalism constitutes a means of *recognizing* cultural diversity. It may also foster state policies that support and help to maintain this diversity. However generous the impulses that animate it, multiculturalism cannot respond to internal nations. Indeed, it is quite inimical to them.

As the term has become commonly used, multiculturalism seeks to recognize a vast array of differences, ranging from the cultural specificity of ethnic groups to the differences among generations to the variety of sexual orientations. In effect, it has come to embrace most forms of difference within a society. Yet, the concept of nation denotes a collectivity that also is marked by social diversity. To the extent that multiculturalism recognizes and celebrates myriad forms of diversity, effectively assigning equal weight and status to all, it undermines the bases of internal nations. It is difficult to see how multiculturalism can accommodate the underlying multinationalism of a state. In effect, it would seem to deny the existence of "internal nations," or at least to reduce them to one more form of difference.[2]

This fundamental contradiction between multiculturalism and multinationalism is commonly ignored, or even denied, in scholarly literature. Indeed, a recent study proposes that Canada should be understood as, at the same time, both multicultural and multinational.[3] To be sure, one could conceive multiculturalism within a multinational framework. It would denote diversity *within* a state's internal nations. But the task would still remain of accommodating multinationalism itself.

Another commonly cited scheme for accommodating diversity is consociationalism.[4] The term refers to methods of elite accommodation through which representatives of the various "subcultures" within a state bargain the terms of state policy. The scheme provides a certain degree of recognition for subcultures within the structures of the state. But, by definition, it does not provide autonomy for them. All the processes of accommodation occur within the state itself. Of course, the very term "subcultures" falls far short of the import of "internal nations."

Decentralization of central state structures so that they can adapt to the particularity of internal nations might constitute a tacit recognition of the existence of these nations. But it does not provide the nations themselves within any degree of autonomy.

The Contradictions of Federalism

A scheme that could provide internal nations with genuine autonomy is, of course, federalism. Under federalism, the terms of autonomy are specified and guaranteed within a constitution, reserving certain functions for the exclusive use of the units that compose the federation. Yet, federalism need not provide internal nations with any degree of *recognition*. In many federations the various units are understood to be based upon purely territorial divisions rather than any cultural, let alone "national," differences among the population. There, the rationale for federalism lies in protecting individual citizens from excessive intrusion by the central state or creating political units that are sufficiently small to facilitate a healthy democratic life. This is an entirely different rationale from multinationalism.

In some cases, federalism *is* based on multinationalism. Belgium and India come to mind: *all* the various units may be openly recognized as based on national or at least cultural differences. But what if, as in Canada, there is a compelling reason for some units to be based instead upon territory? Conceivably, a federation could incorporate both principles: territorialism and multinationalism. Some units would be understood as territorial in nature whereas others would be based upon internal nations. There would have to be some differentiation between the two types of units; the units based on internal nations would need to be recognized as such. Moreover, since they would be concerned with protecting or strengthening the "nation," with its distinctive language and culture, they would in all likelihood need powers additional to those afforded on a purely territorial basis. In effect, the federation would have to be asymmetrical, affording special arrangements for the units that are nations.

As it happens, there is now an abundant literature on the role that asymmetrical federalism can play in accommodating multinationalism.[5] Yet, the Canadian experience points to real difficulties in arranging and maintaining such a federation. It can be readily argued that the Canadian federation was founded on an asymmetrical basis. It was largely because of the insistence of francophone leaders in Quebec that Canada was established on a federal basis. The rationale for the province of Quebec was clearly one of protecting cultural, indeed national, difference. The rest of the federation developed on an essentially territorial basis. In the areas of language and civil law, the *British North America Act* provided for different arrangements in Quebec and the rest of Canada.

During the 1960s, the Quebec government sought to build on these asymmetrical assumptions by securing functions that, in the rest of Canada, were exercised by the federal government. Initially, under the Liberal government of Lester Pearson, this formula was applied in a good number of areas. By the late 1960s, under the leadership of Pierre Trudeau, these arrangements were being phased out on the assumption that Quebec must be treated as a province "like the others." In the late 1980s, the overwhelming rejection of the "distinct society" clause outside Quebec confirmed that for most anglophone Canadians federalism can only be territorial. All provinces, Quebec included, must have the same powers.[6]

The fact of the matter is that there are very few cases of federations that are at the same time territorial and multinational.[7] Indeed, federalism may be unable to handle internal nations if at the same time it is handling territorial divisions elsewhere in the state. In other words, it may difficult to sustain a federation that is based on competing principles.

Over the years, the predominant argument against asymmetrical federalism was framed in terms of the functioning of Parliament. Widely known as the West Lothian question, after the MP who raised it in the British Parliament, the argument asks what is to be the status of MPs from units that enjoy additional powers when bills are debated that do not apply to that unit. The same argument was regularly raised by Trudeau. Still, in Canada, Quebec MPs were not excluded from voting on legislation creating the Canada Pension Plan, even though it did not apply in Quebec. Indeed, two Quebec MPs (Monique Bégin and Marc Lalonde) have been ministers responsible for administering the Canada Pension Plan.

In point of fact, the obstacles may be more purely political. In part, they may involve peoples outside the internal nations for whom the only nation is indeed the nation-state. I have already noted how the Meech Lake Accord debacle demonstrated the refusal of Canadians based outside Quebec to accept that Canadian federalism could at the same time be both territorial and multinational. Beyond that, there is the natural tendency of central states to want to treat all units in a uniform manner. This is especially the case for state bureaucracies, which see asymmetry as a challenge to their own legitimacy. This was clearly a factor in the dismantling of Canada's 1960s asymmetry. By the same token, in both Canada and Spain there have been instances of central officials actively seeking to reduce existing levels of asymmetry by encouraging other units to adopt the same measures. Finally, units of the federation whose rationale is purely territorial may well view unfavourably any concessions to the governments of the internal nations. Such concessions may be seen as slights to their own status and prestige, and they may want to seek the same concessions for themselves.

Devolution and Multinationalism

Considerations such as these suggest that devolution may be a more effective method of accommodating multinationalism, at least when not all parts of the country see themselves first as members of internal nations. Under devolution, arrangements are made specifically for the internal nations; the rest of the state remains unitary. There is no competition between national and territorial units. For that matter, it is quite practical to vary these accommodations from nation to nation.

These days, the most striking instance of such devolution is, of course, the United Kingdom. Under the *Scotland Act* of 1998, the Scottish Parliament was granted authority over a wide range of matters, including health, education, justice and economic development. Despite initial speculation that Scotland was on the "fast track" to independence, financed by North Sea oil royalties and facilitated by integration with the European Union, the independence movement has stalled. The new set of responsibilities appears to be more than enough to occupy Scotland's political class. However feasible Scottish independence may be, there is no inexorable drive to achieve it. In the case of the other beneficiary of devolution, Wales, the new powers are much less extensive. Independence is not even feasible, let alone the focus of major political movement.

Yet, the relative success of devolution in the British case points to the underlying role of another factor in the politics of multinationalism: political culture. This accommodation of multinationalism was possible precisely because multinationalism itself has a legitimacy that it does not have in such states as Canada or Spain. This can be seen in the long-standing practices of organizing distinct sporting teams for Scotland and Wales, issuing Scottish currency through the Bank of Scotland and structuring the military along national lines. In fact, Britain's political leadership regularly uses the term "nation" to refer to Scotland and Wales.

Conclusions

In sum, the institutional accommodation of multinationalism is very much a work in progress, not just operationally but conceptually. In recent years, social scientists have been most effective in signalling the importance of multinationalism. However, they have yet to address satisfactorily the institutional implications of this phenomenon. Meanwhile, most of the world's multinational democracies remain locked in mutual incomprehension. Leaders in the central state insist that the only nation is the one that they represent, while the leaders of internal nations steadfastly proclaim that only they speak for "true" nations, and can usually mobilize the popular support to prove it.

Notes

1. Hechter (1975).

2. This argument is developed in McRoberts (2001, pp. 703-7).

3. Kymlicka (1998, p. 62).

4. Lijphart (1977).

5. Resnick (1994), Kymlicka (2001) and Requejo (unpublished).

6. The argument of these last two paragraphs is elaborated in McRoberts (1997), chapters 2 and 6.

7. In McRoberts (2001, p. 701) I argue that Canada is the only such case.

Bibliography

Hechter, Michael. *Internal Colonialism: The Celtic Fringe in British National Development, 1536-1966.* Berkeley: University of California Press, 1975.

Kymlicka, Will. *Finding Our Way: Rethinking Ethnocultural Relations in Canada.* Toronto: Oxford University Press, 1998.

———. "Minority Nationalism and Multination Federalism," in *Politics in the Vernacular: Nationalism, Multiculturalism and Citizenship,* ed. Will Kymlicka. Oxford: Oxford University Press, 2001.

Lijphart, Arend. *Democracy in Plural Societies: A Comparative Exploration.* New Haven: Yale University Press, 1977.

McRoberts, Kenneth. *Misconceiving Canada: The Struggle for National Unity.* Toronto: Oxford University Press, 1997.

———. "Canada and the Multinational State." *Canadian Journal of Political Science,* Vol. 14, no. 4 (December 2001): 703-7.

Requejo, Ferran. "Federalism and the Quality of Democracy in Plurinational Contexts: Present Shortcomings and Possible Improvements. The Case of Catalonia." Unpublished paper.

Resnick, Philip. "Toward a Multinational Federation: Asymmetrical and Confederal Alternatives," in *Seeking a New Canadian Partnership: Asymmetrical and Confederal Options,* ed. F. Leslie Seidle. Montreal: Institute for Research on Public Policy, 1994.

introduction

1

the conditions of diversity in multinational democracies

Alain-G. Gagnon
Montserrat Guibernau
François Rocher

Most Western nation-states include more than one nation within their territory. However, very few define themselves as being multinational. In a similar manner, Western nation-states are liberal democracies but almost all of them acknowledge the existence of a single *demos* within their territory. As a consequence of this, small nations or parts of nations within their boundaries, while representing a minority, are always politically dependent on the democratic will of a majority since they are not recognized as a separate *demos*.

This book is concerned with diversity in multinational democracies. In particular it considers the theoretical, institutional and legal conditions for the development of nations without states or with partial statehood that are included within the boundaries of larger political institutions. It rejects claims that strengthening democratic nationalisms of nations without a state of their own poses a threat to the stability of the nation-state and is anachronistic and a sign of backwardness. In our view, one should be wary of theories that label substate or minority nationalism as tribal, while they legitimize state nationalism. From this perspective, the "nationalists" are always the "other people," those who "generate trouble," "show dissatisfaction," "pose a threat to the state's integrity" and "question the state's legitimacy." Using the term "tribal" to describe the nationalism of nations without states disregards two crucial points.

First, contemporary forms of nationalism differ substantially from the classical nationalism that contributed to the consolidation of the nation-state in the nineteenth and early twentieth centuries. A sizable number of the nationalisms now gaining salience in nations without states or with partial statehood are grounded upon the defence of democracy and collective rights and are intimately connected with the transformations brought about by globalization – Catalonia, Quebec and Scotland are cases in point. Such nationalisms have developed within multinational democracies and claim the right to develop freely their nation's specificity within a framework of respect and tolerance.[1]

Not all substate forms of nationalism are democratic, and it is vital to distinguish between those based upon democratic principles and those defending an ethnocentric world view grounded upon mechanisms of exclusion, which often involve the use of force. At present, sufficient numbers of democratic minority nationalist movements are emerging in multinational democracies for the social sciences to reflect on them as a distinct phenomenon deserving particular attention.

Second, trotting out the term "tribalization" to refer to the resurgence of all types of substate nationalism is itself anachronistic: it reveals an inability to recognize the connections between the recent rise of substate forms of nationalism and current changes affecting the nation-state system.

Nationalism has traditionally been an uncomfortable topic for social scientists. In the nineteenth and early twentieth centuries we encounter numerous examples of great scholars who paid scant attention to what clearly was one of the major political forces of their time. As Montserrat Guibernau has shown elsewhere, Max Weber, a German nationalist himself, never provided a systematic theory of nationalism. Émile Durkheim and Karl Marx predicted that nationalism would soon disappear.[2] Instead, nationalism has played a key role in the modern age, and it is currently manifesting as a potent force. However, it has often been portrayed in intellectual circles as a sign of backwardness and, as a doctrine, as opposing the cosmopolitan ideal once formulated by Immanuel Kant.[3] Such uneasiness toward nationalism stems from its emotional dimension, which clearly differs from the ideal of rationality defended by the *philosophes* that has, up to now, remained unquestioned. On these grounds, indiscriminate rejection of substate nationalism should be carefully assessed, since it often hides strong forms of state nationalism.

The eighteenth-century concept of popular sovereignty was designed for the "people as a whole." When the revolutionaries in France stated that the principle of sovereignty resides essentially in the nation, they may be taken to have asserted that the nation was more than the king and the aristocracy. National self-determination turned out to be one of the most prominent interpretations of popular sovereignty.

The new ideas of the *philosophes*, emphasizing the cult of liberty and equality and, in particular, the idea of state power rooted in popular consent, were initially applied to the construction and consolidation of the nation-state. Nowadays, democratic nationalist movements in what are frequently termed nations without states invoke the principle of consent and the idea of popular sovereignty to legitimate their claims for self-determination, a concept that is subject to significantly different interpretations. The idea of self-determination has the capacity to challenge the nation-state as a political institution that, in most cases, is based on a cultural and political homogenization of its citizens that is indifferent to internal diversity.

A multinational democracy is a specific type of nation-state that defines itself as democratic and contains a significant degree of internal diversity. At the present time, a large number of nations without states included within multinational democracies are struggling to become global political actors, to provide their members with a strong sense of identity and to make it possible for them to be more active in the political life of their communities. It is our contention that in doing so they contribute to the revitalization of civil society, encourage civic cohesion and reinforce democratic practices.

Themes and Contributions

This book is divided into three parts. Part 1 explores the theoretical conditions of diversity in multinational democracies. Ferran Requejo examines value pluralism as a theoretical perspective of democratic liberalism that, in the case of multinational federations, has at least two advantages over its rivals. First, concerning political liberalism, value pluralism allows us to investigate and constitutionally define individual and collective freedom as well as mutual recognition between different national *demoi* in a more open manner. Second, regarding federalism, it facilitates the application of the liberal and federal logic of the pact when establishing the content of self-government, shared rule and reform processes by diverse national groups that are unable to display any type of normative hierarchy among themselves. Requejo concludes that adopting a perspective of value pluralism may contribute to the accommodation of national pluralism in contemporary liberal democracies. In his view, the experimental nature of federalism continues to be one of its biggest advantages.

Jocelyn Maclure assesses the new meaning of ideas of the nation and the nationalist project and calls for a redefinition of the nation's social imaginary in conditions of deep pluralism. In challenging the understanding of the nation revolving around the idea of commonness, it is important to stress that difference is intrinsic to identity and that identity always contains a trace of alterity. In other words, all nations are made of communities and minorities of different kinds, and all of these groups are segmented by internal diversity and linked to other communities through individuals who uphold multiple "belongings." Nevertheless, the nation remains a source of collective identification. However, rather than being founded on the definition of a "thick" identity, the driving force of the new nationalism is primarily democratic. The sense of belonging is maintained within the nation's internal heterogeneity by the participation of and interaction between diverse citizens who might disagree on the rules and substance of the political association. In this context, the conditions of integration and co-operation in pluricultural and multinational democracies must be examined. Maclure concludes that "the idea of 'commonness' can no longer suture the general economy of nationalism." Nations have to be viewed "as plurivocal and dissensual communities of conversation, self-interpretation and self-determination."

Michel Seymour investigates the objections of most liberal philosophers and political scientists to adopting a politics of recognition for minorities. He presents a reformulation of liberal theory that encompasses collective rights and in which political recognition of diversity can be achieved by rejecting the primacy of ethical individualism without falling prey to reification, essentialism, communitarianism, collectivism or authoritarianism.

Seymour argues for the recognition of collective rights alongside individual rights. In his view, liberal philosophers defend the absolute priority of individual rights and liberties, but they do not realize that, in the context of a multinational state, other fundamental rights equally deserve our attention. It is his contention that "[i]ndividual rights and liberties are fundamental and cannot be overruled by any other principles, but this does not mean that all other principles must be subordinated to individual rights and liberties, for there are also collective rights that are fundamental and cannot be overruled by any other principles. We must endorse a fundamental pluralistic axiology and try to reach a balance between individual and collective rights."

Roderick Macdonald approaches the study of the conditions of diversity in multinational democracies from a legal perspective. He observes that two centuries ago the homogeneity of the relatively small percentage of the population considered to be full citizens meant that competing narratives never surfaced as subjects of public debate. This assertion reveals the struggle for recognition at a time when gender, lack of wealth, religion, social class and ethnicity were excuses for exclusion from political participation. It took more than two centuries for these obstacles to be overcome by Western democracies. Only in the second half of the twentieth century, when the principle of equality between individuals had been accepted, did concerns about collective rights enter the philosophical and political debate.

Seymour points out the need to recognize collective rights, Requejo invokes value pluralism as a principle to be included in federal structures and Maclure advocates citizen participation as a mechanism to develop a sentiment of belonging to a free people or federation of free peoples. In turn, Macdonald stands for a legal pluralistic framework of a radically nonpositivist nature. Law's legitimacy, according to Macdonald, stems from it being the "product of a reciprocal construction within subjects and among subjects acting through the momentary configuration and momentary narration of imposed inherited and chosen institutions." He challenges republican legal theory in favour of legal pluralist theory because, in the end, legal pluralism rejects any theory that places an external determination on the boundaries of law and legal orders. Legal pluralism deals with identity by posing the question of how people recognize their diverse identities in law, thus often contesting official interpretations. In this sense, legal pluralism is clearly an emancipatory practice.

Part 2 offers a comparative politics approach to the study of the institutional conditions of diversity. Catalonia, Quebec, Scotland and the Basque Country are considered in detail, through examinations of the nature of their national identities, nationalist movements, status and degrees of recognition attained within the nation-states within which they are included, and the nature of their political demands.

Montserrat Guibernau establishes a clear-cut distinction between the concepts of state, nation, nation-state and nationalism and focuses on the attributes of nations without states or, as she defines them, cultural communities attached to a specific territory and lacking a state of their own. She presents the political and cultural arguments currently employed by nations without states to legitimize their discourses in the quest for recognition. Using Catalonia as a case study, Guibernau shows that opposing conceptions of the state and the nation coexisted during the Spanish Civil War (1936-39) and the 40 years of Franco's dictatorship, and that there was an attempt to reconcile the two concepts in the transition to democracy and decentralization of Spain. In her view, the optimism experienced by many Catalans during the early stages of the democratic transition, when a new Statute for Catalonia (1979) was ratified and the Catalan government was re-established, stands in sharp contrast to the present feeling of stagnation concerning the evolution of Catalan autonomy, which is expressed in the demands for greater self-rule advanced by the main political parties of Catalan origin. The once dialogic attitudes of large sections of the Spanish political class in the 1970s and early 1980s have been replaced by the neocentralist, neoliberal and neoconservative policies of the Popular Party government that has ruled Spain with a majority since March 2000. These new attitudes are undermining the institutional conditions of diversity agreed to by all Spaniards at the beginning of the transition to democracy.

The symmetrical model of decentralization implemented in Spain contrasts with the asymmetrical model applied in Britain, where Scotland's Parliament enjoys greater powers than the Welsh National Assembly or the Northern Ireland Assembly. David McCrone refers to Britain as a multinational state that until 1999 had a unitary legislature and within which Scotland retained and developed its institutional autonomy in legal, educational and religious matters. He rejects federalism as a feasible option for the UK and signals that, at present, virtually all depends on pressure from below. Support for Scottish independence, always higher among the working class than the middle class, has grown steadily over the last 20 years and reached its peak at the time of the referendum in 1997, when 59 percent thought that independence was likely to come about, regardless of their own personal preferences. McCrone argues that devolution has firmed up Scottish national identity and contributed to the idea that the Scottish Parliament should enjoy more powers. Devolution has also been conducive to the debate about the nature of English identity as distinct from British identity, after many years during which the two were conflated.

In their chapter on culture and identity in Europe, John Loughlin and Michael Keating note that European integration rejects any attempt at creating a homogeneous *demos* with a single culture, language and identity. Quite the opposite, cultural diversity is a fundamental principle of this process. Moreover, European integration has encouraged awareness of regional diversity. Despite this, one may observe a pattern of convergence in terms of language (English becoming the lingua franca of Europe), politics and administration. Indeed, these dynamic factors of convergence, influenced by state restructuring, European integration and globalization, have had important impacts on regions and other subnational levels of government. One can see in the literature that analyzes the regional question in this new context a recognition of the importance of the subnational in terms of both policy-making and democratic practice. The authors state that "the current new regionalism is distinguished by a combination of elements previously thought incompatible: the presence of a regional culture, language and identity is now considered to have a positive relationship with economic development rather than the reverse; political autonomy is now considered important in the context of a wider, competitive Europe."

To explore the various forms of the new regionalism, the authors chose the method of comparative case studies, looking at the same factors in each of eight regions in four countries (France, Spain, Belgium and the United Kingdom). Whether or not there is an emerging Europe of the Regions, the fact is that regions can no longer rely simply on the nation-states to protect and sustain them. The downside of the new regionalism is that competitive regionalism may strengthen strong regions and undermine weak regions. Nonetheless, this process is also a validation of particular regional histories, cultures, languages and identities, these being viewed as assets rather than hindrances to development. Loughlin and Keating stress that institutions and political leadership are both important. Regional governments, where they exist, do matter, not only in fulfilling the tasks of mobilization and collective action but also in providing a symbolic legitimacy to the region as a political space. In that political dynamic, leadership plays a crucial role. They conclude by underlining that regions are now key sites of social and economic regulation.

Stephen Tierney explores the legal accommodation of national minorities in the UK and Canada. He argues that constitutional disputes involving national minorities may end up questioning the overall cultural and, by extension, political neutrality of a constitution, whether in substantive or procedural terms, since the courts having to adjudicate can be seen as an instrument of the dominant culture. Tierney studies the decision of the Canadian Supreme Court in the *Secession Reference* case, highlighting in particular the four organizing and fundamental principles addressed by the Court when issuing its verdict: federalism, democracy, constitutionalism and the rule of law, and respect for minorities, none of which "trump or exclude the operation of any other." He stresses that the Supreme Court's decision broke new ground by conceding that, in certain circumstances, a group may secede by means of a "constitutional" process where the constitution makes no provision for secession. Never before has a domestic constitutional court reached such a decision. For Tierney, this decision reflects a strong relationship between constitutionalism and democracy, an approach that replaces the traditional, isolated-framework vision of constitutions as monolithic structures that cannot be open to amendment. Tierney also points to the questions that remained unanswered by the Court: in a Quebec referendum on independence, what is to be understood as a "clear" question and a "clear" majority, and what are the rights and duties of all parties to and within a subsequent process of negotiation?

François Rocher and Nadia Verrelli offer a more critical approach to the study of the *Secession Reference*. Instead of focusing on its path-breaking aspects, as Tierney does, they analyze its ambiguity, which in part enabled the federal government to usurp the principle of constitutional democracy with the *Clarity Act*, or the *Bill to Give Effect to the Requirement for Clarity Set Out by the Supreme Court in the Secession Reference* (C-20). Their analysis of the *Clarity Act* and the responses to it from the media and academia in both English and French Canada show how the bill "focuses not on how to reconcile unity through diversity but on how to 'deal' with Quebec by rendering its constitutional aspirations nearly impossible."

Part 3 contains four chapters that offer various examples of diversity under stress. Peter Kraus refers to the constraints placed on national minorities as the EU deepens and widens its scope. André Lecours and Luis Moreno examine paradiplomacy as a strategy employed by some nations without states, such as the Basque Country, to promote their national identity abroad, thus breaking the nation-state's monopoly over international relations. Alain-G. Gagnon considers how the promotion of pan-Canadianism strengthens Canada's state nationalism and applies renewed pressure on national diversity within the Canadian federation. Martin Papillon and Luc Turgeon compare the emergence of citizenship regimes in Quebec and Scotland. The four chapters illustrate the difficulties experienced by some nations without states and with partial statehood that are willing to develop their identities and seek cultural and political recognition within the domestic and the international arena.

Peter Kraus argues that the EU protects the national interests and culture of the nation-states forming it and relegates national minorities to second place, largely dependent on the nation-state's will. Within the EU 's institutional setting, this is exemplified by the tension between intergovernmentalism and transnationalism. The former emphasizes the significance of the member states' national cultures, while the latter may encourage the articulation of cultural identities below and beyond the nation-state level and contribute to a new political configuration of identity options. Kraus paints a bleak picture concerning the recognition of national minorities within the EU: in his view, EU decision-making procedures prioritize "equality of states above equality of citizens." Nevertheless, the tension between intergovernmentalism and transnationalism entails a politically productive momentum, keeping things in motion. Thus, the political context of the EU forces the nation-states, that want to see their own identitities receiving institutional protection, to adopt a more open stance toward identity claims raised by nonstate actors.

André Lecours and Luis Moreno reflect on the new prominence achieved by the international activity of regional government's paradiplomacy in the 1990s as a result of both domestic and international changes. It is their contention that while a connection could be established between federalism and paradiplomacy, nationalism is the most important variable conditioning paradiplomacy. The reasons for this derive from paradiplomacy's ability to function as a means for identity construction and consolidation leading to nation-building; as an instrument to promote and sustain specific interest definitions such as cultural preservation; and as a tool for political-territorial mobilization. The theoretical analysis of paradiplomacy is illustrated with an account of the international activities of the Basque Country's government as a case study.

Alain-G. Gagnon challenges the view of many Canadians that minority nationalism poses a threat to political stability and endangers democratic practices. This view ignores the destabilizing effects of the Canadian federal government's attempts to superimpose a pan-Canadian sense of nationhood and to present substate nationhood simply as folkloric expression if not an altogether subversive practice. Gagnon investigates three policy fields: the Social Union Framework Agreement, the Canadian *Charter of Rights and Freedoms*, and international relations, and reveals a growing tendency on the part of the federal government to increase its presence in provincial matters, to restrict the representative role of the provinces in shaping domestic policy and to limit their ability to conduct foreign relations. Gagnon argues that since the 1995 referendum, Ottawa has launched a series of initiatives with the intention of further limiting Quebec's presence in international forums, thus applying a "politics of containment" that places the national diversity exemplified by Quebec under great stress.

Martin Papillon and Luc Turgeon highlight the complex relationship between nationality, state and citizenship and argue that small nations such as Quebec and Scotland are engaged in struggles for the control of the citizenship regime as a tool to refine political boundaries between communities. They suggest that, in both Canada and the UK, the citizenship regime was never fully centralized at the time that the welfare state was being consolidated. This is significant, since the welfare state played a key role in reinforcing both practices "from within" by opening up a debate about the nature and boundaries of communities of solidarity and regimes of access to the state, a process that led to competing definitions of solidarity and community in Scotland and Quebec. The definition of Quebec citizenship emerged in the post-1995 referendum period and was defined in opposition to its federal counterpart as a tool to consolidate solidarity and cohesion from within. Postdevolution Scotland has not witnessed a similar development thus far. In Papillon and Turgeon's view this may be explained by Scotland's multilevel structure, where its status as a nation is recognized within Britain and the EU. Building distinct citizenship regimes from within may provide a third way between independence and assimilation.

The contributions in this book offer a multidisciplinary approach to the theoretical and empirical challenges faced by minority nations included within multinational democracies. They open up new avenues of inquiry centred around the analysis of the political communities emerging in the age of globalization. This book assesses progress being made by some nations without states and those with partial statehood that have acquired various degrees of autonomy in recent years, but it also warns against the tendency of some Western nation-states to oppose or even reverse the processes of recognizing cultural and political diversity within their boundaries.

Notes

1. For a series of such cases, see Gagnon and Tully (2001).

2. Guibernau (1996, chapter 1).

3. Kant (1996).

Bibliography

Gagnon, Alain-G., and James Tully, eds. *Multinational Democracies*. Cambridge: Cambridge University Press, 2001.

Guibernau, Montserrat. *Nationalisms*. Cambridge: Polity Press, 1996.

Kant, Immanuel. "Toward Perpetual Peace" (1795), in *Practical Philosophy*. Cambridge: Cambridge University Press, 1996.

part I
theoretical conditions of diversity

2

value pluralism and multinational federalism

Ferran Requejo

Je hay toute sorte de tyrannie, et de la parliere, et l'effectuelle.
Montaigne, *Essais, Book III, VIII*

Federalism is designed to prevent tyranny without preventing governance.
Daniel Elazar, *Exploring Federalism*

The debate that has taken place over the past decade as to whether liberal democracies are suitably equipped, from a normative and institutional point of view, to deal with cultural pluralism has revealed both the need to revise the way that liberal democracies perceive their own universalist normativity in an increasingly globalized world and the need for liberal democracies to update a number of their institutions. This debate has also shown the cultural limits of traditional liberal theories and the partiality of the theoretical interpretations and practical applications of values such as freedom, equality, autonomy, pluralism and dignity in liberal-democratic multinational federalism.

This paper is mainly concerned with the notion of value pluralism in liberal multinational federations. In the first section I present value pluralism as a theory of the structure of moral normativity in liberal democracies. I defend the greater suitability of value pluralism over its rival theories when one is attempting to revise democratic liberalism from the perspective of the cultural, national and normative pluralism of present-day democracies. In the second section, I link value pluralism with multinational federations in order to discuss the suitability of establishing the recognition of national pluralism, a plurinational division of powers, the participation in the processes of constitutional reform and the constitutional regulation of the right of self-determination, following the 1998 decision of the Canadian Supreme Court in the reference case regarding the secession of Quebec.

Liberal Democracy and Value Pluralism

Two General Observations

Let us start with two general observations. First, when one is attempting to "improve" liberal democracies, both ethically and functionally, in relation to cultural and national pluralism, two strategies may be used:

a) In the first, we place ourselves within the theoretical tradition of political liberalism in order to be able to point out the limits, biases, prejudices and partial interpretations that it displays both in its ethical, anthropological and constitutional aspects and in its institutional aspects – such as federalism. This perspective allows us to carry out a theoretical revision in order to refine liberal values themselves and the legitimation of democracies, and it permits us to put forward a number of proposals for practical reform that are more suitable for refining liberal values. The aim of these refinements and reforms is to achieve a higher degree of accommodation of cultural and national pluralism within contemporary societies.[1]

b) In the second, we use liberal tradition as one of many possible approaches to building democratic polities that go beyond Western liberalism and that are more in tune with the normative, linguistic, historical and cultural diversity of contemporary societies.

In terms of political theory, the first strategy attempts to create a liberal theory of cultural pluralism (or multiculturalism) and national pluralism. The second strategy is designed to produce a more ambitious multicultural theory of democracy and political liberalism.[2]

The second general observation is that it is possible to identify four general types of theory, including liberalism, in relation to how they understand the internal structure of moral normativity – in other words, its basic ontology: 1) monist theories; 2) culturally pluralist theories; 3) pluralist theories without fully rank-ordered values (value pluralism); and 4) pluralist theories with fully rank-ordered values.

By monist theories I mean those that argue for one way of life as preferable to any other, based on a value that is considered to be a priority. Moral monism normally understands its position to be the most "rational" or "human" and of universal application, both for the members of any given collective and for humanity as a whole. This position is usually based on a conception of human nature that is given a moral-ontological superiority over any differences in cultural origin that individuals or groups display. The good life cannot be lived differently to that which is defended, and there are no equivalent good ways of life (for example, Plato and usual interpretations of monotheistic religions). In contrast, culturally pluralist theories establish the impossibility of any anthropology (or ethics) that fails to take into account the cultural characteristics that define individuals and groups. Inevitably, any conception of the good way of life will depend more on the particular cultures of a given group of individuals than on any characteristics that may be shared by all of them. Humanity itself and its moral answers are plural. Cultures and their particular "centres of gravity" (this phrase comes from Herder) are normally understood here to mean autonomous, global, separate, valuable, static and more or less homogeneous groups that should be preserved by each collective (see, for example, Vico and Herder).

On the other hand, pluralist theories without fully rank-ordered values, or value pluralism, defend the existence of a multiplicity of heterogeneous values that cannot be reduced to a single value nor to a permanent and universal order of priority for all individuals and for all cases (Isaiah Berlin is obviously the main reference here).[3] Finally, pluralist theories with fully rank-ordered values accept both the heterogeneity of a series of values that cannot be reduced to a single value and the possibility of establishing a permanent and universal priority of these heterogeneous values for all individuals (for example, the lexicographical priority between Rawls' two principles). In this sense, these theories refer once again to a kind of conception of human nature and rationality. It is important to point out that political liberalism has mainly been based, philosophically speaking, both on monist principles and on pluralist principles with or without a fixed ranking of values. These positions are logically mutually exclusive in philosophical terms.

From now on, we will focus on the first strategy described above and value pluralism (type 3 of the theories). This strategy, of the internal revision of a liberalism, is adopted based on our general interest in the revision and reform of liberal federalism in multinational contexts. The objective is twofold: to improve the normative perspective of liberalism when there is more than one national *demos* within a single democracy, and to establish a more suitable institutionalization for the accommodation of national pluralism than that offered by traditional federalism. In general terms, and using the main Western multinational democracies as our reference point (Canada, Belgium, the United Kingdom and Spain), it appears that disagreement on what is meant by a liberal democracy in a multinational context is related not so much to different ways of life as to issues regarding the national identity of individuals. The reason for adopting value pluralism as a meta-ethical perspective of political liberalism is based on its ability to provide a version of political liberalism that is more sensitive to the goods, values and identities of national and cultural pluralism. This version contrasts with the monist "philosophia perennis" that has so influenced moral and political philosophy from classical Greece until our era.[4] In principle, value pluralism permits a more open and less dogmatic position when establishing any kind of dialogue or deliberation than that permitted by alternative theories. This dialogue, especially in the case of cultural pluralism, is preceded by the difficulty of finding a language that is morally neutral and acceptable to all and is at the same time as open as possible to incorporating the possibilities that cultural frameworks offer as well as their limits.[5] Moreover, this greater theoretical prudence of value pluralism means, in principle, that it is able to show interest in practical experiences and in comparative politics.[6] Finally, value pluralism accepts the inevitability of disagreement in those practical situations that see the coincidence of a series of values that are both desirable and contradictory, values that cannot be synthesized nor easily prioritized.[7]

The perspective of value pluralism also brings us closer to typical cases of rational uncertainty in the moral world and to the dilemmas and rivalry of moral values that are so attractively dramatized in Greek and Shakespearean tragedies. Tragedies are usually beyond the boundaries of human language. We never completely understand the motives of characters whose actions are not totally comprehensible from a rational point of view. But these characters must act, and with their doubts, questions and eventual choices they provoke the participation of our own insecurities. We are faced with an agonistic plurality that will at times be "tragic," not only because it represents some kind of loss but because we cannot avoid negative consequences whatever we decide to do. As we observe the difficulty of finding clear answers to what is happening on stage in such tragedies as Euripides' *Medea* or Shakespeare's *King Lear*, to mention two of my favourites, our moral perspective is brought to the fore, we become more aware of the limitations of our rational systems, whether monist or pluralist, and we may become better moral thinkers.[8] Moreover, and despite the objectivity of Berlin's conception of values, men and women are historical beings that transform themselves, partly because of decisions they have taken. From a more epistemological standpoint, value pluralism also relates to the modern attitude of the humanists of the sixteenth century, an attitude that was more sceptical, tolerant and concerned with the practical aspects of human existence than that resulting from the more systematic theorization of Cartesian philosophy and the scientific revolution of the following century, both of which influenced current moral thought.[9]

Political Liberalism and Value Pluralism

From the perspective of value pluralism within the internal revision of liberalism, the first question is whether there is any compatibility between political liberalism and value pluralism. Berlin himself warns that there is no logical link between them. The Berlinian path leads us to the existence or not of some kind of normative priority for liberty – previously defined – in political liberalism. I believe that Berlin's arguments in favour of compatibility are not totally conclusive, but they are more persuasive when we deal with the political and practical dimensions of value pluralism in diverse cultural and national societies.

One of Berlin's most important contributions is the understanding that the universal content of morality generates unavoidable conflicts among its values.[10] As is well known, value pluralism makes "harmonious" moral and political projects, even those of a liberal character, not only impracticable but incoherent.[11] Berlin's answer to the link between value pluralism and liberalism is negative liberty. This approach has been criticized in several ways; I will mention two. Charles Taylor has emphasized difficulties in the conceptual separation between negative and positive liberties, even when we consider more sophisticated versions of negative liberty (exercise concept) than that of the mere absence of interference from outside sources (opportunity concept). In the *opportunity concept* of freedom an individual is considered free regardless of what he or she does in that sphere. It is included in the classical Hobbes and Bentham approaches. In the *exercise concept*, freedom is linked to some activated human capacity, such as autonomy or self-rule. Here, the lack of outside interference is just a condition of freedom but not a sufficient requirement. Following a path similar to that taken by John Stuart Mill, Taylor defends a qualitative approach to what practices deserve a higher moral status in any consideration about freedom. Noninterference is not a workable discriminatory criterion among negative liberties. Negative and positive liberties cannot but interfere (in education, for example).[12]

The second criticism of Berlin's approach comes from John Gray, who observes that autonomy cannot be considered a fundamental value of liberalism from the perspective of value pluralism – because there are valuable ways of life that are not autonomous but stem from tradition – nor can negative liberty be considered only one value among others. Moreover, negative liberties are also diverse and incommensurable and can be ordered and combined in different ways. By the same token, it is not possible to maintain that liberal democracy is the only legitimate model of political organization; it is simply one of many. So, strictly speaking, it would be a matter of choosing between liberalism and value pluralism. Nevertheless, after a certain basic level of morality has been achieved and the "universal evils" have been avoided (slavery, torture, etc.), it is not acceptable in practice to oblige individuals and groups to accept specific ways of life that they reject. In Hirschmann's terms, it is not the job of a political system to ensure that individuals and groups are *loyal* to a set of values or a certain way of life; it must ensure that they have *voice* within them and an *exit* from them. Although in theoretical terms we cannot have a conclusive defence of the priority of negative liberties (and perhaps a clear criteria of demarcation), they can be usually presented as the moral (and internally potentially agonic) basic layer of liberal politics.

A second question is whether there are models of political organization apart from liberal democracy that are able to ensure the kind of individual freedom represented by dissidence and diversity. This question is more empirical than logical. There are different positions and internal dissidence in all cultures. It seems that it is not legitimate to use culture to justify the repression of internal dissidence. Authors such as Taylor and Gray (and Bhikhu Parekh) are right to urge us to pay attention to certain values and ways of life that are ignored by liberal tradition. Many display moral virtues that liberalism is blind to or barely sees, and their presence is not only acceptable but desirable in democracies that show more normative and institutional sensitivity to cultural and national pluralism. In any case, value pluralism is a perspective that (1) warns about the internal *plural* and *agonistic* nature of morality and politics that Kantist, Utilitarian and other monist theories try somewhat to avoid (I think uselessly); (2) emphasizes that legitimizing criteria in politics are not related always to a universal and non-contextual *moral* perspective but sometimes to some particular and contextual *ethical* perspective; and in which (3) these legitimizing criteria are based not only on *values* – even when functional values such as efficiency and stability are included – but also on partial collective *interests* and particular cultural *identities.*

The conclusion to this second question is that it is more difficult to be persuaded of the practical possibility of pluralism and dissidence within regimes in which negative individual freedom, even in its opportunity concept, and an exit from the dominant ways of life of a society are not guaranteed.[13] Negative liberty belongs to the historical and organizational core of these kinds of democracies. Value pluralism highlights the fact that liberal democracies represent a historical, institutional and practical sedimentation of institutions, procedural rules and decision-making processes that have shown their practical compatibility with those objectives. In any case, defenders of political liberalism tend to be less arrogant when value pluralism is adopted than when monist and fully rank-ordered pluralist theories are adopted.

Legitimizing Poles in Liberal Democracies

Legitimizing normativity is not just about the morality of values. Faced with this normative pluralism, which in general terms includes moral, cultural and functional dimensions, the main political theories (liberalism, conservatism, socialism, communitarianism, nationalism, etc.) have tended to choose one particular dimension or a combination of them by means of a plurality of philosophical approaches (deontological, consequentialist, particularist, theological, perfectionist, etc.). In this way, each one of these theories tends to

- give priority to a number of specific questions on political legitimation;
- use a particular conceptual framework;
- concentrate on specific goods, values, interests and identities;
- propose specific solutions for questions that have been selected as the most relevant in the political sphere: individual freedom and the limitation of power; social equality and the criticism of capitalism; the development of civic virtue and legitimized links with the political community; political stability and social cohesion based on shared feelings, values and customs; or the recognition and promotion of different identities considered as priorities by the individuals of any given group.

On the other hand, these same theories interpret in a different way, marginalize or fail completely to take into account the questions, concepts, values and institutional references defended by rival theories.[14]

In purely descriptive terms, the inevitable and desirable[15] linguistic and normative pluralism that exists in the legitimation processes of the democracies of pluricultural societies may be seen as nine linguistic and normative dominant poles from which the main political traditions have conceived the political legitimacy in liberal democracies (regardless of the perspective and the internal theoretical focus adopted) (see figure 1): the liberal (L) (sphere of individual rights, separation of private and public spheres, limitation and control of power), the democratic (D) (equality of citizenship, participation), the socio-economic (S-E) (production and distribution of goods and services), the social order and security (O-S) (internal peace and external security), the national (N) (collective identity/ies as political unit/s; national group rights), the cultural (C) (religious, linguistic, ethnic and cultural group rights, etc.), the federal (Fd) (territorial self-rule and self-government), the functional (Fn) (stability, efficiency, efficacy), and the postmaterialist (P) (ecology, pacifism). Each pole synthesizes a general type of questions, concepts, epistemological and practical interests, values and goods, identities, institutions and references that the theories usually develop and combine in different ways.

The majority of the edges of the pyramid illustrate the tensions between two poles – for example, the classic clash between the liberal and democratic normative perspectives, which has been developed in some of the political theories of the last two centuries. Other relationships have been developed theoretically

Figure 1
Legitimizing Normative Poles in Liberal Democracies

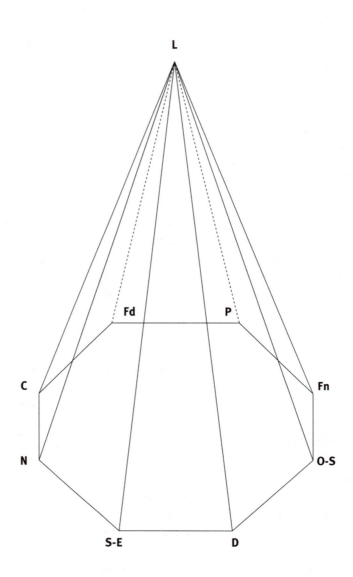

much more recently.[16] There are also tensions within each vertex or normative pole (between liberties and equalities within the liberal pole, for example, and even between liberties themselves).[17] The pyramid illustrates the not so "liberal" nature of the normativity of Western societies. It also allows us to distinguish between "wider" and "narrower" theories of democracy depending on whether they embrace more or less normative poles in their conception of political legitimacy – a question that is not related to the "strong" or "weak" nature of some of the normative poles considered in these theories.[18]

This normative and linguistic complexity, which is present in the legitimization processes of present-day democracies, also endorses the adoption of the theoretical perspective of value pluralism simply for Aristotelian reasons of ethical and epistemological "prudence." None of these theories is able to synthesize these normative poles; none is superior in all theoretical and practical aspects of morality and political legitimation, giving it the right to be the only voice for the development of a "good society." No global normative and linguistic reconciliation is possible. Moreover, in multinational polities, there will be an unavoidable competitive coexistence between different values and national identities that will make any normative synthesis impossible. This kind of pluralism is related to the sense of self-esteem and self-respect of the individuals who share the same democracy (i.e., the political uses of symbols such as flags, anthems, national teams and international projection that makes concrete the self-recognition of those individuals in the public sphere). Traditional universalism has usually taken for granted parochial cultural assumptions, sometimes by way of ignoring what precisely is culturally and nationally not "neutral" from a normative and linguistic perspective. This is a question that, as Berlin also argued, liberalism might incorporate into its theory and put into practice through the pluralization of its normative and institutional bases. If the "minimum moralia" of liberalism must be reviewed in multinational polities, the individual and collective rights, institutions and decision-making processes of liberal multinational federations will probably also be updated.

Value Pluralism and Multinational Federalism

No doctrine which inspires a movement or a party has ever to my knowledge been refuted by argument – it expires as a result of changes in the world

Isaiah Berlin, to Nora Beloff, 1988

Whether federalism is a promising road to take to achieve the political accommodation of national pluralism within a democracy remains an open question. It has received increasing interest in recent years in the fields of political theory and comparative studies. However, there are few empirical cases of multinational federations and almost none are free from structural problems. Canada, India and Spain, to mention only three, have yet to achieve a satisfactory constitutional articulation that is acceptable to all parties in, respectively, Quebec, Kashmir and Punjab, and the Basque Country and Catalonia. This is in spite of the doses of constitutional asymmetry built into some of these cases. Obviously, to ask about federalism's chances is to ask a wider question than one simply about federations. The existence of other kinds of federal agreements (confederations, federacies, associated states, etc.) allows us to respond differently to the possibilities of political accommodation that each offers in relation to multinational societies.

Although it is important to bear in mind that the logic of federalism is applicable not only to federations, in this section and following on from earlier work, I will concentrate on the case of multinational liberal-democratic federations. The key point here is to deal with these federations from the perspective of value pluralism in order to first point out some of the reasons why these federations find it difficult to accommodate national pluralism within the same democratic polity, and to then comment on potential institutional reforms within them. This is the model that I call *plural federalism*.

Two Concealments of Classic Federalism

Multinational federations are currently facing what may be summed up as a liberal, democratic and national challenge to achieve polity-building. This challenge must tackle the implicit conceptual and institutional biases associated with the statist and nationalist monism usually present in democratic federations. The question, in short, is whether it is possible to combine, in the same federation, the perspective of a federal union of different national collectives and the more confederal perspective that tends to predominate in the national constituent units. This question cannot be answered in abstract terms; we must refer to institutional practice and case analysis.[19]

It is well known that, in contrast to some of the premodern federal agreements (cities, leagues, provinces, etc.), the theory and practice of modern federalism have developed in parallel to the theory and practice of the evolution of the state and its territorial element. In the case of multinational societies this point is obviously not a "neutral" one that becomes clearer under the perspective of value pluralism than under the perspective of monist and fully rank-ordered theories. Although this affects the federations more than federalism itself, the situation of federations may, I believe, be described in terms of the overshadowing or concealment of their internal logic.

The history of modern federations is the history of two concealments of classic federalism. Federalism is understood here, in contrast to Elazar, not as a theory that is "designed to achieve some degree of political integration based on a combination of self-rule and shared rule" but more generally as one that is "designed to achieve some degree of political agreement."[20] Federal logic has been concealed, first, by modern processes of state-building and, second, by processes of nation-building promoted by states. As the consequences for federalism of the second concealment have received ample comment, I will deal briefly with the first.

Even though the contribution of contemporary federations to the process of state-building (sometimes based on previous confederations) has been usually regarded as an alternative to the process of creation of centralized states – first with absolutism and then with democratic Jacobinism – federations still share a centralization process with these states that is incorporated into the idea of a common or general authority that demands loyalty from all the individuals within a fixed territory. This in turn defines, first, the notion of subject and, subsequently, that of citizen. In federations it is true that sovereignty and government become plural when faced with the monism of the sovereignty of the king or the people in centralized states. However, when a central or "national" government is established, a form of collective monism may be reintroduced: the people of the whole federation, in competition with the diverse subjects of the federal agreement. How much this phenomenon affects each federation is an empirical question, but it is of crucial importance for multinational federations. In descriptive terms, a multinational federation means not only that there are a number of different nations within a polity; it also indicates, in a value pluralist vein, that these nations have their own ways of interpreting history, valuing their languages, customs and traditions, or understanding what is or should be their political, economic and cultural role in the present and future. These interpretations are likely to be different from those of other national collectives within the polity. They will all be plural, but their plurality will not be identical.

On the other hand, in modern federations it would appear that the tension between the liberal and democratic logics has been "nationally" resolved in favour of the latter. Moreover, the fact that the first and most influential modern federation was the United States of America – which was built on strong uninational foundations with a powerful Supreme Court acting as politics-maker for its practical development – is not unconnected to an evolution of federations that is far removed from the most "confederal" logic of the polities of classic federalism (which in the modern era survived, albeit briefly, in the Netherlands and Switzerland). At the end of the day it would seem that most federations, instead of refuting Bodin's theory that their existence is impossible if one wishes to maintain indivisible state sovereignty, refute only the thesis of indivisibility and not that of a hierarchy that favours statehood or unity in contrast to the diversity of its component parts. Rather than centralization, which as we know is open to a wide range of practical interpretations, this partial evaporation of classic federalism is the product of state political unity.

This first concealment of classic federalism by the state or, in other words, this statist swing of federalism by a number of federations based on the unity of a territorial *demos,* is present in the main conceptions of contemporary liberalism and federalism.[21] This situation is reinforced by the second concealment of federalism: the consequences of the powerful presence of a single, dominant state nationalism in federations. One result of all this has been the difficulties experienced by classic federations in contexts in which "the national *demos*" is not regarded as a single or predominant entity by large groups of citizens. This problem has yet to be resolved by traditional liberalism and constitutionalism.

Naturally, the above does not imply the assimilation of federal state-building processes into the processes of centralized state-building, nor does it ignore the important differences that exist between the two processes and the possible repercussions for the practical functioning of the political system or the political culture of a given collective. In fact, as has been widely recognized, the processes represent two conceptions of democracy: the Jacobin conception fought the federal agreements existing in Europe in the name of democracy. Nor does the above imply any dismissal of the teachings of comparative politics on the instability of confederations in contemporary times. Rather, it is a matter of highlighting the problems that federations will have – albeit fewer than centralized states will have – in developing the normative and constitutional consequences of the existence of a plurality of *demos* (or *demoi*) within the same federal democracy, in contrast to the more frequent statist conception of a single *demos* (and despite the fact that the latter will be described as an internally "plural" reality in terms of language, culture, etc.).

Federalism and Value Pluralism – the "Plural Federalism" Model

Unlike other phenomena associated with cultural pluralism (immigration, indigenous groups), it is sometimes possible to observe a harmony or similarity between the moral values and ways of life of the members of the different national collectives within Western democracies. This kind of pluralism is the product of characteristics and relations related to the history, culture, territory and, above all, power of these collectives. Inevitably, and also unlike other cultural movements, both majority and minority national collectives are the product of processes of nation-building that to a certain extent will have to compete with each other when they try to make collective decisions within the same territory (division of powers, use of political symbols, institutions, presence in the international arena, languages, national holidays, educational curricula, etc.).

Using value pluralism as the theoretical perspective of multinational liberal federations has at least two advantages over rival theoretical perspectives.

- Concerning political liberalism, it allows one to investigate and constitutionally define individual and collective freedom as well as mutual recognition of different collectives or national *demoi* in a more open way. From the beginning, fewer things will be left off the political agenda and the dialogue between the different parties will not be based on deductive theories that display theoretical biases and a lack of information regarding the most relevant aspects of specific political legitimacy. In this way, for example, the legitimacy of collective liberty will not be the exclusive preserve of the state as a collective subject. [22] Value pluralism will also promote agreement between players who are more sceptical of the potential of deductive theories but who do not wish to damage a minimal normative nucleus that is more open to cultural interpretation than in other manifestations of liberalism and constitutionalism.
- Regarding federalism, value pluralism allows for an easier recovery of the liberal and federal logic of the pact when establishing the content of self-government, shared rule and reform processes by diverse national collectives that are unable to show any kind of normative hierarchy between them.[23] This makes it easier to occasionally change the constitutional rules when neither the national federated units nor the federation is in exclusive possession of their unilateral interpretation. These units may display a form of symmetry when they aspire to state-building and nation-building that goes beyond that which federations have enjoyed until the present.[24]

Both points refer to the predominance of freedom, both individual and collective in this case, in value pluralism as a perspective of federal liberalism. There are obviously other basic values and principles of a legitimizing nature (the different interpretations of political equality, respect for minorities, constitutionalism, etc.). However, in the case we are dealing with here, collective freedom plays a similar role to Berlin's negative individual freedom in guaranteeing that undesired external coercion is avoided, adding the positive participatory dimension that defines the shared rule of federations. Once again, "improving" the practical functioning of federal democracies of liberal origin involves doing so both in an ethical sense, which affects how one interprets the legitimizing values and principles, among which is freedom in multinational contexts, and in a functional sense of governance, that is of results and effective conflict management. Or, put another way, to borrow Lincoln's phrase (which has been quoted by Elazar), improving federalism means improving the way it judges individuals (plus national collectives and the federations themselves, I would add), "warts and all."[25] Nevertheless, both objectives (improving normativity and improving governance) may in practice turn out to be contradictory. It will then be necessary, if it is possible in federations, to adopt some kind of balanced solution based on procedures that reflect the accommodation of the national pluralism of the polity.

This is a question that affects the three basic aspects that, in my opinion, make up an adequate federal accommodation of multinational polities – in other words, the three basic aspects of *plural federalism*:

- an explicit and satisfactory constitutional and political recognition acceptable to the main political actors of the national pluralism of the "federation";
- the establishment of a series of agreements – likely of an asymmetrical or confederate nature when necessary or when there is a larger number of federated units than the number of minority nations for a high degree of national self-government of the minority nations of the federation – whose aim is the political defence and development of such national collectives, both in relation to the federation and in relation to the international arena;
- a multinational regulation of the shared rule of the federation and of its reform processes (including clauses of constitutional national secession), which can accommodate the national pluralism of the polity.

These three aspects also highlight the relationship between collective negative and positive liberties in federations that conform to the model of plural federalism.

At this stage it would be appropriate to consider some of the conclusions drawn from the analyses of comparative federalism. Comparative politics shows us, first of all, that multinational federations have normally been reluctant to permit explicit recognition of national pluralism in their constitutional agreements. In fact, this recognition is less common in these federations than the regulation of high degrees of self-government in some federated units. The reason for this may be related to the monism that is a feature of the statist and nationalist conception of the polity in contemporary federal tradition. The political collective, the "federal union," is normally understood to be a unit rather than an expression of national plurality,[26] a fact that has repercussions for the constitutionalization of the internal rules of federal systems as well as for the interpretation of liberal freedom (negative and positive), particularly in individual terms.

Debate in recent years has shown that formal equality of citizenship based on an identical formulation of civic, political and social rights fails to guarantee the recognition of plurinationality and therefore its political accommodation. Citizenship is not available at the same cultural price, in terms of self-esteem and self-image, for all the citizens of the federation. Moreover, in some cases (Canada, Spain) the hegemonic nationalisms of the federation tend to deny their plurinational character in favour of a pluricultural and plurilinguistic conception of a federation that is often considered uninational. In this sense, and from the perspective of value pluralism, I believe that the explicit constitutionalization and institutionalization of a politics of recognition of national plurality is the first element for the accommodation of this kind of society. In Rawlsian terms, it is something that must be included in the "constitutional essentials" and "basic justice" of society. Berlin himself pointed out that nationalism springs, quite often, from a sense of outraged and wounded human dignity and from the desire for recognition. He also stressed that the demand to be treated as an equal is at the core of social and national revolutions and represents the modern version of recognition – "violent, dangerous, but respectable and fair."[27]

Decisive elements for the regulation of recognition are the symbolic and linguistic aspects of each national collective inside and outside the frontiers of the federation.[28] Recognition implies a multilateralness; in other words, it must be done in a number of directions: from each national collective to the others and vice versa. It cannot, therefore, be assimilated into the distribution of a system of freedoms or material resources.

The second point that comparative politics shows us is that minority nations have achieved a variety of levels of self-government. This affects the regulation of collective negative freedom in the federation. In spite of the difficulty of producing uncontroversial and comparable indices of the level of noncentralization and decentralization of different federations, the results of comparative studies and case studies show a lesser gradient for multinational federations in the differences of self-government than for federations in general. The same results also show higher levels of constitutional asymmetry.[29] The interpretation of what "should be" the level of self-government of a national collective within a multinational federation is a question for political debate in each specific case. However, a federated self-government, which in this case is a federated national self-government, should have sufficient symbolic, institutional, legislative, executive, judicial and financial resources to proceed to a set of hegemonic liberal-democratic policies of nation-building. This includes responsibilities, for example, in the spheres of foreign affairs or, if applicable, immigration policy, which in most federations has not been conceded. It will not otherwise be possible to ensure the correct treatment of the collective freedom within the federation.

Third, analysts of federalism agree upon the importance of intergovernmental relations and the institutions that guarantee the participation of federated units for the smooth functioning of the federation. In the same way that the principles of co-operation and "subsidiarity" may attack the logic of the federal division of powers,[30] a wholly confederal approach in the relationship between the federated units and the central power or a very competitive relationship between the units themselves is often an informal but permanent threat to the continuity of the federation. As far as multinational states are concerned, it is easier to develop a "federalism of trust" (or to minimize a "federalism of distrust") if both the rules of participation of the national collectives in the institutions of the union and the possibility of changing those rules include secession as one potential outcome of the collective right of self-determination. The rules of participation and the possibility of changing them also represent manifestations of the collective freedom of national units in federations.

Participation in the union may be achieved through various classical techniques and institutions of federalism: consociational processes and institutions; a second chamber that defends minority rights through, for example, the right of veto for minorities; a supreme or constitutional court whose composition and functions include the national pluralism of the federation. On the other hand, constitutional reform on the initiative of the different national collectives and, above all, the right to self-determination represent a bigger rupture for federations, taking into account the aversion of federal constitutionalism toward the concept of national pluralism and toward the self-determination right for any collective other than the state itself. However, although the debate of recent years on the right of self-determination has produced arguments of a mainly functional nature, based on the stability and the governance of the system, this debate also seems to indicate that there is no definitive normative argument that discourages the regulation of this right in multinational federations (including secession clauses).[31]

Furthermore, even the important decision taken by the Supreme Court of Canada in 1998 regarding the secession of Quebec (the *Secession Reference*) endorsed the legitimacy of the "peoples" of a multinational federation to propose a change to the constitution, as well as the duty of the other members of the federation to enter into a process of negotiation that readjusts the federation through changes to the recognition of multinationality or to the division of powers; results in secession; or establishes a result somewhere between the two. The *Secession Reference* also established the need for a series of procedural rules that do not impede the development of the reform process (a simplified amending procedure). The Supreme Court indicated four inherent principles in the Canadian constitution and its reform process – federalism, democracy, the rule of law and constitutionalism, and the protection of minorities – and added, in a value pluralist token, that none of them predominates over the others and that in this kind of federation the juridical framework can never be considered closed.

In this way, in accordance with the *Reference*, the mere existence of a series of self-governments and federal agreements cannot be seen as sufficient guarantee and expression of the democratic freedom of a multinational collective. This all seems to indicate that it is probably not a good idea that the basic rules of democratic states affecting collectives, including federal collectives, be the same for both uninational and multinational liberal democracies. This issue has sometimes been rejected by traditional democratic constitutionalism when interpreting notions of freedom, equality and pluralism, and when it arbitrarily equates the democratic polity with a single national *demos*.

In fact, the *Reference* established the legitimacy of the right of self-determination for the peoples of a multinational federation. We can say, moreover, that this right is regulated from a federal rather than from a nationalist perspective: unilateral decisions from both sides are constitutionally forbidden; the obligation to negotiate must be implemented according to institutional and procedural rules.[32] And we can also say that the Canadian Supreme Court took a hermeneutic path from the formal and written regulations of the *federation* to the unwritten values of *federalism*. So, what is needed in multinational federations is a new form of constitutionalism in which the right to self-determination embodies the collective freedom of the national groups both in its negative aspect of the defence of the collective personality and in its positive aspect of participation in a general decision-making process that may result in different constitutional results following negotiation with the other members of the federation.

This does not question the potential virtues of federalism in multinational democracies.[33] These processes may be regulated, to implement difficult rules to be followed in the case of secession – time, majorities, referenda, economic imbalances, and so forth – in order to avoid or decrease functional problems or the use of nonreasonable blackmail by political elites.[34] As we saw in the previous section, no political theory of democracy or justice is able to synthesize this complexity of perspectives and theoretical and practical levels. That is why it is crucial to ensure equality among the negotiating parties.

The linguistic and normative pluralism of the negotiation, the different logics or types of rationality that govern the normative questions and issues associated with governance, and the different uses of the language that is involved in the negotiation mean that the agreements reached will inevitably be of the modus vivendi type, at least partially, even when the legitimizing language, rights, institutions and processes are strictly liberal-democratic.[35] Obviously, from this perspective the configuration of the reform procedures and the results will vary according to the specific characteristics of each multinational federation (history, economy, political leadership, the existence of suprastate entities such as the European Union, international relations, etc.). The answers will also be plural and never definitive. Nevertheless, in this way it is possible to safeguard an interpretation of collective freedom that is closer to national pluralism and to the logic of the kind of federalism concealed by contemporary federations.[36] The experimental nature of federalism continues to be one of its biggest advantages in this case.

Nowadays, as I said, the question of whether federal solutions are suitable for achieving a political accommodation of multinational societies remains unanswered. Nevertheless, if comparative federalism teaches us anything it is the desirability of establishing normative and institutional frameworks that are appropriate for each specific case. But in order to do this it is also desirable to overcome the conceptual and practical barriers and biases that the combination of traditional political liberalism and federalism has created in contemporary constitutionalism. From a theoretical standpoint, I believe that adopting a perspective of value pluralism makes it easier to find ways to establish a political accommodation of national pluralism in contemporary liberal democracies. Therefore, I think it would be accurate to say of Berlin what Nelson Riddle, who in 1959 arranged the songs of George Gershwin for a recording by Ella Fitzgerald, said of the New York composer: "He wrote tomorrow's music yesterday."

Notes

1. The debate in recent years between political liberalism and cultural pluralism, among other things, prompts one to: 1) maintain that the "well-ordered society" should include not only political and economic issues (freedoms and resources) but also issues involving political accommodation (cultural rights, recognition and, where relevant, the institutions of self-government and shared rule); 2) distrust those moral theories or theories of "justice" that are strongly deductive in nature (top-down theories) when one is dealing with heterogeneous values, interests and identities. Even if we accept that justice is the main objective in the public arena – which is by no means clear – there appears to be no rational and uncontroversial way to establish its principles or its rules of priority.

2. An example of the contrast between these two intellectual strategies may be found in the debate between Parekh and Kymlicka in *Constellations*, Vol. 4, no. 1 (1997).

3. Information about Berlin and his work is available at *www.wolfson.ox.ac.uk/berlin/vl/*

4. Berlin insists that monism is at the base of any extremism: see Berlin (1998). The classical reference is Berlin (1969).

5. Berlin (1976).

6. As Berlin also stresses, in politics it will be always important to know that there are "regions" in which gardeners obtain better results than in botanicals (1954).

7. Value pluralism is perfectly compatible with partial orderings of values and goods established for specific subjects and contexts. That is, value pluralism is compatible with *particular* and not necessarily fully rank-ordered values. This is one of the potential functions for practical processes of deliberative democracy.

8. For a complementary psychological perspective, see, for example, Harold Bloom's analysis of *Macbeth*: "The enigma of *Macbeth*, as a drama, always will remain its protagonist's hold upon our terrified sympathy. Shakespeare surmised the guilty imaginings we share with Macbeth, who is Mr Hyde to our Dr Jekyll...Clearly the ironies of *Macbeth* are not born of clashing perspectives but of divisions in the self – in Macbeth and in the audience" (1998, pp. 523, 535). For a more "objective" perspective that links political order to facts rather than to thoughts, there is the famous passage from Euripides' *Suppliant Maidens*: "There are three classes of citizens: some are rich and useless, always with a passion for more; others, the have-nots, lack means of livelihood...of the three parts, the one in the middle saves the city and preserves whatever order the city has."

9. Similarly, Toulmin reminds us how, at the beginning of the modern age, Montaigne turned out to be nearer to the linguistic pluralism of Wittgenstein than to the more systematic authors of the seventeenth and eighteenth centuries.

10. This refers to the classic discussion on the incomparability, incommensurability and incompatibility of values. I do not develop this point here. See Raz (1986, ch. 13; 1994), Gray (1995, ch. 2), Walzer (1995), Barry (1990), Galston (1991), Taylor (1982).

11. See other criticisms of monist and culturally pluralist positions as partial and incoherent in Gray (1995, ch. 9) and Parekh (2000, chs. 1 and 2). In this latter work the author says: "Historically speaking liberalism began, at least in the English-speaking world, as a doctrine stressing the contingency of and abstracting away ethnic, religious, cultural and other differences. Not surprisingly it faces acute structural difficulties getting these differences back into its views of man and politics" (p. 346, n 12).

12. Obviously, here we would need to try to establish some kind of rank-ordering of human wants, as well as to decide about some potential transcultural requirements of these wants at the moment of protecting negative liberties in different "background understandings." Berlin is certainly not a systematic thinker. In his theory there is a constant lack of determination about the theoretical status of "values," between a Herderian-Hegelian perspective of self-transformation within specific cultures and a Kantian perspective where values are similar to the categories of the *Trancendental Analytics* of the first *Critique*. However, I think it more helpful to talk about values and criteria than about "principles," which suggests a fully rank-ordered theoretical perspective that is not very sensitive to contextual trends in specific societies. Normative values (and criteria) are semantically closer to a Kantian *general* perspective than to a *universal* one. I have developed this point in Requejo (2001a, ch. 8).

13. Crowder (1998), Weinstock (1997). Gray coherently recommends going from Kantian to Hobbesian legitimizing patterns in politics. What is needed is not a set of common values in society but a set of common institutions that are able to deal with rival values and interests. In fact, he says, the liberal state was born from the

search for a modus vivendi agreement. He also insists that Hobbes did not necessarily need to defend an absolutist perspective in order to maintain peace, in contrast with C. Schmitt's criticism on Hobbes' theory for being "too liberal" when it maintains the distinction between the society and the state. See Gray (2000, ch. 4). However, I think that the limits for any legitimate practical polity are led by the need to protect the value of negative liberty that Berlin had in mind. Under this perspective, liberalism still maintains the *practical* "negative" legitimizing strength based on avoiding evil rather than achieving good in institutions and practical life that is present in Berlin's and (partially) in John Stuart Mill's approaches. This is something more than coexistence. See also Oakeshott (1975).

14. In addition to this *omission strategy*, Charles Taylor has rightly pointed out Berlin's intention in "Two Concepts of Liberty" against what we can call the *redefinition strategy*: "[to] try to finesse the clash between liberty and some other goal – solidarity, justice, social harmony, equality – by telling ourselves that these other goals are internal to the definition of freedom, properly understood...This kind of fudging goes back to Plato, at least...Conflict is finessed by redefinition" (2001, pp. 114-15). Hilary Putnam pointed out something similar in his criticism of epistemological positivism (1997).

15. This paper deals only with the inevitability of pluralism and not its desirability in present-day democracies. For treatment of this issue, see Parekh (2000, chs. 3, 4, 5 and 11) and Requejo (2001a).

16. Depending on the values, questions and so on under consideration, we may also place the theories, the political players, the discourse and so forth on the pyramid like a topographical map. Nevertheless, to take value pluralism as the most promising metapolitical perspective in relation to political liberalism is just a theoretical consideration, and its practical application should be evaluated carefully given that many other normative and contextual factors are included. It would be inconsistent to deduce from value pluralism that every single political decision should be made according only to the principles decided by the corresponding decision-maker (governments, parliaments, courts, etc.). It is likely that such a practice would introduce elements of arbitrariness and political and juridical insecurity, which some principles, such as the defence of "human rights," constitutionalism and the rule of law, attempt to avoid. What one should do is regard value pluralism as a conception of existing democratic liberalism that introduces more open attitudes to the change of

perspective than rival meta-conceptions when one has to take decisions about questions related to cultural and national pluralism. This would probably influence the attitudes and practices of both political decision-makers and public opinion. However, the practical starting point should be located in the political, cultural and institutional reality that already exists in liberal democracies. Here, value pluralism is a promising way to refine the liberal-democratic normativity and to reform its political institutions and decision-making processes.

17. This is not developed in some fully rank-ordered theories such as Rawls'.

18. For example, Habermas' conception of deliberative democracy would be both "narrow," because it only really deals with the liberal and democratic poles, and "strong" in relation to the democratic pole due to its insistence on increasing deliberative and participatory practices.

19. Given the mainly theoretical nature of this paper, this question is not answered directly here. I offer a more institutional analysis in Requejo 1998, 1999a, 1999b, 2001b and forthcoming 2003. See also Moreno (1997).

20. Elazar (1987, p. 84; my emphasis). The term "integration" is ambiguous when it refers to the link between the parties and encourages one to think of a "strong" permanent agreement.

21. Think, for example, of the analyses of federalism as an instrumental, subsidiary, transitory element, or as an element that is associated with the decentralization of the political system, in the works of John Stuart Mill or K.C. Wheare.

22. *Statism* is a position that is also present in liberalism and most minority nationalisms. See Guibernau and Hutchinson (2001), Canovan (1996), Miller (1995), Norman (1995), Tamir (1993).

23. Federalism is also a dynamic institutional and normative perspective that allows us to take into account Taylor's criticism of Berlin's approach: "he seems to have stated the conflict of goods as though it were written into the goods themselves. Whereas I think it arises from the complexity and limitations of human life" (2001, p. 117). Values and their agonistic relationships are historical. This allows a renewal of political pacts and "contracts" within democratic politics that are in the base of a normative and institutional renewal of federalism. As Colin Walters pointed out, "Berlin liked to remind people that when they most believed they know where they are going, that is when they are likeliest to be wrong" (1999).

24. This does not prevent one from recommending caution regarding possible conclusions about multinational federalism given the small number of existing cases in comparative politics of mixed peoples, as well as the biases and mutual differences displayed by the majority of theoretical approaches to nationalism, federalism and liberalism. See Requejo (forthcoming 2003).

25. Elazar (1987, p. 86). Berlin points out that the feeling of belonging to a nation is totally natural and cannot be condemned or criticized in itself. However, his form of "pathological extremism that may lead to unimaginable horrors" is absolutely incompatible with value pluralism. See "Pluralism" in Berlin (1998). Faced with the insistence on the value of the equality of democratic traditions, Berlin and Elazar coincide in considering freedom (negative for the former) as the most important value for liberal democracies and liberal-democratic federalism respectively.

26. An exception is Ethiopia, whose constitution states: "We the Nations, Nationalities and Peoples of Ethiopia...ratified the Constitution of the Federal Republic of Ethiopia," and defines these terms as "a group of people who have or share a large measure of common culture, or similar customs, mutual intelligibility of language, belief in a common or related identity, and who predominantly inhabit an identifiable contiguous territory." See Tewfik (2001).

27. Berlin (1961).

28. Multinational democracies need a more refined and plural legitimacy than uninational democracies. In the former, the ethics of individual and collective *dignity* must be accommodated with the ethics of individual and collective *national diversity*. See Taylor (1992) and Gagnon (2001).

29. Watts (1999, chs. 3, 4, 6 and 8), De Villiers (1995), Agranoff (1999).

30. See Bertelsmann Commission (2000), Noël (1998), Bermann (1994), Rubin and Feeley (1994), Requejo (2001c).

31. Here I am obviously referring to liberal-democratic federal processes in which individual freedom must be guaranteed. See Tully (2001),

McKim and McMahan (1997), Moore (1998) and Buchanan (1997). See also Tully (1994), Gagnon and Rocher (1992), Beiner (1999), McRoberts (1997), MacCormick (1996), Kymlicka (2001), Kymlicka and Norman (2000), Gibbins and Laforest (1998).

32. This right of self-determination has been partly overshadowed by the *Clarity Act* (bill C-20, adopted by the federal government in June 2000). This act interprets in a non-value-pluralist and debatable way the requirements of clarity mentioned but not developed in the *Secession Reference*.

33. Simeon and Conway (2001), Stepan (1999), Linz (1997).

34. Norman (2001).

35. According to Elster, when the parties are a long way from reaching a consensus, the process may include two kinds of verbal exchange – argumentation and strict negotiation – as well as one nonverbal act – voting (see "Introduction" in Elster [1998]). Concerning the main subject of this paper, all three will take place, the first and second among the elites and the first and the third among the citizens. In this latter case, argumentation would appear to be decisive when discussing the existence or not of deficiencies in the recognition of the national pluralism of the federal democracy as well as the advisability or not of changing the federal rules of the game (referenda), while the strict negotiation will be the job of the elites in power at the time.

36. This position implies the predominance of the principle of equality between national groups when one is attempting to guarantee their collective freedoms over the principle of formal equality of the subunits of the federation. See Webber (1994) and Fossas (2001). For an analysis on the debate about the language, constitutionality and the issue of a "clear majority" in the Clarity Act, see François Rocher and Nadia Verrelli, "Questioning Constitutional Democracy in Canada: From the Canadian Supreme Court Reference on Quebec Secession to the Clarity Act," in this collection.

Bibliography

Agranoff, R., ed. *Accommodating Diversity: Assymetry in Federal States*. Baden-Baden: Nomos, 1999.

Barry, B. *Political Argument*. Berkeley: University of California Press, 1990.

Beiner, R., ed. *Theorising Nationalism*. Albany: State University of New York Press, 1999.

Berlin, Isaiah. "Realism in Politics." *Spectator*, no. 193 (1954): 774-76.

————. *Four Essays on Liberty*. Oxford: Oxford University Press, 1969.

————. *Vico and Herder: Two Studies in the History of Ideas*. London: Hogarth Press, 1976.

————. "Rabindranath Tagore and the Consciousness of Nationality" (1961), in *The Sense of Reality: Studies in Ideas and Their History*. London: Chatto & Windus, 1996a.

————. *The Sense of Reality: Studies in Ideas and Their History*. London: Chatto & Windus, 1996b.

————. "My Intellectual Path." *New York Review of Books*. May 14, 1998.

Bermann, G. "Taking Subsidiarity Seriously: Federalism in the European Community and the United States." *Columbia Law Review*, Vol. 94, no. 2 (1994): 331-455.

Bertelsmann Commission. *Disentanglement 2005*. Berlin: Bertelsmann Foundation Publishers, 2000.

Bloom, Harold. *Shakespeare: The Invention of the Human*. London: Fourth Estate, 1998.

Buchanan, A. *"Theories of Secession."* Philosophy and Public Affairs, Vol. 26, no. 1 (1997): 31-61.

Canovan, M. *Nationhood and Political Theory*. Cheltenham, UK: Edward Elgar, 1996.

Crowder, G. "John Gray's Pluralist Critique of Liberalism." *Journal of Applied Philosophy*, Vol. 15, no. 3 (1998): 287-98.

De Villiers, B., ed. *Evaluating Federal Systems*. Cape Town and Dordrecht: Juta and Martinus Nijhoff, 1995.

Elazar, D. *Exploring Federalism*. Tuscaloosa: University of Alabama Press, 1987.

Elster, J., ed. *Deliberative Democracy*. Cambridge: The Press Syndicate of the University of Cambridge, 1998.

Fossas, E. "National Plurality and Equality," in *Democracy and National Pluralism*, ed. Ferran Requejo. London: Routledge, 2001.

Fossas, E., and Ferran Requejo, eds. *Asimetría Federal y Estado Plurinacional. El debate sobre la acomodación de la diversidad en Canadá, Bélgica y España*. Madrid: Trotta, 1999.

Gagnon, Alain-G. "The Moral Foundations of Asymmetrical Federalism: A Normative Exploration of the Case of Quebec and Canada," in *Multinational Democracies*, ed. Alain-G. Gagnon and James Tully. Cambridge: Cambridge University Press, 2001.

Gagnon, Alain-G., and James Tully, eds. *Multinational Democracies*. Cambridge: Cambridge University Press, 2001.

Gagnon, Alain-G., and François Rocher. *Répliques aux detracteurs de la souveranité du Quebec*. Montreal: VLB Éditeur, 1992.

Galston, W. *Liberal Purposes: Goods, Virtues and Diversity in the Liberal State*. Cambridge: Cambridge University Press, 1991.

Gibbins, J., and G. Laforest, eds. *Beyond the Impasse*. Montreal: Institute for Research on Public Policy, 1998.

Gray, John. *Isaiah Berlin*. London: HarperCollins, 1995.

———. *Two Faces of Liberalism*. Cambridge: Polity Press-Blackwell Publishers, 2000.

Guibernau, Montserrat, and J. Hutchinson. *Understanding Nationalism*. Cambridge: Polity Press, 2001.

Kymlicka, Will, ed. *Politics in the Vernacular*. Oxford: Oxford University Press, 2001.

Kymlicka, W., and W. Norman, eds. *Citizenship in Diverse Societies*. Oxford: Oxford University Press, 2000.

Linz, J. "Democracy, Multinationalism and Federalism." *WP 103*. Madrid: Instituto Juan, March 1997.

MacCormick, Neil. "Liberalism, Nationalism and the Post-Sovereign State." *Political Studies*, Vol. 44 (1996): 553-67.

McKim, Robert, and Jeff McMahan, eds. *The Morality of Nationalism*. Oxford: Oxford University Press, 1997.

McRoberts, Kenneth. *Misconceiving Canada: The Struggle for National Unity*. Toronto: Oxford University Press, 1997.

Miller, David. *On Nationality*. Oxford: Clarendon Press, 1995.

Moore, M., ed. *National Self-Determination and Secession*. New York: Oxford University Press, 1998.

Moreno, L. *La federalización de España: Poder político y territorio*. Madrid: Siglo XXI Editores, 1997.

Noël, A. "The Federal Principle, Solidarity and Partnership," in *Beyond the Impasse*, eds. Roger Gibbins and Guy Laforest. Montreal: Institute for Research on Public Policy, 1998.

Norman, W. "Secession and (Constitutional) Democracy," in *Democracy and National Pluralism*, ed. Ferran Requejo. London: Routledge, 2001.

———. "The Ideology of Shared Values: A Myopic Vision of Unity in the Multi-Nation State," in *Is Quebec Nationalism Just? Perspectives from Anglophone Canada*, ed. J. Carens. Montreal and Kingston: McGill-Queen's University Press, 1995.

Oakeshott, M. *Hobbes on Civil Association*. Oxford: Blackwell Publishers, 1975.

Parekh, B. *Rethinking Multiculturalism: Cultural Diversity and Political Theory*. London: Macmillan, 2000.

Putnam, Hilary. "A Half Century of Philosophy, Viewed From Within" ("Scientific Realism" section). *Daedalus*, Vol. 126, no. 1 (1997).

Raz, J. *The Morality of Freedom*. Oxford: Oxford University Press, 1986.

———. *Ethics in the Public Domain*. Oxford: Clarendon Press, 1994.

Requejo, Ferran. "Federalisme, per a què?" *L'acomodació de la diversitat en democràcies plurinacionals*. València: Tres i Quatre, 1998.

———. "Cultural Pluralism, Nationalism and Federalism: A Revision of Citizenship in Plurinational States." *European Journal of Political Research*, Vol. 35, no. 2 (1999a): 255-86.

———. "La acomodación 'federal' de la plurinacionalidad. Democracia liberal y Federalismo Plural en España," in *Asimetría Federal y Estado Plurinacional. El debate sobre la acomodación de la diversidad en Canadá, Bélgica y España*, ed. E. Fossas and Ferran Requejo. Madrid: Trotta, 1999b.

———. "Political Liberalism in Plurinational States. The Legitimacy of Plural and Asymmetrical Federalism: The Case of Spain," in *Multinational Democracies*, ed. Alain-G. Gagnon and James Tully. Cambridge: Cambridge University Press, 2001b.

———. "Federalism and National Groups." *International Journal of Social Sciences*, Vol. 161 (2001c): 41-49.

———. "Federalism and the Quality of Democracy in Plurinational Contexts: Present Shortcomings and Possible Improvements," in *Federalism, Unitarianism and Territorial Cleavages*, ed. U. Amoretti and N. Bermeo. Baltimore: Johns Hopkins University Press (forthcoming 2003).

Requejo, Ferran, ed. *Democracy and National Pluralism*. London: Routledge, 2001a.

Rubin, E., and M. Feeley. "Federalism: Some Notes on a National Neurosis." *UCLA Law Review*, Vol. 41 (1994): 903-52.

Simeon, R., and D.P. Conway. "Federalism and the Management of Conflict in Multinational Societies," in *Multinational Democracies*, ed. Alain-G. Gagnon and James Tully. Cambridge: Cambridge University Press, 2001.

Stepan, A. "Federalism and Democracy: Beyond the U.S. Model." *Journal of Democracy*, Vol. 10, no. 4 (1999): 19-34.

Tamir, Yael. *Liberal Nationalism*. Princeton: Princeton University Press, 1993.

Taylor, Charles. "The Diversity of Goods," in *Utilitarianism and Beyond*, ed. A. Sen and B. Williams. Cambridge: Cambridge University Press, 1982.

———. "The Politics of Recognition, " in *Multiculturalism and the "Politics of Recognition": An Essay*, ed. Amy Gutmann. Princeton: Princeton University Press, 1992.

———. "Plurality of Goods," in *The Legacy of Isaiah Berlin*, ed. R. Working, M. Lilla and R. Silvers. New York: New York Review of Books, 2001.

Tewfik, H. "Ethiopia: The Challenge of Many Nationalities." *Federations*, Vol. 5 (2001): 7-8.

Toulmin, S. *Cosmopolis: The Hidden Agenda of Modernity*. Chicago: University of Chicago Press, 1990.

Tully, James. *Strange Multiplicity: Constitutionalism in an Age of Diversity*. Cambridge: Cambridge University Press, 1994.

———. "Introduction," in *Multinational Democracies*, ed. Alain-G. Gagnon and James Tully. Cambridge: Cambridge University Press, 2001.

Walters, C. "Tracking Romanticism, Root and Branch." *Washington Times*, March 14, 1999, p. B6.

Walzer, M. "Are There Limits to Liberalism?" *New York Review of Books*, October 19, 1995.

Watts, R. *Comparing Federal Systems*, 2nd ed. Montreal and Kingston: McGill-Queen's University Press, 1999.

Webber, J. *Reimagining Canada: Language, Culture, Community, and the Canadian Constitution*. Montreal and Kingston: McGill-Queen's University Press, 1994.

Weinstock, D. "The Graying of Berlin." *Critical Review*, no. 11 (1997): 481-501.

3

between nation and dissemination: revisiting the tension between national identity and diversity

Jocelyn Maclure

In the past few years, nationalism has imposed itself as a central theme of critical reflection for political philosophers and social scientists alike. Previously seen as antithetical to liberal values – the same liberal values that were so often disregarded and violated in the twentieth century – nationalism was more or less seen as the dark side of contemporary politics. Yet, the liberalization of most Western societies did not prompt the dissolution of nationalism as a sentiment of belonging to a (multi)cultural and political community. Countries such as Canada, Belgium, Spain, the United Kingdom and Russia are all facing challenges from minority nations. Aboriginal peoples in the United States, Canada, Australia, New Zealand, Norway, Mexico and other countries of Latin America have begun to frame their political claims in the language of nationalism (hence the appellation "First Nations"). The collapse of multinational countries in central and eastern Europe prompted the return of nations and nationalism in that part of the globe.[1] Moreover, existing nation-states, as a reaction to internal and external pressures, have heightened their nation-building policies. Although this will not concern me here, an exhaustive analysis of the contemporary resurgence of nationalism would need to include some considerations on the forms of nationalism displayed by nation-states or majority nations.

A Liberal and Post-Westphalian Form of Nationalism?

These are the conditions under which a number of *liberal* political theorists such as Yael Tamir, Will Kymlicka and David Miller[2] have made the argument

41

that a notion of "liberal nationalism" is not only nonaporetic, but also necessary in order to ground liberal values. Liberal nationalists argue that the nation provides the background against which stable liberal institutions can endure and flourish. The feeling of belonging to a nation would also foster the solidarity and cohesion required for anchoring redistributive justice. Kymlicka adds that the unfolding of personal autonomy, one of liberalism's core values, demands the existence of a secure cultural context of choice, which is most commonly embodied in the nation. The liberal-nationalist position triggered many responses and, one could say, reduced the reflection on nationalism to the narrow (yet important) debate on the logical compatibility of liberalism and nationalism as two principled categories.[3]

Alongside the work done by political philosophers on the difficult but necessary articulation of liberalism and nationalism, a number of political scientists and sociologists have also made nations and nationalisms their field of inquiry. Leading some comparative analyses and reworking the theories of nationalism elaborated by scholars such as Ernest Gellner, Benedict Anderson and Anthony Smith, a host of social scientists have revealed dimensions of nationalism that have not been thoroughly explored by political theorists.[4] They have, *inter alia*, rearticulated the relation between the nation and the state. We know that, despite their disagreements, the pioneers of the study of nationalism all maintain that nationalism is the movement that endeavours to link the nation and the state. According to Gellner's classic formulation, "nationalism has been defined, in effect, as the striving to make culture and polity congruent, to endow a culture with its own political roof, and not more than one roof at that."[5] Moreover, nationalism entails that the nation and the state "were destined for each other; that either without the other is incomplete, and constitutes a *tragedy*."[6] [my emphasis]. As we know, Gellner believes that nationalism is a fully *modern* phenomenon driven by the complex and sophisticated division of labour characteristic of industrial societies. In contradistinction, Smith maintains that nationalism has deep roots in the premodern world. Nations and nationalism would thus rather emerge from the belief in a shared ancestry and common ethnic descent. Smith nevertheless concurs with Gellner on the idea that, in modern times, the nation and the state must be inextricably linked. Even Anderson, whose redescription of the nation as an "imagined community" has proven extremely helpful in understanding nationality as a social imaginary, takes the Gellnerian paradigm for granted and assumes that "the gage and emblem" of the nation's freedom "is the sovereign-state."[7]

The nation and the state have, however, been dehyphenated in the recent literature on nationalism. The study of non-fully sovereign nations in the West has revealed the inadequacy of the Gellnerian paradigm. Small nations' vigorous struggle for political autonomy cannot be equated with the desire for absolute sovereignty in a given territory. Whilst national minorities such as Quebec, Catalonia, Flanders and Scotland remain fiercely attached to a notion of self-determination, the creation of a nation-state is not seen by these peoples as the necessary pathway to normality, maturity and modernity.[8] The nationalism of minority nations – less romantic, more realistic – has been reframed through the interaction with phenomena such as globalization, political and economic integration, migration, the proliferation of identity politics and new social movements and so on. Minority nations themselves often face demands for recognition, autonomy or for the maintenance of the status quo from internal minorities. Nationalism under these conditions is not antithetical to shared sovereignty. As Keating suggests, "the new minority nationalisms have a view of sovereignty which is highly attenuated by the recognition of interdependence and the limitations of the nation-state...They operate in societies in which citizens have abandoned exclusive notions of identity and can sustain multiple identities at the same time. This gives a new meaning both to the idea of the nation and to the nationalist project."[9]

It is precisely this "new meaning" that I want to investigate in the remainder of this paper. Now that some political philosophers have shown that liberalism and nationalism stand in an agonic but nonaporetic relationship, or at least that practical synthesis between the two is possible, and now that some social scientists have demonstrated that the new nationalisms are not necessarily incongruous and anachronistic under conditions of globalization, a third step remains to be made. Although scholars such as Keating and Kymlicka are well aware of the internal diversity of every (minority) nation, a redefinition of the nation's social imaginary in conditions of deep pluralism is still missing. Put differently, if very few scholars nowadays define the nation as a "homogeneous cultural unit,"[10] a redescription of the nation as a plurivocal and dissensual community of conversation still needs to be formulated.

The Third Step: Challenging the Paradigm of "Commonness"

As I indicated earlier, the contemporary scholars who are studying nations and nationalism in their various and overlapping dimensions respond to the fact that nations cannot be envisaged as homogeneous sites of convergence and fusion. One could argue, however, that the fact of deep pluralism has not sufficiently altered the traditional ways of thinking about the nation as both a political community and a source of identity. For instance, Montserrat Guibernau, although aware that nations without states are not ideal communities free of internal divisions,[11] still wants to define the nation as a "human group conscious of forming a community, sharing a common culture, attached to a clearly demarcated territory, having a common past and a common project for the future and claiming the right to rule itself."[12] We understand from that Rousseau-inspired definition that nationality is mainly about commonness and shared experiences. As I will try to argue, this is only one important dimension of the nation.

Understandings of the nation have always revolved around that idea of commonness. This is, of course, due to the powerful homogenizing and unifying capacity of the nation since the nineteenth century. In effect, the nation has turned peasants, workers, immigrants and so on into national subjects. The (sometimes violent) practice of nationalism was, and still is, used to create "nations" out of groups of people criss-crossed by identity-related differences and similarities. This process of homogenization is, however, rarely fully successful. France, which represents one of the most powerful attempts to erect a common and transcending republican identity on the ashes of local differences, can hardly turn a blind eye to the demands of recognition coming not only from abroad (Corsica) but also from Bretons, Basques, Provençals, immigrants from North Africa and second-generation immigrants.[13] The nation, then, no different from any other mode of collective identification in this regard, cannot be made intelligible without a perspicuous representation of its internal dissonance and ambivalence. An epistemic breach has been opened in the reflections on identity and difference in the past decade. What is proper to a cultural identity, Jacques Derrida argues, "is to not be identical to itself."[14] An identity, as a narrative or as a process of interpretation of self and other, always already includes an element of difference, a rebellious aspect that eludes the act of representation. In other words, difference is intrinsic to identity or identity always contains a trace of alterity.[15] The old – but still pervasive – understanding of difference as what is external to a homogeneous self is endlessly refuted by the daily transgression of cultural boundaries by people, problems, ideas, imaginaries and so on.[16] So if Quebec, to take an example, can correctly be described as a multicultural and multinational democracy, that is as a community composed of a francophone majority, a historical anglophone minority, 11 aboriginal nations and a great number of immigrant citizens and communities, all of these groups are themselves segmented by internal diversity and linked to other communities through the numerous individuals who uphold multiple belongings.[17] So First Nations, who are often thought of as largely homogeneous, are made of men and women, urban Aboriginals and Aboriginals living on reservations, traditionalists and nontraditionalists, elders and youngsters (who, because of part assimilation policies, sometimes literally do not speak the same language), and so forth. The descendants of French Canadians, which some sovereignist leaders like to see as a uniform group, live with differences of sexuality, gender, generation, political allegiance, lifestyle, class and profession. These lines of commonness and differences shift and recompose themselves from one context to the next. "What unity there is, and what is identity," as Clifford Geertz points out, is "negotiated, produced out of difference."[18]

The nation nonetheless presents itself as an all-encompassing identity and as a unitary political subject – thus as a sphere of belonging capable of creating the One out of the Many. According to Craig Calhoun, "the nationalist claim is that national identity is categorical and fixed, and that somehow it trumps all other sorts of identities, from gender to region, class to political preference, occupation to artistic taste."[19] National identity, according to the nationalist interpretation, is of another kind than sexual, gender, class, ethnic, generational, religious and political identities. Nationality's prerogative or *chasse-gardée* would lie precisely in its capacity to synthesize or reconcile diverging identifications into an all-encompassing, categorical, almost transcendent identity. However, if the nation was, with the great religions, the most efficient system of hierarchizing, subsuming and suppressing multiplicity,[20] it is not clear that it can or should, under our present conditions, hold on to that role and status. Globalization encourages the multiplication and dissemination of the axes of collective identifications.[21] If we can concur with thinkers such as Charles Taylor and Axel Honneth on the embedded and dialogical character of identity formation, we also have to recognize that the meaning-giving intersubjective spheres are multiple, overlapping and sometimes even conflicting. Supranational, transnational and regional forms of human co-operation coexist and sometimes rival the nation for people's loyalty. The rejection of the hypothesis of the nation's dissolution should not blind us to the fact that we are also witnessing both a deterritorialization and a reterritorialization of the modes of belonging and political mobilization. The either local, transnational or supranational character of problems faced by citizens stimulates investment in communities of action other than the nation. This is not to say that the nation has definitively or necessarily lost its preferential status as a marker of identity and its structuring capacity. It is rather to argue that we cannot assume that the nation is always capable of subsuming alternative sources of identity. We are witnessing the desanctification and reconfiguration of the nation, not its supercession.[22]

This fissure in the nation's imaginary has been investigated and narrated by Homi Bhabha. According to him, "the nation is no longer the sign of modernity under which cultural differences are homogenized in the 'horizontal' view of society. The nation reveals, in its ambivalent and vacillating representation, an ethnography of its own claim to being the norm of social contemporaneity."[23] Now that almost everyone agrees that the nation cannot be thought of as an ideal *Gemeinschaft*, the language of commonness must be supplemented by a discourse truly permeated by the idea that difference is woven into the fabric of the nation. The nation-space, Bhabha suggests, must be thought in "double-time," as the complex and fluid formation that emanates from the tension between the will to unity and cohesiveness (the pedagogical) and the ceaseless translation, iteration and transformation of the norms of public discourse (the performative or the counternarrative). There is a rift between the pluralized life-worlds of national subjects and the representation(s) of the nation as a self-identical site.[24] According to the nationalist pedagogy, simultaneously historical and teleological, "the scraps, patches and rags of daily life must be repeatedly turned into the signs of a coherent national culture."[25] Internal cohesiveness and temporal depth is posited to the nation.[26] The nation, as a political space, must thereby be thought of as a fluid configuration of power/knowledge relationships. Groups within the nations make use of these power relations to hegemonize discourses and practices, to impose narratives and to discard others. Hence, for instance, the propensity of a particular trend among Quebec nationalists to defend a uniform and Jacobin conception of citizenship. This also explains why, according to Taylor, "attitudes have become steadily more rigid in English Canada toward any possible accommodation of Quebec's difference during the last ten years."[27] Yet it is this very process of unification and homogenization that is being hampered by the struggles for disclosure and recognition of various minorities. Although always operating, the pedagogical's capacity to screen out or normalize difference is weakened by minority struggles. The voices from the margins, Bhabha continues, act as reminders of the ambivalent character of national identities: "minority discourse acknowledges the status of national culture – and the people – as a contentious, performative space of perplexity of the living in the midst of the pedagogical representations of the fullness of life."[28]

Yet, the conclusion that the nation is imploding and succumbing to the forces of fragmentation does not follow from this attempt to reframe the imaginary of the nation. The nation remains, despite its constitutive ambivalence, a powerful source of collective identification. A sizable majority of the diverse citizens of Quebec, Catalonia and Scotland, with all their identity-related differences and similarities, recognize themselves as Quebecers, Catalans and Scots. The driving force of their nationalism is, as I will argue in the following section, primarily democratic or political, rather than founded on the definition, defence and promotion of a "thick" identity.

New Nationalisms as Quests for Democratic Freedom

The struggles of minority nations for recognition do not revolve primarily around an ethics of authenticity understood as the defence and promotion of a substantive identity that ought to survive the "threat" of globalization and uniformization. National identities, even those defined as highly homogeneous, always include an intractable element of ambivalence, dissonance and dissensus. This dilation of the trace of difference within the nation under conditions of globalization does not only eventuate in the increasing multiculturalization of contemporary societies. Undoubtedly, citizens of diverse ethno-cultural backgrounds have to find ways of living together within the same political community. But, moreover, and more importantly for any attempt to think differently about the national imaginary, difference also pervades the boundaries of communities based on common ethnicity, culture or language. As I already pointed out, diverse class, sexual, gender, generational, religious and political identities cut across and intersect with the cultural identity shared by francophones from Quebec.[29] Pluralism is not only the coexistence of, and interaction between, different cultural forms of life but also the interplay of identity-related differences and similarities *within* a form of life. These different layers of diversity are irreconcilable with essentialist interpretations of national identity. National identity is *aspectival*: its form and character are shaped by the angle and position one takes to observe it.[30]

The nation's internal heterogeneity explains why democratic freedom – namely the nation's will and capacity to continuously decide on its norms of public recognition, its socio-economic orientations, its conditions of membership, its articulation of the rule of law and democracy principles, its place in the global order; thus on what it is and what it wants to become – rather than a consensual identity, is the driving force of the new nationalisms. This is to say, again, not that national identities are dissolving, but rather that the "commonness" that allegedly characterizes them should not be exaggerated. The character of a national identity is internally contested and changes over time: dissenters, immigrants, new generations and mutations within the identity of the majority trouble the hegemony of the dominant narrative. What resists these tribulations, I want to argue, is the will to self-determination (understood in the context of the attenuated and deflationary notion of sovereignty discussed earlier). A feeling of belonging to a national community, as the nationalisms of Quebec, Catalonia and Scotland tend to show, is maintained and heightened not by focusing on a consensual identity to defend but by the incessant participation of, and interaction between, diverse citizens who disagree over the rules and substance of the political association.[31] As Renan anticipated, attachment to the ongoing activity of self-interpretation and self-determination lies at the core of national consciousness. Reappraising the inalterable tension between the nation and its diversity does not necessarily lead to fragmentation but, potentially, leads to the creation of bonds of belonging between citizens who can deliberate (without covering up their identity-related differences) on the future of their political community and on their place in that future. This attachment to popular sovereignty or collective self-determination, rather than definitive agreement on a set of rights or on a shared identity, is the main facet of this new imaginary of belonging.[32] In some of its variants, minority nationalism would thus be less a static quest for cultural survival than a struggle for the capacity to decide collectively which aspects of culture should be reproduced.[33]

The politics of minority nations is thus an instance of what is now called "identity politics." The struggles of women, gays and lesbians, and immigrant, linguistic and religious minorities are in many ways different from the nationalism of minority nations, but are all primarily driven by the will to participate in an equitable (i.e., nonassimilative) fashion to the elaboration of the rules they must abide by. Minority nationalism, in this context, flirts with separatism only when this postsovereignist democratic freedom is thwarted by majority nations' centralism.[34]

Social Integration Revisited

Reappraising the tension between national identity and diversity leads us to the wider debate on the conditions of integration and co-operation in multicultural and multinational democracies. The way of seeing national identity and nationalism sketched out above suggests that the liberal-nationalist argument that unity and stability depend in the final analysis on a shared national identity needs to be revised. Rightly rejecting the view that unity and stability are grounded in shared values, Kymlicka concludes that "people decide who they want to share a country with by asking who they identify with, who they feel solidarity with. What holds Americans together together, despite their lack of common values, is the fact that they share an identity as Americans."[35]

This argument is surely partly right, as a feeling of belonging together contributes to keeping political communities stable, but it still raises some questions. Shared identities are said to be founded on a collective memory and on common visions for the future. But these sources of identity, even in a mononational community, are themselves contested and debated by citizens interpreting history differently and cherishing discrepant ideas of the common good. Of course, American citizens can defend conflicting interpretations of the past, narratives of identity and political visions and yet still identify themselves as Americans. But can this common identification account for social unity, stability and co-operation? Much more needs to be done to ground that hypothesis. Is a shared national identity, even when hotly debated, always sufficient to prevent fragmentation? It did not seem to be the case in Belgium, as a pan-Belgian identity preceded the consolidation of Flemish and Walloon identities.[36] And what if another identity-marker (such as religion) interposes itself between fellow citizens and trumps nationality as the most politically salient identity (think of the civil war in Lebanon, for instance)?

Moreover, as Kymlicka recognizes, the liberal-nationalist position is inadequate in the case of multinational states wherein the shared national identity is the source of much debate and instability. Turning to Charles Taylor, Kymlicka wonders whether stability in multinational settings lies in the respect for and affirmation of deep diversity, that is in the acceptance that there is a plurality of ways of belonging to the larger community (such as feeling attached to Spain through Catalan identity). This argument makes a great deal of sense. But liberal nationalists still have to explain why a shared national identity, albeit lived and interpreted differently, cannot ground stability and solidarity in multinational associations. After all, Spanish and Canadian identities are recognized and affirmed, to varying degrees, by a majority of Basques and Catalans and Quebecers respectively. Is the counterfactual argument, that people can only identify with a single national identity, implicit in the liberal-nationalist position?

If a nation is a continuous and polyphonic process of interpretation and narration, and debates over the character of its identity ongoing and rarely free of dissent, stability and cohesion must perhaps in the end rest on something "thinner" than the sharing of a national identity. But what is it that holds nations together if it is not, at least in the first instance, a shared national identity? Political theorists and scientists tend to link stability and cohesion to social harmony. Yet, for a variety of reasons, such as the reasonable pluralism of world views and of schemes of interpretation (heightened by cultural diversity), the limits and fallibility of the faculty of judgment (the burdens of judgment), and the persistence of unequal power relationships and real-time constraints, consensual resolutions of political debates are scarce and, at best, provisional. In line with the argument sketched out above, it is worth exploring the possibility that social integration does not depend on consensual agreement over controversial political issues, such as the substance of a shared national identity, for instance, but more fundamentally on the continuous activity of reworking the political community. Agreement over basic rights, constitutional essentials, dispute-resolution procedures, conceptions of the common good or the substance of a shared identity can facilitate and consolidate social co-operation and stability, but cannot be considered *sine qua non* preconditions.

The democratic process of exchanging reasons and visions with others not only spurs the capacity to develop a reflexive stance toward our own judgments and to see the association from a plurality of perspectives, but it also, as a byproduct, cultivates a thin or second-order form of belonging that can withstand punctual disagreement on substantive or procedural matters. It is a thin and second-order sentiment of belonging because it is engendered by means of and as a result of civic participation (*en passant,* so to speak). While more substantial forms of identification with a shared national identity or with the founding principles of a political community tend to be reflexively articulated and publicly affirmed, this thinner allegiance stays in the background and discloses itself through unnoticed actions and decisions, such as the acquiescence to express discontent publicly rather than violently, the endurance to persist with the game of argumentation in spite of frustration and tenacious disagreement and the willingness to water down one's wine when compromises are in reach. The bonds created through participation are thin also because they can be severed by repeated setbacks or by permanent bias in the procedure of public deliberation. When minorities and dissenters cannot effectively partake in the game or when the rules of the game are biased against them, they regroup in other loci of opinion- and will-formation and imagine ways of either transforming or destabilizing the wider political community.

Social integration under circumstances of pluralism and disagreement would thus lie, as the argument goes, in the ongoing possibility of challenging prevailing decisions and political stabilizations. Citizens who disagree with each other or with public officials can still identify with the community insofar as they can voice their dissent and initiate new rounds of public deliberation. Tully presents this argument:

> Citizens develop a sense of identification with the principles and the association to which they are applied not because a consensus is reached, or is on the horizon, but precisely because they become aware that, despite its current imperfections and injustices, the association is nonetheless not closed but open to this form of democratic freedom. It is a free association. This legitimacy-conferring aspect of citizen participation generates the unique kind of solidarity characteristic of constitutional democracies in the face of disagreement, diversity and negotiation.[37]

Civic bonds are most severely weakened when the capacity of dissenting citizens to contest controversial resolutions is blocked and when they feel it is no longer worthwhile to struggle for the reformation of the polity's institutions, norms, laws and policies. Ending on the losing side of a particularly intense battle obviously undermines one's allegiance to the community, but the overall stability of a regime is preserved if the game goes on. Social integration, understood as the threshold of stability and co-operation required for ensuring peaceful co-existence, rests in the final analysis on the processual and gamelike character of democratic politics. Decision-making is an unavoidable moment of politics, but it is a moment that almost unavoidably produces exclusion and injustice.

Dissenters can still confer legitimacy to the political process if they can express their particular and generalizable public reasons and listen to the reasons and stories of others, are able to initiate a second-order discussion on the procedures of public reason if needed, and have good reason to believe that they will be able to bring the resolution back to the moment of deliberation if new evidence proves their position right. When these demanding conditions are respected, dissenters' broader political or civic identity can withstand the shock of outrage and disappointment caused by punctual defeats because it is on the basis of that identity that they will get to initiate new public challenges.[38] In sum, the legitimacy of and identification with a regime of citizenship partly hangs on a complex and nonideal framework of agonistic public deliberation.

To take an example, when the conversation is going, as it is now, Aboriginal peoples in Quebec do not attempt to destabilize the state of Quebec.[39] This is obviously to suggest not that *talk* can in itself satisfy minorities and ensure stability in any context (talk must be supplemented with action) but that a vibrant and continuous democratic process fosters a thin form of belonging capable of grounding to a certain extent social co-operation in conditions of ethical pluralism and cultural diversity. The laborious democratic dialogue between Quebec and Canada partly explains the fact that, in spite of the defeat of the sovereignist party in power (the Parti Québécois) at the 2003 election, support for sovereignty in Quebec has fluctuated between 40 and 44 percent since the 1995 referendum.[40]

Liberal nationalists could perhaps agree with the argument that it cannot be agreement in a thick sense, on the substance of a shared national identity, that grounds social co-operation and political stability, given that debates over the substance and contours of a shared national identity are ongoing, but they would still add that the nation *is* the political space that enables democratic participation. Yet, as the age of the nation-state comes to a close (which is not to say that nations and nation-states are withering away), infranational and transnational sites of political deliberation and action are proliferating. Groups and minority nations that have been excluded or marginalized within nation-states are regrouping, entering into processes of will- and opinion-formation and challenging the sovereignty of the state. Environmental, financial, migration and security problems that disregard national borders have forced the creation of transnational public fora. The nation-state is, therefore, one pre-eminent and distinct political space among others.

Conclusion

The aim of this paper was to shed some light on an elided aspect of nationalism, not to provide a normative theory of nationalism.[41] My suspicion is that nationalist manifestations around the world are too diverse for such a theory to get off the ground. The differences between various nations and nationalisms might be as important as the similarities between them.[42] Furthermore, it was very remote from my intention to suggest that the nationalisms of small nations such as Quebec, Catalonia and Scotland are univocal. Quebec, Catalan and Scottish nationalists disagree on what constitutes their respective nations and on what kind of nationalism they should promote. If an important majority of nationalists from these three countries are devoted to a civic, inclusive and pluralist conception of the nation,[43] countertrends are also being voiced. Ethnicism, xenophobia, assimilationism and the evilization of the Other inside and outside have not vanished from some of the nationalist discourses of small and big nations all over the world.

Yet, now that a number of scholars are trying to show that nationalism does not stand in an aporetic relation with both liberal values and political frameworks founded on shared sovereignty, the tension between national identity and diversity needs to be re-evaluated. Nations such as Quebec, Catalonia and Scotland, which simultaneously constitute majorities within their boundaries and minorities within wider states or federations, should be seen not as standard cases capable of explaining any minoritarian form of nationalism, but rather as laboratories for the experience of this new symbolic and dynamic form of nationalism. The idea of "commonness" can no longer suture the general economy of nationalism. Scholars must explore how nations, as plurivocal and dissensual communities of conversation, self-interpretation and self-determination, can articulate collective action, social co-operation and common belonging with internal difference and enduring political disagreement.

Notes

An earlier version of this paper was presented at the "Stateless Nations" conference at the University of Edinburgh (January 2001) and to the Research Group on Plurinational Societies at McGill University.

1. Brubaker (1996), Laitin (1998).

2. Tamir (1993), Kymlicka (1995) and Miller (1995).

3. For further developments on the liberal nationalism debate, see, among others, Weinstock (1996), Mason (1999), Buttle (2000), Patten (1999) and Moore (1999, 2000).

4. See Keating (1996), Brubaker (1996), Guibernau (1996, 1999) and Calhoun (1997, 1994).

5. Gellner (1983, p. 43).

6. Gellner (1983, p. 6.

7. Anderson (1991, p. 7).

8. For example, see Laforest (1995), Maclure (2003) and Gagnon (2001) for the case of Quebec, and Guibernau (in this volume) for that of Catalonia.

9. Keating (1996, p. 53). See also Guibernau (1999), Castells (1997) and Dieckhoff (2000). This new meaning, I believe, cannot be captured by the "civic-ethnic" dichotomy proposed by Ignatieff (1994). Most nations, as Ignatieff (2000) himself now recognizes, are made of both civic and ethnic elements. The German constitution, for instance, includes various civic dispositions – even if Germany is usually used as a trope for the ethnic nation. In addition, every "civic" nation is driven by an "ethnic" majority. Public institutions are never fully culturally blind. See Kymlicka (1995), Kymlicka and Straehle (1999) and Seymour (2000).

10. Gellner (1983, p. 125). However, for some noticeable exceptions, see Tully (1995, 2002a), Hedetoft (1999) and Bhabha (1994).

11. Guibernau (1999, p. 31).

12. Guibernau (1999, p. 14.

13. Wieviorka (2001), Amselle (2001).

14. Derrida (1991, p. 16).

15. Tully (1995, p. 13), Hall (1996, p. 4), Geertz (2000, pp. 68-88), Karmis and Maclure (2001).

16. Clifford (1997).

17. As the last part of the sentence makes clear, Quebec is submitted to the dynamics of multiculturalism and multinationalism on the one hand and to interculturalism, *métissage* and mutual contamination on the other.

18. Geertz (2000, p. 227).

19. Calhoun (1994, p. 314).

20. Balibar (1995), Anderson (1991).

21. Karmis and Maclure (2001), Nootens (1999).

22. Maclure (2003).

23. Bhabha (1994, p. 149).

24. This does not mean that each and every national subject will feel the nation the way Bhabha or numbers of migrants do. The point is not to universalize *that* experience of nationness but rather to highlight the potential dissonance between the experience of nationality and its representation. In conditions of deep pluralism, a feeling of *dépaysement* often affects the non migrant citizen even at "home."

25. Bhahba (1994, p. 145).

26. Calhoun (1997, p. 11).

27. Taylor (1999, p. 277).

28. Bhahba (1994, p. 157). This subjectivist picture of the nation is obviously at odds with the objectivist view, which holds that people feel they belong together because they *really* share various features together, such as culture, religion, language, understandings of the past and projects for the future. But what is missing from the subjectivist interpretation, embraced in different ways by J.S. Mill, Renan, Anderson and others, is a more thorough thematization of the nation's constitutive ambivalence. For a nuanced objectivist position, see Miller (1995). It is worthwhile noting that a subjectivist position does not have to deny that a nation actually shares some "objective" features, but needs only to suggest that objective features are not sufficient to create a common self-consciousness and that people have different (and sometimes incompatible) interpretations of the objective elements they share.

29. Maclure (2003, ch. 4).

30. Tully (1995, p. 11).

31. This emphasis on self-rule is particularly strong in multinational units constituted by overlapping and often conflicting spheres of

legitimacy. See the chapters gathered in Gagnon and Tully (2001).

32. Tully (2002a).

33. This aspect is present in Taylor's founding essay on the politics of recognition, but should, I believe, have been emphasized more (1994).

34. Keating (2001), Guibernau (in this volume).

35. Kymlicka (1995, p. 188).

36. Karmis and Gagnon (2001).

37. Tully (2002b, p. 211).

38. Tully (2002a).

39. I am referring here to the process that led to the reactualization of the James Bay Agreement with the Cree in 2001-02 and to the current negotiations with the Innu.

40. Much more needs to be done for grounding this thesis on stability. For a more detailed but still tentative demonstration, see Maclure (unpublished).

41. For such an attempt, see Norman (1999).

42. Taylor (1997, p. 52).

43. Keating (1996), Carens (1995).

Bibliography

Amselle, Jean-Loup. *Vers un multiculturalisme français. L'empire de la coutume.* Paris: Champs-Flammarion, 2001.

Anderson, Benedict. *Imagined Communities,* 2nd edition, revised and extended. London and New York: Verso, 1991.

Appadurai, Arjun. *Modernity at Large: Cultural Dimensions of Globalization.* Minneapolis: University of Minnesota Press, 1996.

Balibar, Etienne. "Culture and Identity," in *The Identity in Question,* ed. John Rachman. New York: Routledge, 1995.

Barry, Brian. *Culture and Equality.* Cambridge: Polity Press, 2000.

Bhabha, Homi. *The Location of Culture.* London: Routledge, 1994.

Brubaker, Roger. *Nationalism Reframed: Nationhood and the National Question in the New Europe.* Cambridge: Cambridge University Press, 1996.

Buttle, Nicholas. "Critical Nationalism: A Liberal Prescription?" *Nations and Nationalism,* Vol. 6, no. 1 (2000): 111-27.

Calhoun, Craig. "Nationalism and Civil Society: Democracy, Diversity and Self-Determination," in *Social Theory and the Politics of Identity,* ed. Craig Calhoun. Oxford: Blackwell Publishers, 1994.

———. *Nationalism.* Buckingham: Open University Press, 1997.

Carens, Joseph H. "Liberalism, Justice, and Political Community: Theoretical Perspectives on Quebec's Liberal Nationalism," in *Is Québec Nationalism Just? Perspectives from Anglophone Canada,* ed. Joseph H. Carens. Montreal and Kingston: McGill-Queen's University Press, 1995.

Castells, Manuel. *The Information Age II: The Power of Identity.* Oxford: Blackwell, 1997.

Clifford, James. *Routes: Travel and Translation in the Late Twentieth Century.* London: Harvard University Press, 1997.

Connolly, William E. *Identity/Difference: Democratic Negotiations of Political Paradox.* Ithaca: Cornell University Press, 1991.

———. *The Ethos of Pluralization.* Minneapolis: University of Minnesota Press, 1995.

Derrida, Jacques. *L'autre cap.* Paris: Les Éditions de Minuit, 1991.

Dieckhoff, A. *La nation dans tous ses États. Les identité nationales en mouvement.* Paris: Flammarion, 2000.

Foucault, Michel. "Le sujet et le pouvoir," in *Dits et écrits volume IV.* Paris: Gallimard, 1994.

Gagnon, Alain-G. "The Moral Foundation of Asymmetrical Federalism: A Normative Exploration of the Case of Quebec and Canada," in *Multinational Democracies,* ed. Alain-G. Gagnon and James Tully. Cambridge: Cambridge University Press, 2001.

Gagnon, Alain-G., and James Tully, eds. *Multinational Democracies.* Cambridge: Cambridge University Press, 2001.

Geertz, Clifford. *Available Light.* Princeton: Princeton University Press, 2000.

Gellner, Ernest. *Nations and Nationalism.* Ithaca: Cornell University Press, 1983.

Guibernau, Monserrat. *The Nation-State and Nationalism in the Twentieth Century.* Cambridge: Polity Press, 1996.

————. *Nations without States: Political Communities in a Global Age*. Cambridge: Polity Press, 1999.

Hall, Stuart. "Introduction: Who Needs 'Identity'?" in *Questions of Cultural Identity*, ed. Stuart Hall and Paul Du Gay. Thousand Oaks, CA: Sage, 1996.

Hedetoft, Ulf. "The Nation-State Meets the World: National Identity in the Context of Transnationality and Cultural Globalization." *European Journal of Social Theory*, Vol. 2, no. 1 (1999): 71-94.

Ignatieff, Michael. *Blood and Belonging: Journeys into the New Nationalism*. London: Vintage, 1994.

————. *The Rights Revolution*. Toronto: Anansi, 2000.

Karmis, Dimitrios, and Jocelyn Maclure. "Two Escape Routes from the Paradigm of Monistic Authenticity: Post-Imperial and Federal Perspectives on Complex and Plural Identities." *Ethnic and Racial Studies*, Vol. 24, no. 3 (2001): 361-85.

Karmis, Dimitrios, and Alain-G. Gagnon. "Federalism, Federation and Collective Identities in Canada and Belgium: Different Routes, Similar Fragmentation," in *Multinational Democracies*, ed. Alain-G. Gagnon and James Tully. Cambridge: Cambridge University Press, 2001.

Keating, Michael. *Nations against the State: The New Politics of Nationalism in Quebec, Catalonia and Scotland*. London: Macmillan, 1996.

————. *Beyond Sovereignty: Plurinational Democracy in a Post-Sovereign World*. Les Grandes Conférences Desjardins, Programme d'études sur le Québec, March 2001.

Kymlicka, Will. *Multicultural Citizenship*. Oxford: Clarendon Press, 1995.

Kymlicka, Will, and Christine Straehle. "Cosmopolitanism, Nation-States, and Minority Nationalism: A Critical Review of Recent Literature." *European Journal of Philosophy*, Vol. 7, no. 1 (1999): 65-88.

Laforest, Guy. *De l'urgence. Textes politiques 1994-1995*. Montreal: Boréal, 1995.

Laitin, David D. *Identity in Formation: The Russian-Speaking Populations in the Near Abroad*. Ithaca: Cornell University Press, 1998.

Maclure, Jocelyn. *Quebec Identity: The Challenge of Pluralism*. Montreal and Kingston: McGill-Queen's University Press, 2003.

————. "Breaking with the Social Harmony Tradition: Social Integration in Conditions of Diversity." Unpublished paper on file with author.

Mason, Andrew. "Political Community, Liberal-Nationalism, and the Ethic of Assimilation." *Ethics*, Vol. 109 (1999): 261-86.

Miller, David. *On Nationality*. Oxford: Oxford University Press, 1995.

Moore, Margaret. "Beyond the Cultural Argument for Liberal Nationalism." *Critical Review of International Social and Political Philosophy*, Vol. 2, no. 3 (1999): 26-47.

Nootens, Geneviève. "L'identité postnationale: itinéraire(s) de la citoyenneté dans la modernité avancée." *Politique et Sociétés*, Vol. 18, no. 3 (1999): 99-120.

Norman, Wayne. "Theorizing Nationalism (Normatively): The First Steps," in *Theorizing Nationalism*, ed. Ronald Beiner. Albany: State University of New York Press, 1999.

Patten, Alan. "The Autonomy Argument for Liberal Nationalism." *Nations and Nationalism*, Vol. 5, no. 1 (1999): 1-17.

Seymour, Michel. "Quebec and Canada at the Crossroads: A Nation within a Nation." *Nations and Nationalism*, Vol. 6, no. 2 (2000): 227-57.

Tamir, Yael. *Liberal Nationalism*. Princeton: Princeton University Press, 1993.

Taylor, Charles. "The Politics of Recognition," in *Multiculturalism*, ed. Amy Gutmann. Princeton: Princeton University Press, 1994.

———. "Nationalism and Modernity," in *The Morality of Nationalism*, ed. Robert McKim and Jeff McMahan. New York and Oxford: Oxford University Press, 1997.

———. "Democratic Exclusion (and its Remedies)," in *Citizenship, Diversity, and Pluralism: Canadian and Comparative Perspectives*, eds. A.C. Cairns, J.C. Courtney, Peter MacKinnon, Hans J. Michelmann and David Smith. Montreal and Kingston: McGill-Queen's University Press, 1999.

Tully, James. *Strange Multiplicity: Constitutionalism in an Age of Diversity*. Cambridge: Cambridge University Press, 1995.

———. "Introduction," in *Multinational Democracies*, ed. Alain-G. Gagnon and James Tully. Cambridge: Cambridge University Press, 2001.

———. "Reimagining Belonging in Circumstances of Cultural Diversity: A Citizenship Approach," in *The Postnational Self: Belonging and Identity*, eds. Ulf Hedetoft and Mette Hjort. Minneapolis: University of Minnesota Press, 2002a.

———. "The Unfreedom of the Moderns in Comparison to Their Ideals of Constitutional Democracy." *Modern Law Review*, Vol. 65, no. 2 (2002b): 211.

Walker, Brian. "Modernity and Cultural Vulnerability: Should Ethnicity Be Privileged?" in *Theorizing Nationalism*, ed. Ronald Beiner. Albany: State University of New York Press, 1999.

Webber, Jeremy. *Reimagining Canada: Language, Culture, Community, and the Canadian Constitution*. Montreal and Kingston: McGill-Queen's University Press, 1994.

Weinstock, Daniel. "Is There a Moral Case for Nationalism?" *Journal of Applied Philosophy*, Vol. 13, no. 1 (1996): 85-100.

Wieviorka, Michel. *La difference*. Paris: Balland, 2001.

4

rethinking political recognition

Michel Seymour

This paper discusses the reluctance of liberal philosophers and political scientists to engage in politics of recognition for minorities. This reluctance is especially strong with respect to the entrenchment of the collective rights of minority nations and "linguistic national minorities" (understood as extensions of neighbouring national majorities) in constitutional documents. I first sketch the theoretical framework that can support such political recognition and then discuss some of the objections to political recognition that have been raised from a liberal perspective. As I understand it, politics of recognition must translate into constitutionally entrenched collective rights, and this can coherently be done within a liberal framework as long as the approach is inspired by political liberalism. My hope is that by answering those objections, I can pave the way for a liberal theory of collective rights.

Political Liberalism as a Theoretical Framework

The liberal framework that I use here is that of political liberalism, that is, the view according to which liberalism must avoid any commitment to comprehensive theses in metaphysics.[1] It is founded upon a political conception of the person as well as a political conception of peoples (nations), and it is neutral toward issues of personal identity, moral psychology and social ontology. Individuals have an institutional identity and are conceived as citizens no matter how they represent themselves from a metaphysical point of view (single or multiple identity, individualistic or communitarian, narrative or essentialist, dualistic or materialistic, religious or secular, etc.). Nations also have an institutional identity quite apart from representing themselves as ethnic, civic, cultural, socio-political[2] or diasporic. Political liberalism does not imply a commitment to the view according to which persons are "prior to their ends." We can be neutral in the debate between individualists, who believe that persons are individuated as independent from any moral or religious beliefs, and communitarians, who reject that view. The crucial point is that our institutional identity must be understood as distinct from our metaphysical identity, and this entails, among other things, that we must distinguish between institutional and moral identities. While our moral identity may change, our institutional identity remains the same whether or not we can be considered under those circumstances as having as well the same personal identity. Rawls reminds us that, on the way to Damascus, Saul of Tarsus became Paul the Apostle. Individualists say that he remained the same person but changed his moral beliefs. Communitarians say that Saul of Tarsus became another person. Without engaging in the debate, Rawls suggests that we can acknowledge that his institutional identity remained the same.[3] We can say that we are confronted with the same citizen, even if communitarians *may* be right in thinking that we are not dealing with the same person, in the metaphysical sense.

Similarly, peoples can be described as having a certain institutional identity. We can thus introduce a political conception of peoples that parallels that introduced for persons.[4] Using Kymlicka's terminology, we can describe them as "societal cultures" involving common languages, common "structures of cultures" and common histories.[5] These institutional features belong to all sorts of nations, whether their populations also conceive themselves as ethnic, civic, cultural, socio-political or diasporic.

Political liberalism also entails that individuals are not the ultimate sources of moral worth, for peoples too have an autonomous moral worth. I am favourable to an axiological pluralism in virtue of which the equal moral importance of individuals and peoples is asserted. This leads to the admission of two distinct original positions, one for individuals and one for peoples.[6] Ultimately, it also implies that we are seeking an equilibrium between individual and collective rights. We reject both ethical individualism and ethical collectivism. Individual rights must not override collective rights and collective rights must not override individual rights. So we are not favourable to approaches that attempt to derive collective rights from arguments that ultimately rely only on claims made by individuals. We reject both accounts that treat the subjects of collective rights as individuals and arguments purporting to show that collectivities only have instrumental value for individuals. We must make room for full-blooded collective rights and not only for "group differentiated rights."[7] Collective rights are claimed not on behalf of individuals but on behalf of peoples. The subjects of these rights are not individuals, they are peoples, and their relevance is not to be explained by the value individuals ascribe to their own cultural affiliations. Peoples are valuable because they contribute to cultural diversity and because there is a growing overlapping consensus on the value of cultural diversity.

As this argument does not presuppose ethical individualism or ethical collectivism, I disagree with Kymlicka on the appropriate justification for collective rights. He is certainly right to claim that peoples understood as societal cultures provide necessary conditions for the implementation of liberal values. But Kymlicka is also aware that this is not sufficient to justify the promotion and protection of many different societal cultures, for the claim is compatible with the existence of a unique societal culture for all mankind. Nor is it sufficient to suggest that most citizens favour, among other things, the protection of their own cultural affiliations, for the population may equally favour many other sorts of group affiliations and the state cannot provide assistance to all the groups. So Kymlicka must provide an argument that justifies the special character of *cultural* protection, and must thus find a justification for saying that societal cultures should be the primary targets of the politics of recognition (whether they are minority nations, linguistic national minorities or immigrant groups).

To do this, Kymlicka is forced to postulate in the minds of persons the existence of a rational preference toward *their own particular cultural affiliation.*[8] This additional premise allows him to justify a certain cultural protection for many different minorities within the constraints of ethical individualism. The trouble is that it is simply not true that among all the possible group affiliations most people prefer their own cultural affiliation. Individuals rank their allegiances very differently, and they even change their minds from time to time. Some do not care about their cultural affiliation. Others rank it very low. The inevitable conclusion is that the individualistic justification for collective rights fails.

But the approach presented here does not postulate such a problematic rational preference, because it does not try to justify collective rights solely by relying on individuals as sources of moral worth. Of course, I accept that as a matter of fact societal cultures are necessary conditions for the implementation of a system of rights and liberties. I also accept that the majority of citizens must be favourable to the protection of their own societal cultures, for if they were not, assimilation would no longer constitute a moral harm. But I disagree with the suggestion that there is a consensus among the population to the effect that cultural affiliation occupies centre stage among all group affiliations. On the contrary, we have to acknowledge the wide variety of multiple identities within the population and acknowledge their dynamic character. So we have to seek another argument, and I suggest that an anti-individualistic justification that relies on the value of cultural diversity provides exactly what we are looking for.

Let us consider for instance the principle of the instrumental value of cultural diversity relative to the human species. It is not to be confused with a thesis regarding the intrinsic value of cultural diversity,[9] nor with a view asserting the instrumental value of cultural diversity for the individual.[10] The survival of the human species is seen as having an intrinsic moral worth in addition to the moral worth of individuals, and it is relative to the survival of the human species that we can acknowledge the value of cultural diversity. Just as a diversified economy can be a necessary condition for prosperity, the protection of cultural diversity is an insurance policy against the disappearance of the human species.[11]

On the basis of this first premise asserting the value of cultural diversity, we can develop an argument for political recognition. We accept that there are many different concepts of the nation (ethnic, civic, cultural, socio-political and diasporic) that are irreducible to one another and we choose to acknowledge this irreducible diversity. This is our second premise. So let us accept such an irreducible conceptual pluralism regarding the nation. It entails a tolerant attitude toward the different ways of conceptualizing peoples.

We should add, as a third premise, that nationhood is at least in part a matter of self-representation and, as an empirical observation, that many different populations entertain different self-representations involving these different concepts of the nation. Indeed, many communities are engaged in a nation-building process in which they articulate their national consciousness in accordance with different national self-representations involving different concepts. Some may even be engaged simultaneously in many different national self-representations.

Finally, we must also acknowledge that these different self-representations contribute to cultural diversity. This is certainly the case when the self-representations are articulated with a different concept, for the self-representations suppose different ways of understanding human communities. Aboriginal peoples often see themselves as ethnic nations. Other populations insist on the importance of language, culture and history. Some populations hail the virtues of civic identity. There are also national groupings that try to steer a course between civic and cultural identities by putting forward a socio-political model. Finally, some diasporic nations will also emerge and try to survive in spite of their diasporic nature. Accepting these different self-representations is one of the best ways we have to ensure that human diversity is preserved. Even when two communities are the same sort of nations, there are important differences that serve the purpose of cultural diversity.

If we agree with all those claims, then we must realize that together they provide a philosophical justification for adopting a policy of recognition toward peoples.

In other words, it is claimed that we must first adopt an attitude of tolerance toward different concepts of the nation, since this pluralism has led to a formidable diversity in the self-representations of peoples. And it is claimed that we must grant a political recognition in the public sphere to these different national identities, since they serve the purpose of cultural diversity and cultural diversity is instrumental for the survival of the human species. Just as individuals with different views of themselves may all be recognized as citizens, peoples having different national representations may be recognized as societal cultures.

I said that the kind of liberalism I favour is political liberalism. In this regard, it is important to point out that political liberalism is not ultimately founded upon the value of individual autonomy but rather upon the value of tolerance. But this idea of tolerance should not be understood as implying that liberals must tolerate anti-liberal political regimes. Tolerance applies first and foremost to different conceptions of persons and peoples. In other words, it stems from the acknowledgment of an irreducible diversity of metaphysical views concerning the person and the people. For this reason, it can bring about in the public realm a mutual recognition between citizens and between societal cultures that can lead to consensus on the political conception of the person and the political conception of the people. Tolerance also inevitably applies to the irreducible variety of moral ideals held by these different individuals and peoples, which can then bring about political liberalism. But it need *not* imply that political liberalism itself should be relativized and that we should be tolerant toward anti-liberal regimes. Once we agree on the political conceptions of the person and of the people and agree on the irreducibility of reasonable views about the good life or about common good, we can then proceed to derive political liberalism. And since the conceptions of persons and peoples are universal in character, we must also agree that political liberalism is itself a universal doctrine. Consequently, there is no reason to conclude that tolerance involves a commitment to a certain form of political relativism.

Now, it is true that Rawls argued both for political liberalism and for tolerance toward hierarchical (anti-liberal) societies, but there is no logical connection between these two views. Let me emphasize that point, since people generally reject political liberalism precisely on the grounds that it leads to relativism.[12] Rawls was led to embrace this view of toleration toward nonliberal regimes because he also held the view that the normative principles and the conception of the person on which political liberalism is based are the result of a historical consensus that has been achieved within our own political culture. Rawls thus interprets political liberalism as a particular historical achievement within democratic societies. When we understand it that way, we inevitably see it through the lens of a relativistic approach. But one can reject this communitarian turn that took place simultaneously with the Rawlsian defence of political liberalism. The consensus reached concerning the political conception of the person need not be founded solely upon tradition, since it can be re-enacted through deliberation and discussion.

Moreover, one must acknowledge the existence of a global basic structure and reject Rawls' idea that there are only local basic structures. Rawls mistakenly believes only in the basic structures that exist within traditional nation-states, and he seems to ignore completely the effects of globalization. *Pace* Rawls, there is indeed a global basic structure that perhaps does not entirely replace the local ones but that still has an enormous influence over our lives. The cosmopolitan conception of the person can thus be introduced within an amended Rawlsian framework, as long as we accept the extension of the notion of basic structure at the global level. The cosmopolitan person is just the political person in a global basic structure. The veil of ignorance, a device by which individuals accept to ignore their own specific social, economic, class and ethnic affiliations in order to reach impartiality, can therefore be applied to cosmopolitan persons in a second stage within Rawls' first original position, whereby individuals belong to a single, homogeneous people.

We must also leave behind Rawls' propensity to avoid complexity. We live in multi-ethnic societies and not within closed societies that we enter only by birth and leave only by death. So a consensus reached through deliberation between citizens of different origins at the local level could be seen to indicate that the same consensus can also be reached at the level of the global structure. Unfortunately, Rawls has chosen to work within simplified models only. This is perhaps initially a reasonable methodological choice, since it allows him to distinguish between justice within a people and justice between peoples, but working only with the simplified model of an ethnically uniform society can also lead one to downplay the cosmopolitan virtues of political liberalism. If political liberalism can be implemented anywhere, it must be within our own democratic societies. These are increasingly polyethnic, pluricultural and multinational. If it can be accepted by citizens of different origins within our societies, we cannot continue to argue that the consensus cannot be exported to the global structure.

In summary, one can remain faithful to political liberalism without having to become tolerant toward nonliberal regimes. In order to secure this position, we must make amendments to the initial doctrine of political liberalism. We can disentangle political liberalism from its own historical roots through discussion and deliberation. We can also widen the scope of application of the veil of ignorance to the global society by acknowledging that there is after all a global basic structure. And we can treat the consensus reached at the local level between individuals having different origins as an empirical indication that confirms the results we have reached under the veil of ignorance at the global level. Political liberalism can then itself be seen as a realistic utopia even within the international arena if it can work in our multi-ethnic societies. So, even if it is founded upon the value of tolerance between different metaphysical views of the person and of the people and between different moral ends, it does not lead to tolerance toward nonliberal regimes.

It may be surprising to see Rawls' political liberalism used in an argument for political recognition, especially since we have also criticized Kymlicka. I agree that Rawls has had almost nothing to say concerning the problems of cultural protection for linguistic national minorities and minority nations, and I agree that Kymlicka has done a fantastic job in this regard. But I disagree with Kymlicka's ethical individualism, for I believe that one cannot appropriately derive an adequate account of collective rights if one adopts ethical individualism.[13] This is why I find Rawls' approach so appealing. Rawls defends a liberal approach that is not founded upon ethical individualism, nor upon any other comprehensive doctrine. He can thus work with a watered down political notion of peoples as well as a watered down political notion of person. It is for this reason that he can also acknowledge the autonomous moral value of peoples, and allow for a second original position involving peoples.

It is true that the "peoples" discussed by Rawls in his *Law of Peoples* are those that already have their own states. He almost never discusses in his work the fate of stateless peoples. This is not a theoretical failing but rather the result of a simplified methodology. Rawls has chosen to consider in first approximation only the simple case of peoples that already have their own states. Just as he considers for the sake of simplicity a first original position involving individuals belonging to a single homogeneous people, he assumes that the law of peoples must in first approximation deal only with an international order in which all peoples would have their own states. The eight principles that Rawls describes as forming the basis for a consensus reached in such an international order apply to peoples as organized into states. In both domestic and international justice, these are extreme simplifications. But it is clear that Rawls' approach is perfectly compatible with developments that increasingly take into consideration the complexity of our own societies. Rawls explicitly claims that the eight principles should be complemented by rules for federations of peoples, and he crucially adds that there must also be rules concerning the self-determination and secession of peoples. He states that a "people" should not in the course of secession subjugate the rights of another "people."[14] In these particular occurrences, the word "people" does not apply to the owners of a state, for it refers to a population seeking to create its own nation-state or to minority nations that are part of a seceding people. Rawls also briefly discusses in a footnote the illegitimate character of the Confederate States during the American Civil War.[15] Whether or not the Southerners formed a people, secession would have been illegitimate because its segregationist character would have violated the fundamental obligation to protect basic human rights that is expressed in the law of peoples. Once again, the people involved in this argument is not the owner of a state, and the law of peoples has applications within the state and not only in the international realm.

The clarifications I gave above and the proposed amendments lead to a reformulation of Rawls' theory. It should be clear that I favour a cosmopolitan law of peoples in which the rights and obligations of individuals and peoples are asserted and have application locally in the domestic realm and globally in the international realm.

I want to argue for the political recognition of peoples within multination states. Let me, however, close these preliminary remarks by saying that my approach is not meant to serve as an argument against nation-states. It is true that it is concerned with the viability of multination states, but this does not mean that I endorse only this model of political organization. On the contrary, just as I am willing to tolerate different views of the person and of the people, and different moral views held by them, I also wish to recognize the existence of a wide variety of political models. These include nation-states, multination states (for example, multinational federations) and confederations of nation-states.

As it is now customarily suggested, nation-states are weakened from above through globalization and from below through the pressures exerted by cultural minorities. But globalization and cultural minorities do not announce the end of nation-states as such. Globalization may indeed create a need to establish political supranational organizations, but these organizations should, among other things, be understood as a means of protecting nations against the negative effects of globalization, and these nations include those that are organized into nation-states. There is also certainly a need to recognize cultural diversity within sovereign states, but that too must not entail the dissolution of the nation-state. At best, it affords reasons for developing a *de jure* pluricultural conception of the nation-state, based on a pluricultural view of the nation.

Indeed, there should not necessarily be a tension between nation-states and cultural pluralism. Those who think that there is very often presuppose an outdated conception of the nation. They wrongly believe that nations must be ethnically or culturally homogeneous. But this need not be so. There is no oxymoron involved in the idea of a pluricultural nation, one that allows for an explicit recognition of minority cultures (linguistic national minorities and immigrant minorities). And so there is no contradiction between nation-states and politics of recognition of minority cultures within the state.

We should, therefore, adopt a pluralist approach and realize that some peoples could develop into nation-states while others could engage in confederations with other peoples. Some will want to form federations with other peoples, and others, like those within the European Union, for instance, will find that the most appropriate model is a hybrid mixture involving federative and confederative features. So in a sense, even if the traditional ethnically and culturally homogeneous nation-state is outdated, we cannot say that the nation-state model as such is outdated. It is just that it can no longer be the only political model available and that where it survives it has to go through important transformations, for it must involve a political recognition of cultural minorities. The nation-state should not be ruled out and replaced by a single alternative political model for, to repeat, *cultural* pluralism calls for *political* pluralism, and political pluralism requires the recognition of a wide variety of political models such as the nation-state model itself. So, far from entailing the dissolution of the nation-state, cultural diversity more subtly calls for a pluralist approach at the political level, which in turn may lead us to accept in certain cases the creation of new nation-states.

Furthermore, if we truly are cultural pluralists, we should be willing to fight for a political recognition of cultural diversity. When a state contains many different national groups, we should make sure that this cultural pluralism is reflected in the constitution, in the institutions and in the many different administrative arrangements within the multination society. But if a state refuses to recognize its minority nations, then they will have a moral argument for secession and thus a moral argument to create a new nation-state. So one cannot simply announce the end of nation-states just by invoking cultural pluralism, globalization or multiple identities. A failure to defend cultural pluralism by the encompassing state could, on the contrary, lead us to a different form of political recognition of cultural diversity; that is, the creation of new sovereign states.

This is, in rough outline, what I take to be the general theoretical framework behind the politics of recognition. It provides the philosophical background for politics of recognition in a multination state. It is an argument based on justice and not on stability for the multination state, although it might be argued that serving the cause of justice may be the best way to ensure in the long run the stability of the state. Of course, arguments based on stability may also be invoked for politics of recognition. It can be argued that in order to ensure the viability of multination states, we should implement politics of recognition of the component nations belonging to those states. The rationale behind this is that one cannot expect a nation to be willing to accept a devolution of its sovereignty to an encompassing state while failing to be recognized as a nation within that state. So I wish to claim that those who argue for multination states and against politics of recognition defend an unstable position. In order to avoid such a problem, one must make room for the entrenchment of collective rights of peoples in the constitution of multination states. I shall not develop this particular argument any further, however, but turn instead to objections that have been raised against political recognition.

Reification?

Some of the objections raised against the political recognition of peoples have to do with the ontology of collectivities. It is claimed that the defender of collective rights for peoples must postulate a dubious collective entity, a macrosubject that is problematic from an ontological point of view. But this objection can easily be countered if the general framework adopted is political liberalism. I have argued that political liberalism is founded upon a political conception of the person and of the people.[16] By "political conception of the person," Rawls understands a consensual and publicly available self-representation of individuals who see themselves in the political realm as "moral persons," that is, as having a certain rational autonomy as far as their institutional identity is concerned. This consensual self-representation has gained credence within our modern political culture. It is well suited to account for the concept of citizen, that is, for our "institutional identity." It does not involve factual claims concerning our moral psychology.[17]

If liberalism is supported by a political conception of the person, this creates favourable conditions for similarly introducing a political conception of peoples who see themselves as constituting full societal cultures. Nations are, at least in part, "imagined communities,"[18] and we do not need to postulate their existence out there in the real world as independent metaphysical entities. From a strict metaphysical point of view, there could be good reasons to believe that there are important ontological problems in admitting the existence of peoples. But the situation is quite different if we rely just on a political conception. In this case, we make use of a consensual self-representation that does not have any metaphysical import and that applies only in the political realm. Indeed, many social groups may represent themselves as peoples (or nations) in a way that parallels the self-representation of individuals as moral persons. And so there seems to be no reason to oppose the introduction of a political conception of peoples in addition to the political conception of persons as the subjects of rights. For that reason, the qualms expressed by many concerning the social ontology behind a theory of collective rights are now simply out of place. We do not need to reify groups in order to allow them public recognition in a constitution.

Essentialism?

Contrary to what has often been suggested, political recognition of deep cultural diversity does not presuppose an essentialism concerning the nation. The reason is that, according to the approach presented here, nations do not exist apart from the self-representations of the individuals. They are at least partly subjective and they can thus change through time because the self-representations of whole populations can also change through time. This view of the nation allows us to see it in constant transformation, even if these changes take place very slowly. We are therefore not committed to the view that they have a permanent essence or a stable ontological status. I reject "primordialism" or "perennialism" as it is sometimes applied to nations.[19] There used to be a time when nations did not exist, and there will be a time when they no longer exist. We are thus not presupposing an essentialist definition of the nation in terms of necessary and sufficient conditions. There are many acceptable definitions of this concept, and these must be understood as "stereotypes," in Hilary Putnam's sense of the word.[20]

The problem, however, is that many philosophers believe that in order to avoid essentialism, we must accept a radical metaphysical thesis according to which "existence precedes essence." Since persons do not have a nature, they are what they do and must therefore be understood as the result of their own actions. If we accept this approach and accept the view that self-representations are also constitutively related to nations, then identity can be equated with narrative identity. The identity of a person will be the result of the relevant actions that have shaped her life, in accordance with the way in which she chooses to tell the story of her life. The choice of the relevant actions thus depends on the narrative construal that she decides to adopt. Now, narrative identity is such that it may lead the person into a constant reappraisal of her own projects, goals and moral ends, which means that one's identity constantly changes. Accepting narrative identity is accepting a radical, metaphysical and dynamic account of personal identity. It is, according to many philosophers, the only way to avoid essentialism.[21]

Now, this is apparently bad news for any constitutional political recognition, since constitutions are meant for long-term policies and require the postulation of fixed identities. The problem is that according to this new narrative account, group affiliations are subject to important changes and vary in accordance with one's narrative construal. So constitutions can perhaps contain references to basic human rights but not to group rights as such. Once again, the reason is that narrative identity implies multiple and variable group identities. This apparently explains why people do not address identity issues in the courts. It is because everyone accepts that, in these matters, differences are important between individuals and that one's identity may also vary through time. In other words, everyone presumably understands that we have entered a realm where it is impossible to work with established, fixed identities. So the constitutions that avoid postulating groups are in a way quite faithful to this radical variability of personal identity.[22]

What reply can be made here? My first response is that since the argument rests on the metaphysical thesis of narrative identity, it does not do justice to the fact of pluralism. As I pointed out earlier, there are many different ways of conceptualizing persons as well as peoples, and applying the principle of tolerance forces us to acknowledge the irreducible disagreement that we have on these issues. The minimal consensus that can be achieved involves only institutional identities (of the person and of the nation). We can all recognize each other as citizens with different metaphysical views about ourselves. Some believe in fixed essences, while others believe in narrative identity. These disagreements are instances of a reasonable pluralism. So it is foolish to try to build a political consensus in a pluralist society by relying on particular controversial claims in metaphysics.

I also do not understand why an argument concerning the radical variability of views on matters of identity should lead us to believe that individuals but not groups can be the object of provisions in a constitution. In political philosophy, we must resist reifying all entities, individuals as well as peoples. There is as much variability on issues of personal identity as there is on issues concerning group affiliations. If we agree to entrench provisions concerning individuals in spite of the deep gulf that separates us on metaphysical issues, why can't we do the same for groups? Since individuals have been recognized as citizens in the constitution, why can't we allow for peoples a similar recognition as "societal cultures"? I said that there was a time when nations did not exist and that there will be a time when they no longer exist. But this remark also applies to individuals. There used to be a time when there were no individuals and there will unfortunately be a time when there are no longer individual human beings in this world. But that is not a reason for denying them rights. Similarly, I want to suggest that we should not refuse rights to peoples on the basis of their contingent, historical character. Once again, political liberalism allows us to argue in favour of political recognition for peoples without falling prey to essentialism.

If we entrench the collective rights of peoples in the constitution, there will most probably be many national groups that finally raise their voices and seize the courts for past grievances and injustices, just like many individuals seized the Supreme Court of Canada when Canadians decided to entrench a charter of rights and liberties. So the actual status quo does not reflect an absence of consensus on the need for political recognition. Indeed, it is wrong to suggest that the silence of populations on "identity" issues in the courts explains the silence of the constitution. It is, on the contrary, the silence of the constitution that explains why the population is itself silent.

Nations are partly subjective. We must, however, distinguish between two different senses of the word "subjective." It is one thing to argue that nations do not exist apart from our self-representations, along with a minimal loyalty and the collective will to live together, and quite another to suggest that our rational preferences and emotional ties are also relevant. I agree that there is a deep diversity of views concerning the nature of our national affiliations, but even those who disagree on these issues can see themselves as part of the same nation, and have minimal loyalty and a will to live together. So a minimal consensus can be reached regarding our institutional national affiliations as long as only some subjective features are treated as relevant, for it is only then that the account becomes compatible with different ontological views. Those who insist on the importance of individual rational preference and emotional ties presuppose an individualistic justification for cultural protection that I find problematic. I shall return to this point later.

Communitarianism?

I now want to remove an even more important prejudice that liberal philosophers entertain toward political recognition. It must be emphasized that recognition of deep diversity does not necessarily lead to communitarianism; that is, the view according to which the state must promote a particular conception about the good life or about the common good. But this is how many liberals interpret political recognition. It is claimed that the promotion and protection of a particular group amounts to the promotion and protection of particular interests. The problem becomes salient especially for those who believe that essentialism can only be avoided by endorsing a narrative account of identity, for it then becomes impossible to separate identity from the goals, projects and moral ends that we entertain. Our national identity will itself be intermingled with plans, goals, projects and moral ends. It is very often with such a view of narrative identity that communitarians are led to think that the state must promote a particular moral view. According to the communitarians, individuals and communities are individuated by specific sets of values, goals and projects. Members of the same community entertain similar views about the common good or about the good life. Promoting and protecting the individuals and their national communities must go hand in hand with promoting and protecting the particular moral views that are held by them.

But my approach avoids the pitfalls of communitarianism. Nations may be understood only as "societal cultures," involving (1) a common public language (or many official common languages); (2) a common public culture understood as a "structure of culture" (i.e., common institutions offering a "context of choice"), compatible with the existence and recognition of local public minority cultures; and (3) a common public history, compatible with the existence and recognition of different local minority histories. The concepts of "societal culture," "structure of culture" and "context of choice" are all borrowed from Kymlicka.[23] Once again, political liberalism allows us to make such a move.

Recognition of the collective rights of nations within the multination state need not involve a partial commitment in favour of specific sets of values if peoples (or nations) are construed as political societies involving only common public languages, common public cultures and common public histories. The notion of a common public culture, in particular, refers only to a common set of institutions (political, social, "cultural" and economic institutions). It refers to a "structure of culture" and not to a "character of culture." Individuals are individuated partly in terms of specific institutional affiliations. They have a specific national identity, but this must not be confused with a particular moral identity. Rawls' distinction between our institutional identity and our moral identity can thus be applied at the collective level. Rawls suggested that our moral identity could change even if our institutional identity remains the same. The same kind of remark can be made regarding the structure of culture: the structure of culture may remain the same even if the character of culture changes.[24] This is why Rawls' distinction between institutional identity and moral identity at the individual level parallels Kymlicka's distinction between the structure of culture and the character of culture at the collective level.

These three "goods" (common language, culture and history) are not "particular" goods, for they are basic ingredients in the concept of a common civic identity that, in turn, is required in any society. So promoting these goods is not the same as promoting particularism, for the features in question are universal traits belonging to any society. Individuals can be multilingual, have multiple cultural affiliations and even be members of nations within nations, and thus entertain multiple national identities. And they can share at the same time the same societal culture as long as the latter is understood as involving a common public culture and as long as it is implementing a politics of recognition for its minority cultures. This pluralism must not remain a de facto pluralism. It must become also *de jure* pluralism. And we can do it without falling prey to communitarianism.

Collectivism?

Politics of recognition have nothing to do with collectivism, that is, the view that the collective rights of peoples have absolute priority over the fundamental liberties of individuals. One can and, indeed, one must allow for an equilibrium between individual and collective rights. Both sorts of rights are fundamental and cannot be violated. One can be both anti-individualist and an anti-collectivist liberal, just like Rawls. As we have seen, political liberalism enables us to reach such an equilibrium.

The debate has been confused partly because we fail to distinguish between two distinct sorts of questions: those that concern the debate between liberalism and communitarianism, which ultimately rests on whether moral principles, values or goals are constitutive of one's identity, and those that concern the debate between individualism and collectivism, which determines the priority to be afforded to individual rights as opposed to collective rights. It is possible to reject communitarianism in favour of liberalism without embracing individualism, since we are willing to grant collective rights on a par with the fundamental individual rights and liberties. Individuals may have a moral priority over communitarian ideals, perfectionist virtues or utilitarian goods, but not necessarily over societal cultures.

We subscribe to the fundamental claims of liberals, for we assert that 1) individuals and communities are not institutionally individuated by to their moral identities; 2) individual rights are fundamental and cannot be subordinated to any other rights; 3) there is a priority of justice over common good; and 4) the state must be impartial and practise a benign justificational neutrality toward any particular view of the common good.

But we are not individualists, because, unlike so many liberals, we do not assert the absolute priority of individual rights over collective rights. As societal cultures with a common civic identity, peoples or nations may also have fundamental rights in a liberal society. I would thus reject the ethical individualism that now prevails in the literature and that affects even the work of Kymlicka. Actually, Kymlicka does not really wish to defend collective rights as such. He prefers to talk about "group differentiated rights," and the distinction between the two sorts of rights is more than just a matter of terminology. For Kymlicka, the essential idea in the notion of "group differentiated rights" is the object of the right and not the subject. It is the collective good and not the collective subject of the good. So for him, individuals can be the subject of such rights. Moreover, allowing for group-differentiated rights apparently fulfills a fundamental individual requirement. Societal cultures are primary goods and individuals assign the status of a primary good to their own societal culture. Their national affiliation is of fundamental value to them. So for Kymlicka, these collective goods are goods for the individual. By protecting and promoting these so-called primary goods, we are protecting and promoting individuals, for we are protecting and promoting something that is of crucial importance to them. Finally, Kymlicka restricts the application of group-differentiated rights to minorities, and he accepts them only as external protections and not as internal restrictions.

There are, of course, many philosophers who believe that Kymlicka has successfully shown that ethical individualism is compatible with a regime of collective rights, even if Kymlicka's argument has been attacked by numerous liberal philosophers. Unfortunately, I am afraid that Kymlicka's attempt fails, for the reasons previously mentioned. Individuals do not necessarily give absolute priority to their national affiliations. They have different allegiances, and some are more important than others. For many citizens, national ties are less important than those they entertain toward their family, fellow workers, sexual orientation, neighbourhood, city or region. The fundamental principle of equal respect must be applied in those instances, for different individuals may chart their allegiances differently and those allegiances may change from time to time. So it is simply not true that individuals give the status of a primary good to their own national affiliations. Buchanan has used this argument in order to conclude, contrary to Kymlicka, that nations are not special among all cultural groups.[25] Pogge has used a similar argument in order to conclude that many cultural groups, and not necessarily ethnic groups, could make a claim for political recognition.[26] Weinstock has shown that since the argument could lead us into a proliferation of group rights, it could serve as a *reductio ad absurdum* against most arguments in favour of such rights[27]: affording collective rights would lead to an irremediable proliferation of groups seeking the same kind of recognition, and this presumably shows that it would be a mistake to engage in such recognition.

Answering these objections completely would require a theory that imposes enough constraints on the subject of the right, and that would justify the inclusion of certain groups and the exclusion of others. I shall leave this task for another occasion. For present purposes, it is enough to note that these arguments work only if we assume ethical individualism. The idea is that according to ethical individualism, cultural protection can be justified only if it is claimed on behalf of individuals. It must, in other words, be based on their rational preferences or emotional ties. Kymlicka's opponents are quite happy to share this premise with him. But it is then noted that individuals have a wide variety of cultural allegiances and that national allegiance does not occupy a central position for all of them. All sorts of groups can count among their favoured allegiances. So if political recognition is to be granted to groups, it must be granted to all the groups that are important for individuals. Political recognition is problematic because we cannot expect a constitutional document to recognize all the groups.

The arguments of Buchanan, Pogge and Weinstock do not affect the approach presented here because we do not subscribe to ethical individualism. Unfortunately, there are literally hundreds of liberal philosophers who declare that ethical individualism is an essential, constitutive doctrine of liberalism. Ethical individualism is 1) a comprehensive doctrine, according to which 2) individuals are prior to their ends and 3) are the ultimate source of legitimate moral claims, and according to which 4) individual autonomy is the most fundamental liberal value. On that basis, some reject altogether the idea of collective rights.[28] Others distinguish between acceptable and unacceptable sorts of collective rights (for example, Kymlicka's distinction between external protections and internal restrictions).[29] Some argue that collective rights are acceptable only if they are individuated by their object and only if the ultimate subject of the right is the individual.[30] Others assert that collective rights are not special to ethnic groups.[31] In all these cases, philosophers tend to ignore in different ways the importance of recognizing collective rights for what they are. The picture is distorted because ethical individualism is simply assumed without argument.

For Kymlicka, group-differentiated rights are required for the protection of individual attachments or preferences toward particular groups. He thinks that the only justification for collective rights is one that postulates not only that there are primary collective cultural goods for the individual but also that individuals rationally prefer their own societal culture. But we have to acknowledge the fundamental plurality of our emotional ties, cultural attachments and national sentiments. We also have to acknowledge an irreducible variety in our preferential ranking of these various allegiances. But does it mean that one cannot provide a justification for the implementation of a regime of collective rights? Not really. What it shows, essentially, is that such a foundation cannot rest upon ethical individualism.

So how can we justify the special status of peoples? First, Kymlicka is quite right to claim that the protection of societal cultures is not only compatible with individual liberties but is, as a matter of fact, a condition of possibility for the exercise of individual liberties, for societal cultures provide a context of choice that enables us to exercise them. So the protection of societal cultures is on a par with liberal ideals. Second, we could add that societal cultures are necessary conditions for the occurrence of a chart of different allegiances in the minds of individual citizens. There could not be different rankings from individual to individual and from time to time if there were no societal cultures in the first place. Third, far from creating problems for political recognition, the existence of multiple identities provides evidence that, in a sense distinct from Kymlicka's, nations are special for individuals. Indeed, plural identities paradoxically reinforce the importance of national belonging. It is because we can be part of many groups and rank them as we choose that national identity can reveal its importance. If we had to choose only one group affiliation, many would prefer another, but if we are allowed to choose many, it appears that national affiliation, no matter how it is ranked, is part of everyone's chart, while sexual orientation or allegiance to a trade union or a professional group appears only in some charts and not in others. For instance, many heterosexuals will not mention their heterosexual orientation; many Montrealers will not think of mentioning their Montreal affiliation, and many Canadian philosophers will not think of mentioning their affiliation to the Canadian Philosophical Association. But the vast majority of Canadians (or Quebecers) will sooner or later mention that they are Canadians (or Quebecers).

Of course, the above remarks are not meant to suggest that politics of recognition can be justified by new arguments in moral psychology. They serve only to prove that national affiliation is somehow special. To repeat, the justification for cultural protection is that the existence of different societal cultures is an instance of cultural diversity and that there is an overlapping consensus over the value of cultural diversity.[32]

We tend to forget that there are different versions of liberalism. While some are founded on ethical individualism, others are founded on toleration. There is almost a conspiracy to criticize this alternative form of liberalism, but, as I have argued, it is a preferable theoretical framework for the politics of recognition. I have shown that Rawls, for instance, defends such a framework. Even if he is still under the spell of the traditional nation-state model, and even if he has done very little (especially when compared to Kymlicka) on the subject of deep national diversity, there is much to be said in favour of an approach inspired by his political liberalism for politics of recognition. His brand of liberalism is not based on a comprehensive doctrine such as ethical individualism, so the collective rights of peoples are not derivatively introduced on the basis of considerations pertaining to individuals. They do not merely have an instrumental value for individuals. Collective rights are not justified by the rational preferences of individuals, because peoples "as such" have a right to self-determination (although they may have only a remedial right to secede, as suggested by Buchanan). I believe that a liberal theory that can welcome collective rights in this way puts us on the right track.

This is what is explicitly taking place in *The Law of Peoples*. Many commentators have been very critical of the book.[33] They are right to criticize its important limitations for international justice and, in particular, they are right to denounce Rawls' failure to appreciate the existence of a global basic structure, his abandonment of fundamental liberal principles in the realm of international relations and his tolerance toward nonliberal regimes. But they also fail to appreciate the virtues of the book, and this is because they read him through the lens of ethical individualism.

Authoritarianism?

There is another objection that can be levelled against the claims I have been making. When we try to show the importance of peoples in political philosophy, we must treat them as subjects having emotions and attitudes. There must, in particular, be a reference to the general will of the people as something that is supposedly different from a mere collection of individual volitions. But if there is such a distinction to be made, the main problem is to determine who is able to interpret the general will of the people, and who is able to speak on its behalf. If the international community of peoples is to engage in an international social contract, who is going to speak on behalf of each people?

There is thus another argument to be made against the present approach. If we are minimally concerned about "letting the people decide," and if we are prepared to accept a minimal democratic constraint, the law of peoples will have to be approved by their populations. So it appears that the will of the people is nothing over and above the will of the population. Consequently, "the people" must ultimately be reducible to a collection of individual citizens, and societal cultures must themselves be construed as associations of individual citizens. To put it differently, talking about collective rights and about the irreducibility of peoples as collective bodies is problematic and enters into a tension with the democratic principle. So from a democratic point of view, collective entities should not be understood as distinct from republics of individual citizens.

Once again, individualism wins the day, but this time it is not through an argument that concerns the ultimate *justification* for group protection. It is rather because of a problem about the ultimate *legitimation* of group protection. So-called collective rights can only be accepted if, as a general principle, they are the result of consensus among concerned individual citizens. There is no legitimacy to the idea of the general will of the people if it cannot somehow be reduced to the individual volitions of all its ordinary citizens. For Habermas, for instance, civic (negative) liberties and political (positive) liberties have the same origin[34]: they must all originate from the deliberations of the individual citizens. If we want to accept any principles, it can only be because these principles have legitimately been established through a consensus in a republic of fully participating citizens. But this shows that the will of the people is nothing over and above the collection of willing individual citizens. Once again, individuals must have absolute priority. This time it is not because they are the ultimate source of justification for valid moral claims, but rather because they are the ultimate source of the legitimation of valid moral claims.

However, this argument can be sustained only if groups are understood as purely objective entities existing independently of the self-representations of individuals. There is the implicit assumption that we have a choice between seeing the group as an *objectively* irreducible social entity and seeing the group as a collection of citizens. But social groups need not be construed as purely objective entities, and thus need not be understood in opposition to a republic of individual citizens.

We can accept that, as a matter of principle, the general will of the people does not exist independently from the interpretation made by its individual citizens, but we do so without reducing it to a collection of individual wills. Since the group exists only if each of its members has an appropriate self-representation, accepting that it does not exist independently from the will of each citizen does not cause the dissolution of the group. The fact that each member has a say in what counts as the will of the people does not mean that there is no such thing as a social entity called "the people," for there is a big difference between trying to express one's own will and trying to interpret the general will of the people. Even if the will of the people does not exist apart from the self-representations of all the citizens, the opinion of each citizen is an opinion concerning what is good for the group as a whole and thus concerns what the group desires as a group, and that is very different from having to decide what is good for oneself.

So we can accept a general democratic constraint on the general will of the people without having to reduce the people to a collection of individual citizens. In order to meet a truly democratic challenge and legitimize the collective rights of peoples, one needs to understand peoples as being, at least in part, "imagined communities." They do not exist apart from the self-representations of citizens. Of course, this must not be interpreted as a claim in social ontology, for the version that we accept is the political conception of the people. Such a conception is also one according to which peoples do not exist apart from the self-representation of the population, but as we saw, it must not be confused with an ontological claim. In any case, the citizens belonging to those imagined communities can have their own interpretation of what they see in their minds as "the will of their own community."

The will of the people is the result of the democratic decision of the population. It is the result of a shared interpretation by the majority of individual citizens concerning what each one sees as "the will of the people." If a majority of citizens votes in favour of a particular policy for the people, we can conclude that this is the will of the people. In other words, we accept the majority rule as the correct interpretation for the democratic principle. This rule is acceptable as long as everyone has an equal right to participate in the decision, and as long as the minority is allowed to continue defending its own alternative option and to try convincing the majority about this alternative option. It is acceptable also only if the decision of the majority does not go against fundamental individual rights and fundamental minority rights. Futhermore, members of the minority must not be forced to remain within the political community. In other words, if the majority makes a decision that minorities believe runs against their interests, they are entitled to leave.

In general, majority rule is acceptable only if we are able to prevent the tyranny of the majority by a counterbalanced political recognition for minorities. This, by the way, answers indirectly another objection often levelled against politics of recognition for minority nations: what are the virtues of such policies if the adopted measures lead to a large number of restrictions on minorities within those minority nations? The answer, of course, is that we must also implement a policy of recognition for those internal minorities.[35]

Finally, I would add that when crucial issues like secession are involved, majority rule is acceptable only if both the minority and the majority win in the situation. The correct interpretation of the democratic principle remains in this case the majority rule, and so if a majority chooses to secede, then secession becomes acceptable. But those who wish to remain within the encompassing state must also win in some sense. When a seceding entity contains minorities that have strong emotional ties with the citizens of the encompassing state, there must be partnership relations between the two states. One can think of a confederation of nation-states, for instance. So it is not necessary in the case of secession to modify our interpretation of the democratic principle by introducing new rules of a qualified majority. The majority rule can be maintained, but we can creatively imagine other solutions to make sure that it is a win-win situation, for both majorities and minorities.

My view is that there are individual and collective interests. Citizens can participate in the deliberations concerning those two different sets of interests, but they do it in two different ways. They consider individual arguments of rational acceptance (why is it good for the individual?) when their individual interests are involved, and they consider collective arguments of rational acceptance (why is it good for the people?) when collective interests are involved. The ultimate criterion of individual rational acceptance is based on the principle of individual consent, but the ultimate criterion of collective rational acceptance is the democratic principle, interpreted as the majority rule.

Conclusion

Many philosophers question the moral priority afforded the nation-state, but most of them still fail to promote politics of recognition. Much literature has been published in the last 10 years concerning the end of nation-states and the virtues of constitutional patriotism, postnational identity, federalism, multicultural citizenship, cosmopolitanism, and so on. Many philosophers have been engaged in a critical assessment of nation-building policies, but only a few have considered politics of recognition. But it should be realized that the appropriate model of political organization is perhaps not the important point. Whether we are dealing with nation-states, multination states or supranational organizations, all these political arrangements must incorporate politics of recognition. In addition to full protection of human rights, we must implement the politics of recognition at all levels. Single nation-states must recognize the existence of linguistic national minorities (extensions of neighbouring nations) and immigrant communities, multination states must recognize the existence of minority nations and national minorities, and supranational organizations must recognize nation-states and multination states, as well as the minority nations and national minorities that form them.

Political recognition of deep diversity is indeed compatible with liberalism, as long as liberalism is conceived as political liberalism. Individual rights and liberties are fundamental and cannot be overruled by any other principles, but this does not mean that all other principles must be subordinated to individual rights and liberties, for there are also collective rights that are fundamental and cannot be overruled by any other principles. We must endorse a fundamental pluralistic axiology and try to reach a balance between individual and collective rights.

I would thus be inclined to say, along with Charles Taylor, that there are two sorts of liberalism: liberalism 1, which asserts the absolute priority of individual rights over collective rights and of the individual over society, and liberalism 2, which gives room to what Taylor calls "collective goals" as well as individual liberties. Taylor uses the phrase "collective goals" and not "collective rights" because of his penchant for communitarianism. As a good communitarian, he rejects the priority of justice over common good and rejects for the same reason the priority of rights over moral obligations. So he does not like to talk about rights. His idea of political recognition is strictly political and has only a minimal effect on constitutional arrangements. But if we remove the communitarian orientation that is at the heart of Taylor's approach, we could reformulate liberalism 2 as asserting an equilibrium between individual and collective rights.

I have argued that one can provide room for the collective rights of peoples without committing oneself to reification, essentialism, communitarianism, collectivism or authoritarianism, and that we can achieve this as long as we reject ethical individualism. It is true that most liberals subscribe to ethical individualism, but not all do. Rawls, for instance, argues for a law of peoples in which the fundamental rights of peoples are asserted alongside with the fundamental rights and liberties of individuals. The main task of this paper has been to show that this is the correct approach.

Notes

1. Rawls (1993).

2. Seymour (2000).

3. Rawls (1993, p. 31).

4. This is precisely what Rawls (1999) does.

5. Kymlicka (1995, pp. 76-79).

6. See Rawls (1999, pp. 33-34) for an account that allows us to treat peoples as self-authenticating sources of claims.

7. Kymlicka (1995).

8. Kymlicka (1989, p. 166).

9. For such a thesis, see Parekh (2000). For a critical assessment, see Bauböck (2001).

10. As far as I know, no one holds this particular view. For a critical assessment of the view, see Kymlicka (1995, pp. 121-23).

11. National diversity is perhaps intrinsically connected with cultural diversity, but cultural diversity may be neither intrinsically nor ultimately valuable. Rather, it may be instrumentally valuable for the survival of the species. So there could very well be a time when this will no longer be so. On the distinction between intrinsic and ultimate value, see Raz (1986, pp. 177-78).

12. See, for instance, Tan (2000).

13. See Seymour (2004).

14. Rawls (1999, p. 38).

15. Rawls (1999, p. 38, n 45).

16. For the political conception of persons, see Rawls (1993, pp. 29-35); for the political conception of peoples, see Rawls (1999, especially pp. 23, 34).

17. Rawls (1985, p. 245).

18. Anderson (1991).

19. Geertz (1963).

20. Putnam (1975, pp. 249-51).

21. Taylor (1985, 1989, pp. 47, 50-52) and Ricoeur (1990).

22. Taylor is of course a defender of both narrative identity and politics of recognition, and the argument may sound problematic for that reason. But it should be remembered that Taylor avoids any talk of collective rights in Taylor (1994). Political recognition must be granted concerning the "collective goals" of minority nations and national minorities, not their collective rights. So he is not clearly favourable to politics of recognition that formally entrench collective rights for peoples.

23. Kymlicka (1989, 1995).

24. Kymlicka (1995, p. 77).

25. Buchanan (1996).

26. Pogge (1997).

27. Weinstock (1999).

28. Barry (2001), Habermas (1994), Hartney (1995), Narveson (1991), Tamir (1999).

29. Kymlicka (1994, 1995, ch. 3).

30. Green (1991) and Réaume (1988).

31. Buchanan (1996), Pogge (1997), Weinstock (1999).

32. I do not accept Kymlicka's arguments against using the value of cultural diversity to justify implementing collective rights. Kymlicka's criticisms work only because he presupposes that the value of cultural diversity can only be instrumental to the individual. But it can be an instrumental value relative to the species and not to the individual, or it may be intrinsically valuable.

33. See, for instance, Beitz (2000), Buchanan (2000), Kuper (2000), Pogge (1994, 2001), Tan (2000).

34. Habermas (1995).

35. Green (1994).

Bibliography

Anderson, Benedict. *Imagined Communities*. New York: Verso, 1991.

Barry, Brian. *Culture and Equality*. Oxford: Polity Press, 2001.

Bauböck, Rainer. "Cherishing Diversity and Promoting Political Community." *Ethnicities*, Vol. 1, no. 1 (2001): 109-15.

Beitz, Charles. "Rawls's Law of Peoples." *Ethics*, Vol. 110 (2000): 669-96.

Buchanan, Allen. "What's So Special about Nations?" in *Rethinking Nationalism*, ed. J. Couture, Kai Nielsen and Michel Seymour. Supplementary volume, *Canadian Journal of Philosophy*, University of Calgary Press, 1996.

———. "Rawls's Law of Peoples: Rules for a Vanished Westphalian World." *Ethics*, Vol. 110 (2000): 697-721.

Geertz, Clifford. "The Integrative Revolution: Primordial Sentiments and Civil Politics in the New States," in *Old Societies* and *New States*, ed. Clifford Geertz. New York: Free Press, 1963.

Green, Leslie. "Two Views of Collective Rights," in Collective Rights, ed. Michael McDonald. Special issue of *Canadian Journal of Law and Jurisprudence*, Vol. 4, no. 2 (1991): 315-27.

———. "Internal Minorities and Their Rights," in *Group Rights*, ed. Judith Baker. Toronto: University of Toronto Press, 1994.

Habermas, Jürgen. "Struggles for Recognition in the Democratic Constitutional State," in *Multiculturalism and the Politics of Recognition*, ed. A. Gutmann. Princeton: Princeton University Press, 1994.

———. "Reconciliation through the Use of Public Reason." *Journal of Philosophy*, Vol. 92, no. 3 (1995): 1995.

Hartney, Michael. "Some Confusions Concerning Collective Rights," in *The Rights of Minority Cultures*, ed. Will Kymlicka. Oxford: Oxford University Press, 1995.

Kuper, Andrew. "Rawlsian Global Justice: Beyond the Law of Peoples to a Cosmopolitan Law of Persons." *Political Theory*, Vol. 28, no. 5 (2000): 640-74.

Kymlicka, Will. *Liberalism, Community and Culture*. Oxford: Clarendon Press, 1989.

———. "Individual and Community Rights," in *Group Rights*, ed. Judith Baker. Toronto: University of Toronto Press, 1994.

———. *Multicultural Citizenship*. Oxford: Clarendon Press, 1995.

Narveson, Jan. "Collective Rights?" in Collective Rights, ed. Michael McDonald. Special issue of *Canadian Journal of Law and Jurisprudence*, Vol. 4, no. 2 (1991): 329-45.

Parekh, Bhikhu. *Rethinking Multiculturalism: Cultural Diversity and Political Theory*. London: Macmillan, 2000.

Pogge, Thomas. "An Egalitarian Law of Peoples." *Philosophy and Public Affairs*, Vol. 23, no. 3 (1994): 195-224.

———. "Group Rights and Ethnicity," in *Ethnicity and Group Rights*, ed. W. Kymlicka and I. Shapiro. New York: New York University Press, 1997.

———. "Rawls on International Justice." *Philosophical Quarterly*, Vol. 51, no. 203 (2001): 246-53.

Putnam, Hilary. "The Meaning of 'Meaning,'" in *Mind, Language and Reality*, ed. Hilary Putnam. Cambridge: Cambridge University Press, 1975.

Rawls, John. "Justice as Fairness: Political Not Metaphysical." *Philosophy and Public Affairs*, Vol. 14, no. 3 (1985): 223-51.

———. *Political Liberalism*. New York: Columbia University Press, 1993.

———. *The Law of Peoples*, Cambridge, MA: Harvard University Press, 1999.

Raz, Joseph. *The Morality of Freedom*. Oxford: Clarendon Press, 1986.

Réaume, Denise. "Individuals, Groups, and Rights to Public Goods." *University of Toronto Law Journal*, Vol. 38 (1988): 1-27.

Ricoeur, Paul. *Soi-même comme un autre*. Paris: Seuil, 1990.

Seymour, Michel. "On Redefining the Nation," in *Nationalism and Ethnic Conflict*, ed. Nenad Miscevic. Chicago and La Salle: Open Court, 2000.

———. "Collective Rights in Multination States: From Ethical Individualism to the Law of Peoples," in *The Fate of the Nation-State*, ed. Michel Seymour. Montreal and Kingston: McGill-Queen's University Press, 2004.

Tamir, Yael. "Against Collective Rights," in *Multicultural Questions*, ed. C. Joppke and S. Lukes. Oxford: Oxford University Press, 1999.

Tan, Kok Chor. *Toleration, Diversity and Global Justice*. University Park: Pennsylvania State University Press, 2000.

Taylor, Charles. *Sources of the Self*. Cambridge: Harvard University Press, 1989.

———. "The Politics of Recognition," in *Multiculturalism*, ed. A. Gutmann. Princeton: Princeton University Press, 1994.

———, ed. "Self-Interpreting Animals," *Human Agency and Language, Philosophical Papers*, Vol. 1. Cambridge: Cambridge University Press, 1985.

Weinstock, Daniel. "La boîte de Pandore," in *Nationalité, citoyenneté et solidarité*, ed. Michel Seymour. Montreal: Liber, 1999.

5

the legal mediation of
social diversity

Roderick A. Macdonald

This essay considers two models for the *legal* (as opposed to the political or economic) recognition of social diversity in what have been variously called "multi-ethnic," "multicultural" and "multinational" states. Part 1 sets out and critiques traditional, state-based conceptions of how the law should apprehend the task. It questions the view that social diversity is best protected through constitutional and quasi-constitutional arrangements attributing, and facilitating the adjudication of, rights-based identity claims. Part 2 argues for an alternative theoretical perspective – legal pluralism – that explicitly acknowledges the capacity of diverse groups (whether social, psychological, affective or virtual) to generate identity-forming legal rules, institutions and processes of ordering. Moreover, it claims that the mediation of interests, not the adjudication of rights, is the optimal procedural mode for legally framing and acknowledging social diversity.

Four caveats are in order. The first is this: all theoretical perspectives in law are hypothetical. A legal theory typically encapsulates a set of strong commitments concerning society and community, freedom and agency, equality and identity, culture and solidarity, justice and the good, love and hate, and so on. As such, it invites reflection on whether it is a helpful way of imagining the real, and modelling this real according to values one actually claims to uphold. A legal theory is not a descriptive account of "objective" social facts that can be falsified by empirical testing. No legal theory can be either true or false. It can, of course, be judged as more or less coherent. But in the end, every theoretical perspective has a feel that either does or does not resonate with the person being asked to carry it on board. The theoretical perspective presented here, then, is not necessarily more connected to brute social facts than any other. It is, rather, a statement of belief about identity, human agency and interpersonal relationships.[1]

The second caveat relates to framework and scope. Given its focus on the *legal* recognition of social diversity, this paper is unconcerned with many structural distinctions commonly drawn in political science analyses of the state. It does not, for example, differentiate between (1) those "multinational" states with a long history – France, the United Kingdom, Canada, New Zealand, for example; (2) those "multinational" states having a more recent postcolonial history – Nigeria, Indonesia, Brazil, for example; and (3) those that are emerging in attempts to build suprastate governance institutions – the European Union and the Commonwealth of Independent States, for example. However different the practical politics of state formation may be, the sociology of diversity in all these cases is the same. Indeed, given this paper's claim that the modern political state is best conceived as a conjunctional arrangement of territory – with no necessary or a priori political, economic, geographic, linguistic or ethnic rationale – the logic of social diversity that it presents applies even to states that explicitly hold themselves out not to be multi-ethnic, multicultural or multinational. As a matter of law, the key issue is not what states assert about their citizenry but rather what citizens assert about their states.

The third caveat speaks to the manner in which this paper treats social diversity itself. Liberal theory typically assesses responses to social diversity by distinguishing between two types of identity claims. On the one hand, there are those identities to which it attributes a right of political self-determination. These identities are said to be "deep," structural, constitutive or necessary for modelling citizen loyalty to a given political organization. They are invariably characterized as "national" identities and are wielded in support of the argument that nations must become states. On the other hand, there are those identities that are considered to be more personal to the individual claiming them. As adopted by or attributed to individuals, these have often been the cause of discrimination or exclusion from general social and political life. They are wielded in support of the argument that "equal protection" or "equality" principles must explicitly protect individuals who adopt or who are ascribed such identities. This paper draws no distinctions between types of identity claims. It takes identity to be an assertion that individuals make about themselves, not a category of being attributed by the state. Hence, it assumes neither a closed inventory of cognizable identity claims nor a preordained lexical ordering of their importance to any given person.

Finally, because the purpose of this essay is to consider the legal mediation of social diversity, it addresses a relatively narrow range of policy options. Over the past two centuries, states have dealt with social diversity in a variety of ways. Often their objective has been to suppress or eliminate diversity of all types. Many tools and techniques have been called in aid.[2] Ethnic cleansing aims at mass migration of peoples. Territorial expulsion accomplishes the same goal by migrating geography. Genocide destroys diversity by physically destroying peoples; assimilation destroys diversity by destroying their identity. None of these policy options is addressed here. Group defamation as reflected in Holocaust denial or homophobia; sterilization of "defectives"; gender-, religion- and race-based electoral exclusions; and marginalization by repressive policies directed at public symbolic expression (such as the prohibition of religious, cultural or linguistic icons or artifacts) are similarly excluded policy assaults on diversity. This paper explores only the range of legal possibilities that take for granted the continuing presence of psycho-socio-demographic minorities (and perhaps even the continuing absence of a psycho-socio-demographic majority in the hypothesis of multiple psycho-socio-demographic minorities).

The Legal-Republican Consensus

Mainstream legal theory presents law as a systematic assemblage of official rules of general conduct attributing various types of rights to individual, discrete, legal subjects. The integrity of a legal system and the rights that it establishes are said to be guaranteed by independent adjudicative bodies such as courts. Although increasingly contested in North American law faculties, this classical theory still holds a powerful sway in certain other corners of the academy (for example, political science, economics and philosophy departments), where informal normative orders are not routinely conceived as legal. Many of the virtues of liberal-democratic political systems – most notably the idea of the rule of law – are directly ascribed to the postulates of mainstream legal theory, even though none of its underlying principles actually requires law to be legitimated through democratic practices of enfranchisement.[3]

As translated into the domain of public politics, mainstream legal theory rests on three affirmations. First, the notion of law is to be exclusively associated with the normative products of the state. Law in any other infra- or suprastate context has no meaning. Necessarily, the legal recognition and protection of social diversity implies state action. This affirmation may be described as a postulate of "legal centralism."

Second, there can only be a single legal order in any geographic territory. Even in federal systems the legal order is unitary, because a supreme constitution authoritatively allocates law-making authority to different legislatures (for example, jurisdictional rules) and provides mechanisms for resolving normative conflicts that may arise (for example, paramountcy rules). Necessarily, the legal recognition and protection of social diversity implies a fully integrated set of norms, processes and institutions. This affirmation may be described as a postulate of "legal monism."

Third, law is always the explicit product of official institutions like legislatures, courts and executive agencies. The outputs of these institutions are law simply because of their origin; nothing can be law other than what emanates from these institutions. Necessarily, the legal recognition and protection of social diversity implies an institutional formality that enables those norms that count as democratically legitimated rules to be distinguished from other, merely social, norms. This affirmation may be described as a postulate of "legal positivism."

Together these postulates of centralism, monism and positivism make up the core of what may be described as the "republican" consensus about law in the political state. In a nutshell, this consensus holds that law does not create the state: the state creates law. Moreover, the consensus holds that law is an explicit, consciously undertaken, top-down exercise of will by political actors; law is not a tacit, iterative adjustment of assertions and expectations generated in everyday social interaction. And the republican consensus decrees that political authority is legitimated not through, say, the will of God, or even through the traditions and informal social practices of multiple groups and communities, but only through the formal consent of a population seen as a singular entity; the congeries of legislation and agencies reposing in the state are the ultimate coercive instruments and institutions of a geographically determinate, self-governing people. The third idea in particular sustains the conception of the territorial state as the political and legal reflection of a "general will" that embodies the "nation."

In republican legal theory, citizenship is the nexus between membership in the nation and membership in the state. One's sense of "nation" is channelled by citizenship into enfranchisement in the state. Of course, in many contemporary cases – especially postcolonial multinational states and newly formed states emerging from ethnic separatist movements – the state actually deploys the notion of citizenship to suppress prior "national" sentiment and to coerce membership in the putative nation through a concept of "civic nationalism." In post-Enlightenment thinking, state law was meant to deploy one of the central philosophical concepts of the Enlightenment – the individual (the person) – to ground the notion of the citizen. Two centuries ago, the idea that human beings should be conceived in law as discrete individuals was a powerful vehicle for laying to rest the status-based assumptions of feudalism. No longer were people to be judged by, and their life choices to be limited because of, the accident of birth and pedigree. Human beings were to be seen as at least predominantly autonomous agents, vested with natural and inalienable rights as persons and, more importantly for present purposes, as citizens. Republican citizenship presupposed and still presupposes individual human agency beyond that allowed by a preordained role, and it presupposed and still presupposes that these individual human agents would have no particular identities in their role as citizens.

A number of socio-political factors evident at the end of the eighteenth century explain the extraordinary success of the republican model of state and citizen in Western thought. Among the more obvious are the following. In the revolutionary epoch, the percentage of the population considered as full citizens was relatively small and socio-culturally homogeneous. As a result, radically discordant conceptions of individual agency (personal identity) rarely surfaced in public political debate; those wielding political power in the name of democracy and popular sovereignty either were or conceived themselves to be remarkably similar. Again, the character of the population and the economy was relatively stable. Consequently, there was little immediate pressure on official law to reflect or accommodate a changing socio-demography; class analysis had yet to fracture the presumed uniformity of the third estate. And still again, the state and its emanations played a relatively limited role in people's daily lives. For this reason, official law was not generally called upon to transact with multiple citizen identities forged through the diverse normative orders of a dynamic, everyday social intercourse.

Of course, none of these socio-political factors of the revolutionary epoch obtains in quite the same manner today. The population of liberal democracies is more heterogeneous along almost every demographic dimension. Indeed, the twentieth century revealed the general population of any state to be incorrigibly plural. The electoral franchise is broader; immigration and migration have diversified populations; and, just as importantly, people are much more aware of the vast array of their individual characteristics that distinguish them from others. However easy it once may have been to conceive the state as the reflection of an ethno-culturally homogeneous population, it is infinitely more difficult to do so today – even in Europe's apparently "national" states.

Too, the general patterns of interaction associated with largely rural, religious and premarket societies are no longer as settled, shared and significant. Improvements in transportation and communication, urbanization and the development of a wage labour economy mean that neighbourhoods and even semi-isolated villages are in constant mutation. In both psychological and physical dimensions, the sense of an unchanging and impermeable community *chez nous* – a rural Beauce, or an urban Pointe-St-Charles, or even a societal

Newfoundland if you will – is no longer fully sustainable. Of course, the Beauce is still the Beauce and not "the Point," but what makes it the Beauce is how Beaucerons negotiate between their past, their present and their future, not some essential immutable character of the region or its inhabitants.[4] However easy it once may have been to conceive the state as the institutional and political reflection of a stable, inbred, necessarily determinate, social Arcadia, it is infinitely more difficult to do so today.

Finally, over the past two centuries, and especially over the past half century, the state has assumed a larger social – welfare and economic – regulatory role. Notwithstanding more recent attempts at the privatization and deregulation of governmental functions, even today direct, instrumental, public sector activity remains more significant than it was in the eighteenth century. The initial, liberal idea of the jurisdictional state as a location for attributing space for community, group and individual action has given way to the idea of the regulatory state as governor and orchestrator of all manner of human agency. However easy or difficult it once was to conceive the state as relatively inactive in the detailed management of everyday life, it is infinitely more difficult to do so today.

It is not just that the "homogeneity" of the "citizen" in a given state is no longer a plausible presumption. The complementary presumption – the purported political understanding (the descriptive hypothesis) of an abstract citizenship that lay at the origins of the republican state – has been exposed as myth. While the republican aspiration (the prescriptive hypothesis) continues to this day in some high-level political theory, it is now acknowledged that the putative citizen of the revolutionary period was not, in fact, disembodied or decontextualized. Rather, citizenship was constructed upon three deep psychosocial identities: religion, language and ethnicity (or in its sanitized, more "acceptable," early-twenty-first-century version, culture).

These key identities, never directly expressed in France although patent in nonliberal nineteenth-century German republican legal-political theory, together constituted the badge of "national" identity to be protected and promoted by the state. Thus, for example, however much "citizen Robespierre" made universalist claims about humankind and however much he decried religion, he was firmly grounded in eighteenth-century Catholic ideology. These three embedded identities have vexed republican constitutionalism for 200 years largely because they are embedded, and therefore their exclusionary consequences are unacknowledged. Indeed, the difference between aspiration and reality is all the more evident nowadays in view of the increasing, or at least increasingly recognized, socio-demographic diversity of contemporary states just noted.

In large part, psychosocial identity "nationalism" has proved problematic in legally sustaining social diversity because it originated in an impoverished view of what it means to be an individual. Today a much richer appreciation of the multiple dimensions of identity prevails. The totalizing identities of religion, language and ethnicity – just like the totalizing identities of feudal status before them – no longer dictate the full range of personal action and belief; people no longer have automatic reflexes given by, nor even seek or find "necessary" responses to everyday life encounters through direct appeal to, religious precept, ethnic origin or language. Increasingly, people recognize themselves and their perceptions as given not exclusively by their character as, for example, anglophones, Moravians or Buddhists. Of course, other world views – vegetarian or vegan, environmentalist, Shriner – can be equally totalizing. Still, most people today do not claim for themselves a singular identity given by a totalizing ideology, or even a fixed identity given by a small number of complementary totalizing ideologies.

More than this, because people now have a better understanding of themselves as being socially located and as becoming themselves through their complex and shifting interactions with others, they do not consider themselves as being simply disembodied, discrete individuals; nor even do they consider themselves as disembodied, discrete individuals interacting with other disembodied, discrete individuals. They are members of groups – and multiple groups at that. These groups, of course, have fluid contours and boundaries: they can be of all types – psychological, sociological, visible, invisible, physical, virtual, psychoanalytic and so on. The more people find and acknowledge their individuality in the multiple groups they choose to be associated with or to reject, or with which they feel an obligation of association or rejection, or to which they are assigned by others who are nonmembers, or to which they are claimed by others who are members, the more they come to express that affiliation or membership in the language of identity.

The republican legal consensus, especially in its conception of "national" identity, rests on three assumptions about individual identity that many find unattractive.[5] First, it only recognizes certain identities. Over the past few decades in Western liberal democracies, the state has discovered identities beyond language, religion and ethno-culture. Most of these "new" identities are characterized in republican theory as personal identities, not national identities; in their regard the state aims at no more than acknowledgement and equal protection. Thus, the state has typically pursued equality by reference to a number of externally visible identity characteristics that it deems as constituting individual personhood and that it presumes have led to exclusion or discrimination in the past.

Over vast tracts of state legal regulation, people are considered to be constituted by these identity characteristics – for example, their age, their sex and the colour of their skin. Of course, not all such physical characteristics are deemed constitutive of identity: for example, height, weight, body type, eye colour, hair colour, baldness and jowls do not today attract the same legal regard. Even more than this, while some nonphysical and non-externally-visible characteristics are also seen as identity-giving – for example, being gay, lesbian or bisexual – others are not. Thus, state law does not now conceive people to be constituted by their timidity or temerity, their capacity or incapacity to intellectualize, or their overall world view as pessimist or optimist. This legal neglect persists notwithstanding that much of a person's daily interaction with others depends on deploying strategies to exploit or hide all these sociological and psychological identity-giving traits.

In other words, many key identities for people today – both psychological and sociological – are beyond the reach of law; no current conception of antidiscrimination law takes account of them. Other identities are enormously resistant to legal capture and palliation through state institutions; here official law preserves the appearance of its egalitarian project by characterizing these identities either as a "social condition" (for example, class, or being a vagrant or a hermit) or as a "personal preference" (for example, being a vegetarian or a bridge player), and not as an identity. There comes a point where even the most comprehensive state artifacts like human rights codes and charters of rights wash out particular identities. In the contemporary state, not all personal identities are legally cognizable, regardless of how important they may be to any given person. Classification and restrictive enumerations are the stock-in-trade of republican legal analysis – whether in public law or private law.

Second, the republican consensus presumes that some of the identities that it does acknowledge are more important than others: these "key" identities are said to define the identity of the state. In the past, these "defining" or "national" identities were not really perceived as such – that is, as privileged personal identities. But once the state expands the number of particular identities that it is willing to contemplate as forming state-constructed personal identity, the three psychosocial identities at the historical root of "national" identity are out of the closet. In respect of language, religion and culture, the goal of the republican state has traditionally not been to ensure the equal protection of diverse, and typically marginalized, identities. Quite the contrary. It has been the explicit protection and promotion of a singular identity: one language, one religion, one ethnicity (people). By contrast with the modern antidiscrimination ethos about identities – the ethos that all particular identities of, for example, a sexual, racial, age and ethnic nature are deserving of equal respect – in these three cases the republican state has often deployed law to advance a single exclusive "national" identity, with the conscious aim of denying alternative identities.

Of course, liberal democracies recognize the inappropriate exclusionary objective of two of these psychosocial "national" identities. Religion and ethnicity have generally been abolished or attenuated as markers of "national" identity. In most states, a singular religion has lost its role as formally constituting national identity, although some "secular" states still claim to be grounded in a notion of Christianity, of the Judeo-Christian tradition or even of some undifferentiated conception of God – as expressed, for example, in the preamble to the Canadian *Charter of Rights and Freedoms*, or more obliquely, in the rules on the solemnization of marriage that mimic canon law. In general, however, the acknowledgement of religious pluralism has resulted in religion being reconceived not as a national identity but as a particular identity – like sex or age – meriting antidiscrimination protection. Indeed, most modern liberal states claim not to be theocracies (even though this may not be true in theory, as in "Anglican" England, or in certain practices, as in the "Bible belt" United States, or in theory and practice, as in Israel): religious "nationalism" is now rejected as official ideology in the republican model. Likewise, ethnicity has gone through a transformation. In the main, it has been reconceived as a particular, rather than as a national, identity. But, while ethnic "nationalism" has, at least in public political rhetoric, gone the way of religious "nationalism," its underlying exclusionary impetus has resurfaced in the sanitized concept of a civic "nationalism" based on language and culture.

In many liberal-democratic states, language and ethnoculture survive unproblematized as badges of "common" or national" identity. Of course, the project of a secular or civic "nationalism" is not new. Whatever the facts, it was the aspiration of the French revolutionaries. At bottom, Marx too sought a secular rationale for political authority – class consciousness – that would provide an identity-giving "nationalism," or more accurately an identity-giving "internationalism." But even Marxism presumes an excluded Other – the bourgeoisie. Modern forms of civic "nationalism" are no different in this respect. On what basis may it be said that a socially constructed culture – Canadian culture, Quebec culture – is less exclusionary than a socially constructed ethnicity?

Of course, some socially constructed ethnocultures are less exclusionary and sustain less aggressive state policies than others: compare, for example, French nationalism of the Third Republic with German nationalism of the National Socialist regime. Still, even French nationalism today represses Bretons, Basques, Corsicans and Provençales, not to mention Muslims from the Magreb. To the extent a state deploys language and culture as markers of "national" identity, it continues to promote the logic of exclusionary identities. In such a state neither language nor culture can be characterized – like religion, sex or ancestry – simply as a legally protected reflection of a particular personal identity.

There is a third unhappy feature of the republican conception of identity: its tendency to essentialize identity for the purposes of giving or denying legal recognition. There are several facets to this essentializing motif. To begin, seeing personal identity as congruently tied through membership to a fixed identity ascribed to a group misses the fluidity of group identities. Affirming that people are just the sum of their multiple preconstituted group identities is as troublesome as denying that group identities can shape personal identity; both deny the interactive, iterative character of all identities. Hence the problem. Once the state takes on the role of recognizing and legitimating certain particular identities, it finds itself obliged to announce criteria for determining what constitutes the essence of that identity. Yet the complexity of personal identities defies legal taxonomy. What is linguistic identity of a true bilingual? What is the ethnic identity of a Métis? What is the gender identity of a cross-dresser? How many categories of age, of sexual orientation, of "marital status," of citizenship are identity-constituting?

The complexity of particular identities suggests a further difficulty: individual identity is not unidimensional; identities are cumulative, intersecting, overlapping. Consider the psychological and sociological identities noted earlier. When a person reflects, reacts, speaks or presents himself or herself in public, upon what basis does he or she do so? That person might think or even claim to be doing so "as" a white, or a heterosexual, or an anglophone, or a male, or a lapsed Protestant, or a 55-year-old, "as" someone who is legally trained, or a bald person, or a resident of Montreal and so on. How does one know whether another is speaking as several of these things (of these particular identities)? As all of these things? Or as none of these things? Because republican theory posits categories of identities and typically limits its view of antidiscrimination protection to "discrete and insular" minority identities, it presumes to answer these questions only by reference to a priori categories of identity, and to only one of these at a time.

Just as important as inquiring into how cumulative, intersecting and overlapping personal identities can be individuated is asking "who is to decide?" It is as demeaning to be told – say, by Parliament, by the courts, by the police – that one's voice is being heard only "because of" its partiality as it is not to be heard at all. Tokenism takes partiality as the criterion of inclusion, as if the speaker had no other claim to be heard. Likewise it is as demeaning to be told that one's voice is being heard only in its register as one of these partial identities. Once the state hears citizens as reflecting only a group perspective, it ceases to hear them as citizens. Of course, to be rooted in one's partiality is to recognize that people are always telling partial truths about themselves. They consciously negotiate and renegotiate how to tell their partial truths to each other. These partial truths, like their partial selves, must be constantly reinterpreted and reunderstood as such, lest their partiality be mistaken for the whole.

In the end, the partiality of self and other is for each person to discover and appropriate. There is no litmus test for identity – say, as a francophone, as a mulatto or as a woman – that can trump self-ascription. It is not for the state to say that Félix Leclerc is a white, male, francophone singer if he himself claims to be a black, female, hispanophone painter. The state can only pose hypotheses about how its institutions and, by ricochet, citizens should prima facie respond to Félix Leclerc's identity claims. The state, just like Félix Leclerc's *concitoyens*, may view certain identity claims as less plausible than others, but the question of plausibility is always itself interactive and iterative. The republican conception of identity – whether of national identities or of particular identities – peremptorily denies to individuals the possibility of negotiating with others the contours and contents of their multiple identities.[6]

The relationship between republican legal theory and modern understandings of individual identity is complex and twice disquieting. Most importantly, republican theory implicitly claims that certain identities are necessary to sustain a state. For example, republican theorists usually claim that, at a minimum, a state requires a common language or languages of public political discourse – a claim to which multilingual states, and especially multilingual suprastate organizations, seem to call into question. Democratic deliberation presupposes intersubjective communication, but communication occurs in several symbolic discourses and often through translation (whether of multiple natural languages or of "coded" political messages). Indeed, as the everyday experience of bilinguals attests, true communication is often impaired by a false linguistic homogeneity.[7] When the state attempts to promote certain particular identities – identities such as those that in international law are said to carry the right to "self-determination" – it promotes a conception of "national" identity that by definition is exclusionary. This conception not only relegates all nonprivileged reflections of that particular identity trait (for example, various other languages or cultures) to the realm of the Other, but also makes the selected traits the point of first reference for identity formation. It indicates to citizens how they must first apprehend who they are, and who others are.

Second, when the state attempts to delimit the scope of equal protection on identity grounds, in republican theory it can do so only by essentializing, prioritizing and discriminating among particular identities. In some ways this is inevitable. Given the vastness of social diversity, the state, just like individual human beings, is unable as a matter of pure cognitive reach to perceive, reason, make choices and explain without categorizing and classifying – intellectual activities that when applied to human identity are reductionist. But there is a gulf between reduction and essentializing. A reductionist characterization is self-consciously contingent and is understood as approximation; an essentialist characterization finds its logic not in an invitation to complexification but in the denial of further complexity. In essentializing, legal republicanism puts barriers in the way of citizens as they choose their particular identities and keep these choices open to constant revision. Yet it is in their very choices about individual identity that people imagine their life possibilities. It is through these choices that others imagine these same possibilities – in the way they offer goods and services, pay remuneration or allow shared participation in daily activities. And it is through these choices that people imagine like possibilities for others.

There is, nonetheless, a laudable obverse to these problematic identity features of the legal republican perspective. In relation to both individual and national identity, republican legal theory is fundamentally nonsubstantive (acknowledging, nonetheless, that the project of a priori characterization is inextricably a legal project and that, consequently, some distinctions will have to be drawn). That is, any particular configuration of identity-recognition in any particular state is given by politics and political theory, not by republican legal theory.

There are no inherent legal limits on the inventory of particular identities for which states may mandate equal protection. Thirty years ago, sexual orientation and social status as welfare recipient were only beginning to appear in human rights codes; today, we see emergent identity claims relating to height (police force cases), weight (extra charges for airline seats) and being a pet owner (exclusion from condominium ownership); 30 years from now, these codes may well embrace identity claims relating to eye colour, toenail shape and eating habits.

There are also no inherent legal limits on the inventory of particular identities that states may select for inclusion as characteristics of "national" identity. Constitutionally, national identities may be thick or thin. They may be constituted by one, two or 20 particular identities.

More than this, there are no personal identities that are inherently "national" identities. Republican theory does not mandate language, religion or culture as necessary indicators of identity. Nor does it exclude them, or any other such badges – sex, sexual orientation, race, height, ancestry, bloodline.

Finally, there is no inherent singularity to "national" identities in republican theory. Just as individuals may claim at any one time several particular identities (including several particular identities singled out for equal protection treatment), states may also claim at any one time several "national" identities.

This is true however the particular components of personal identity selected for recognition as "national" identities are chosen.

It follows that republican legal theory is, at least in principle, indifferent to both the specific content and the specific number of personal identities promoted as "national" identities in a given state. And it is indifferent as to the singularity or plurality of the individuated personal identities privileged within each category of "national" identity. There is, in other words, no legally relevant difference between uninational and multinational states – whatever the specific identity components of that "nationality" might be.

The argument of this first part can be summarized as a series of propositions about individual identity and about the republican consensus concerning how law should manage the social diversity that these identities both constitute and reflect.

Take first the notion of identity. This paper asserts a subjectivist, agency-driven conception of identity that embraces five elements.[8] First, individual identity is both self-created and ascribed by others; while individuals make their own identities, they do not do so free of the constraints of others. Second, some individual identities are sociological – that is, formed in interaction with social groups; some identities are psychological – that is, formed in interaction with one's understanding of how one conceives others; and some identities are psychoanalytic – that is, formed in interaction with one's understanding of how one conceives oneself. Third, some identities are tacit or immanent and some are explicit or kinetic; an identity is no less an identity for being unacknowledged. Fourth, some identities are apparently given and some are apparently chosen; while a physical trait may be given – possibly gender, body type, bloodline and so on – the identity constructed from this physical trait is not inevitable. Fifth, each person is constantly constructing and reconstructing the lexical order of the social-group relationships with others (particular identities) that together constitute his or her identity.[9]

What, then, of the republican consensus about how the law and the state should manage the social diversity that these features imply? To begin, for a particular identity to be formed, to take root and to be recognized as such, it requires expressive forms, processes and institutions. In republican theory, the state is typically called upon to provide this formal, procedural and institutional recognition through law. As a matter of law, however, some identities are ignored, some are actively repressed, some are protected and some are mandated. No identities (including "citizenship," which is formally constituted by the political state) exactly map the territorial frontiers of any legal or political order; all are either substate or suprastate in scope. Whether uninational or multinational, a state can deploy law to promote "national" identity; republican legal theory imposes no limits on the number of identity characteristics that may be considered as forming a "national" identity. But, however they are promoted, "national" identities implicitly marginalize all non-national particular identities, and they explicitly exclude and disrespect all alternative expressions of the identity characteristics being promoted.[10]

The Legal-Pluralist Alternative

Despite the sometimes awkward fit between the socio-demographic character of contemporary territorial states and the assumptions and value choices inherent in legal-republicanism, the theory continues to be attractive even to political scientists and legal scholars who are broadly sympathetic to diversity claims. There are several reasons for this, the key one being that republican theory appears to simplify the task of recognizing and accommodating social diversity by denying the juris-generative power of particular identities. The multiple, overlapping normative communities (whether territorial, affective, affiliative, economic or virtual) in which people live their everyday lives (as, for example, children, parents, siblings, spouses, neighbours, friends, co-religionists, workers) and in which they discover, negotiate and order their particular identities can be conceived not as sites of law but simply as brute facts. Republican theory holds that, however worthy of legal regard these brute facts may be, they can acquire legal significance only through the instrumentality of state recognition.

Contrast the theory of legal pluralism.[11] Legal pluralism posits law in every site, at every moment and through every mode of human interaction. It rejects the republican postulates of centralism, monism and positivism. Human agents participating in different psychosocial milieux create and negotiate both their own normative standards to shape and symbolize social behaviour and their own institutions and processes to reinforce or apply these standards. Even the simplest legal regimes are constituted by a plurality of law-generating sites, moments and modes. These regimes are in constant interaction, mutually influencing the emergence of each other's rules, processes and institutions through trajectories of normativity that are both varied and unpredictable. That is, in a legal pluralistic approach normative regimes – including those normative regimes of the political state – are not stable, unambiguous and self-contained within clear jurisdictional and territorial boundaries. Every particular identity creates and is reflected in a legal regime.

Legal pluralism also posits that there is no permanent hierarchy among these legal regimes and no permanent hierarchy of particular identities privileged by these regimes in any individual's life. Each person is constantly deciding and redeciding (and refusing to decide) which regimes provide the symbol structure for evaluating claims about law and about identity in any given situation. Each person is constantly deciding the relative weight of rules, processes and values amongst the multiple legal regimes that attract, invite or demand loyalty and commitment. Legal pluralism understands legal artifact, social milieu and particular identity as mutually constituting and constituted, as an unsystematic *mêlée* of interacting components.[12]

For a legal pluralist, the state's pretence to unify or to rank these multiple legal regimes is at best contingent (both in space and through time), and its pretence to specify which identities are juris-generative is illusory. No inventory in a human rights code, for example, can ever capture the meaning of particular identities for individual legal subjects.[13] Nonetheless, even though individuals comprise a multiplicity of legal subjects reflecting a multitude of particular identities, they constantly attempt to achieve an iterative integration of their particular identities. This is pursued through a continuing narrative of meaning through which each identity is held open to evaluation – by itself and by all other particular identities. On this account, a legal regime is not pre-existing but is a process of creating and maintaining normative realities, of creating and maintaining self-understandings and identities.[14]

The legal subject negotiates and iterates identities in every site of interaction – with the state, society, community, workplace, family and so on. Each of these normative sites reacts through the several (the hundreds, the thousands) of other legal subjects narrating themselves and being narrated there. Particular legal subjects are shaped by the knowledge and identities they inherit, create and share with other legal subjects. The different sites of law – the different legal regimes – are constituted by the knowledge they possess, the knowledge they create and the knowledge they share through particular legal subjects. By imagining law as a mode of giving particular sense to particular identities and particular interactions in particular places, legal pluralism shifts inquiry toward thinking of law as meaning, not machinery. On this account, legal knowledge is about discovering sources of normativity in identity claims.[15]

In a legal pluralist framework, then, law is presented and represents itself as radically noncentralist, nonmonist and nonpositivist. By contrast with the theoretically decontextualized, unitary and integrated citizen of republican legal theory, the pluralist legal subject is an individual who both self-identifies in multiple fashions and is identified by others in multiple fashions. Membership in any given legal order is contingent upon whatever criterion of identity the legal subject and his or her interlocutors choose to adopt at any given moment. A particular identity claim – for example, sexual orientation – may be the impetus through which a particular narration of self is occasioned. It does not, by that fact, become a privileged identity – a "national" identity –

for the legal regime being iterated through that identity. More to the point, because the content and boundaries of a legal order will always be found in the minds of legal subjects – in the plurality of their conceptions of their particular identities and the particular identities of others – the legal pluralist perspective holds that the "national" identity of even the political state as a legal regime will also always be contingent. Finally, for the same reason, legal pluralist theory denies that any particular legal order, including that of the state, can determine the content and boundaries of any other legal order.[16]

These legal pluralist hypotheses about the relationship between assertions of identity and law do not, of course, fundamentally affect the way in which the legal issues presented by conditions of social diversity are cast. Simply pluralizing sites, modes and sources of normativity does not change the diversity challenge to "national" identities. Queer Nation confronts gender-identity claims that put its conception of citizenship to the test; the United Church confronts "heretical" claims that contest how doctrinal orthodoxy defines the "faithful"; an Aboriginal nation confronts "psychic identity" claims that stand in opposition to "blood quantum" as the test of membership and belonging.

In each case, the legal issues remain those elaborated in the introduction to this essay: which of law's institutional resources – for instance, formalized constitutional and quasi-constitutional arrangements attributing rights – are best suited to inviting and apprehending identity claims? And second, what processes of social ordering – for instance, the strict adjudication of these rights before official courts – are most conducive to recognizing and accommodating multiple diversity claims? By acknowledging the juris-generative capacity of individuals pursuing identity claims in group interaction, and by focusing on narrative iteration and mediation as the optimal procedural modes for framing and acknowledging social diversity, the legal pluralist approach offers a radical alternative to republican legal theory for addressing these issues.

The focus in republican legal theory on the political state has tended to give priority to formal (primarily constitutional) aspects of institutional design as these relate to rules, institutions and processes of social ordering. In republican theory the questions are: what identities give rise to identity rights? And by what means should these identity rights be guaranteed? There is, of course, utility in considering how formalized systems structure the recognition of social diversity. After all, any constitution – be it of the state, a corporation, a club or a family – serves an identity-constituting function. The constitution often does so explicitly in a text, although in the common-law tradition most of the identity-constituting function of constitutions is normally left tacit. A constitution usually defines who are the members of the polity in question; it typically states a raison d'être – a telos for the group; it invents and allocates the organic branches of governance – executive, legislature and judiciary, for example. It specifies the legitimating processes for these organic branches – election, nomination and so on; it decides and establishes whether governance is unitary, confederal or federal and so on; it indicates how revenue is to be raised and spent; it sets out countermajoritarian constraints such as bills of rights; it elaborates institutions and processes for its interpretation; and lastly, it provides for its amendment.[17]

Within this inventory, given the premises of republican legal theory, some items appear more obviously related to the recognition of identity claims than others – notably, the criteria of membership, the telos, federal or confederal governance regimes, protected amendment procedures and, especially, countermajoritarian constraints. But institutions of identity-recognition are not all imagined and legitimated through a formal constitution and the "rights" it guarantees. No one would think that, for example, one's permissible identity as a bridge player and the manner in which this identity finds expression in the activities of the Montreal Bridge League would be exclusively determined by "constitutional rights" attributed by, hypothetically, the World Bridge Federation. As a matter of legal pedigree, there are at least five broad procedural frameworks for imagining governance and regulation in a manner that acknowledges particular identities: call them political (legislative), legal (judicial), administrative (executive), constitutional (constitutive) and external (extrasystemic).[18]

Political procedures and institutions speak to the legislative process: issues like entitlement to vote, guaranteed constituencies and requirements of supermajorities in certain cases. They are directed primarily at law-making processes and the idea of actual or virtual political vetoes. Legal devices seek to limit the capacity of legislative or executive governance by inbuilt limitations on action. Charters of rights and antidiscrimination and equality norms are good examples; typically these are focused on the judicial process. Administrative processes and frameworks seek to insulate the management of institutions from the governance and control of those of a different (typically dominant) identity. School, hospitals, universities, social service agencies, local municipalities, marketing boards, professional corporations and other executive agencies are often designed to frame governance practices and everyday management to acknowledge particular identities.

A fourth set of identity-promoting norms are those associated with constitutive constitutional norms. These include the creation of a federal system, a bicameral parliament and the allocation of certain governance powers in counter-intuitive ways – for example, in Canada, marriage and divorce, judicial appointments, the declaratory power. The final series of practices and procedures can be characterized as external. These are suprasystemic, involving a direct appeal to authority outside the constituency. Adherence to international treaties and conventions, membership in UN agencies and the use of appeals to world public opinion by Aboriginal peoples are contemporary examples of how external mechanisms and processes can be deployed in aid of identity recognition.

These five archetypes can be re-imagined so that the juris-generative energy of social diversity is harnessed to limit the capacity of the state to reconstitute particular identities into "national" identities. Consider the recent controversies in Quebec involving school attendance by young Muslim girls wearing the *hijab* and young Sikh boys carrying the *kirpan*. Authorities insisted that the children could not be admitted to class wearing a *hijab* or carrying a *kirpan*. Various grounds for the exclusion were raised: first, these were said to be the mark of a religion, not acceptable in a secular institution; second, the *hijab* connotes the submission and inferiority of women, unacceptable in a society committed to equality of the sexes; third, the *hijab* made the identification of students difficult; fourth, the *kirpan* is a dangerous weapon. It is unnecessary here to do more than briefly allude to the spurious nature of all these rationales: do not some Roman Catholic students wear a cross and some Jewish students a *yarmulke*? Do not other religions exclude women from full participation in social life – from the priesthood, for example? Is one's face the only external means of identification? How is a dulled *kirpan* more dangerous than a fork in the school cafeteria? It is more important to consider how questions of particular identity may be framed as legal issues.

The immediately precipitating event for these controversies was the massive restructuring of public education in Quebec following, first, the enactment of legislation requiring, *inter alia*, immigrant attendance at French-language schools, and second, the replacement of religious school boards by linguistic school boards in the 1990s. Previously, there were four categories of schools: Roman Catholic French-language and Roman Catholic English-language, under the former Roman Catholic School Board of Montreal (CÉCM), and Protestant French-language and Protestant English-language, under the former Protestant School Board of Greater Montreal (PSBGM). The schools under the PSBGM had become more secular in the 1920s, when they began to admit Jewish students who had been excluded from Roman Catholic schools. Moreover, the combined effect of greater social diversity from increased non-European immigration beginning in the 1960s, the exclusion of the children of non-Catholic immigrants from CÉCM schools, and the requirement that immigrants study in French obliged the PSBGM to confront diversity in the early 1970s, and to do so by creating its own French-language schools. The process of significant ethnocultural accommodation within PSBGM schools had thus been engaged for three decades by the late 1990s.

The restructuring of the 1990s resulted in far fewer new English-language schools (notwithstanding the incorporation of a small number of English-language schools from the former CÉCM), but these were nevertheless as socio-demographically diverse as the English-language and French-language schools in the former PSBGM. The new French-language schools became populated (through the incorporation of several French-language schools from the PSBGM) by a much more diverse group of students than had been found in the French-language schools of the CÉCM. For the first time, administrators and school directors of French-language schools previously dominated by *fran-cophones de souche* of Roman Catholic faith had to cope with a large number of immigrant children, most of whom were not Roman Catholic, many of whom were not from Europe and at least some of whom were studying in the French language against their will. As well, those schools that were inherited from the CÉCM were undertaking the first steps toward becoming secular institutions. Administrators were presented with a dual challenge.

The first challenge was the simple fact of having to cope quickly and massively with a new diversity among the student population – ethnic, racial, linguistic and, above all, religious. The second challenge was the fact of having to cope with a new student population whose education had been heretofore forged in the crucible of a minority-dominated educational system. Even though the religious minorities transferred to the new school board – Muslim, Sikh – were not the same as those – ostensibly Protestant – that historically formed the catchment of the PSBGM, they had internalized the diversity ethic of a minority board. That is, most parents of these former PSBGM students did not share the "statist" ideology of the former CÉCM, and many (especially those who were refugees from countries where "statist" ideology was dominant) considered such an ideology as reflecting an exclusionary "cultural" nationalism.

In view of this socio-demographic history, it is not surprising that, of the four former categories of schools, only in the Roman Catholic French-language schools (especially in the bedroom communities surrounding the City of Montreal) did the controversy over wearing the *hijab* and carrying the *kirpan* erupt. Those schools in the new French-language board whose population, professors and administration were transferred from the former PSBGM suffered no such paroxysms. Given this context, how would republican legal theory and legal pluralism differ in the manner of their conception of the identity claims at issue?

One might begin by noting that in the case of both the *hijab* and the *kirpan*, the minority wished to participate in public institutions. They did not seek to construct their own institutions that would mandate a badge of "national" inclusion – Muslim schools, Sikh schools. This is, in other words, a quite different situation from that arising when socio-demographic minorities actually make a claim for separate identity-forming institutions: schools, hospitals, social service agencies and so on. Yet, consistently with republican legal theory, the public institutions within which they sought to participate compelled their exclusion on the grounds that education was secular education for civic virtue. (This despite the continued presence of crucifixes and other religious iconography in the classrooms, and despite the fact that these socio-cultural minorities had not previously sought to have this iconography removed.)

Second, the republican response overemphasizes "rights" as a way of expressing identity claims. Rather than considering whether current constitutive processes for school boards are likely to produce a fair reflection of social diversity, and rather than considering whether the internal administrative organization of schools can better reflect this diversity (as has been done elsewhere in Canada), the republican response presumes that the issue at stake is the "constitutional right" to wear the *hijab* and carry the *kirpan* – a right the contours of which can and must be litigated before the courts. Notwithstanding that civic nationalism (in the aspirational sense) would not explicitly deny alternative identities, the contemporary republican vision of civic nationalism requires schools (indeed, all state institutions) to articulate and reinforce the "national" identities of the state and to deny a public presence to all other particular identities.

The legal pluralist sees the issue quite differently. Legal pluralists understand public institutions as meeting grounds for all citizens claiming all identities – as privileged sites for corroding the hard edge of essentialized identities, be these the "national" identity of the state or of any group. Rather than being construed as a place to promote a "national" identity against which only rights claims may prevail, the school is cast as a *lieu de rassemblement* within which different identity claims may be articulated, mediated and conciliated. On a legal pluralist analysis, one has to conclude that by failing to recognize how their own ethno-cultural "national" identity defines and excludes other identities, the CÉCM administrators are inviting (even compelling) these diverse "nationalities" – Muslim, Sikh – to become "states."

Because a pluralist analysis sees legal regimes as constituted in the iteration of identities, the most effective institutional responses are not those that imagine "minority" identity claims being argued over and as against "national" identity claims. A pluralist perspective challenges school administrators to acknowledge how the "national" identity claims they make are simply surrogates for the particular identity claims of presumed majorities. On this account, the legal recognition of social diversity is grounded in enfranchisement – in everyday administrative arrangements within public institutions that do not lexically rank particular identities. Through these arrangements, the state both disclaims its own "essentialized, national" public identity and removes inducements for particular identity claims to reconstitute themselves as "essentialized, national" identities in competition with that previously privileged by the state.

Sometimes, however, people who claim particular identities do not do so with the ambition of participating or seeking enfranchisement in public institutions, even when these public institutions are explicitly meant to be *lieux de rassemblement*. Rather they proclaim their own legal regimes and institutional sites within which they pursue and validate these particular identities. Consider the data collected in an empirical survey of plaintiffs in the Montreal Small Claims Court in the mid-1990s. The aim was to determine if the institutional design of the court facilitated greater access by people who self-ascribed subordinated particular identities.[19] The catchment of the court maps one of Canada's most socio-demographically diverse census districts. The court is organized to promote access by removing barriers – cost, complexity and delay (and lawyers) – from the process. Moreover, its judges are given power to participate actively in the adjudication, even to the point of becoming mediators. Finally, most judges have received social-diversity "sensitivity training." Despite these structural and procedural adjustments, the data showed no increase in the access to the court by those who would characterize themselves as claiming subordinated particular identities.

The study examined all court plaintiffs for an entire year, sorting them by reference to socio-demographic criteria collected in prior data sets: age, sex, language, education, income, ethnicity, citizenship, race, religion and so on. The results obtained were then compared with census figures on the same questions for the court's catchment. The study found that well-educated, white male citizens who were either English-speaking Quebecers or *francophones de souche* and aged between 35 and 55 with a good income were grossly over-represented among the court's plaintiff population. No nonrandom distributions of the relevant types of conflict or nonrandom distributions of personality traits – fighters versus lumpers – skewed the socio-demography of the plaintiff cohort.[20] In other words, a state institution specially conceived to be responsive to populations most likely to make nonmainstream identity claims had almost no impact on the use of the institution by these populations.

How should this outcome be interpreted? If conflict cognizable by state legal institutions is randomly distributed, one would predict that all citizens should be equally disposed to use the disputing facilities provided by the state. That is, *ceteris paribus*, the extent to which citizens litigate should not correlate to any particular identity characteristics other than (hypothetically) a particular identity framed around an inclination to litigate. According to republican legal theory, the statistically significant relative absence of plaintiffs from disfavoured population sectors cannot be ascribed to individual identity choice but can only be seen as a symptom of a pathology. It appears to show that an official institution explicitly designed to enhance participation by those who would be most likely to claim a subordinated particular identity will not always guarantee quantitatively equal participation.

Of course, depending on political ideology, republican theorists have diverse remedies for this pathology, which they characterize as a problem of access to justice. Socialists could be predicted to argue for more legal aid, more systemic remedies and so forth. Liberals would argue for procedural adjustments to the litigation system to make it less intimidating to those likely to assert subordinated particular identities. Libertarians might see the remedy in replacing state institutions by state-delegated private courts or consensual arbitrations. Communitarians likely would seek to develop soft official solutions like state-managed conciliation processes. All these are statist strategies that postulate relationships between people created and regulated by abstract, impersonal, official, rights-attributing rules. The characterization of people – as consumer, tenant, employee – is given by the jurisdictional criteria proper to these institutions. Other characterizations – as a spouse, father, resident of a neighbourhood, friend, tenant, francophone, Hindu, senior citizen and so on – are excluded. So while the court may be responsive to those citizens claiming subordinated identities, under republican legal theory it must still require that the claims actually being advanced be framed as pre-existing identity-neutral rights.

Once again, the legal pluralist sees things differently. The preponderance of white, male, francophone professionals in the Small Claims Court may not be pathological at all. Perhaps certain plaintiffs have opted out of the court not for reasons of "personality" but because they have their own means for recognizing and negotiating conflict. In this light, the pathology might rather be that, as a response to conflict, and especially personal identity conflict, mainstream legal ideology sees this absence as a problem. Might there be processes of social ordering and practices for recognizing particular identities that stand in counterpoint to traditional conceptions of rights adjudication? Perhaps informal, ambiguous and contradictory rules, iterated in multiple normative sites, reveal citizens to be engaged in building their own legal regimes and negotiating their own responses to identity conflict. The idea of debating and mediating conflict in nonstate institutions may be more the proof of an open, tolerant society than a pathology to overcome.

If law is a hypothesis for acknowledging and building identities and relationships, the focus should be on the interactions between state and other manifestations of legal normativity. Access to state legal institutions would be conceptualized not as formally mandated but as constantly being negotiated.

Local or community institutions would be seen not as subordinated, unofficial counterpoints to state institutions but as competing legal regimes. Decisions would have to be re-imagined as the mediated outcome between contesting parties who deploy unofficial institutions in order to assert and negotiate the contours of their particular identities in a language and characterization that acknowledges these identity claims.

It follows that the pluralist hypothesis is more democratic and less *dirigiste* – that is, more respectful of the idea that the assertion of particular identities against presumed "national" identities lies at the foundation of a liberal democracy – than mainstream republican legal theory. Republican legal theory ascribes to the state the exclusive role of characterizing identity in any particular site of human interaction (including a site of conflict) and of organizing this interaction on the basis that conflict must produce winners and losers. Where this involves conflict between different externalized modes of identity expression it demands that citizens become only tenants, or consumers, or spouses, or victims, or dependants, or "discrete and insular minorities."

The legal pluralist approach denies categorical distinctions between state normativities and multiple nonstate normative regimes. In conceiving all these normative sites as legal regimes that compete for human loyalty and commitment, it enfranchises citizens to define the context of interaction (including the context of a dispute). It also authorizes them to define how the relationship in issue should be characterized – for example, as an identity claim or not; and if so, of what identity? And it permits (indeed invites) citizens to negotiate their identity with others over time, rather than crystallizing it once and for all in the language of rights.

Conclusion

A legal pluralist approach does not deal with particular identities by asking how state law recognizes social diversity. Rather, the pluralist inquiry is how do people recognize and iterate their diverse identities through law. The aspiration is to contest interpretations of identity given and demanded by the state and its officials. In this sense, legal pluralism denies that there can be multinational states because it denies that there can be uninational states. "National" identities are no more than a conjunctional privileging of certain particular identities. "National" identities are found in the belief and behaviour of those whose narrative of their particular identities succeeds.

Insofar as law's attempt to recognize particular identities is concerned, it is erroneous to imagine legal subjects only as the physical presentations of a series of narrating selves constructed by gender, race, class, language and culture.

There is, and can be, no presumptive priority to any social category: class, gender, race, tortfeasor, tenant, spouse, child, timid, aggressive, bald, blue-eyed, tall, obese, queer, abled and so on are all partial understandings of subjects.

In the end, for a legal pluralist, the way we hold up each of our narrating selves to the critical scrutiny of our other selves and the way we hold ourselves up to the critical scrutiny of all the other narrated selves projected upon us by others are the measures of identity. Mediating these hypothetical, shifting and ambivalent iterations is then the measure of law. For the mediation that we undertake between the diverse identities that we attribute to ourselves and which are attributed to us by others is the first step to a mediation between these diverse identities in the public sphere. And in this mediation, there can be neither permanent particular identities nor permanent "national" identities.

Notes

An earlier version of this essay was presented to the session "The Legal Mediation of Diversity" at the conference "The Institutional Accommodation of Diversity," Saint-Marc-sur-le-Richelieu, Quebec, held September 20-22, 2001, under the auspices of the Research Group on Multinational Societies. I should like to thank my colleagues Richard Janda and Nicholas Kasirer and my research student Simon Chamberland for their assistance in revising this essay for publication.

1. For a further, more detailed elaboration of this point see Macdonald (1998b).

2. The character of these diversity-denying policy responses is developed in greater detail in Macdonald (1996b).

3. For an excellent contemporary discussion see Tremblay (1997).

4. For a touching evocation of the permeability of local rural identities see Cliche and Ferron (1972).

5. Consider the arguments of Harris (1989-90) and Higgins (1996).

6. Compare Sharpe (2002).

7. The point is developed at length in Macdonald (1997).

8. Some have called this conception "postmodern." See, for example, Stychin (1995) and Wicke (1991).

9. This position has close affinities with that argued by Iris Young. See, notably, Young (2000, pp. 99-103).

10. For an alternative conception of the possibilities of republican constitutionalism, see Stychin (1994).

11. For a summary review of the origins and variations of legal pluralist thinking see Merry (1988) and Macdonald (1998a).

12. The idea of a *mêlée* is taken from Sampford (1989). For its application to pluralist theory see Macdonald (1993b, 1996a).

13. This claim is nicely illustrated in Iyer (1993) and Kropp (1997).

14. The implications of viewing legal regimes as constituted by narrating legal subjects are traced out in Macdonald and Kleinhans (1997).

15. For an elaboration of this approach to law see Sousa Santos (1995a, 1995b). See also Macdonald (2002).

16. On the hypothesis of boundary negotiation of legal regimes see Kasirer (2002).

17. Macdonald (1991a, 1991b).

18. I have developed these features with particular reference to Canadian practices in Macdonald (1996b). For another elaboration see Macdonald (1993a).

19. The findings of the study are reported in Macdonald and McGuire (1996, 1997, 1998, 2000).

20. The potential impacts of personal disputing styles are explored in Paquin (2001).

Bibliography

Cliche, Robert, and Madeleine Ferron. *Quand le people fait la loi : la loi populaire* à St-Joseph de Beauce. Montreal: Hurtubise, 1972.

Gaudreault-Desbiens, Jean-François. "Angoisse identitaire et critique du droit de la 'critique juridique identitaire américaine' comme objet et source de réflexion théorique." *Revue interdisciplinaire d'études juridiques* (forthcoming 2003).

Harris, Angela P. "Race and Essentialism in Feminist Legal Theory." *Stanford Law Review*, Vol. 42 (1989-90): 581-616.

Higgins, Tracy E. "Anti-essentialism, Relativism, and Human Rights." *Harvard Women's Law Journal*, Vol. 19 (1996): 89-126.

Iyer, Nitya. "Categorial Denials: Equality Rights and the Shaping of Social Identity." *Queen's Law Journal*, Vol. 19, no. 1 (fall 1993): 179-207.

Kasirer, Nicholas. "Le droit robinsonien," in *La solitude en droit privé*, ed. Nicholas Kasirer. Montreal: Thémis, 2002.

Kropp, Douglas. "'Categorial' Failure: Canada's Equality Jurisprudence – Changing Notions of Identity and the Legal Subject." *Queen's Law Journal*, Vol. 23, no. 1 (fall 1997): 201-30.

Macdonald, Roderick A. "Meech Lake to the Contrary Notwithstanding: Part I." *Osgoode Hall Law Journal*, Vol. 29, no. 2 (1991a): 253-328.

———. "Meech Lake to the Contrary Notwithstanding: Part II." *Osgoode Hall Law Journal*, Vol. 29, no. 2 (1991b): 483-570.

———. "The New Zealand Bill of Rights Act: How Far Does It or Should It Stretch?" in *Proceedings of the 1993 New Zealand Law Conference*. Wellington: New Zealand Law Society, 1993a.

———. "Recognizing and Legitimating Aboriginal Justice: Implications for a Reconstruction of Non-Aboriginal Legal Systems in Canada," in *Aboriginal Peoples and the Justice Systems: Report of the National Round Table on Aboriginal Justice Issues*. Ottawa: Royal Commission on Aboriginal Peoples, 1993b.

———. "Les Vieilles Gardes: Hypothèses sur l'émergence des normes, l'internormativité et le désordre à travers une typologie des institutions normatives," in *Le Droit soluble: Contributions québécoises à l'étude de l'internormativité*, ed. Jean-Guy Belley. Paris: L.G.D.J., 1996a.

———. "The Design of Constitutions to Accommodate Linguistic, Cultural and Ethnic Diversity: The Canadian Experiment," in *Dual Images: Multiculturalism on Two Sides of the Atlantic*, ed. K. Kulcsár and D. Seabo. Budapest: Institute for Political Science of the Hungarian Academy of Science, 1996b.

———. "Legal Bilingualism." *McGill Law Journal*, Vol. 42, no. 1 (February 1997): 119-67.

———. "Critical Legal Pluralism as a Construction of Normativity and the Emergence of Law," in *Théories et émergence du droit: pluralisme, surdétermination et effectivité*, ed. Richard Janda, Andrée Lajoie, Roderick A. Macdonald and Guy Rocher. Montreal: Thémis, 1998a.

———. "Metaphors of Multiplicity: Civil Society, Regimes and Legal Pluralism." *Arizona Journal of International and Comparative Law*, Vol. 15 (1998b): 69-91.

———. *Lessons of Everyday Law*. Montreal and Kingston: McGill-Queen's University Press, 2002.

Macdonald, Roderick A., and Martha-Marie Kleinhans. "What Is a *Critical* Legal Pluralism?" *Canadian Journal of Legal Studies*, Vol. 12, no. 2 (fall 1997): 25-46.

Macdonald, Roderick A., and Seana C. McGuire. "Judicial Scripts in the Dramaturgy of the Small Claims Court." *Canadian Journal of Law of Society*, Vol. 11, no. 1 (spring 1996): 63-98.

———. "Small Claims Court Cant." *Osgoode Hall Law Journal*, Vol. 34, no. 3 (fall 1997): 509-51.

———. "Tales of Wows and Woes from the Masters and the Muddled: Navigating Small Claims Court Narratives." *Windsor Yearbook of Access to Justice*, Vol. 16 (1998): 48-89.

———. "For Whom the Court Toils." Unpublished manuscript dated July 2000.

Merry, Sally Engle. "Legal Pluralism." *Law and Society Review*, Vol. 22, no. 5 (1988): 869-96.

Paquin, Julie. "Avengers, Avoiders and Lumpers: The Incidence of Disputing Style on Litigiousness." *Windsor Yearbook of Access to Justice*, Vol. 19 (2001): 1-38.

Sampford, Charles. *The Disorder of Law*. Oxford: Blackwell, 1989.

Sharpe, Andrew. *Transgender Jurisprudence: Dysphoric Bodies of Law*. London: Cavendish, 2002.

Sousa Santos, B. de. *Toward a New Common Sense*. New York: Routledge, 1995a.

———. "Three Metaphors for a New Conception of Law: The Frontier, the Baroque, and the South." *Law and Society Review*, Vol. 29, no. 4 (1995b): 509-84.

Stychin, Carl F. "A Postmodern Constitutionalism: Equality Rights, Identity Politics, and the Canadian National Imagination." *Dalhousie Law Journal*, Vol. 17, no. 1 (spring 1994): 61-82.

———. "Essential Rights and Contested Identities: Sexual Orientation and Equality Rights Jurisprudence in Canada." *Canadian Journal of Law and Jurisprudence*, Vol. 8, no. 1 (January 1995): 49-66.

Tremblay, Luc B. *The Rule of Law, Justice, and Interpretation*. Montreal and Kingston: McGill-Queen's University Press, 1997.

Wicke, Jennifer. "Postmodern Identity and the Legal Subject." *University of Colorado Law Review*, Vol. 62, no. 3 (1991): 455-74.

Young, Iris Marion. *Inclusion and Democracy*. Oxford: Oxford University Press, 2000.

part II
institutional conditions of diversity

6

between autonomy and secession: the accommodation of minority nationalism in Catalonia

Montserrat Guibernau

The nation has become one of the most contested concepts of our times. The multifarious definitions of the nation focus on cultural, political, psychological, territorial, ethnic and sociological principles according to the different scholars, politicians and political activists willing to shed light onto such a disputed term. Their lack of agreement suggests a major difficulty in dealing with such a complex phenomenon. The crux of the difficulty probably lies close to the link that has been established between nation and state and to the common practice of using the nation as a source of political legitimacy. Recognition as a nation entails different rights for the community that claims to be one, since being a nation usually implies attachment to a particular territory, a shared culture and history, and vindication of the right to self-determination. Defining a specific community as a nation involves more or less explicit acceptance of the legitimacy of the state that claims to represent it, or if the nation does not possess a state of its own, the state then implicitly acknowledges the nation's right to self-government, involving some degree of political autonomy that may or may not lead to a claim for independence.

State, Nation and Nationalism

The nation, however, cannot be viewed in isolation; I argue that a clear-cut distinction needs to be drawn between four concepts: state, nation, nation-state and nationalism. By "state," taking Weber's definition, I refer to "a human community that (successfully) claims *the monopoly of the legitimate use of physical force* within a given territory,"[1] although not all states have successfully accomplished this, and some have not even aspired to accomplish it. By "nation," I refer to a human group conscious of forming a community, sharing a common culture, attached to a clearly demarcated territory, having a common past and a common project for the future, and claiming the right to rule itself. This definition attributes five dimensions to the nation: psychological (consciousness of forming a group), cultural, territorial, political and historical. The "nation-state" also needs to be defined and distinguished: it is a modern institution, characterized by the formation of a kind of state that has the monopoly of what it claims is the legitimate use of force within a demarcated territory and that seeks to unite the people subject to its rule by means of cultural homogenization. Finally, by "nationalism" I mean the sentiment of belonging to a community whose members identify with a set of symbols, beliefs and ways of life, and have the will to decide upon their common political destiny.[2]

Nation, state and nationalism form a triad characterized by constant tension between the three components. Changes in the definition of one have the capacity to influence and, to some extent, even alter the definitions of the other two. For instance, if belonging to a nation is defined in terms of common descent, the definition of the state and with it that of citizenship, as an attribute conferred upon the members of the state, will have to include descent as a *sine qua non* condition for membership. Consequently, any nationalist movement emerging in this circumstance will focus upon common descent as a prerequisite for inclusion in the nation that the movement's members want to defend and promote. Where common ancestry is replaced by territory or by the will to be a member of a particular nation as the primary condition for membership of a particular state, the definition of nation and the character of nationalism are altered accordingly.

This example refers to conditions for membership, that is, to elements considered indispensable for distinguishing between those who belong and those who do not belong to the nation. But alterations in the definitions of nation, state and nationalism are not restricted to conditions for belonging or criteria for membership.

The state's self-definition as a unitary, a federal or even a multinational political institution holds significant consequences for the peoples living within its boundaries. Any one of these self-definitions, once adopted by a specific state, has the capacity to influence the definition of the nation. This is particularly evident in the case of a state that declares itself to be multinational, thus assuming the coexistence of more than one nation within its territory. Such a position entails an automatic distinction between nation and state that challenges the commonly accepted coincidence between the two. A multinational state explicitly acknowledges its internal diversity and, in so doing, influences the diverse definitions of nationalism that may emerge within its territory. First, in these cases the nationalism instilled by the state will necessarily involve acceptance of the diverse nations included within its borders. This type of nationalism tends to focus on shared constitutional rights and principles as elements able to hold together an otherwise diverse citizenry. Second, the nationalism emerging from the national minorities within the state is strongly influenced by the state's recognition of their status as nations. The minorities' nationalism is bound to focus upon demands for greater power and resources that will allow them to further the degree of self-government they enjoy – assuming that they already have some political autonomy.

In a similar way, alterations in the definition of nationalism also have the power to impact upon the definitions of both the state and the nation. A nationalist discourse based upon the rejection and dehumanization of those who do not belong to the nation and upon their portrayal as "enemies" and a "threat" will feed xenophobia and ethnic hatred. This type of nationalism tends to foster a narrow definition of the nation that is based upon the exclusion of the different and the belief in the superiority of one's own nation above all others. A state endorsing this sort of nationalism is likely to have as policy the marginalization and sometimes even the elimination of "others" within its territory, and/or to pursue a consistent assimilation policy. This type of state often engages in conflicts with other states as a result of an aggressive economic and/or territorial expansionist policy.

These examples show how differences in the nature and definition of one constituent of the triad create substantial variations in the definitions of the other two. Further consideration suggests that different definitions of nation, state and nationalism coexist simultaneously in different parts of the globe. Hence, the relation between the three can be analyzed by focusing on two different levels. The first, as I have shown above, involves the study of how changes in the definition of one constituent affect the other two. The second considers those external factors that are capable of altering the nature of the triad by shifting the balance of power between its constituents, to undermine one at the expense of another. Here we are confronted with radical transformations that are able to break the more or less stable equilibrium existing within the triad by affecting the relationships of the constituents at a structural level, well above the particular situations considered when analyzing individual cases.

At present, the main challenge to the relationship between the elements of the triad concerns those radical and rapid transformations that are now affecting the traditional nature of the state. The proliferation of supranational institutions, the increasing number of multinational corporations and the emergence of substate nationalist movements are contriving a novel political scenario in which the state's traditional role is being fundamentally undermined. Signs of this have already become apparent: the radicalization of state nationalism, the rapid increase in ethnic and national conflicts and the state's resistance to giving up substantial aspects of its sovereignty all point to the urgent need for the state to recast its nature. We are now witnessing the rise of what I call "nations without states": potential new political actors able to capture and promote sentiments of loyalty, solidarity and community among individuals who seem to have developed a growing need for identity. Various political and economic arguments may also be invoked when accounting for the relevance that nations without states may acquire in the foreseeable future.

Nations without States

A nation without a state is based upon the existence of a cultural community that is endowed with a stable but dynamic core containing a set of elements that have generated a specific national identity. The state, that is, the political institution with which the nation should ideally identify, is missing. This creates a political scenario in which the cultural unit lacks a political institution that its members can regard as legitimate.

The members of a stateless nation regard the state containing them as alien and maintain a separate sense of national identity generally based upon a common culture, history, attachment to a particular territory and the explicit wish to rule themselves. Self-determination is sometimes understood as political autonomy and stops short of independence; in other cases it involves the right to secede. Catalonia, Quebec, Scotland, the Basque Country and Flanders represent but a few nations without states currently demanding further autonomy. It could be argued that some of these nations do have some kind of state of their own since substantial powers have been devolved to their regional parliaments. But in my view political autonomy and even federation fall short of independence since they tend to exclude foreign and economic policy, defence and constitutional matters, and this is why it continues to make sense to refer to them as nations without states.

The main attributes of the nation-state, which somehow favour the assimilation of otherwise culturally diverse citizens, are its power to confer rights and duties upon its citizens; its ability to provide for their basic needs – a function that since the Second World War has materialized in the establishment of various types of welfare systems; and its power to maintain order in society while controlling defence, immigration, foreign policy, education, communication systems and the economy.

The relationship between nation and state has shifted from the nineteenth and early twentieth centuries, when the state and its role in nation-building was given pre-eminence. In contrast, since the second half of the twentieth century we have been confronted with the re-emergence of nationalism in nations without states. This involves "state-building" strategies being used by stateless nations seeking to construct their own state or, at least, their own "quasi state."

The rise of nations without states is closely connected to two interrelated factors: the intensification of globalization processes, and transformations affecting the nation-state. The nation-state has traditionally based its legitimacy upon the idea that it represents the nation, even though, once created, the state often had to engage in nation-building processes aimed at the forced assimilation of its citizens. It is now becoming apparent that, in many cases, these processes have largely failed; the re-emergence of nationalist movements in nations without states proves it. It seems that the state is becoming increasingly unable to fulfill its citizens' needs, and as a result of this they are turning away from it and searching for alternative institutions.

Most so-called nation-states are not constituted by a single nation that is coextensive with the state; internal diversity is the rule. The nation-state, after a long process of consolidation that involves constructing a symbolic image of the community endowed with a particular language and culture, creating symbols and rituals to emphasize its unique character, and fixing its territorial borders, is being forced to respond to challenges from within.

The nations or parts of nations included within a single state do not share similar levels of national awareness. What is more, while some will define themselves as nations, others will be happy to be referred to as provinces or regions. Nations are not unique or fixed, and it is possible to find throughout history the disintegration of nations that have played a prominent role during a particular period, followed by the creation of new ones.

The state has a strong tendency to absorb functions and a great reluctance to delegate control over any task it considers an integral part of its sovereignty. The argument for state centralization is closely connected to the idea of state sovereignty, understood as full control over all matters concerning the social, political and economic life of the citizens living within its boundaries. The increasing number of international organizations, multinational companies and supranational social movements and the technical sophistication of modern warfare are currently challenging this classic concept of state sovereignty. The state is exposed to pressure from above, while at the same time it lays itself open to increasing pressure from within to modify its traditional centralist nature and acknowledge the existence of territorially circumscribed cultural communities within itself that show varying degrees of national self-consciousness and put forward different socio-political demands. The origin of most of these communities can be traced back to an era prior to the founding of the nation-state, when diversity was generally diluted under the centralist and homogenizing practices of a then incipient nation-state.

The Quest for Recognition

The nationalism of nations without states currently employs two major sets of arguments to legitimize its discourse. First, a political argument stemming from the French and American revolutions endorses democracy and popular sovereignty as leading principles to legitimize the construction of the modern state. In late eighteenth-century France, sovereignty was taken from the king and aristocracy and placed in the hands of the nation as the "whole people," even though it was assumed at first that the most educated and enlightened citizens would have to guide the people and bring them gradually into political life.

Second, a cultural argument that emphasizes the richness of linguistic and cultural diversity. This argument is closely related to the principles of Romantic nationalism, in which cultural and linguistic diversity are valued and promoted, thus reinforcing the specific identities based upon them.

The nationalism of nations without states often clashes with ignorance, neglect or lack of will from the state, which tends to resist pressure to grant the right to self-determination to national minorities living within its borders. In most cases, nations without states remember both a past in which they enjoyed their own autonomous institutions and the conflict and oppression that generally ended that earlier autonomy. Berlin defines nationalism as "the result of wounds inflicted by someone or something, on the natural feelings of a society, or of artificial barriers to its normal development."[3] In the nationalist discourses of nations without states currently seeking recognition it is common to find a detailed list of grievances against the state. In Berlin's words, "Nationalism springs, as often as not, from a wounded or outraged sense of human dignity, the desire for recognition."[4] The struggle for recognition entails the desire to be regarded and treated as an equal, as a nation with a voice, able to participate in the political processes affecting its future. Recognition involves many dimensions that sometimes overlap. There are moral, social, political and even financial consequences for a state that decides to acknowledge the existence of different nations within its territory. In the process of recognition, pride and moral sentiment take precedence over economic compensation. Berlin writes,

Recognition is demanded by individuals, by groups, by classes, by nations, by states, by vast conglomerations of mankind united by a common feeling of grievance against those who (they rightly or wrongly suppose) have wounded or humiliated them, have denied them the minimum demanded by human dignity, have caused, or tried to cause, them to fall in their own estimation in a manner that they cannot tolerate. The nationalism of the last two hundred years is shot through with this feeling.[5]

The relationship between nations without states and the state is often marked by: 1) political dependence; 2) limited or frequently nonexistent access to power and resources; 3) restricted or even absent economic powers; and 4) in many cases, a restrained capacity to develop and promote the nation's own culture and language. Nations without states claim the right to be recognized as political actors and to have a say in different fora, entrance to which has been up to now restricted to nation-states. Some may argue that recognizing nations without states adds further complexity to current international structures, and they may add that this might lead to increasing fragmentation and oppose the advancement of internationalism.

I argue that such positions ignore the right of peoples to preserve and develop their cultures and decide on their political future. Contemporary democratic nationalist movements in nations without states invoke the right to self-determination, a principle advanced by Woodrow Wilson after 1918. This right involved, at first, "equating the popular principle of sovereignty with the attack on the remaining dynastic empires in Europe, and later with anticolonialism generally. Secondly, it involved abandoning the constitutional mode of settling disputed claims in favour of political settlements."[6] In Mayall's view, the historical fate of the principle of national self-determination is doubly ironic: it has tended to legitimize the state and only the state, and it has elevated and institutionalized the progressive view of human affairs by attempting to freeze the political map in a way never seen before.[7] He points to two major challenges to the internal order: irredentism as the main essentialist challenge, and secession as the main rationalist challenge. Irredentism in modern political usage has come to mean any territorial claim generally based on historical and/or ethnic arguments made by a sovereign state to lands within another. Secession refers to the creation of an independent state out of territory previously included within another state from which it has now separated. The term is also often employed to describe unsuccessful separatist rebellions against the state, which may or may not involve the use of violence.

A crucial distinction between irredentism and secession concerns the level at which they originate. Irredentism is usually instilled by state elites and emerges within the existing system of interstate power rivalries. "Secession," Mayall stresses, "depends on group sentiment and loyalty not just on a disputed title to land or a doctrine of prescriptive right."[8] Secession constitutes a standing challenge to an international order based on the sovereign state.

> It does so because, on the one hand, it belongs to the modern "rationalist" world in which the right to self-determination is held to be a fundamental human right, while, on the other, aggressive war, and therefore the possibility of acquiring title by conquest, is proscribed under the United Nations Charter. The only way out of this impasse is to resort to the conventional interpretation of national self-determination as reflected in the existing state order. This is so obviously a fiction that it must in turn constitute a provocative invitation to secessionist nationalists.[9]

In my view, the recognition of nations without states as global political actors does not necessarily involve them becoming independent. My argument is that while some nations without states may secede, most are likely to achieve greater political autonomy within the political institutions that are currently being developed. In the rest of this paper I examine the accommodation of Catalonia within the new democratic Spain as an example that illustrates some of the tensions between political autonomy and secession.

Between Autonomy and Secession: The Catalan Case

Opposing conceptions of the state and the nation were at stake in the Spanish Civil War. Franco defended a highly centralized and uniform image of Spain that rejected the progressive government of the Second Spanish Republic (1931-38) and abhorred the process of decentralization initiated by it. During the Second Republic, statutes of autonomy were sanctioned in Catalonia (1932), the Basque Country (1933) and Galicia (1936), although it was only in Catalonia that the statute had been implemented at the time of Franco's rising.

The Francoists, or "nationals," emphasized unity and condemned all forms of cultural diversity. Their nationalism emerged as a reaction against ideologies such as socialism and anarchism that in their view threatened the country's traditional socio-political structure, and it was based on a conservative centralist and Castilian-centred ideology that would stop the path toward modernization initiated by republican Spain and sustain the traditional structures defended by large Catholic sectors. The Francoist victory resulted in the suppression of all regional political institutions and laws, and also in the prohibition of the Catalan and Basque (Euskera) languages and all sorts of symbolic elements (flags, anthems) of the Catalan and Basque identities.[10]

The transition to democracy that began after Franco's death in 1975 can be seen as an attempt by the political class to synchronize Francoist institutions with the requirements of a modern society. During the seventies, the profound dislocation between the social and political spheres became increasingly alarming and highlighted the political system's inability to solve the multiple problems facing Spanish society. Yet, although Francoism endorsed significant changes in trying to modernize, it proved obsolete, unable to run a society that had experienced dramatic transformations since 1939. With one million unemployed and inflation standing at 30 percent in 1975, the inadequacy of Francoist policies became patently clear.[11]

Spain was no longer a rural country. Heavy industrial zones were concentrated in Catalonia and the Basque Country. A demographic explosion took place in the sixties and, together with great internal migrations, this led to the growth of urban areas. A new middle class emerged and some sectors of the bourgeoisie that had once supported Franco now pushed for reforms. With the Spanish economy practically isolated, these new sectors pressed for the integration of Spain into the then European Community. Illiteracy had decreased substantially, from 50 percent in 1931 to 11 percent in 1981.[12] Furthermore, conservative Catholicism, one of the main pillars of Franco's regime from its early stages, had entered an irreversible decline, giving rise to a new secular society. These changes took place in the context of a new international political scenario within which Spain could be fully accepted only if it adhered to Western democratic values. It became urgent to generate a new political system based upon democratic principles and capable of replacing Spain's image as a backward, homogeneous and conservative country.

Rupture or reform were the two options Spaniards faced after Franco's death. The political establishment opted for reform, but, as Cebrián points out, the outcome was a democratic break with the past.[13] In the light of Francoist law, the regime prompted its own suicide by opening the way to democratic rule. The break was initiated from above, and as a result a peculiar situation arose: although the Francoist regime had disappeared, the public administration and institutions of the state remained intact. In such a context, Solé Tura argues that the transition to democracy succeeded only by a combination of three factors.[14] First, institutional stability was provided by the leading role played by King Juan Carlos I in backing the reforms. Second, there was a concerted effort by the various political factions to reach a consensus over the terms under which the transition should be made, once political reform had been sanctioned by the Spanish people and the first democratic elections held in 1977. Finally, large sectors of the population actively mobilized in favour of democratization, in contrast to the primarily restrained attitude of the Catholic Church and the army. The process of disentangling what, according to Franco's political last will, was "tied up and well tied down" reached a turning point in 1978 when Spaniards ratified the new constitution. It was now necessary to substitute a "culture of resistance" with a "culture for democracy."[15]

The National Question in the New Democratic Spain

Probably the most dangerous consequence of Francoism was the intensification of the question of the national minorities, an issue embittered by the regime's inexorable centralism. After almost 40 years of division and resentment between the "winners" and "losers" of the Civil War, there was growing pressure for what the left and some progressive Catholic groups called "national reconciliation."

The 1978 Spanish constitution was the product of the consensus achieved between the main political parties that had emerged from the first democratic elections. The need to obtain the support of both Francoist reformists and anti-Francoists generated endless discussion in the writing of the constitution and contributed to the incoherence and lack of precision of some parts of the text. Nevertheless, for the first time Spain had a constitution that was not the result of one single political force opposing all others, and, despite the limits and deficiencies, the political model advanced by the constitution "was not exclusive or divisive, but an integration model."[16] Theconstitution questioned the radically conservative character of the Spanish nationalism defended by Francoism, and it not only aimed at transforming Spain into a democratic state but also acknowledged the existence of national minorities within its territory.

The preamble to the Spanish Constitution acknowledges the will of the "Spanish nation to protect all Spaniards and all the peoples of Spain in the exercise of human rights, their cultures and traditions, languages and institutions."[17] Article 2, probably the most controversial in the whole text, exemplifies the tension between the unity of Spain and the social pressure to recognize historic nations such as Catalonia, Galicia and the Basque Country: "The Constitution is founded upon the indissoluble unity of the Spanish nation, the common and indivisible *patria* of all Spaniards, and recognizes and guarantees the right to autonomy of the nationalities and regions integrated in it and the solidarity among them."[18]

By emphasizing the indissoluble unity of Spain while recognizing and guaranteeing the right to autonomy of the nationalities and regions, the constitution put forward a radically new model of the state. It sought to reconcile unity with diversity within the Spanish state, described as a single nation containing "nationalities and regions."[19] It does not, however, define "nationalities" or "regions."

The Spanish Autonomous System
During the Francoist regime, nationalism and democracy stood together in Catalan demands for Spain's transformation into a democratic state, able to

recognize diversity within itself and ready to alter its recalcitrant centralist nature. The makers of the constitution opted for a model based upon a symmetrical decentralization of Spain that was referred to as "coffee for everyone" (*café para todos*). Instead of responding directly to the nationalist demands of Catalonia[20] and the Basque Country as nations, they divided the territory of Spain into 17 Autonomous Communities, some historically and culturally distinct, like Catalonia, the Basque Country and Galicia, and others artificially created, like La Rioja, Madrid and many others.

Yet, while the so-called "historical nationalities," that is, Catalonia, the Basque Country and Galicia, could start the process toward full autonomy immediately, other regions had to fulfill a five-year "restricted autonomy" period first. Once full autonomy is achieved, however, the constitution makes no distinction between communities. During the early stages of the Autonomous Communities System, substantially greater powers were devolved to the historical nationalities. This helped to fulfill the nationalist demands of Catalans and Basques and, in some cases, caused resentment among the communities enjoying fewer devolved powers.

In spite of varying powers being devolved to different communities, all communities are structured in a similar manner. Each community has a regional legislative assembly consisting of a single chamber. Deputies are elected on the basis of proportional representation and usually the leader of the majority party or coalition assumes the presidency of the community. The president heads a regional executive of ministers in charge of departments that mostly, but not always, follow the Spanish state's pattern – this depends to a certain extent on the number of powers devolved to each community.

In many respects, the autonomous governments act as states, or at least they do so with respect to most of the powers that have been devolved. The Catalan and Basque governments, for example, provide services in education, health, culture, housing, local transportation and agriculture, and they have even gained control of their police force. The Spanish government holds exclusive jurisdiction over defence, the administration of justice, international relations and general economic planning. A compensation fund administered by the government allocates special resources to poorer regions and is intended to promote equilibrium and solidarity among all the communities.

Catalonia: A Nonsecessionist Nationalism?

Does regional nationalism pose a threat to the governance of Spain? Does decentralization help destabilize the central government? Analyzing the role played by the main Catalan nationalist party and its contribution to the governance of Spain sheds light on these questions.

The tension between the acceptance of Catalonia as part of Spain and the desire to extend its autonomy lies at the core of the nationalist discourse of the Convergence and Union Coalition (*Convergència i Unió*, or CiU). They have been in power since 1980, and the leader, Jordi Pujol, has since been re-elected six times as president of Catalonia. The CiU defines Catalonia as a nation but does not question Spanish unity. The CiU supported the Socialist government from 1993 to 1995, when it lost its majority in the Spanish Parliament, and supported the conservative Popular Party (PP), also short of a parliamentary majority, between 1996 and 2000. This illustrates Pujol's idea of Catalan nationalism as a nonsecessionist movement. In his view, it is feasible to be a Catalan nationalist and, at the same time, contribute to the governance of Spain. Pujol granted support to the Spanish Socialist Workers' Party (PSOE) in a climate fraught with constant corruption scandals affecting socialist leaders. During this period (1993-95) he managed a substantial development of the Catalan Statute of Autonomy, while the right to retain 15 percent of the taxes collected in Catalonia was probably his greatest achievement. Since 1997, after negotiations with the Popular Party, the Catalan government (*Generalitat*) has retained 30 percent of the taxes collected.

In Catalonia, so far, decentralization has not bred pro-independence nationalism. The only Catalan party standing for an independent Catalan republic to be achieved by democratic means is the Republican Left of Catalonia Party (*Esquerra Republicana de Catalunya*, or ERC), which has generally obtained around 8.5 percent of the vote in regional elections since 1980. The ERC has recently been increasing its influence in Catalan politics following fundamental transformations in its structure and political ideology in 1988 and a decisive leadership change in 1996.

After 25 years of autonomy, Catalans and Basques are not fully satisfied with their current status and want to be recognized as nations within Spain. They demand special treatment and show an increasing reluctance to accept the "coffee for everyone" option set up in the 1978 Magna Carta. Asymmetrical decentralization is regarded as an arrangement that would more accurately reflect Spanish reality. The decentralization of Britain, where Scotland and Wales are being granted substantially different degrees of political autonomy according to the intensity of their nationalist claims and national identity, is usually referred to as a model that Spain should follow. Two recent initiatives, the 1998 Declaration of Barcelona and the 2001 Catalan Self-Government Report, exemplify the growing demand for greater autonomy in Catalonia.

The 1998 Declaration of Barcelona

In July 1998, the main nationalist parties in Galicia, the Basque Country and Catalonia – the Galician Nationalist Bloc (*Bloque Nacionalista Galego*, or BNG), the Basque Nationalist Party (*Eusko Alderdi Jeltzalea-Partido Nacionalista Vasco*, or EAJ-PNV) and the CiU – signed a joint declaration in which they demanded that Spain be defined as a multilingual, multicultural and multinational state. In their view, after 20 years of democracy Spain continued to have a unitary character and had not resolved the national question. In their own words:

> During this period we have endured a lack of juridical and political recognition, and even social and cultural recognition of the specificity of our national realities within the Spanish state.
> This recognition, which if fair and democratic, is absolutely essential in the context of a Europe enmeshed in the process of political and economic re-structuration which in the medium term will involve the redistribution of political power amongst its different layers of government. A Europe whose union should be based upon respect for and the structuring of its different peoples and cultures.[21]

The main demand of the nationalist parties subscribing to the Declaration of Barcelona is that Catalonia, Galicia and the Basque Country be recognized as nations within the Spanish state. As was described earlier, the 1978 constitution stated that Spain is formed by a single nation containing some "nationalities and regions," but these were never defined. The consequences of recognizing Catalonia, the Basque Country and Galicia as nations would be twofold. First, it would imply a substantial change to the constitution, which acknowledges the existence of a single Spanish nation. Second, it would involve accepting that Spain can be defined, at least, as a "nation of nations."

The Declaration of Barcelona has obtained a negative response from the representatives of the two main Spanish parties, the PP and the PSOE.

The 2001 Catalan Self-Government Report

In December 2001, the main political parties of the Catalan left – the ERC, the Catalan Socialists' Party (*Partit dels Socialistes de Catalunya*, or PSC [PSC-PSOE]), the Citizens for Change civic association (*Ciutadans pel Canvi*, or CpC) and the Initiative for Catalonia-Greens (*Iniciativa per Catalunya-Verds*, or IC-V) – launched the Catalan Self-Government Report.

The report was notable as the first collective proposal advanced by the Catalan left in over 21 years of political autonomy. Its drafting and publication coincided with the announcement that Catalan president Jordi Pujol would not stand for re-election in the 2003 Catalan contest. Pujol's statement intensified an already heated debate about both his succession and the future of the CiU coalition, which has since turned into a federation. The report was also released amid a centralist conservative campaign launched by the Popular Party.

The key objective of the Catalan Self-Government Report is to achieve greater autonomy for Catalonia. It contains over 90 specific proposals to strengthen Catalan's self-government and endorses the reform of the 1979 Catalan Statute of Autonomy and the 1978 Spanish constitution. Its main demands are the redefinition of Spain as a plurinational state and for Catalonia to be granted the right to have an institutional presence within the EU and other international organizations.

Toward a Radicalization of Catalan Nationalism?

In spite of current criticism and increasing pressure to modify the autonomous system by conferring special status upon Catalonia, the Basque Country and Galicia, Spain's current decentralization model deserves a positive evaluation as a tool that facilitated the peaceful accommodation of regional nationalism after 40 years of dictatorship.

The decentralization of Spain, however, has not been free from conflict and tension between regional and central governments. For instance, the demand for further resources to be allocated to the autonomous institutions and for greater powers to be devolved has characterized most of the relations between the *Generalitat* – Catalan government – and the central government in Madrid. Conflict arose in discussion on the percentage of taxes collected in Catalonia that should be retained by the *Generalitat* without having to wait for their redistribution by Madrid. Conflict came to the fore again when different laws concerning the use and promotion of the Catalan language issued by the *Generalitat* were challenged by the central government and subsequently examined by the Spanish Constitutional Court (*Tribunal Constitutional*), which ratified their constitutional nature. Further confrontation has emerged whenever other Autonomous Communities, usually those that are "nonhistorical," have complained about what they perceive as better treatment from the state received by the "historical" communities.

For over 20 years, the majority of the Catalan population has supported the CiU's nonsecessionist nationalism, which is based on the definition of Catalonia as a nation with a specific history, language and culture and a strong desire for self-government. But could matters change in the near future? Are there new variables that could trigger the rise of pro-independence nationalism in Catalonia?

Since 1993, Pujol's coalition has accounted for its support to the PSOE and later to the PP as contributing to the governance of Spain and benefitting Catalonia. In particular, Pujol sought to appease the alienation felt by many of the CiU's supporters when it backed the PP from 1996 to 2000 by pointing out the economic advantages Catalonia obtained in return.

The socio-political landscape was fundamentally transformed on March 12, 2000, when the PP obtained an overwhelming majority in the Spanish general election that, among other things, annihilated the CiU's bargaining power. While the CiU's support was needed in Madrid, the PP was sympathetic to Catalan claims. Soon after the 2000 election, sympathy and understanding were replaced by a neocentralist political discourse charged with conservative overtones. Since then, the PP has been dismissive of claims for greater autonomy by the historical nationalities and become arrogant toward its former political allies.

It has thus become increasingly difficult and almost unpalatable for Pujol to account for the CiU's continuous and now unnecessary support for the PP in Madrid. A significant number of CiU voters have become critical of this policy and would prefer the nationalist coalition to seek the support of a Catalan party, such as the ERC, rather than rely on the PP.

Spanish political pundits defend the unchanging nature of the 1978 constitution by defending a notion of "postnationalism" that is based on a vulgarized concept of Habermas' "constitutional patriotism." In their view, the constitution exemplifies and guarantees civic consensus and, for this reason, should remain untouched (this is the position of Prime Minister José María Aznar, for instance, who had opposed the constitution on nationalistic grounds when it came up for popular ratification in 1978). The conservative national majority, the so-called "constitutionalists," define the Magna Carta as a rigid document, but "the problem with this representation arises when the document is not understood as a flexible frame for the evolving nature of social coexistence but as a fetish that freezes the moment of its mythical foundation."[22] Opposed to them are the "nationalists," who are, in practice, neither more nationalist nor less constitutionalist. The "nationalists" represent national minorities and defend the idea that constitutions are intrinsically adaptable to new historical circumstances. In particular, they seek to amend the Spanish constitution in order to rectify the partialities and selective constraints that are bound up with the circumstances in which it originated.

The Spanish media have fully adopted the false dichotomy between "constitutionalists" and "nationalists" without questioning the strong Spanish nationalism espoused by the "constitutionalists." The media often defend the "sentinels of a sealed constitution" and demonize those who advocate revisiting the social contract under less urgent conditions than were obtained at its drafting, after Franco's death and in a climate of great tension about whether a peaceful transition to democracy would be possible.

Further to this, the PP is currently engaged in a strategy to promote a new brand of Spanish identity, one that was previously fostered by socialist governments. This "new" identity defines Spain as a modern, industrialized, decentralized, pro-European and secular society; under the PP's ascendancy it is also conservative and hostile to Spain's internal diversity, which is often referred to as a nuisance, a remnant of the past and a threat to the unity of Spain.

What are the consequences for Catalonia of such radicalization of Spanish conservative and centralist nationalism?

First, if pursued, the centralism of the PP threatens to alienate large sectors of Spanish society, especially in the Basque Country, Catalonia and Galicia. The delicate equilibrium among the various political tendencies, which enabled a successful transition to democracy, could suffer under the renaissance of attitudes more akin to previous political periods. The democratic nature of Spain might be compromised by the temptation to restrict dialogue between its constituent parts, or to rule by acquiring a concentration of forces great enough to ruin the balancing of the state by social forces, leading to what Alexis de Tocqueville called the "tyranny of the majority."

Second, the radicalization of centralist nationalism is contributing to a re-examination of Catalan nationalism. In particular, it has fostered an open debate about whether Catalans should be content with the current arrangement or whether they should embrace claims for greater autonomy, federalism or even independence. The 1998 Declaration of Barcelona and the 2001 Self-Government Report illustrate the desire for greater autonomy, at least among the Catalan political elite. This debate is not restricted to discussions about the relation between Catalonia and Spain, however, but also extends to the ideal status of Catalonia within an expanding European Union that is engaged in a process of political integration.

Traditionally, only a small minority has supported secession in Catalonia. This minority is now growing. According to a 2001 poll conducted by the Centro de Investigaciones Sociológicas in Madrid, 35.9 percent of Catalans were in favour of Catalonia's independence and 48.1 percent were against, while the ERC was the party perceived as having improved the most during the previous year. To understand such a significant change in public opinion, it is worth considering: 1) the ideological and generational renewal undertaken by the ERC under its new leadership; 2) the progressive erosion of support for the CiU after 20 years in government and its alliance with the conservative PP; 3) the conservative neocentralist policies of the PP government; 4) the inability of the Catalan Socialists to present themselves as an autonomous party and not merely an appendix of the PSOE; and 5) the retirement of Jordi Pujol.

In this political scenario, the ERC's secessionist discourse may attract new supporters, consolidating the party as Catalonia's third political force and placing it in a key position, particularly if neither the CiU nor the Catalan Socialists can achieve a majority in the forthcoming 2003 Catalan election.

Conclusion

Current Catalan demands for greater autonomy and, in particular, claims for the recognition of Catalonia as a nation within Spain are a strong force acting on the triad formed by the nation, the state and nationalism analyzed at the beginning of this paper. While the conservative Popular Party focuses on the "indissoluble unity of the Spanish nation, the common and indivisible patria of all Spaniards," the main Catalan political parties, through the Declaration of Barcelona and the 2001 Self-Government Report, argue for Catalonia's recognition as a nation within Spain. In so doing they invoke the reference made in the constitution to "the nationalities and regions forming Spain."

The ambiguous wording of the constitution confers legitimacy on both claims, but the restrictive interpretation of the government now in office frustrates the demands of those who support greater decentralization and a redefinition of Spain as a multinational state. The PP understands Spain as a state formed by a single nation. Political parties in Catalonia define the community they represent as a nation and regard the Spanish state as multinational. Conflict between these, so far, unreconciled positions feeds the renewal of a brand of Spanish nationalism that is focused on the Castilian language and culture and charged with conservative overtones. It also fosters Catalan nationalism and contributes to a rising distrust of the good will once shown by Spanish political parties when dealing with Catalan demands. Such demands traditionally have involved not secession but rather the claim for greater decentralization within Spain.

Attitudes toward Catalonia's status within Spain are currently far more conservative and restrictive than those exhibited when the constitution was ratified in 1978. The danger in pursuing these attitudes lies in the progressive radicalization of both Spanish and Catalan nationalism, which threatens to reverse the inclusiveness once attributed to the constitution and applied and interpreted in a generous manner by peoples, such as the Catalans, who endured 40 years of political, cultural and economic oppression during the Francoist regime.

Notes

1. Weber (1991, p. 78).

2. Guibernau (1996, p. 47).

3. Berlin (1996, p. 248).

4. Berlin (1996, p. 252).

5. Berlin (1996, p. 256).

6. Mayall (1992, p. 50).

7. Mayall (1992, p. 56).

8. Mayall (1992, p. 61).

9. Mayall (1992, p. 63).

10. See Benet (1973).

11. See Solé Tura (1985).

12. Tezanos et al. (1989, p. 106).

13. Cebrián (1982, pp. 13-24).

14. Solé Tura (1985, p. 80).

15. Abellán (1982, p. 33).

16. Solé Tura (1985, p. 84).

17. *Constitución Española: edición comentada* (1979, p. 19).

18. *Constitución Española: edición comentada* (1979, p. 26).

19. As Solé Tura notes (1985, p. 101), it is highly controversial and juridically ambiguous to stress the unity of a "nation" at the same time as recognizing the existence of "nationalities" within it.

20. For an analysis of Catalan nationalism during the Spanish transition to democracy, see Guibernau (1997).

21. *Declaració de Barcelona* (1998, p. 1).

22. Resina (2002).

Bibliography

Abellán, J.L. "La función del pensamiento en la transición política", in *España 1975-1980: Conflictos y logros de la democracia*, ed. J.L. Cagigao et al. Madrid: Editorial J. Porrúa Turanzas, S.A., 1982.

Benet, J. *Catalunya sota el règim franquista*. Paris: Edicions Catalanes de París, 1973.

Berlin, I. *The Sense of Reality*. London: Pimlico, 1996.

Cebrián, J.L. "La experiencia del período constituyente", in *España 1975-1980: Conflictos y logros de la democracia*, ed. J.L. Cagigao et al. Madrid: Editorial J. Porrúa Turanzas, S.A., 1982.

Centro de Investigaciones Sociológicas. Estudio no. 2410. *Situación social y política de Catalunya*, March 2001.

Constitución Española: edición comentada. Madrid: Centro de estudios constitucionales, 1979.

Declaració de Barcelona. Bloque Nacionalista Galego, Eusko Alderdi Jeltzalea-Partido Nacionalista Vasco, Convergència i Unió. Barcelona, 1998.

Elliott, J.H. *The Revolt of the Catalans: A Study in the Decline of Spain (1598-1640)*. Cambridge: Cambridge University Press, 1963.

Giner, S., ed. *La Societat Catalana*. Barcelona: Institut d'Estadística de Catalunya, 1998.

Guibernau, Montserrat. *Nationalisms*. Cambridge: Polity Press, 1996.

———."Images of Catalonia." *Nations and Nationalism*, Vol. 3, no. 1 (1997): 89-111.

———. *Nations without States: Political Communities in the Global Age*. Cambridge: Polity Press, 1999.

———. *Nacionalisme Català: Franquisme, Transició i Democracia*. Barcelona: Pòrtic, 2002.

Institut de Ciències Polítiques i Socials. *Sondeig d'opinió* (1996) *Catalunya*, vols 1989-1996.

Mayall, J. *Nationalism and International Society*. Cambridge: Cambridge University Press, 1992.

Resina, J.R. "Postnational Spain? Post-Spanish Spain?" *Nations and Nationalism*, Vol. 8, no. 3 (2002): 377-396.

Solé Tura, J. *Nacionalidades y nacionalismos en España: Autonomía, Federalismo, Autodeterminación*. Madrid: Alianza Editorial, 1985.

Tezanos, J.F. "Modernización y cambio social en España", in *La Transición Democrática Española*, ed. J.F. Tezanos et al. Madrid: Editorial Sistema, 1989.

Vilar, P. *La Catalogne dans l'Espagne moderne*. Paris: Flammarion, 1977.

Weber, M. *From Max Weber: Essays in Sociology*. H.H. Gerth and Wright Mills, eds. London: Routledge, 1991. First published 1948.

7

redesigning the UK:
the politics of devolution

David McCrone

In these days, when the world is becoming smaller and comparisons are drawn from far and wide, Kenneth McRobert's book *Misconceiving Canada* (1997) provides a powerful stimulus for looking at the UK vis-à-vis Canada and at Scotland vis-à-vis Quebec. On the face of it, there are some interesting parallels as well as obvious differences. Both states belong to the same family of parliamentary democracies; both contain territories – Scotland and Quebec – that consider themselves indubitably nations rather than regions; the possibility of secession is for both a central part of the political agenda. As the UK decentralizes to the nations and regions of its island archipelago, so the previously insular Brits cast around for lessons and examples of what not to do, as well as what to do. Conferences abound on nations that are not conventional states (not "stateless," but perhaps "under-stated" might be a better term). While one may, with justice, dispute the epithet "stateless" – there are powerful legislatures in, for example, Scotland, Quebec and Catalonia – we have much to learn from each other.[1]

This paper explores the analytical value of comparing the UK with Canada, and Scotland with Quebec, the opportunities as well as the limitations. It argues that the UK has a key contradiction at its heart: its hitherto unitary nature, set alongside its multinational character, compounded by an unwritten constitution. This has allowed constitutional change to happen relatively easily and without recourse to constitutional courts and formal structures of federalism.

The lack of definition of British citizenship until fairly recently, coupled with acceptance across the political spectrum that Scotland is a nation in its own right (as is Wales), has meant that the UK is not so much "misconceived" as "underconceived." Finally, this paper reviews the evidence for the demand for constitutional change in Scotland and argues that the debate is less a matter of conflict between rigid constitutional categories than a matter of locating Scotland on a shifting continuum of constitutional change, of self-government.

Comparing Britain and Canada

One of the apparently strong differences one finds in comparing the two states is that devolution in the UK seems to evoke less angst, less venom, than in Canada. Assuming this is a fair assessment of the two situations, one might ask why. It might be that in the UK, a hitherto overly centralized state, the novelty of devolution has not yet worn off, and sooner or later, once that novelty has worn off, Scotland and Wales will hit the constitutional buffers just as Quebec has done. In other words, critics point out, battling around the issue of ultimate sovereignty is a zero-sum game. As well, Quebec has had "devolution" much longer than have the nations of the UK, and it is much more extensive. But this is a wager on history, and only time will tell.

Perhaps, however, straightforward comparisons between the UK and Canada and between Scotland and Quebec are only of limited value. Perhaps the constitutional niceties are less important than the historico-sociological processes involved. The first and most obvious difference between Scotland and Quebec and between the UK and Canada is the suprastate framework of Europe (or its absence), which is described by Neil MacCormick as a theatre of opportunity rather than a threat to identity.[2] In other words, the geopolitical framework of the European Union is much more significant than NAFTA. The EU framework allows a much looser relationship between statehood and sovereignty, so that the constitutional debate revolves around which level of governance should have which powers, rather than becoming a battle to the death between competing sovereignties. The EEC/EC/EU has evolved in large part as a means of "exporting" national issues such as agricultural support and industrial development in the postwar period onto the supranational level.[3]

In comparing Scotland and Quebec, the most obvious aspect to focus on relates to the origins of the two states containing them. Both Britain and Canada have claims to be described as "state-nations" rather than the more conventional term "nation-states" insofar as – whether as "two solitudes" or "historic nations" – some level of "national" identity clearly existed before their founding. One can debate with scholars in the UK whether or not Britain is a "nation" or simply a state – a political umbrella for constituent nations – but there is little doubt about the historical pedigree of Scotland, England and even Wales as nations prior to the Treaty of Union in 1707. That term, "treaty," gives the game away. One can only have treaties between nations (states), not regions within a state, and indubitably Scotland is, in Anderson's phrase, an imagined national community.[4] To be sure, "region" can be used, but only in an administrative context, such as economic region. Scotland's (and Wales') nation-ness is both cause and effect of the absence of formal symmetrical federalism in the UK. As in Spain, the British nations relate quite differently to central state power.

What is of key interest here is the *mentalité* issue. According to McRoberts, the Trudeau government embarked on a process from the 1960s that had all the classic marks of nation-building, including repatriating the constitution and culminating in the aggressive stance taken by the present Chrétien administration. Nothing comparable has happened in the UK. There was the Thatcher factor, but she was a Little Englander – still is – with very little feel for how a genuinely multinational United Kingdom might be developed. Indeed, home-rulers in Scotland and Wales have much to be grateful to her for, for no one – unwittingly – did more for their cause. Hers was a Faustian bargain that gave her supreme power in a country whose constitution encouraged such things, just as the price is being paid by her unfortunate successors: Major, Hague and now Duncan Smith moving ever further to the right, with ever-diminishing electoral credibility. After the Blair government was elected in 1997, there was a fairly fatuous PR attempt at repackaging the UK as "cool Britannia," but that died under a hail of mirthful scorn.

Canada, of course, has to live with an elephant problem: its neighbour to the south, which makes the issue of national identity north of the 49th parallel omnipresent. Again, there is nothing comparable in the UK, apart from the congeries of Little Englanders who have captured the Conservative Party for the moment. The UK is the rump of an erstwhile imperial state that has progressively lost territory – dominions, colonies and even "home countries" like Ireland as recently as 1921, a mere 80 years ago – and this means that chain-rattling to the effect that Britain will end if territory is given up is an empty gesture. The Brits have been especially good at acceding, usually with reasonable grace, to the demands for self-government from former colonies without losing what they consider the essence of their own "national" identity. Like an iceberg slowly sailing into warmer waters, the UK diminishes in size while still being recognizable: Britannia is downsized, that is all. The UK's imperial identity has translated successfully into a state one, without running too much of a risk of obliterating itself completely. Even such a fervent supporter of Union as John Major, the last Conservative prime minister and maybe the last for some time, was moved to declare that the UK had no "strategic interest" in holding on to Northern Ireland, as if it were not "really" British despite being more Unionist than the Unionists. The malcontents of the English conservative Right have been less hostile to devolution than to the European Union.

What seems crucial is that Canada does not have the equivalent of England, a territory with 85 percent of the UK population that has always seen itself as the core, with a few Celtic add-ons. The national identity of the English is not dependent on the Celts, who are too few in number and, anyway, are not the unfavoured Other against which English identity is constructed. That distinction is normally reserved for the French or the Germans. The pike, after all, measures itself not against the minnows but against much bigger fish in the pond.

Witness, for example, the fairly sanguine approach to Scottish (and presumably Welsh) home rule to be found in England. In the British Social Attitudes survey of 1999, 40 percent said they would be sorry if Scotland left the UK, and only 7 percent would be pleased.[5] Their preferred option for Scottish government largely mirrors that in Scotland itself. Twenty-four percent of people in England favoured an independent Scotland (compared with 30 percent of people in Scotland); 54 percent a home rule parliament (compared with 55 percent in Scotland); and 13 percent no parliament at all (12 percent in Scotland). One does not get a sense of a people whose very identity is threatened by secession, or even by modest home rule. To be sure, there does seem to be a rising trend of people in England who describe themselves as "English" (57 percent), compared with 70 percent who say they are "British," and the self-styled English are more likely to want an independent Scotland, and incidentally to be more right wing in their political views, but as yet the conceptual difference between "England" and "Britain," at least in everyday parlance, is weakly developed. Maybe it always will be, and in the event of Scottish (and Welsh) independence the (con)fusion of England and Britain will be complete. It simply will not matter any more. Northern Ireland, on the other hand, despite Unionist protestations, is not really British to many on the "mainland," as the British in Ireland quaintly call it.

The Scottish Anomaly

One might be tempted to dismiss these observations as a sociologist's musings on highly fluid identity data, but the argument is set on firm constitutional bedrock. Neil MacCormick pointed out in his British Academy lecture in 1997 that at the heart of the British constitution lies the Scottish anomaly.[6] England, he argued, saw the Union of 1707 as the completion and consolidation of the soi-disant "glorious revolution" of 1688, not a step in a quite different direction.

Hence, the English legal theorist A.V. Dicey promulgated what became the conventional view, that it was an "incorporating" Union, not a federal or quasi-federal one. Thus, to speak of the *Act* of Union rather than a *Treaty* of Union, as the Scots did (and do), reflects a *mentalité* that still lies at the heart of the constitutional process. MacCormick observes: "In form, the Union constituted a new state with a new name. But in substance, the underlying assumption was that the larger partner [England] was a continuing entity."[7] Underlying this difference, he argues, is a more basic philosophical difference. Whereas the old English constitution was unwritten, derived from custom, convention, common law and the absolute and sovereign authority of Parliament (the Crown in Parliament), the Scottish tradition was based on *ius regni*, the law of the realm, on popular assent authorizing and limiting monarchical power: rule by "community of the realm." MacCormick argues that we have an English constitution underpinning a British state, and within that a "Scottish anomaly" in which "Scotland was incorporated, but Scotland stayed different."[8]

What does this have to do with the argument at hand? It implies that, as writers such as David Marquand have observed,[9] there is something "unmodern" about the UK, not in the sense that it is socially and economically unreconstructed – Britain was, after all, the home of the Industrial Revolution and almost single-handedly invented market capitalism – but that in constitutional-political terms it has not resolved (nor really tried to resolve) its inherent contradictions. The capacity of the British state to reform itself within its famously "unwritten" constitution allows it to be Janus-faced: one side holding onto "historic" institutions like the monarchy and the other side changing as times demand. Historian Eric Hobsbawm commented that "tradition" in the UK resembled a patina of age: something quite modern was quickly encrusted with the legitimacy of the past, largely a *trompe l'oeil* to protect social, especially class, interests.[10] Thus, the UK is a multinational state that until 1999 had a unitary legislature. Scotland in particular retained and developed its institutional autonomy in matters legal, educational and religious. Devolution, observes Neil MacCormick, replaced managed quasi federalism with democratic quasi federalism. The British worried far less than most about the theoretical contradictions of this position.

If one then tries to understand devolution since 1997 as part of some grand plan for territorial decentralization and constitutional modernization in these islands, one will be disappointed, as are constitutional modernizers such as Anthony Barnett and other reformists in Charter 88.[11] The reform of the House of Lords has replaced (some) unelected peers with political appointees: hardly the stuff of democratic revolution. The battle for English regionalism has barely begun, and there is no game plan for bringing it about, short of acceding to those regions (such as northeast England) who clamour loud and long enough. We shall see. At present, some of the more peripheral regions like northeast England seem to be the favourites in the race for regionalism in England. They are, nonetheless, no less English for that; their argument is based on the practicalities of regional power, not on the symbolism of national identity.

There is a problem for would-be constitutional reformers. Given that the UK government has no grand plan to roll out by way of reform, virtually all depends on pressure from below, a point acknowledged by the government. Show us the popular demand for regional reform, they say, thus betraying the lack of an overall constitutional strategy of their own. Theirs is a reactive plan, amounting to no real plan at all. Indeed, the parliament for Scotland was acceded to as the outcome of a long (Scottish) battle for home rule that the Labour government was required to implement as the price of election north of the border in 1997: less a matter of choice, more of fulfilling a bargain. It had precious little to do with constitutional reform *tout court*, just as Wales got its national assembly as a reward for Labour loyalty during the dark years of Conservative rule (to say nothing of the threat from Welsh nationalists to Labour hegemony in the Principality).

Others would look outwards to international experience: to Spain, in the first instance, as the example of asymmetrical federalism in the West. It is hard to convince British politicians and commentators that the Spanish case is relevant. After all, they observe, it is a developing, southern European country, and one that created home rule in the process of recovering democracy after dictatorship, barely 25 years ago. What, they inquire, has that to do with the self-styled mother of parliaments? The British have entered the new century with a patchwork of constitutional solutions and precious little pressure for a wider settlement. In any case, if McRoberts is correct, imposing a neat, symmetrical federal solution on this patchwork that is the postimperial United Kingdom is simply asking for the fragile garment to be rent asunder. Watching the legal-constitutional struggles in the Canadian courts does not fill one with confidence that even new countries, never mind old ones, can easily make new constitutions out of pieces of the past. More importantly, the Canadian conjuncture is decidedly different: repatriating a constitution from the mother country, an aggrieved Quebec smarting from the rebuff of Meech Lake, an aggressive nation-building project from the Canadian centre.

Would federalism work in the UK? This is the assessment of a sociologist, not a constitutional lawyer, but one might argue that 1) the time for federalism has probably been and gone (in the 1880s when Ireland was to be the first recipient of "home rule all-round" – which didn't happen, of course, largely because the Tory and Liberal Unionists defeated it); 2) there is the English problem:

England is too big, and there is no serious push for English regionalism as yet; 3) federations tend to be created either in largely empty settler countries such as Australia and Canada or to reinforce democratic institutions in erstwhile totalitarian countries (Germany and Spain). Besides, in Scotland there is little talk of federalism – it sees itself as a nation, not a minority province – and more than a suspicion that federalism would allow other "regions" to gang up on Scotland out of suspicion and jealousy, much as we perceive has happened to Quebec.

The Brits, anyway, are not great constitutionalists – at least for themselves (writing such things for foreigners is fine: since the end of empire, writing other people's constitutions has been something of an industry for constitutional lawyers). There are now writers, like Tom Nairn, who have set themselves the task of writing the Scottish constitution, with a bill of rights, entrenching self-governing powers and so on, but few seem to share Nairn's enthusiasm for the task, even in Scotland. France, one of the great modern republics, has had to battle with its *dirigiste* sense of Frenchness, and has struggled with permitting a more multicultural view of citizenship. The periodic rise of the National Front reflects this linear view of French identity, and even when defeated at the polls, the mainstream parties are constrained to pay attention to its nationalistic agenda. In a world in which the so-called nation-state appears to be losing many of its capacities to control its own affairs (while retaining and developing others, of course) and in which Europe feels threatened by political refugees and "economic migrants," it is hard to argue that state solutions dreamt up in the late eighteenth century are as relevant in the twenty-first.

Who Are the British?

The British have adopted a "muddling through" approach and developed what David Marquand has called an "unprincipled society." He observes:

> Thanks to the upheavals of the seventeenth century – thanks in particular to the victory of the English landed classes over the Stuart kings – one cannot speak of a "British state" in the way one speaks of a "French state" or in modern times of a "German state." The UK is not a state in a continental sense. It is a bundle of islands (including such exotica as the Channel Islands and the Isle of Man which are not even represented at Westminster), acquired at different times by the English [*sic*] crown, and governed in different ways.[12]

He continues: "Its inhabitants are not citizens of a state, with defined rights of citizenship. They are subjects of a monarch, enjoying 'liberties' which their ancestors won from previous monarchs." That is a point worth pondering. Are the Brits citizens at all? And if so, since when? They seem to have acquired formal citizenship by a legislative sleight of hand when the 1948 Nationality Act made them "citizens of the UK and colonies," and largely because they were forced into it by others, such as the Canadians. Prior to that date, they were deemed "subjects" of the Crown, a descriptor extended, whether they liked it or not, to those inhabiting the imperial territories. *Civis britannicus sum* would have a similar evocation to its Roman predecessor: you would not actually have to live in the homeland to be counted in. Many Australians, New Zealanders and Canadians of a certain age long held on to the motherland in this way.

The Second World War finally brought that idea crashing to the ground. Former parts of the empire like India and Canada wanted to control their own ingress and egress of citizens and would-be citizens, so the British government had to define the remaining inhabitants as British citizens. Governments of both right and left would have much rather stayed with people being subjects of the Crown first and citizens of nation-states second. That, with hindsight, might have seemed an odd thing for socialists to do (Labour governments were happy to describe themselves thus in those days). The Left, however, wished to encourage a non-ethnic definition of being British to encompass nonwhite peoples in their liberation struggles. The Right was happier to develop a more ethnic definition, and that culminated in the 1980s when Thatcher legislated in a "patriality" clause based on the essentially white origins of some Commonwealth citizens in terms of right of residence. Thus, *ius soli*, the law of territory, and *ius sanguinis*, the law of blood, were fused into fuzzy meanings of British citizenship and identity. Robin Cohen has it thus:

> British identity shows a general pattern of fragmentation. Multiple axes of identification have meant that Irish, Scots, Welsh and English people, those from the white, black and brown Commonwealth, Americans, English-speakers, Europeans and even "aliens" have had their lives intersect one with another in overlapping and complex circles of identity-construction and rejection. The shape and edges of British identity are thus historically changing, often vague and, to a degree, malleable – an aspect of British identity I have called "a fuzzy frontier."[13]

This is the Britain we inhabit today, a Britain that the reforming constitutional world of modernity appears to have largely passed by. Just when we have belatedly got around to it, it seems to have gone out of fashion. We can debate alternative scenarios without being able to do a great deal to bring them about. The pessimistic scenario is that British identity is thin and feeble: for the English, it is simply a synonym, England and Britain to be used interchangeably; for the Celts, it is a state veneer that served its time at the height of empire, Union and Protestantism (the reason why most of the Irish could never be "British," even if they wanted to be). This matrix is no more, and one prediction is that it will simply fade and give way to the "genuine" nationalities of these islands. Empire no more: Britain no more. On the other hand, more optimistically for those who believe in the United Kingdom, this loose sense of Britishness might be tailor-made for postmodern times in which pick'n mix identity is the order of the day. Be whoever you want to be. Somehow, the UK has become a multicultural, postmodern society without really trying, still less understanding how it has come about.

To overstress the sense of choice is dangerous. We know that we do not have control over being British or being anything, still less being English. We know that black and brown people in England largely feel they cannot claim to be "English" because it is a term with ethnic (white) connotations.[14] Being British is different, for that indicates which passport you carry and where you have the right to settle. We also know that (white) people in England who say they are British (rather than English) tend to be more liberal and left of centre than those who say they are English. That is interesting, because in Scotland the reverse is true.[15] There, the self-styled Brits are more conservative and right of centre than either Brits in England or, indeed, people (8 out of 10) in Scotland who give their identity as Scottish and are on the leftist end of the spectrum. Beware, then, easy assumptions about the fixity of labels such as "British": it can mean quite different things north and south of the Scottish-English border. Such labels are operated by people as political and cultural cues, ways of signposting their political and cultural allegiances in an ever-shifting debate. To coin a phrase, one is dealing here with identities not as roots but as routes.

Much of my argument so far, especially concerning the unwillingness of the British to engage with matters constitutional and theoretical, may simply reinforce one's view that the people of the British islands are intellectually lazy and insufferably self-satisfied. That may be true, and a judgment to make. The argument, though, is concerned with what one finds on the ground rather than what one would like to happen.

The political realm helps little in this respect because the Conservative Opposition is engaged in a fractious internal civil war that may wound it so deeply that it is out of power for at least the rest of the decade. There is Thatcher's Faustian deal 20 years ago: the time is up, the debts are being called in and the party may be no more. (Canadians, of all people, know about disappearing Conservatives. Maybe they just become Liberals, or, in the British case, New Labour?) British Tories seem far more concerned about their cousins across the

Channel than what is happening over their northern border. (In passing, one might wonder on the English claim to the [English] Channel in its naming conventions, when the French are happy to leave it as an allusion, *La Manche*). There is less talk about "saving the Union" these days on the Right, in part because many believe that the battle was lost with devolution in 1999. They may be right. Perhaps they dimly perceived that home rule would change – change utterly, to borrow from the Irish poet William Butler Yeats – the nature of the complex and implicit relationship between the remaining territories of our islands. After all, one can sense that things are being lost without having much of a clue as to why they are happening. Scotland, in large measure, is an irrelevance to the Tories, and for the moment the reverse is also true.

Is, however, Britain an irrelevance to the Scots? The rest of this essay is concerned with what Scots are thinking, by looking at recent survey work pre- and postdevolution to test the water as regards the future of the UK. It is, in passing, interesting that Britain and Canada are, possibly with Belgium, the Western countries where we can have a discussion premised on the possibility that the states we belong to may implode or in some other way cease to exist in the way we have known them. One could, of course, lose Scotland (and Quebec for that matter) and carry on determinedly as if nothing much had happened. So be it, even though it would be like having a limb amputated and getting on with life. So, will Scotland secede? Stands the Union where it did? Alas, poor Britain?

The Politics of Self-Government

Over the past 20 years or so, there has been in Scotland a steady if uneven increase in support for independence. Such support has two options: either within the EU (such that Scotland becomes like Ireland and Denmark, for example) or outside the EU (like Norway). Broadly speaking, twice as many support the former over the latter. Taking both together, between 1979 and 2001 support for independence in either form virtually trebled, from under 10 percent to 27 percent, with a high of 37 percent at the time of the 1997 referendum on a devolved Scottish parliament. Outright opposition to any extension of self-government fell from 26 percent to 9 percent over the same period. Support for devolution (that is, home rule within the UK) stood at 60 percent in 2001, but it is important to acknowledge that since 1979 this has been the dominant position in Scottish public opinion. In short, the failure to achieve a devolved parliament over the previous quarter of a century was the result not of Scots going cold on the idea, but of the failure of successive governments to translate these aspirations into constitutional reality, that is, until Labour was elected at Westminster in 1997.

The relationship between constitutional preferences and party allegiance is also complex in Scotland. For example, around two-thirds of supporters of independence do not vote for the Scottish National Party (SNP) (most are Labour voters), while almost four out of every 10 SNP voters claim they do not support independence.[16] A further complication is that a majority of people (51 percent) who say that their preferred national identity is Scottish and not British support neither the SNP nor independence.

What is going on here? If one visualizes these variables as a Venn diagram, there is only loose alignment in Scotland between national identity, constitutional preference and party allegiance. One might have expected that support for independence would be strongly correlated with being Scottish and with voting for the overtly nationalist party, the SNP, such that this becomes the "core" nationalist position. The relative lack of alignment might suggest that nationalism in Scotland is somehow weaker than, and by implication somewhat deviant from, the putative norm.[17] This, however, is to make assumptions about other countries, for we do not have systematic evidence that the situation in Quebec or Catalonia, for example, differs. "Being Scottish," as it were, seems to be bounded in different ways: political, constitutional and cultural, and much of the internal debate has to do with which version should be dominant. The SNP, for example, presents itself as "Scotland's party," a title disputed by Labour, its major competitor, which argues that Scotland's interests are best served by remaining within the Union.

Regardless of people's preferences, what do they think will happen? At the time of the referendum in 1997, 59 percent thought that independence was "very likely" or "quite likely" in the ensuing two decades (made up of 76 percent of those who supported that option and 48 percent of those who did not). In 1999, 51 percent took this view (75 percent of those who supported it and 43 percent of those who did not). In like manner, between 1997 and 2000 fewer people expected Scotland to leave the UK as a result of devolution. Whereas in 1997, 42 percent thought that having a Scottish Parliament made it more likely that Scotland would leave the UK, by 2000 this had fallen to 27 percent. This was not because they thought home rule made it more likely that Scotland would stay in the Union, but because they felt that devolution in itself would make no difference either way. The "slippery slope" argument put forward by the Conservatives and other Unionists, that devolving power to a legislature while keeping it within the UK would lead ultimately to full independence, does not conform to the expectations of the Scottish electorate.

Further evidence that support for independence is broad yet thin in Scotland comes from cohort data gathered by the British Election Panel Study, which had waves of collection annually between 1997 and 2000.[18] These data show that support for the independence option in any wave is around half of that in other waves. This is not to imply that there is a sharp falling away in each annual wave, because there is broad support of similar magnitude in waves that are further apart. What does this imply? Around half (55 percent) say that they never support independence in any of the waves, nearly half (45 percent) have done so on at least one occasion and 7 percent have done so at every opportunity. There are two ways of looking at this. On the one hand, many more people have supported independence on at least one occasion than have supported the SNP, who get around 30 percent in the polls. On the other hand, support for the SNP can be described as broad and thin, with only 1 in 14 giving independence constant support. Support for independence also contrasts with 9 out of 10 people who have supported devolution on more than one occasion, and three-quarters of whom have never opposed it on any of the waves in question. Opponents of devolution are reduced to a mere 1 in 10.

It would seem, then, that devolution – a home rule Parliament, which Scotland now has – is the preferred option by far, and that support for independence is a minority pursuit. There is certainly truth in that as a statement of the new status quo, but that is to reify the constitutional debate in Scotland somewhat. This is perhaps inevitable, given that Scotland's main political competition is structured around these two constitutional options and between Labour and the SNP. This, however, is to ignore the high degree of flexibility and nuance that is involved. Thus, for example, while two-thirds of people in 2000 said that the UK government at Westminster actually has the most influence over how Scotland is run (and only one in eight think it is the Scottish Parliament), fully three-quarters believed that the Scottish Parliament *should* be the institution with most powers. Similarly, two-thirds of Scots wished the new Parliament to be given more powers, including the same proportion of supporters of devolution (9 out of 10 supporters of independence want Parliament's powers extended). Further, this position had actually strengthened since 1999, reflecting their experience of the Scottish Parliament.

This implies that the Scottish electorate views the constitutional debate less as a matter of choosing from a range of mutually exclusive options (reinforced of course by the party battle itself, which reifies the choice in hard-and-fast terms) and more as positioning the governance of Scotland along a continuum of self-governance. They are currently happy to work within the new constitutional set-up for the UK, but they are open-minded when it comes to the future. The issue is less one of constitutional categories than one of moving Scotland along a continuum as and when circumstances arise. This also helps to make sense of the apparent confusion between party allegiances, constitutional preferences and preferred national identities. Previous work[19] reveals quite clearly that Scots wanted a parliament to make Scotland a better place to live in with regard to social and economic conditions, and had less interest in either making a statement about symbolic identity or, more narrowly, improving democratic accountability in and of itself. To revert to the Venn diagram metaphor, the Scottish political agenda is framed by the outer boundaries of the three circles, rather than by overlap at the core. Hence, the debate is about whether Scotland's interests are best resolved by remaining within the British state, and under what conditions; about which party or parties can best be trusted to maximize those interests; and about how people choose to configure their identities as Scottish or British, and in what mix of these, and for what purposes. There is, for example, nothing remiss about being Scottish for some purposes or occasions and British for others, and varying these through time.

Conclusion

The strong message that comes out of analysis of public opinion pre- and post-devolution in Scotland is that facile claims that it has immediately strengthened or weakened the Union are not borne out. On the one hand, Scots have down-sized their expectations from the high point at the time of the 1997 referendum, yet there is a clear dissonance as regards which parliament, Scottish or British, matters most. Most recognize that London holds the purse strings, and yet they want Edinburgh to have more powers. We find that dissatisfaction with the Scottish Parliament comes not from people who did not want one in the first place but from those who think it should be more powerful.

While constitutional theory might treat the Scottish Parliament as the subordinate one of the two, that is not how it appears to people in Scotland. This is reflected in terms of which parliament Scots trust most to work in the country's long-term interests. Westminster's highest rating occurred in 1997, the year Labour were elected at Westminster and the Scottish referendum took place, when 35 percent of people in Scotland thought they could trust it all or most of the time (compared with a massive 84 percent for the Scottish parliament-to-be). While both parliaments have fallen somewhat in the eyes of Scots, a mere 17 percent trust Westminster compared with 53 percent who trust Edinburgh, a ratio of three to one. Similarly, Scots are pretty sure that England does much better out of the Union than does Scotland. Fully 59 percent thought that Scotland got less than its fair share of UK spending, and only 10 percent that it got its fair share. Again, almost three times as many think it is the English economy, rather than the Scottish one, that benefits from having Scotland in the UK (43 percent to 16 percent).

How, then, have people in Scotland made sense of devolution? It appears that they are much more in sympathy with the old Liberal concept of home rule –

self-government – than they are with the narrowly constitutional sense of devolution: powers delegated, but sovereignty retained by London. There has been no headlong rush to independence, but there has been a firming up of Scottish national identity coupled with a growing belief that the Scottish Parliament has insufficient powers to govern in the way the people want.

In truth, Scotland's position in the Union was always more complex than either orthodox nationalists or dyed-in-the-wool Unionists allowed. Scots seem relatively content with their Parliament, while seeing it as unfinished business, part of a longer-term process to enhance its powers as and when its people judge. For the moment, Scotland remains British, but in a distinctive manner that suits its interests. Perhaps it was ever thus.

Notes

1. See the conference proceedings published in MacInnes and McCrone (2001).

2. MacCormick (1999).

3. See, for example, Milward (1992), who argues that far from being a threat to national sovereignty, the EEC shifted difficult problems such as these onto another plane.

4. I have developed this argument more systematically in my book *Understanding Scotland* (2001).

5. The data referred to in this paper are taken from the following series of studies: Scottish Election Surveys of 1979, 1992 and 1997; Scottish Referendum Survey of 1997; Scottish Social Attitudes Surveys of 1999 and 2000. These are described in greater detail in McCrone (2001, ch. 7).

6. MacCormick (1999).

7. MacCormick (1999, p. 139).

8. MacCormick (1999, p. 142).

9. Marquand (1988).

10. Hobsbawm (1988).

11. Barnett (1997).

12. Marquand (1988, p. 152).

13. Cohen (1994, p. 35).

14. See Modood (1998).

15. The British (and Scottish) Social Attitudes Surveys make this plain.

16. See Bond (2000) and Bond and Rosie (2002).

17. This argument is developed at greater length in McCrone and Paterson (2002).

18. See, again, McCrone and Paterson (2002).

19. See Brown et al. (1999).

Bibliography

Barnett, Anthony. *This Time: Our Constitutional Revolution*. London: Vintage Books, 1997.

Bond, Ross. "Squaring the Circles: Demonstrating and Explaining the Political 'Non-Alignment' of Scottish National Identity." *Scottish Affairs*, Vol. 32 (Summer 2000): 15-35.

Bond, Ross, and Michael Rosie. "National Identities in Post-Devolution Scotland." *Scottish Affairs*, Vol. 40 (Summer 2002): 34-53.

Brown, Alice, David McCrone, Lindsay Paterson and Paula Surridge. *The Scottish Electorate: The 1997 General Election and Beyond*. London: Macmillan, 1999.

Cohen, Robin. *Frontiers of Identity: The British and Others*. London: Longman, 1994.

Hobsbawm, Eric. *Industry and Empire*. Harmondsworth: Penguin, 1988.

MacCormick, Neil. "The English Constitution, the British State and the Scottish Anomaly." "Understanding Constitutional Change," special issue of *Scottish Affairs* (1999): 129-45.

McCrone, David. *Understanding Scotland: The Sociology of a Nation*, 2nd ed. London: Routledge, 2001.

McCrone, David, and Lindsay Paterson. "The Conundrum of Scottish Independence." *Scottish Affairs*, Vol. 40 (summer 2002): 54-75.

MacInnes, John, and David McCrone, eds. "Stateless Nations in the 21st Century: Scotland, Catalonia and Quebec," special issue of *Scottish Affairs* (2001).

McRoberts, Kenneth. *Misconceiving Canada: The Struggle for National Unity*. Oxford: Oxford University Press, 1997.

Marquand, David. *The Unprincipled Society*. London: Fontana, 1988.

Milward, Alan. *The European Rescue of the Nation-State*. London: Routledge, 1992.

Modood, Tariq. *Ethnic Minorities: Diversity and Disadvantages*. London: Policy Studies Institute, 1998.

8

culture, identity and development in European minority nations and regions

John Loughlin and Michael Keating

Europe, understood as the 15 member states of the European Union and the countries to both east and west gravitating around them, is a fascinating scenario of diversity and convergence. Within the European Union itself there coexist a number of distinct state traditions,[1] state forms ranging from federalism to centralized unitary states, as well as diverse policy styles. Stein Rokkan, in his conceptual map of Europe, has laid out the main features of this diversity in terms of the historical processes of nation- and state-building.[2] Esping-Andersen identifies different kinds of welfare states, which he describes as the "three worlds of welfare capitalism," a theme taken up in somewhat different terms by Castles, who uses the term "families of nations."[3] More recently, scholars have distinguished varying approaches to local government in northern and southern Europe,[4] and between Anglo-Saxon, Germanic and French traditions, to which might be added the Scandinavian tradition.[5] In addition to this political and administrative complexity is the great diversity in culture, language and identity across the continent, including the newly liberated countries of eastern and central Europe.

It is sometimes claimed by Eurosceptics that this remarkable diversity would be flattened out and homogenized by the process of European integration. But one fundamental difference between traditional processes of nation-state building and the process of European integration is that the latter explicitly rejects any attempt to create a homogeneous *demos* with a single culture, language and identity. Indeed, the preservation of cultural diversity became a principle of the Union with the Treaty of Maastricht. It is true that Maastricht referred primarily to the diversity of national traditions found in the member states and paid scant regard to the even greater cultural and linguistic diversity found in the large number of regions, as well as in immigrant groups. Indeed, European integration is one factor among several that have encouraged awareness of this regional diversity in recent decades.

Nevertheless, signs of increasing convergence along a number of dimensions must balance this picture of diversity. Perhaps the most important element of convergence is that resulting from what has been loosely termed "globalization," at least in terms of lifestyle habits but also in terms of attitudes and values.[6] The traveller in Europe is struck by the similarities of dress, custom and attitudes, particularly among younger people, even while more traditional cultures survive, just as international fast food outlets coexist alongside national and regional cuisine. Linguistically, it is striking that English has become the lingua franca of Europe, as it has in the rest of the world. Indeed, English has replaced French as the preferred second language of minority language groups.

One can also note patterns of convergence in politics and administration. First, there are the fads and fashions of institutional and policy design and public administration reform. After the Second World War the welfare state and Keynesian approaches to economic policy were adopted by most Western states. In the 1980s this was challenged by neoliberalism, a rather loosely defined but politically effective ideology that attempted to reverse the basic tenets of the welfare state. International organizations such as the OECD, the World Bank and the World Trade Organization have spread these models of public policy and administration around the globe, with the sanction of cuts in financial aid. These forces for convergence have been at work in Europe too, but the most powerful tool of convergence on that continent has, of course, been European integration. After a long period of sclerosis, this took off in the 1980s, driven by Jacques Delors' Single Market project and the drive toward economic and political union as formulated at Maastricht in 1993. Today, there is a single currency, a European Central Bank and the aptly named "convergence criteria," all of which together have imposed a financial and monetary discipline for those countries seeking to enter the eurozone. In the end, all but three countries have joined euroland, and of the three who chose not to join (although they undoubtedly met the criteria), Sweden voted against entry in a referendum and the UK will probably stay outside, mainly because of public opposition to abandoning the pound as a symbol of sovereignty.

These dynamic factors of convergence, coming from state restructuring, European integration and globalization, have had important impacts on regions and other subnational levels of government. A now quite extensive literature describes and attempts to analyze afresh the regional question in this new context, as well as responses to these factors.[7] Although there is general agreement that we are not witnessing the emergence of a "Europe of the Regions," what is striking in this literature is the recognition of the importance of the subnational level in terms of both policy-making and democratic practice,[8] even if this is not yet satisfactorily institutionalized at the level of the EU itself. Furthermore, with the decline or disappearance of Keynesian approaches to economic development and the withdrawal of the state in areas such as regional policy, regions have been left to fend for themselves in a situation of competitive regionalism. It is true that national governments usually work closely with regions to help them compete, but regions have also been forced to reinvent themselves according to what has come to be known as the "new regionalism," a vague and diffuse term with several different meanings.[9] Increased EU funding for declining and peripheral regions has increased this competitive element, and regions across Europe have mobilized in order to win some of this funding, limited though it is and was. Thus, the "new regionalism" has come to include several different elements and become, to some extent, the ideological component of this mobilization.

What is "new" about this regionalism is not that it is "modernizing," since at least some strands of the regionalism of the 1950s and 1960s in regions such as Brittany or Corsica were also modernizing, but that it developed in the context of the hegemony of neoliberalism and the withdrawal of the state where the earlier form developed in the context of the welfare state and state intervention. The current new regionalism is distinguished by a combination of elements previously thought incompatible: the presence of a regional culture, language and identity is now considered to have a positive relationship with economic development rather than the reverse; political autonomy is now considered important in the context of a wider, competitive Europe. By the late twentieth century it was possible to formulate a hypothesis, contrary to the old modernization wisdom, that in the new conditions of production a distinct local culture might be an asset for development and a means of coping with globalization. Research has shown the extent to which this model of new regionalism is shared by regional and local elites right across Europe.[10] Yet, for all the agreement on the importance of values, behaviour and identities in mobilizing actors around development projects, there is little systematic work on just what the key factors are. Too often, explanations are reduced to vague formulations about "social capital" or to essentially descriptive accounts of success stories.

The Research Project

This, then, is the context of European diversity and convergence of our research project on the relationship between culture, institutions and development in eight regions in four European countries. Our interest is in the rise of new spatially specific forms of social regulation and collective action beyond the state. We focus on the regional level, identifying the region as an intermediate level between the state and the local, with a certain sense of common identity and institutions. Rather than taking these territorial systems of action for granted, we are interested in the way they are constituted under conditions of economic, cultural and institutional change in the context outlined above. We wish to avoid two pitfalls. The first is a certain functionalist determinism that assumes that political and institutional form follow from the functional demands of the global economic system. The second is a tendency to cultural reductionism, the belief that change is driven by embedded cultural patterns and values largely immune from political or institutional influence; related to this is the tendency to reify "identities," giving them a certain primordial essence and stretching the concept to cover too much. We examine regional development as a complex project, with economic, social, cultural and political dimensions, the balance among which varies from one case to another.

In order to explore these issues we chose the method of comparative case studies, looking at the same factors in each of the eight regions. The four countries possess a variety of state forms: Belgium has a federal state, Spain a strongly regionalized state, France a regionalized unitary state and the United Kingdom what is best characterized as a "Union" state, which is currently undergoing a significant program of devolution. This allows us to examine whether similar factors (the broad similar processes of convergence) will lead to similar results despite this variety. If the outcomes in all eight regions are basically similar, then it might be hypothesized that institutions, at least at the national level, are of little relevance. On the other hand, we might find that outcomes, while having similarities, are expressed according to the particular state tradition.

Within these states, we chose what seemed to be, prima facie, a "strong" region and a "weak" region: Flanders (strong) and Wallonia (weak); Catalonia (strong) and Galicia (weak); Brittany (strong) and Languedoc-Roussillon (weak); and Scotland (strong) and Wales (weak). By comparing these regions within the same state, the state form is held constant, allowing us to analyze variations and similarities that might be attributable to other factors such as level of economic development, socio-economic features, political leadership, institutional capacity, the existence or not of a minority language and identity and its uses. We cannot actually control for all of these. All we can do is show that different patterns of regulation are possible within the same state.

Our concern was also to go beyond a merely static institutional analysis, by examining the political dynamics of regional development. This we did by tracing the strategies and development styles emerging from the dominant political and social coalitions in each region. The emphasis was on economic development, but to assess the qualitative rather than the quantitative aspects we looked at cultural and linguistic policy, social inclusion and environmental policy. Thus, the comparative dimension of our project compared regions within particular states but also across state traditions. In this way a picture could be built up of convergence and divergence and the dimensions along which these are occurring.

Culture, Collective Action and Development

Our first finding was that there is indeed convergence toward common patterns and outcomes. In all eight regions, our research showed that culture and norms mediate between individuals and institutions and cannot be reduced to one or the other. Second, we found that culture is neither primordial nor something that can be created *ex novo* merely by an act of will. It is the result, rather, of actors working with existing materials, reshaping them in the process. What is interesting, however, are the politics of identity and the uses to which actors can put them in development projects. By promoting a common identity forged by regional culture, political elites can reconcile discordant themes that might otherwise be sources of fragmentation and internal conflict: 1) the opposition between tradition and modernity, 2) the tension between inward- and outward-looking conceptions of regional identity, 3) the clash between economic development and social cohesion and 4) the tension between the market and regional culture.

Tradition and Modernity

Although we reject the primordialist conception of identity, it is clear that the raw materials do matter and that there is a degree of historical path-dependency. Both tradition and modernity are social constructs and draw on the same historical materials, but these are used in quite distinctive ways to the advantage or disadvantage of the region, as is clear from our eight case studies. It is striking that it is the "strong" regions that have used these most successfully as part of their mobilization for development. Catalonia and Flanders have a "usable" past as historic trading regions in which the economic dimension plays an important role in the imagination of the territory. Brittany can count on traditions of collective action and on a legacy of Christian Democratic efforts to modernize tradition as a condition of survival. Scotland draws on memories of independent nationhood and on the institutions of civil society – the Church, education and law – that survived the 1707 Act of Union. Among the "weak" regions,

Languedoc-Roussillon lacks even a memory of a definable space or any tradition of autonomy. Galicia, Wales and Wallonia do have such memories, but they also have self-images of failure that are hard to shift. Wales, like the west of Scotland and Wallonia, has a history of domination by heavy industry, big firms and Fordist production methods that has left a legacy of class polarization, lack of social co-operation and a poor record of entrepreneurship. In all eight regions, these distinct patterns have become somewhat self-perpetuating and produce vicious or virtuous circles and positive and negative stereotypes that involve certain features of territorial societies being applied to the society as a whole to create a larger story of success or failure.

Yet regions are not completely trapped in their past, and change can sometimes come quite rapidly in response to external shocks such as those outlined above, as well as to internal political and economic changes. The transition of Scotland and Wales from old industrial societies under the Conservative governments of the 1980s and 1990s involved massive disruption, and both nations were excoriated for being trapped in "collectivism" and a "dependency culture." There was a certain effort to rebuild a business class in Scotland, but this flew in the face of the overall effort to insert the economy into global markets, although it is true that an indigenous bourgeoisie may be the precondition for insertion into global markets as in, for example, Quebec. There was also strong hostility to political devolution on the part of the Scottish business class. One reaction to this hostility emphasized precisely the common territorial and cultural identity, and the resulting political and social mobilization may have helped Scotland (and Wales, in a similar pattern) move from the politics of opposition to more constructive institution-building after 1997. Brittany, on the other hand, had a less brutal and more successful transition from the 1950s onwards, with a role for the new local elites or *forces vives,* who shifted the image of the region from one of backwardness to one of modernity.

Wallonia, like Scotland and Wales, was hit by a massive industrial crisis in the 1980s that dealt a severe blow to regional self-confidence and self-perception. Recently, however, local management of change has helped forge a more positive self-image, rescuing elements of the industrial culture rather than consigning it all to the waste bin. Catalonia's economic restructuring in the 1980s was less radical but still substantial, and it was managed partly by local leadership committed, for political reasons, to sustaining a common vision. Languedoc-Roussillon's economic restructuring in the 1970s and 1980s was dominated in the early stage by the central state, which, as it had no commitment to sustaining a regional vision, served to further fragment local identities and collective capacities. Regionalists failed to produce a counterbalance in the form of modernized tradition and were rendered largely irrelevant. Even when decentralization came in the 1980s, it was the city leaders in towns such as Nimes and Montpellier who were the beneficiaries. A regional theme is now hardly available for development efforts.

Inward and Outward Conceptions of Identity

"Europe" has been an increasingly important factor in questions of regional mobilization and identity. In fact, it is still unclear as to whether European integration has enhanced or hindered the position of regions within their states and in the European Union policy-making system. Evidence can be gathered to support both positions. On the one hand, the availability of regional funding has been important in inciting the mobilization of regions, and this and some of the European Commission transnational programs have encouraged regions to establish links directly with the EU institutions as well as with other regions beyond the frontiers of their states. European integration has also relativized the previously absolute position of national governments, and regions, with other subnational authorities, are now policy actors in their own right. Without going as far as claiming that there is now a Europe of the Regions, we can claim that there is a Europe with the Regions. On the other hand, in some respects European integration has actually undermined regions, at least in the constitutional sense that the EU recognizes only its own institutions and the member states and not subnational authorities. The latter are only weakly recognized in the Committee of the Regions. This means that in cases such as Germany and Spain the prerogatives of the Länder and the Autonomous Communities in certain policy areas might be undermined by the fact that the commission deals only with the national government. In the area of regional funding in France it is not the regions but the central state agency, the DATAR, that deals with the commission in preparing and monitoring regional funding programs.

Despite these limitations, it remains that, at least in the more diffuse and less technical area of culture and identity, Europe provides an overarching framework that helps to reconcile inward and outward conceptions of identity. This dimension is found in all our case studies. Europe helps regional elites to buy into the theme of modernity and progress and to give legitimacy to regionalism by dissociating it from parochialism and tying it to the future. By encouraging mobilization toward the exterior, it allows elites to encourage internal mobilization, thus strengthening internal identity. At the same time, the new regional paradigm validates this identity as a progressive tool in the armoury of economic development.

For regional nationalist parties, it also helps to blur the difference between independence and devolution within the state. This has proved immensely important in Catalonia and Flanders, which have pressed for more autonomy in tune with steps toward European integration and which have been active in the Europe of the Regions movement. The very lack of definition of the goals of the European project helps actors with rather different aspirations to co-operate in the pursuit of regional influence and European resources. Scotland and Wales came to the European game later than Catalonia and Flanders, but since the late 1980s Europe has transformed their self-understanding to the point that their nationalist parties are the most pro-European in the United Kingdom (with the possible exception of Northern Ireland's SDLP). Neither Galicia nor Languedoc-Roussillon, on the other hand, has developed a shared vision of Europe.

Economic Development and Social Cohesion

Shared culture and identity do not, in our cases, banish class conflict in favour of solidarity and social cohesion. Class politics are still played out, but in a new framework in which the region plays a role, albeit not an exclusive one, in social mediation. Culture and identity can provide a basis for collaboration, although they are not, as is sometimes imagined, a substitute for class identity. Both labour and capital are torn between local and broader identities and solidari-ties, but we detected a tendency in the more successful regions for both sides to strengthen their territorial presence. There is a strong regional bourgeoisie in Flanders that is closely identified with the regional project and a weaker one in Catalonia. Scotland has a class of industrialists and financiers who identify with the territory, although their numbers declined steadily throughout the twenti-eth century. Wales, Galicia and Languedoc-Roussillon have very weak business classes, while the Walloon bourgeoisie is strongly Belgian in orientation and tied to the old heavy industries.

Labour has been willing to play the regional card but is also torn by its com-mitment to statewide solidarity and redistribution, especially in former indus-trialized regions such as Wales and Wallonia. In all our cases with the exception of Galicia, trade unions are statewide organizations. At the same time, they have to be responsive to demotic regional and nationalist sentiment. Scotland, Wales and Wallonia, which have strong labour and socialist traditions, have empha-sized social cohesion. The Scottish Parliament, especially, and the Welsh National Assembly have developed policy options that vary considerably from those developed at Westminster for England. In Flanders and Catalonia the ruling parties are right of centre and exemplify bourgeois regionalism, which is more sympathetic to market principles while remaining conscious of the necessity of maintaining social cohesion within the region. In this sense, these parties are closer to Christian Democracy; this is also the case in Brittany. In Galicia and Languedoc-Roussillon, there are struggles for ideological hegemony between conservative and modernizing regionalists (Galicia) and between a conservative left and a modernizing right (Languedoc-Roussillon). Whatever the ideological hue, however, it remains true that regional elites in all our case studies emphasize solidarity and cohesion within the region.

In three of the weaker regions (Galicia, Languedoc-Roussillon, Wales), we found that relations between the regional population and the state are marked by clientelism, a complicated concept that is sometimes difficult to distinguish from other forms of interest representation. One aspect of clientelism is of key importance here: the ability of the clientelist system to exploit territorial identities and encourage territorial expression of grievance but then to satisfy these by providing divisible goods that discourage broad political mobilization. This is both a structural and a cultural phenomenon. In Galicia, Wales (at least in part) and Languedoc-Roussillon, political structures have been shaped so as to require the presence of intermediaries in order to get things done, giving opportunities for patrons and, later, political parties to fill the gap. In Brittany, Catalonia, Flanders and Scotland the immediate reciprocity of the clientelistic exchange is replaced by the more diffused reciprocity characteristic of high trust societies.

Market and Culture

Language use and policy best illustrate the tensions inherent in this dimension. Among the strong regions, Catalonia and Flanders have most successfully incorporated language policy into a modernizing project. In Catalonia, the Catalan language has been successful in imposing itself as the dominant language of the region despite the coexistence of Castilian and also some hostility from the Madrid government. As one of the wealthier regions in Spain, Catalonia has demonstrated that the existence of a regional language is not necessarily an obstacle to economic development. In Belgium, Flanders has overtaken Wallonia both economically and linguistically in the sense that today English has replaced French as the second language after Dutch in that region.

Among our other case studies, the positive link between language and successful economic development is less clear-cut. In both Galicia and Wales, the regional languages have survived and even experienced a certain revival. However, it is still far from certain that they have been successfully incorporated into the regional development project as in Catalonia and Flanders. In Languedoc-Roussillon, there are two minority languages, Catalan and Occitan, and, as in other aspects of the region's political and cultural situation, these are divided both against each other and against the region. In Scotland, Gaelic is marginal in the nation's self-identity and language is not much of an issue. In Wallonia, there is no minority language. However, in both regions, culture and dialects may replace language as such as a component of the new paradigm of regional development. What is clear is that, whatever the degree of success or failure in the language policies in each of our case studies, there is a general adoption of the notion that regional culture and language are important elements of the new development paradigm and should be supported and encouraged by public policies. There is great variation in the actual policy commitment in real financial terms, but at least lip service is being paid to the idea; it is rare to find the sentiment that regional languages and cultures ought to disappear if the development project is to be successful.

Conclusions

The vast processes we identified initially – globalization, Europeanization, state restructuring and societal transformation – have affected all eight of the studied cases. Furthermore, regional elites within all eight nations and regions have responded to these challenges in similar ways, despite the great differences in constitutional status, political and institutional capacity, socio-economic development and degree of political mobilization. All eight cases have bought into the idea that there is an emerging Europe of the Regions, however this is defined, and that this new Europe presents them with both a challenge and an opportunity. The challenge is that this is a competitive Europe, and regions can no longer rely simply on the national states to protect and sustain them. To some extent they are now on their own, and they must reinvent themselves in order to compete successfully against other regions. The opportunity is that the new paradigm of regional development in effect validates their particular histories, cultures, languages and identities. For the first time, these are now seen as assets rather than hindrances to development. Thus, the eight regions illustrate empirically what is sometimes put forward as a mere theoretical construct: that globalization has, paradoxically, led to a new appreciation of the local and regional, as expressed in the barbarous neologism "glocalization." The particular, the local and regional – the customized – become part of an economic and cultural process that is truly global. Of course, much of the new paradigm might be dismissed as pure ideology and wishful thinking.[11] On the other hand, it could also be seen as thoughtful wishing and, in any case, almost all political and social realities can, at some point, be dismissed as mere "constructs." What is important here is that the ideology of the new regionalism has begun to affect political and policy choices at both national and regional levels.

At the same time, the downside of the new, competitive regionalism may be that the strong regions will become even stronger and the weak weaker. To some extent, this is borne out in our case studies. Here we can discern what seem to be the conditions for success in mobilizing around a regional development project. First, the already existing level of economic performance is important. Thus, Flanders and Catalonia are at or above the European average and Scotland is just below it. Brittany, however, is among the four weak regions in poorer performance. Second, there needs to be a shared territorial identity that is both open and flexible. This means that the nation or region is never complete but always being built, the future never closed but always open to divergent paths. Catalonia, Flanders and Scotland illustrate this feature. Languedoc-Roussillon has no shared identity, while in Galicia and Wallonia identities are not very flexible. Wales and Brittany are somewhere in the middle as each region attempts to modernize its identity. Third, there are weak ties that facilitate social co-operation but do not lock actors into dysfunctional patterns of behaviour. Again, Flanders, Brittany and Catalonia illustrate this with their "light" forms of development policy, which allow government to intervene to help development but to pull out of projects if they fail. On the other hand, in Galicia and Languedoc-Roussillon clientelistic links have hampered flexibility. Scotland, with its continuing civil society based on institutions and memories rather than strong ethnic solidarities, has a stronger network of actors than Wales, where internal divisions are greater. Fourth, the uses of history and myth are important and the more successful nations and regions, such as Brittany, Catalonia, Scotland and Flanders, have developed a positive and dynamic self-image, while the weaker ones have more negative self-images.

Finally, institutions and political leadership are both important. While elected regional governments in themselves cannot change a regional culture and social relations, they do play a role. Our studies suggest that regional government, where it exists, does matter and that mere governance will not always fulfill tasks of mobilization and collective action. Elected government gives a symbolic legitimacy to the region as a political space and endows it with the one form of legitimization that, in a democratic society, trumps all others. Of course, something more than just elected government is necessary, as the comparison between Brittany and Languedoc-Roussillon or Catalonia and Galicia shows. In each case, the region has exactly the same kinds of institutions, but it is necessary for the other conditions to be met for these institutions to be effective. This brings us to the importance of political leadership. In effect, this involves a complex process of synthesizing divergent elements, including symbolic representation, social cohesion and policy, into a project for a region. Our strong regions have strong political leadership capable of this. This does not necessarily mean that the weak are destined to remain weak forever. Radical change is possible, as the Celtic Tiger phenomenon demonstrates. Furthermore, although we have emphasized the competitive aspect of the new Europe of the Regions, we should not forget that there are also collaboration and policy learning among regions through EU bodies, such as the Committee of the Regions, and the vast range of interregional associations, such as the Assembly for European Regions. While regional competition in Europe does impose some common imperatives, there is still scope for diversity. This is not limited to culture or folklore but includes basic questions about the insertion of the region into the European and global economies. Regions are not replacing nation-states, but in a post-sovereignty world, regions are key sites of social and economic regulation.

Notes

1. Dyson (1980), Loughlin and Peters (1997).

2. Rokkan (1987).

3. Esping-Andersen (1990), Castles (1993).

4. Goldsmith and Page (1987).

5. Loughlin (2001).

6. Mendras (1997), Crouch (1999).

7. Keating and Loughlin (1997), Keating (1998), Le Galès and Lequesne (1998), Jeffery (1997).

8. Loughlin (2001).

9. Keating (1998)

10. Kohler-Koch et al. (1997).

11. This is the interpretation of Lovering (1997).

Bibliography

Castles, Francis. *Families of Nations: Patterns of Public Policy in Western Nations.* Aldershot: Dartmouth, 1993.

Crouch, Colin. *Social Change in Western Europe.* Oxford: Oxford University Press, 1999.

Dyson, Kenneth. *The State Tradition in Western Europe: A Study of an Idea and Institution.* Oxford: Martin Robertson, 1980.

Esping-Andersen, Gøsta. *The Three Worlds of Welfare Capitalism.* Cambridge: Polity Press, 1990.

Goldsmith, Michael, and Edward C. Page, eds. *Central and Local Government Relations: A Comparative Analysis of West European Unitary States.* London: Sage, 1987.

Jeffery, Charlie, ed. *The Regional Dimension of the European Union: Towards a Third Level in Europe?* London: Frank Cass, 1997.

Keating, Michael. *The New Regionalism in Western Europe: Territorial Restructuring and Political Change.* Cheltenham, UK, and Northampton, MA.: Edward Elgar, 1998.

Keating, Michael, and John Loughlin, eds. *The Political Economy of Regionalism.* London: Frank Cass, 1997.

Kohler-Koch, Beate, et al. *Interaktive Politik in Europa: Regionen im Netzwerk der Integration.* Opladen: Leske + Budrich, 1997.

Le Galès, Patrick, and Christian Lequesne, eds. *Regions in Europe.* New York: Routledge, 1998.

Loughlin, John. *Subnational Democracy in the European Union: Challenges and Opportunities.* Oxford: Oxford University Press, 2001.

Loughlin, John, and B. Guy Peters. "State Traditions, Administrative Reform and Regionalization," in *The Political Economy of Regionalism,* ed. Michael Keating and John Loughlin. London: Frank Cass, 1997.

Lovering, John. *Misreading and Misleading the Welsh Economy: The New Regionalism.* Cardiff: Department of City & Regional Planning, University of Wales, 1997.

Mendras, Henri. *L'Europe des européens: sociologie de l'Europe occidentale.* Paris: Gallimard, 1997.

Rokkan, Stein. *Centre-Periphery Structures in Western Europe: An ISSC Workbook in Comparative Analysis.* Frankfurt: Campus, 1987.

9

the constitutional accommodation of national minorities in the UK and Canada: judicial approaches to diversity

Stephen Tierney

The role played by constitutional law in mediating the relations of power between the constituent units of multinational states is evident primarily in the institutional design of the state. It is, however, also made manifest as these power relations play themselves out in everyday legal discourse – in particular as sub-state national communities agitate for improved recognition and enhanced self-government, which, they contend, can be accommodated through differing and increasingly creative approaches to constitutional interpretation. This paper focuses upon constitutional interpretation, examining recent attempts by the courts to negotiate autonomy claims advanced by national minorities in cases that test the capacity of existing constitutional arrangements to manage the institutional conditions of diversity within plurinational democracies.[1]

The paper concentrates largely upon the judgment of the Canadian Supreme Court in the *Quebec Secession Reference* case,[2] and by way of comparison it turns at different points to the recent devolution process in the United Kingdom and the challenges faced by the UK judiciary as it attempts to work through the asymmetrical division of powers set out in the UK's new constitutional arrangements. In both states the courts are being called upon to recognize Canada and the UK respectively as multinational democracies, a process that challenges judges to reconceptualize a number of well-established and perhaps overly formalistic constitutional assumptions.[3] For example, at the heart of the *Quebec Secession Reference* case is the question of how sovereignty is divided within the Canadian federation, a question that seemed to raise the issue of provincial self-determination. In discussing the *Secession Reference*, analogies will be drawn with Scottish devolution, since there is already evidence that fundamental questions surrounding sovereignty and self-determination may not be buried very deeply beneath the surface of the new settlement represented by the *Scotland Act*, 1998. When such questions come before the courts, judges are themselves under pressure in terms of their capacity to deal with fundamental cleavages within the state. When political disputes surrounding sovereignty and self-determination crystallize as questions of law, courts become embroiled in attempts to provide objective legal resolution to intensely disputed and heavily politicized questions. These questions test the very legitimacy of the constitutional system and threaten the continued existence of the state within which, and in defence of which, judges are expected to act. Of course, few disputes involving the fundamental issues of sovereignty and secession come before the courts in federal or devolved systems. But when they do, as the Canadian experience has shown, it can fall upon the courts to retrieve the constitution's credibility in times of such crisis. It is from these disputes that the most interesting judicial insights into the nature of a particular constitution and, indeed, of constitutionalism in general can be made, and within such disputes that the capacity of a particular set of constitutional arrangements to manage and mediate cultural diversity in multinational democracies is put most fully to the test.

Courts, Substate Nations and Constitutional Change

Courts and Constitutional Decision-Making – a "Higher Form of Republican Deliberation"?[4]

Constitutional disputes surrounding the issue of autonomy for national minorities go to the heart of a constitutional order's normative structure, raising fundamental questions about the political legitimacy of both the constitution and the state itself. It was in this context that the Canadian Supreme Court, fully conscious of the degree to which the ongoing disagreement over Quebec's status was straining Canadian constitutional self-understanding, set out in the *Secession Reference* to articulate the norms and values that underpin Canada as a multinational constitutional democracy. The Court was also conscious that fundamental constitutional disputes of this kind raise prima facie questions about the political nature of law, law's internal legitimacy and, consequently, the capacity of law or a particular legal system to balance interests fairly. Disputes concerning the autonomy of substate national groups can present law with particular difficulties because the status of the legal order may itself be

the constitutional accommodation of national minorities in the UK and canada under challenge, when the group involved, or at least important political actors within it, seek to remove that group to a greater or lesser extent from the jurisdictional writ of the state's constitutional system. Leaving aside for one moment the specific issue of secession or sovereignty, it is worth dwelling a little longer on the issue of law's capacity for independent operation within a broader polity. It is a central tenet of liberal constitutionalism that law, and in particular adjudicatory devices within a democratic constitution, can be distinguished from other political institutions and processes in important and self-sustaining ways. If law is perceived to be substantively transparent and if its adjudicatory processes are conducted by judges who are perceived by the parties to be sufficiently independent and impartial, the legal system is deemed capable of constituting a fair set of rules and procedures even by parties whose substantive positions are diametrically opposed. Law might thereby help to depoliticize these disagreements by providing a credible forum for the playing out of highly contentious disputes, including those involving intercommunal social and political relations. In doing so, it might make the process and outcomes of adjudication legitimate in the eyes of both winners and losers. Central to this notion is the idea that legal adjudication can be distinguished from more overtly "political" structures and processes, in particular those of law-making.[5] The idea of law as somehow separable from, and independent of, prevailing political, material and other deterministic tides is of course strongly contested from a number of political positions. This creates extensive areas of debate surrounding law's ontology and the relations between law and other political and social processes, issues that are largely outside the scope of this paper. Instead, the focus here is upon the constitutional systems of specific plurinational liberal democracies and upon the narrower question of the degree to which these particular constitutional and legal systems are deemed legitimate in the eyes of competing parties to disputes concerning the accommodation of diversity in these multinational states. In other words, this paper is primarily concerned with the subjective sustainability of particular legal systems rather than with issues of law's objective value.[6]

Since the systems dealt with here (Canada and the UK) are liberal democracies, most of the discussion is structured within the confines of liberal debate on the nature of law and constitutionalism. Narrowing this focus further to adjudication, it can be said that the debate within liberalism on the nature of judges has moved on considerably from the traditional nineteenth-century doctrine of the English common law, where judges were attributed with the characteristics of politically neutral philosopher kings, operating above the political process and bringing credibility to their task from this elevated position of objectivity. Modern debates on the appropriate judicial role were transformed in the early decades of the twentieth century by legal realism, which has substantially undermined the notion that judges are, or should hold themselves out as being, value-neutral arbiters whose adjudicatory work can be detached from their political and philosophical commitments and preconceptions. The debate on the proper judicial role intensifies in times of constitutional change or constitutional malaise, and it is perhaps no surprise that it has recently returned in these two contexts in the UK and Canada respectively.[7]

In the UK, devolution and a new bill of rights together promise to involve judges ever more in issues of great political moment, just as the Charter of Rights and Freedoms and the "federal question" have so engaged the Canadian bench. The surviving apologists for the English common law myth of the judge as a political eunuch are increasingly challenged from the realist position, with calls for judges in a mature democracy to locate themselves appropriately within the body politic rather than to attempt disingenuously to elevate themselves above it. For example, Carol Harlow, a prominent English constitutional lawyer, reflecting upon constitutional change in the UK, has argued: "Law cannot endure as a world neutrally detached from the content of political argument but must take its proper place as a facet of political society rather than as an autonomous and external force acting upon it."[8] This realist attitude is not an implicit criticism of judges for failing to live up to our high expectations. On the contrary, it is a recognition, first, of the central role courts play within any democratic system of governance beholden to the rule of law and, second, that this role is uniquely valuable in restraining the excesses of the other branches of government and, thereby, in sustaining the legitimacy of the constitution as a higher set of norms operating above, and from this position regulating, the fast and loose manoeuvrings of the "political" constitution. As the first United States Chief Justice, John Marshall, is said to have asked rather bluntly as long ago as 1788: "To what quarter will you look to remedy an infringement of the constitution, if you will not look to the judiciary?"[9]

Substate Nations and the Legitimacy of the Courts

In the specific context of aggrieved substate nations pressing for greater autonomy either by way of better accommodation within an existing state or through secession, the credibility of law and adjudication comes under particularly acute pressure precisely on this question of value neutrality. The level of disillusionment with the judicial system will inevitably be part of a broader sense of dissatisfaction with the state's constitutional structure, which is often perceived by substate nations to consolidate the institutional dominance of the state's majority culture. As writers like Will Kymlicka and Yael Tamir have argued, this level of disaffection is to be found even in ostensibly liberal, democratic and tolerant societies, which, they contend, are not culturally neutral as purported but which in fact promote, and indeed impose, the prioritization of a particular societal culture, often through constitutional devices such as an official language or an established religion.[10] Therefore, specific constitutional disputes involving national minorities can lead to a deeper questioning of the overall cultural and, by extension, political neutrality of the constitution, whether in substantive or procedural terms. In this environment, the difficulties facing the courts in bringing legitimacy to the process of adjudication become very great, particularly as the court, too, can be seen as an instrument of the dominant culture.

Before turning to the *Secession Reference*, it should be noted that the Canadian Supreme Court has been subjected to precisely this type of critique for the way in which it has acted in important cases involving Quebec over the past 20 years.[11] An example of this is the way in which the legitimacy of both the Canadian constitution and the courts was called into question by prominent political actors in Quebec at an early stage in the litigation that would eventually result in the *Secession Reference*. This reference arose from proceedings brought by Guy Bertrand, who sought to challenge before the Superior Court of Quebec the constitutional validity of the Quebec draft bill that authorized the staging of a referendum on sovereignty to be held in 1995 and that anticipated a process of "accession to sovereignty" in the event of a Yes vote. He also filed a motion claiming that the referendum would violate his rights as a Canadian citizen under the Canadian Charter of Rights and Freedoms and seeking an injunction that would prevent the referendum being held. The attorney general of Quebec sought a motion to dismiss Mr. Bertrand's action on the basis that this was an attempt to interfere with the legislative powers, functions and privileges of the province's National Assembly. When Mr. Justice Robert Lesage on August 31, 1995, refused to dismiss Mr. Bertrand's application on the jurisdictional question and proceeded to hear substantive arguments, the attorney general of Quebec withdrew from further participation in the proceedings, with Premier Jacques Parizeau announcing on September 2: "We can't subjugate Quebecers' right to vote to a decision of the courts. That would be contrary to our democratic system. Quebecers want to vote. They have a right to vote. And they will vote."[12]

It is difficult to imagine how, in terms of the legitimacy of the constitution, the nature of the dispute at this point could have been more debilitating for Canada. The Government of Quebec was not arguing simply that the National Assembly had more powers than Mr. Bertrand was claiming and leaving it to the courts to determine the outcome of the dispute. If this was the only issue, then it would have been a very ordinary federal dispute. Instead, the Government of Quebec was contesting the power of the federal courts to decide the question, bringing into play the issue of *Kompetenz-Kompetenz*.[13] There are parallels between the *Kompetenz-Kompetenz* dispute that has arisen in the EU context, where the dispute is between member states and the central organs of the EU (in particular, the European Court of Justice), and that which has arisen in Canada. In the latter case the debate is not only about the respective powers of centre and federal subunit but about which institution, if any, has the constitutional power to determine such jurisdictional and competence questions.[14] In terms of judicial authority, if there is a claim by a federal subunit like Quebec that the federal courts do not have the constitutional competence unilaterally to set the limits of provincial constitutional competence, particularly on such a vital issue, then when courts reassert the federal constitution's normative power, the resulting clash will inevitably call into question the status of the court itself as the highest-ranking forum for the settlement of constitutional disputes within the state. This seems to be precisely what occurred when Mr. Justice Lesage decided that the substance of Mr. Bertrand's motion should be heard by the Superior Court. As the Quebec government confirmed in withdrawing from the Bertrand litigation, "We submit that the only judge and the only jury of the future of the Quebec people will be the people of Quebec themselves."[15]

Both Mr. Justice Lesage and the federal government were aware of the threat this posed to the judicial system. In the first stage of the Bertrand proceedings, Mr. Justice Lesage, in giving judgment, declared that in a federal system the division of powers must be enforceable by the courts,[16] and when the litigation continued after the referendum, the federal government intervened, citing its "duty to protect the integrity of the Constitution and to uphold the role of the courts as the prime defenders of the Constitution and the Rule of Law."[17]

It was in the context of such a high level of disputation, and with the Quebec government having withdrawn from proceedings, that the Canadian Supreme Court was called upon by the federal government in the *Secession Reference* case to provide an opinion on Quebec's right, under domestic and international law, to secede. In this context it seems that, beyond the immediate question of the legality of secession, at a deeper level the Supreme Court also faced the task of attempting to relegitimize the federal constitution, particularly for those in Quebec who seemed to be calling into question the absolute nature of its authority. The stakes here could not have been higher. A court in this situation is not only seeking to revive the authority of a constitutional order as a body of rules and a political process through which a substate national group is happy to seek accommodation; it is, in addition, engaged in retrieving its own authority, which is also under pressure as a central institution of the crisis-ridden constitutional order.[18] This seems to illustrate the point made in the introduction: when the judiciary attempts to mediate diversity in multinational states, it is also engaged in the task of reassuring both sets of parties of its own legitimacy to engage in such a management role.

Constitutional Reform in the UK: Towards a New Constitutionalism?

Before examining the Canadian Supreme Court's judgment in the *Secession Reference* (which may be seen perhaps as an attempt to resuscitate faith in the constitution), we will begin to explore the new challenges being faced by UK judges following a period of ad hoc but extensive devolution aimed at the better accommodation of substate national groups.[19] Judges in the UK are now being called upon to confront a formalization of the traditionally loose constitutional structures, and in doing so, to articulate a new constitutionalism for a devolved UK. With the present wave of constitutional reform in the UK (which also includes a new bill of rights through the *Human Rights Act,* 1998) we might anticipate the emergence of a new political idiom in the UK. The ad hoc "political" constitution that British constitutional lawyers have had to work with for so long is undergoing a period of almost unprecedented restructuring. Traditionally the British system of government has been discussed more in political than in constitutional terms, with the language of the British constitution constrained by a very flexible institutional context that has largely disabled any meaningful assessment of the constitutionality of political behaviour. This may now be changing as the UK moves, perhaps, from a political constitution to a new constitutional politics. One important by-product is that, as the Westminster Parliament has begun to articulate constitutional principles through legislation, this process has elevated judges to the position of pivotal constitutional actors, particularly as the courts are called upon to define the details of the institutional plate changes taking place below the political surface. What will be of interest in the context of devolution are the ways in which, and the extent to which, judges in the UK will interpret the legal framework of the new institutional infrastructure in an attempt to better accommodate national diversity within the state.

Later in the paper we will return briefly to the ways in which the Scottish courts have begun to meet these early constitutional challenges. This follows a review of the *Secession Reference,* which represents the most dramatic example of how courts can become involved in managing the constitutional accommodation of national difference within the state.

The Quebec Secession Reference

Background

The prominent role that the Supreme Court played in settling contentious disputes arising from the "patriation" of the Canadian constitution in the early

1980s enabled the Court to define contested provisions in the Canadian constitution. However, it also served to implicate the Court in a process of constitutional reconfiguration that was widely felt in Canada to have ridden roughshod over Quebec's conventional rights. In particular, the issue of Quebec's right to veto constitutional change was hugely contentious. Denied such a right by the Court, Quebec, as a partner in Canadian confederation, felt betrayed. The Supreme Court's decision in the *Veto Reference* case[20] was, in the view of one commentator, the issue over which "Quebec and the rest of Canada had their most dramatic falling out,"[21] and it suggested to many Quebecers that the Supreme Court was filling gaps in the constitution to Quebec's disadvantage.[22] As Michael Mandel puts it: "though [former Prime Minister] Trudeau passed the first constitutional amendment against Quebec's will, it was the Supreme Court of Canada that said it was constitutionally acceptable to do so."[23] It was from the maelstrom of the early 1980s that doubts really arose in Quebec concerning the Supreme Court's capacity to adequately account for national diversity in Canada.

Beyond the question of Quebec's particular dissatisfaction with both the process and the substance of patriation, some have pointed to a broader problem of democratic deficit in the entire patriation process, which, it has been argued, did not involve much in the way of popular participation throughout Canada as a whole. During the process, there was no reaffirmation of popular will by way of, for example, a referendum. It has subsequently been asked what, in the absence of a popular reconstitution of the state's political order, actually sustains the legitimacy of the now indigenous Canadian constitution in the eyes of the country's citizens: "If the Canadian people never ratified it, and if the Westminster Parliament which enacted the greatest part of it is no longer a part of the Canadian legal system, then what is supporting the constitutional structure?"[24] In particular, how could the Supreme Court assert so confidently in the *Veto Reference* that "*The Constitution Act, 1982* is now in force. Its legality is neither challenged nor assailable"[25]? It is interesting to note that the legitimacy of the constitution was being questioned by critics on democratic grounds, and in light of this it is perhaps no coincidence that the Supreme Court chose to place such emphasis upon the principle of democracy in the *Secession Reference*. It is also interesting, from the point of view of those who see the *Secession Reference* decision as an attempt by the Supreme Court to distance itself from its *Veto Reference* judgment, that when the Court restated in the *Secession Reference* the "neither challenged nor assailable" passage from the previous case, it did so with the proviso that the constitutional texts enumerated in section 52(2) of the 1982 act are not exhaustive and that the constitution also "embraces unwritten as well as written rules."[26] In other words, the *legality* of the 1982 act is not assailable, but to some extent its *meaning* is up for grabs. With this gap opened up, the Supreme Court of Canada would go on to explore the unwritten principles within the constitution, several of which (democracy, federalism and minority rights) encompass the value of diversity within the Canadian federation.

There are, it seems, interesting parallels between the constitutional context within which constitutional changes have taken place in Canada and that within which devolution has been implemented in the UK in the last few years. First, in both cases, constitutional change took place in a fairly ad hoc fashion, and rather than involving a rewriting of constitutional fundamentals *ab initio*, change has built on the existing constitution. For example, in the course of Canadian history, the transition from colony to independent state was gradual. Second, Canada's constitution evolved from the UK and was initially modelled on the UK system.[27] These two factors combined to ensure that, even until 1982, the doctrine of Westminster's parliamentary sovereignty retained some influence upon constitutional developments.[28] In Scotland, of course, this doctrine, whereby the UK Parliament asserts its self-declared supremacy, remains very much the spectre at the constitutional reform feast. A third point of possible comparison is that, although Canada has a written constitution, it seems that the written aspect of the constitution is nonexhaustive,[29] which is again perhaps the legacy of an inchoate process of constitution-building over a long period. It therefore relies, perhaps to a greater extent than other written constitutions, both on the hidden wiring of the unwritten norms and principles that help any constitutional structure to function and, to a particularly high degree, on the Supreme Court to articulate these norms and principles. Again, there are similarities here with the UK constitution, which to an even greater extent is held together by unwritten conventions and by the English common law doctrine of Parliament's legislative supremacy. It seems, therefore, that within the UK constitution it will also be possible for substate national groups to raise arguments about unwritten principles within the constitution, which might encourage the courts to embark on processes aimed at the better accommodation of these communities and of national diversity in general.

The Litigation

It is difficult to escape the conclusion that, in handing down its opinion in the *Secession Reference,* the Supreme Court's hand was swayed by Quebec's general dissatisfaction with the previous two decades of attempted constitutional reform. As has been already suggested (and will be discussed further below), it is perhaps partly on account of Quebec's disillusionment with the Supreme Court's role in the early 1980s that the Court turned so dramatically to the unwritten as well as the written dimensions of the constitution, and that the coverage of its decision extended much further than many observers expected.[30] Whatever the reasons for the Court's approach, there is no doubting the seriousness of the issue or the high level of disputation it found itself confronted with. If the issue at stake in the *Secession Reference* is characterized as a dispute between constitutionalism and democracy, then it is clear that the federal government and Quebec (which of course played no formal role in proceedings before the Supreme Court) took up polarized positions on either side of a fairly crude divide with respect to these core constitutional values, the federal government stressing the primacy of the rule of law and Quebec sovereigntists that of democracy. This prompted Kenneth McRoberts to comment later: "As long as the public debate over Quebec sovereignty was framed in terms of two mutually exclusive principles, the rule of law and the democratic legitimacy of a Quebec referendum, it could only result in an impasse, and an increasingly bitter one."[31] The Supreme Court in the *Secession Reference* was charged with the task of resolving this impasse.

On September 26, 1996, the Canadian government, taking up the case begun by Mr. Bertrand, announced that it would send a reference case to the Supreme Court. It did so on September 30 with the following questions:

- Under the Constitution of Canada, can the National Assembly, legislature or government of Quebec effect the secession of Quebec from Canada unilaterally?
- Does international law give the National Assembly, legislature or government of Quebec the right to effect the secession of Quebec from Canada unilaterally? In this regard, is there a right to self-determination under international law that would give the National Assembly, legislature or government of Quebec the right to effect the secession of Quebec from Canada unilaterally?
- In the event of conflict between domestic and international law on the right of the National Assembly, legislature or government of Quebec to effect the secession of Quebec from Canada unilaterally, which would take precedence in Canada?[32]

With the Quebec attorney general still refusing to participate, the Supreme Court appointed André Joli-Coeur, a lawyer from Quebec City, to act as *amicus curiae* and put forward arguments from the sovereignist position.[33]

The Decision
The Supreme Court's decision, given on August 20, 1998, was unanimous. This paper deals only with the Court's disquisition of the first question put to it by

the federal government, since the issue under discussion here concerns domestic constitutional law rather than international law. The Court recalled that the *Constitution Act* of 1982 did not provide an exhaustive definition of the constitution. The constitution of Canada "embraces unwritten, as well as written rules," including "the global system of rules and principles which govern the exercise of constitutional authority in the whole and in every part of the Canadian state."[34] In particular, the Court addressed four "fundamental and organizing principles,"[35] namely federalism, democracy, constitutionalism and the rule of law,[36] and respect for minorities, none of which "trump or exclude the operation of any other."[37]

Turning then to the issue of secession, the Supreme Court made clear that the answer to the federal government's first question was "no." A constitution binds individuals and groups together in a complex web of shared responsibilities, and, accordingly, the court held that Quebec could not secede simply pursuant to a referendum without prior negotiations with the other "participants in Confederation."[38] The Court noted that secession would also require an amendment to the constitution because an act of secession would "alter the governance of Canadian territory in a manner which undoubtedly [would be] inconsistent with [Canada's] current constitutional arrangement."[39] On the other hand, if a "clear majority" of the Quebec population voted for secession based on a "clear" referendum question, this would constitute a "clear" repudiation of the existing constitutional order, and, provided Quebec respected the "rights of others," the other "participants in Confederation" would thereupon come under a "reciprocal obligation" to negotiate in good faith with Quebec. In these negotiations all parties would be required to respect all four constitutional principles referred to by the Supreme Court in its decision. Having gone thus far, the Supreme Court did not clarify what it meant by "clear majority" or "clear question"; which amending formula should be used; or any of the process questions begged by this idea of a negotiation process. These questions, at least for the time being, were left to the political process.[40]

The Duty to Negotiate:
"Quebec is only the engine on this journey, not the driver"?[41]

This decision clearly broke new ground. It was the first time a domestic constitutional court had conceded that, in certain circumstances, a province may secede by way of an ostensibly "constitutional" process where the constitution makes no provision for secession. Peter Hogg was prompted to suggest that the duty to negotiate was a "stunningly new element that the Supreme Court of Canada added to the constitutional law of Canada."[42] The first question this raises concerns where the duty of "the participants in Confederation"[43] to negotiate the secession of Quebec comes from. It is difficult to present this simply as a manifestation of the democratic principle rooted in the Canadian constitution. For example, if the democratic will of the whole of Canada was opposed to such negotiations or to an outcome that would result in Quebec sovereignty, how would these competing manifestations of the same principle be respectively prioritized? Similarly, the principle of federalism does not appear to provide an answer, since appeals to this principle could again be made by all sides. As Hogg puts it, "The vague principles of democracy and federalism, which were relied upon by the court, hardly seem sufficient to require a federal government to negotiate the dismemberment of the country that it was elected to protect."[44]

To begin with, we might consider three possible explanations for the Court's construction of this duty to negotiate secession. It could be argued, first, that the nonexhaustive nature of the written constitution and the lack of any reference to secession in the written constitution allowed the Supreme Court to find that such a duty was an implied constitutional provision in terms of the "fundamental and organizing principles" the Court used to supplement references to substantive textual provisions. But this argument faces considerable problems both in terms of precedent and by the measure of relevant comparators. In terms of precedent, constitutional silence on secession has never before, certainly to my knowledge, been taken by a court to imply a right to secede. Looking to comparable situations, no written constitution is without gaps that need to be filled by the courts, nor is absolute clarity on every important constitutional provision to be found in any constitution. Furthermore, most constitutions are silent on the question of secession precisely because it is considered, like revolution, to be out of the question. On this basis, the materials the Canadian Supreme Court had to work with are much the same as those available to any constitutional court operating within a written constitution when the specific question of secession arises. Nonetheless, the unwritten principles that it identified within the constitution influenced the Court to a great extent:

> Underlying constitutional principles may in certain circumstances give rise to substantive legal obligations...which constitute substantive limitations upon government action. These principles may give rise to very abstract and general obligations, or they may be more specific and precise in nature. The principles are not merely descriptive, but are also invested with a powerful normative force, and are binding upon both courts and governments.[45]

The Court seems to suggest that such principles may even give rise to a specific duty to negotiate secession.

A second possible reason for the court's novel approach in positing a duty to negotiate secession is the unique nature of this very issue. Unlike most constitutional disputes, this case did not involve two parties seeking a solution within the constitution. The scenario to be addressed by the Court was one in which a province (which was absent from proceedings) seemed to reject the authority of both the constitution and the Supreme Court. In this respect the Court was faced with the political reality of the state's possible breakup, and when this scenario reaches a certain point it ceases to become an issue of law at all. As Peter Hogg puts it:

> Even without the court's ruling, the political reality is that the federal government would have to negotiate with Quebec after a majority of Quebec voters had clearly voted in favour of secession. It is safe to say that there would be little political support for a policy of attempted resistance to the wish of the Quebec voters. The court's decision simply converts political reality into a legal rule.[46]

The Supreme Court was, therefore, confronted with having to find a constitutional solution to what was in many ways an extraconstitutional problem, and arguably this is what led to its novel approach, the alternative being to withdraw and leave the issue entirely to the political arena.

The uniqueness of secession seems to be a major factor behind the Supreme Court's approach, but there is also perhaps a third feature underpinning the Court's conclusion that a duty to negotiate may exist: namely, the genuine desire to accommodate Quebec in recognition of its unique position within Canada. It is in this notion that the issue of institutional accommodation of national diversity really begins to emerge in the Court's judgment. By combining the values of democracy and federalism, the Supreme Court recognized the political reality of Quebec's distinctiveness in the history of Canada's constitution. Even if that distinctiveness is not yet enshrined in the written constitution, it is central to the structure of the Canadian union:

> The principle of federalism facilitates the pursuit of collective goals by cultural and linguistic minorities which form the majority within a particular province. This is the case in Quebec, where the majority of the population is French-speaking, and which possesses a distinct culture. This is not merely the result of chance. The social and demographic reality of Quebec explains the existence of the province of Quebec as a political unit and indeed, was one of the essential reasons for establishing a federal structure for the Canadian union in 1867.[47]

Some commentators doubt whether the Supreme Court is choosing to single out Quebec as a "special" province with special rights since it does not do so unequivocally,[48] but it should be borne in mind that, given both the level of political sensitivity surrounding this issue and the fact that any such declaration would arguably conflict with the principle of equality of the provinces enshrined in section 41 of the Constitution Act, 1982, the Supreme Court would have had extreme difficulty in making explicit either that Quebec has unique status or that it is entitled to special rights. Although the Supreme Court makes no such explicit endorsement of special rights for Quebec, it may well be thought that the use of the key word "distinct," which was central to the Meech Lake process, must be of some significance.[49]

By reading the duty to negotiate as, at least in part, an attempt to accommodate Quebec's distinctiveness, it can be argued that the Court was seeking to re-energize the constitutional system in the eyes of the disaffected people of Quebec. As such, it has been suggested, above and by others, that the Supreme Court was attempting to mitigate some of the dissatisfaction felt in Quebec with the decisions in the *Patriation Reference* and *Veto Reference* cases and with the general failure by the rest of Canada in the last two decades to recognize, within the constitution, Quebec's unique position in Canada. As Jean Le Clair puts it: "Backtracking from the dubious reasoning it expressed in the Quebec Veto Reference, the court recognized the need to take into account Quebec's specificity in Confederation. In other words, in the eyes of the court, the federal principle is not an ethereal concept universally applicable in all federations; it is historically contextualized."[50]

To conclude these initial comments on the duty to negotiate, it seems that Quebec's distinctiveness may well have been an important part of the Supreme Court's formulation of this duty. This issue will be returned to in detail below, when we discuss how, implicitly if not explicitly, the Court is suggesting in this recognition of Quebec's status that Quebec enjoys a qualified right of "external" self-determination within the Canadian constitution.[51] Before doing so, it is useful to explore further the issue of constitutionalism in the context of the *Secession Reference*.

The *Secession Reference*, Constitutionalism and Democracy

Democratic constitutionalism typically requires that the exercise of power within a polity accords with a particular set of rules determined through a popularly agreed process, and that these rules should be open to amendment. Another important element within democratic models of constitutionalism is that the practices of political actors be reviewable in terms of these rules, in accordance with a transparent and consistent set of procedures, and by way of adjudicatory mechanisms displaying popularly credible levels of independence and impartiality. Hence the legitimacy of political behaviour can be tested in a democratically validated forum by reference to an overarching and popularly affirmed structure – the constitution. By this construction, the constitutional order is inextricably bound to the democratic infrastructure that underpins it and that provides it with its legitimacy.

It has been mentioned briefly above that the issue at stake in the *Secession Reference* has been widely seen as a tension between constitutionalism and the rule of law on the one hand and democracy on the other. In addressing these two principles, the Supreme Court stated, in recognition of their fluidity: "In our constitutional tradition, legality and legitimacy are linked."[52] The Court also suggested that the linkage between the two principles of democracy and constitutionalism is not a conflictual one: "Constitutionalism facilitates – indeed, makes possible – a democratic political system by creating an orderly framework within which people may make political decisions. Viewed correctly, constitutionalism and the rule of law are not in conflict with democracy; rather, they are essential to it."[53]

James Tully has addressed this issue in an interesting way.[54] Tully notes that just as constitutional practice in the contemporary era is changing and becoming more open-ended, the work of theorists is also becoming more fluid as they reconceptualize constitutionalism. He views the Supreme Court's decision in a very positive light for the way in which it recognizes a close relationship between constitutionalism and democracy. Indeed, the reciprocal relationship between these two values is at the core of Tully's model of "radical democratic constitutionalism." Central to this idea is a process-based approach to constitutionalism, in place of the traditional "isolated framework" vision of constitutions as monolithic structures resistant to change. Instead, constitutions should be open to amendment, and the rules governing democratic practices of deliberation should also facilitate change. This emphasis on process seems to reflect the political reality that agreed outcomes are difficult to reach in divided societies, but that some necessary flexibility is offered by ongoing patterns of deliberation, discussion and participation involving the norms of constitutionalism and democracy. The first task of the theorist in engaging with this radical democratic project is not simply to observe this new fluidity but to investigate its "critical potential" and its capacity to aid individuals and groups struggling for recognition and inclusion in the public sphere. A second task is to resist the danger that process-based constitutionalism will be captured and neutered by constitutional elites. The principle of democracy referred to by the Supreme Court in the *Secession Reference* seems to reflect a more process-based approach to constitutionalism along the lines observed by Tully. For example, in the scenario of Quebec's journey toward possible secession, the referendum provides the constitutional momentum for the initiation of a process of constitutional change through negotiation. By this plebiscitary device, the democratic will of "the people" is expressed directly and not through elected representatives. In this sense it becomes an organic, legitimizing device that creates the democratic imperative for the activation of the process of constitutional change.

Not surprisingly, the federal government and commentators who share the federalist position have preferred, in reading the Supreme Court of Canada's decision, to focus upon the Court's references to constitutionalism and the rule of law rather than the references to democracy. In particular, they stress that the constitution remains important even in the negotiation process. Therefore, the principle of democracy invoked through a referendum in Quebec may create a duty to negotiate change, but this process of negotiation will take place within the confines of the constitution, and parties to the negotiations must each act in accordance with all four of the constitutional principles to which the Court referred.[55] The essence of this "federalist" reading of the decision is that the democratic principle must be seen as a constitutional principle, enunciated as part of the constitution and not competing with it as a rival source of legitimacy or authority.[56] Therefore, the obligation that flows from it – that is, the duty to negotiate – is also essentially a constitutional duty and one that will both be regulated by the constitution and apply to all parties. A consequence of the duty to negotiate, applying to all sides, is that the negotiation process must be a genuine one and not simply a rubber stamp of Quebec's aspirations.[57]

Even in this federalist reading, however, there is recognition that new ground is being broken, that the Supreme Court is taking an expansive approach to the constitution to meet extraordinary circumstances and that the Supreme Court's decision recognizes that a legitimate path towards constitutional change may begin with the referendum process.[58] Warren Newman notes the Supreme Court's position that democracy cannot be called upon to trump the other constitutional principles. At the same time, however, he cites with approval the Court's position that the Canadian constitutional order cannot remain indifferent to the clear expression of a clear majority of Quebecers that they no longer wish to remain in Canada: "Otherwise, this would mean that the other constitutional principles necessarily trump the clearly expressed democratic will of Quebecers."[59] It seems, therefore, that Newman approves both the way in which the Supreme Court has to some extent risen above a technical reading of the constitution and its radical suggestion that political legitimacy is now a necessary concomitant of constitutional legality.[60] Newman's "constitutional" reading of the decision certainly suggests that even though the Supreme Court has opened the door onto a constitutional path to secession, the process that the

Court requires to be followed makes this radical step acceptable to federalists. The Supreme Court, he argues, has welcomed sovereigntists "back into the fold." All political causes are valid "so long as that cause and those who propound it respect the legal framework and basic constitutional values that govern the making of political choices in a free and democratic society like ours."[61] Therefore, accommodation within the constitution can even stretch to secession if the rules are followed.

What seems to come out of the different readings of the decision offered by commentators such as Tully and Newman is a shared focus on the way in which the decision, whilst weaving together a series of constitutional principles in a complex way, concludes that none outbids any other or, to put it another way (borrowing an expression used by James Tully in a different but related context), that these important constitutional values are "equiprimordial."[62] The Supreme Court's assertion of the enduring authority of the constitution need not be cast as constitutionalism trumping democracy; the interconnection between the two principles is far more complex than this. The Canadian constitution is a democratic organism, and in large part its popular authority derives from the implicit recognition of its democratic validity, a validity that can be reinforced through the self-affirming vitality of an accessible amendment process. Central to the constitution are values and underlying principles of which a central one, recognized by the Supreme Court itself, is democracy. In a sense what the Court is saying is not that the formal constitutional text overrides popular sovereignty but rather that the constitution must be able to adjust to accommodate popular sovereignty in order to replenish its own legitimacy as a responsive and democratic instrument. In this process of adjustment it should be guided by universal principles that are themselves enshrined within the constitution, and it should respond positively to specific claims made from the perspective of democratic legitimacy whilst remaining mindful of the other interests at stake within the constitutional framework and the range of norms that must inform and guide the process of change.

The *Secession Reference* and Self-Determination

Having discussed how the issue at stake in the *Secession Reference* has been posited as a struggle between the competing principles of democracy and constitutionalism, we can consider whether the Supreme Court, in finding that in certain circumstances the rest of Canada may have a duty to negotiate Quebec's secession, brings into play an additional principle, namely self-determination. We can also consider whether this principle must be seen as an implicit value of the Canadian constitution, together with the explicitly articulated principles of democracy and constitutionalism (and indeed federalism and the rights of minorities), if the Court's construction of the rest of Canada's duty to negotiate secession is to be fully understood.

By holding a referendum on sovereignty, Quebec was in fact putting forward the specific democratic will of a self-ascribed, self-determining unit in contradistinction to both the notion of democracy in the abstract and the competing principle of the popular sovereignty of the whole people of the Canadian state. As such, the Quebec position is more accurately categorized, as it often has been, as a self-determination claim than as a democratic claim. Of course, to describe Quebec's claim as one of self-determination is not to say that it is *un*democratic – indeed far from it – but to recognize that, at least in legal terms, there is a notable distinction between the principles of democracy and self-determination. As the international lawyer Thomas Franck observes, "self-determination is not an early version of democracy...While democracy invokes the right of each person to participate in governance, self-determination is about the social right of a people to constitute a nation state."[63] In other words, as a self-determination claim, the Quebec government's position is not that the people of Quebec are entitled to participate in a democratic form of governance (this right, the right to "internal" self-determination, they already have within Canada) but that Quebec as a people possesses the right to trump the immanent authority claimed by the democratic constitutional order to which Quebec belongs, even to the extent of effecting secession. This issue remains important in terms of the prospects for success of any future negotiation process, because it appears that both sides could enter such a process with very different attitudes to what the purpose of the negotiations should be. I will return to this issue below, but for now the crucial question is whether the Supreme Court in the *Secession Reference* was in any way open to Quebec's self-determination claim.

The starting point is perhaps the Supreme Court's explanation of why, in reference to the principle of constitutionalism, unilateral secession through a majority vote in a province-wide referendum is not by itself enough to effect secession. The Court noted that it is superficially persuasive that "the notion of popular sovereignty underlies the legitimacy of our existing constitutional arrangements, so the same popular sovereignty that originally led to the present Constitution must (it is argued) also permit 'the people' in their exercise of popular sovereignty to secede by majority vote alone."[64] But this is unsound. The Canadian system is not one of simple majority rule: "Constitutional government is necessarily predicated on the idea that the political representatives of the people of a province have the capacity and the power to commit the province to be bound into the future by the constitutional rules being adopted."[65] However, the notion that the commitments of earlier generations predetermine a province's destiny is qualified, since a province can press for changes within the federal system and the constitutional rules can be amended "through a process of negotiation which ensures that there is an opportunity for the constitutionally defined rights of all the parties to be respected and reconciled."[66] Furthermore, a requirement that constitutional change may be effected only by super-majority consent is not incompatible with democracy. Through the power of constitutional amendment "our belief in democracy may be harmonized with our belief in constitutionalism."[67] As the Court continues: "Constitutionalism facilitates – indeed, makes possible – a democratic political system by creating an orderly framework within which people may make political decisions. Viewed correctly, constitutionalism and the rule of law are not in conflict with democracy; rather, they are essential to it."[68]

The question remains, however, how can the Supreme Court move from a province's power to initiate a process of constitutional amendment (which is important in terms of the principles of democracy and federalism) to what seems to be an endorsement of Quebec's right to secede (albeit following negotiations)? Or, put another way, how does the Supreme Court, in balancing democracy and constitutionalism, and indeed the other two foundational principles it finds within the constitution, arrive at a duty on the rest of Canada to negotiate the secession of Quebec?

Before exploring this issue we may pause to consider how the Supreme Court dealt with the federal government's first question and whether it addressed it fully. This question, it will be recalled, hinged on whether Quebec could, under the Canadian constitution, secede *unilaterally*. In defining secession, the Court adopts a narrow meaning of the term "unilateral":

> In one sense, any step towards a constitutional amendment initiated by a single actor on the constitutional stage is "unilateral." We do not believe that this is the meaning contemplated by Question 1, nor is this the sense in which the term has been used in argument before us. Rather, what is claimed by a right to secede "unilaterally" is the right to effectuate secession without prior negotiations with the other provinces and the federal government. At issue is not the legality of the first step but the legality of the final act of purported unilateral secession.[69]

This suggests that Quebec is permitted to propose a constitutional amendment. But if all Quebec was being offered by the Supreme Court was the right to ask the rest of Canada to amend the constitution in order to allow Quebec to secede, at which point the rest of Canada could say "no," Quebec would be receiving nothing new, except perhaps a fast-track process by which to propose constitutional amendments. It seems, however, that the novelty of the decision rests in the fact that the Supreme Court goes further than this; that it is recognizing a prima facie right to secede that the rest of Canada may not frustrate provided Quebec negotiates the details of that secession in good faith. This reading of the opinion seems to lie behind Peter Hogg's view that the duty to negotiate secession is a "stunningly new element" added to Canadian constitutional law.[70] If so, then it may be argued that this right is not very far from being a right to secede unilaterally, albeit a right that is qualified by the duty to negotiate the practicalities of separation. In other words, if Quebec gets a clear majority on a clear question and is prepared to negotiate, then the rest of Canada has no right to refuse the principle of secession. It can negotiate only the method of that secession – and this, after all, is a normal, practical step in any agreed secession.[71] Indeed, in the postwar process of African and Asian decolonization, in which self-determination was unequivocally a unilateral right under international law, the process followed by many nascent states was not dissimilar to this. Therefore we might ask two further questions. First, is the Supreme Court really offering Quebec a prima facie right (albeit a qualified one) of unilateral secession? Second and concomitantly, if such a right does now exist, why is that the case and, in particular, why is the rest of Canada expected, under the constitution, to accede to secession in the course of those negotiations?

Turning to the first of these questions, although the Court says, "Quebec could not purport to invoke a right of self-determination such as to dictate the terms of a proposed secession to the other parties: that would not be a negotiation at all,"[72] it qualifies this considerably: "we are equally unable to accept the reverse proposition, that a clear expression of self-determination by the people of Quebec would impose no obligations upon the other provinces or the federal government. The continued existence and operation of the Canadian constitutional order cannot remain indifferent to the clear expression of a clear majority of Quebecers that they no longer wish to remain in Canada."[73] Such indifference "would amount to the assertion that other constitutionally recognized principles necessarily trump the clearly expressed democratic will of the people of Quebec."[74] It seems clear that Quebec has a right to secede, albeit following negotiations (which the other provinces and the federal government have a duty to enter into) if a clear answer to a clear question is achieved in the preceding referendum. "The clear repudiation by the people of Quebec of the existing constitutional order would confer legitimacy on demands for secession."[75]

The second question following from the conclusion that Quebec seems to have a prima facie right to secede is why this is the case, and why in particular is the rest of Canada expected to accede to Quebec's secession in the course of negotiations. Earlier in the paper three possible reasons were suggested for the Court's articulation of this duty to negotiate secession. Here I will elaborate on the third of these, namely Quebec's distinctiveness, which seems somehow to entitle it to a form of self-determination. This is of particular relevance because it is on this issue that the Supreme Court of Canada seems to grapple with national diversity within the Canadian federation. The principles of democracy and federalism are applied by the Court in building both Quebec's right to initiate secession and the rest of Canada's duty to negotiate it in the event of clear majority support based on a clear question. But are these two principles sufficient in themselves to construct both this right and this duty? It seems that, in order to understand how the Court arrives at this right and this duty, the crucial phrase in its opinion is the "clear expression of self-determination by the people of Quebec." If Quebec's claim of a right to move toward sovereignty through negotiations is seen only as a "democratic" claim and not, more specifically, as one of self-determination, then why, for example, should it trump the democratic right of a majority of Canadians to resist either, at the very least, negotiations or secession at the end of these negotiations (which it seems to do if Quebec negotiates in good faith)?[76] After all, the principle of democracy must apply to the whole of Canada as much as to Quebec. As the Supreme Court says: "No one majority is more or less 'legitimate' than the others as an expression of democratic opinion...Canada as a whole is also a democratic community in which citizens construct and achieve goals on a national scale through a federal government acting within the limits of its jurisdiction."[77] Furthermore, constitutionalism surely weighs into the debate on the side of the territorial integrity of the state should a majority in the whole country reaffirm, in a democratic way, their commitment to it. Linked to this is the Court's recognition that "[t]he Constitution is the expression of the sovereignty of the people of Canada."[78] Therefore, if this duty to negotiate secession is to be analyzed only through the prism of democracy, it seems that the Supreme Court is, first, elevating one particular application of the principle of democracy over other applications and, second, according priority to democracy over the other principles within the constitution, something that it said cannot be done.

To reiterate, and to recall Peter Hogg's comment about dismembering the country,[79] it is difficult to see how the principle of democracy, even when coupled with the principle of federalism, imposes upon a sovereign people the duty to negotiate the secession of a territorial subunit.[80] A majority vote in a referendum in Quebec may well "confer legitimacy on the efforts of the government of Quebec to initiate the Constitution's amendment process in order to secede by constitutional means,"[81] but presumably a democratic expression of resistance to Quebec's secession in other provinces would confer equal legitimacy on provincial governments to oppose such an amendment. It seems, however, that such opposition to the principle of secession is a right that the other provinces are denied, provided Quebec negotiates in good faith: "The rights of other provinces and the federal government cannot deny the right of the government of Quebec to pursue secession, should a clear majority of the people of Quebec choose that goal, so long as in doing so, Quebec respects the rights of others."[82] Quebec's right to secede, therefore, seems to override the right of the "sovereign" people of Canada to preserve the country's territorial integrity even if a democratic commitment to the state's boundaries is endorsed overwhelmingly by a majority of the Canadian people.[83]

This brings us back to the idea that "no one majority is more or less 'legitimate' than the others." The Supreme Court suggests that the negotiation process "would require the reconciliation of various rights and obligations by the representatives of two legitimate majorities, namely, the clear majority of the population of Quebec, and the clear majority of Canada as a whole, whatever that may be. There can be no suggestion that either of these majorities 'trumps' the other."[84] But surely a party that has a prima facie right to secede before the negotiations begin has already trumped the other on the core issue? For good measure, the Supreme Court even discusses the issue of state recognition with a thinly veiled threat of international embarrassment for the rest of Canada if it fails to co-operate with Quebec's quest for secession: "a Quebec that had negotiated in conformity with constitutional principles and values in the face of unreasonable intransigence on the part of other participants at the federal or provincial level would be more likely to be recognized than a Quebec which did not itself act according to constitutional principles in the negotiation process."[85] Although this is also a warning to Quebec to negotiate in good faith, the novel implication of the Court's logic is that if it does negotiate in this way, Quebec is entitled to secede.

It is, therefore, difficult to see how the self-determination element within Quebec's right to secede through negotiation can be addressed simply as the natural extension of the democratic principle. If democracy, or one particular manifestation of it, popular sovereignty, is used to entitle secession from a prevailing constitutional order, it must first be asked which group of people is claiming this power, upon what basis, and what it is that makes this particular substate group a viable self-determining unit. The Supreme Court has said that the people of Canada are sovereign, but in concluding that no one majority is more or less legitimate than the others, and that a majority in Quebec can call upon the rest of Canada to negotiate secession, the Supreme Court is also suggesting that at a fundamental level Quebec also is sovereign, provided that the exercise of this sovereignty leading to secession is endorsed clearly by the Quebec population and involves bona fide negotiations with Quebec's partners in the Canadian confederation.[86]

This decision may be seen as a genuine and imaginative attempt to recognize Quebec's distinctiveness within the Canadian constitution, but it nevertheless begs the question whether it came too late to save a federation that has lost the faith of many Quebecers.[87] Although a commitment to democracy and to other values may open a genuine negotiation process, the fundamental disagreement on the nature of sovereignty, and ultimately on the question of where the last word on the settlement of constitutional issues lies, may be the undoing of any such process.[88] Constitutional negotiations require the initial will on both sides to work toward an agreed polity. If this is lacking, then the negotiations are not "constitutional" at all, and the issue becomes one not of democracy against constitutionalism but of self-determination opposed to the territorial integrity of the existing state. In this scenario, no matter how fluid and accommodating a constitutional structure might be, if it does not at a fundamental level represent a territorially bounded society to which all sides feel a commitment or a desire to belong, then it becomes clear that the dissident group is seeking not the power to express a radical constitutional voice of dissent but the capacity to procure its exit from the state. By taking part in negotiations this group is not attempting a popular reclamation of its role within the polity but offering a courteous farewell before heading for the door – a political and not a legal act, as the Supreme Court has recognized.

UK Devolution, Sovereignty and the Courts

UK Courts and Constitutional Change

The ways in which the recent and, indeed, ongoing process of constitutional reform in the UK promises a prominent role for the courts were introduced above, and in this part of the paper I address how even in this early period of reform the courts have begun to articulate their vision of the devolution settlement in Scotland. It would be premature to read too much into these early cases since no dramatic decisions similar to the *Secession Reference* have been handed down, but it is possible that they portend more dramatic developments in the future. Whether UK courts will develop the imagination displayed by the Canadian Supreme Court remains to be seen.

Judges in both Scotland and England are now faced with the difficult task of attempting to reach an appropriate balance between activism and restraint in the task of constitutional adjudication. Given that the *Scotland Act* 1998 effectively rewrites major areas of the UK's constitution and that it contains a significant number of open-ended provisions that invite judicial elaboration, greater involvement by judges in what have traditionally been seen as political aspects of the constitution is perhaps inevitable. As such, eyes are already being

cast toward Canada and other jurisdictions given that there are important provisions within the *Scotland Act* that will require the courts to consider the purpose of the devolution settlement as a whole.[89] For example, cases will arise
involving questions of *vires* and the limits of devolved competence, and in the
course of these disputes, arguments will be presented that ask the courts to go
beyond the literal meaning of the statute to consider the fundamental constitutional parameters within which the act as a whole operates and through which
it interacts with other seminal pieces of legislation (most obviously the *Human
Rights Act* 1998).[90] At the heart of these disputes, differing visions of what the
entire devolution project seeks to achieve may emerge, and this will consequently draw the courts into implicit, or indeed explicit, renderings of what
they understand to be the guiding norms of the new relationship the *Scotland
Act* is carving out between Edinburgh and Westminster. Questions of this type
also beset the Canadian Supreme Court in the *Secession Reference*, and it is not
inconceivable that a Scottish court or the Judicial Committee of the Privy
Council (which is vested with the task of adjudicating competence disputes)
will embark upon an articulation of underlying norms in a way similar to that
of the Supreme Court in the *Secession Reference*.

Differing Visions of the *Scotland Act*

On one level the *Scotland Act* can be understood as just another Westminster
statute that, by the doctrine of parliamentary sovereignty, can be repealed or
amended as easily as any other. There are, however, two doctrines that emerge
from Scotland's constitutional tradition – one historical and one modern – that
take issue with the monolithic power of parliamentary sovereignty, at least
insofar as it applies to Scotland. The first is the contention that a distinctive
constitutional tradition in Scotland survived the Union of 1707, a suggestion
that has been hinted at from time to time by the Scottish courts.[91] The feeling
in certain quarters was that the *Scotland Act* provided an opportunity to revitalize this tradition. Second, from the mid-1980s onward, a popular movement
for Scottish self-government gathered momentum that largely eschewed any
search for an indigenous praxis stemming from Scotland's pre-1707 constitutional arrangements and that instead propagated an essentially political vision
of sovereignty. This movement argued plainly that the Scottish people were
entitled to self-government by political right, a claim advanced by national
minorities in numerous countries, not least in Canada.

Turning to the first doctrine, certainly the Scottish courts have, on occasion,
suggested that the Scottish legal system preserves a different constitutional tradition that accredits higher status to the Acts of Union than to ordinary legislation, and they have thereby insinuated that Parliament itself may be bound by

some of their more important terms. The dictum of Lord President Cooper in *MacCormick v Lord Advocate* is the most widely cited statement of this view:

> The principle of the unlimited sovereignty of Parliament is a distinctively English principle which has no counterpart in Scottish Constitutional Law...Considering that the Union legislation extinguished the Parliaments of Scotland and England and replaced them by a new Parliament, I have difficulty in seeing why it should be supposed that the new Parliament of Great Britain must inherit all the peculiar characteristics of the English Parliament but none of the Scottish Parliament, as if all that happened was that Scottish representatives were admitted to the Parliament of England. This is not what was done.[92]

There have, however, been few such glimpses of a different and enduring Scottish tradition,[93] leading some to argue that the Acts of Union do not survive in any real legal sense as fundamental constitutional texts. This is particularly so given the numerous repeals and modifications to which they have been subjected,[94] not the least of which is section 37 of the *Scotland Act*, which provides that the two Acts of Union are to "have effect subject to this Act."

The more relevant and seemingly more important doctrine is that of popular sovereignty. The impetus for constitutional reform in the modern era began in earnest with the Campaign for a Scottish Assembly, which was launched in 1985. In 1988 it issued the Claim of Right for Scotland, which was drafted by a committee appointed by the Campaign for a Scottish Assembly and which, in declaring the right of Scotland to self-government, had as its main thrust the claim that sovereignty in Scotland rests with the Scottish people. The Claim of Right called for a Scottish Constitutional Convention, which was subsequently established (meeting for the first time in 1989) and vested with the task of drawing up proposals for home rule. With the legitimacy it enjoyed amongst Scotland's political elite, involving *inter alia* the Labour and Liberal Democratic parties, local authorities, churches and the Scottish Trades Union Congress, the Scottish Constitutional Convention acquired a high media profile that was reflected in the publicity attracted by its most important publication, "Scotland's Claim, Scotland's Right."[95] This set out a detailed blueprint for devolution remarkably similar to the model eventually enacted through the *Scotland Act*. What is particularly interesting about this document (bearing in mind the strong involvement of the Scottish Labour Party in the Scottish Constitutional Convention) is that the Convention shared the earlier commitment of the Campaign for a Scottish Assembly to the idea of popular sovereignty. As the Scottish Constitutional Convention declared, "we, gathered as the

Scottish Constitutional Convention, do hereby acknowledge the sovereign right of the Scottish people to determine the form of Government best suited to their needs..."[96]

So far, the courts have not been confronted by any major issues equivalent to the *Secession Reference*. The only glimpse so far of the judicial approach to the broader issues in devolution has been the case of *Whaley*,[97] where the Court of Session (Scotland's main civil court) was asked to examine the privileges of the Scottish Parliament. In the course of this case Scotland's most senior judge (Lord Rodger, the Lord President) took the opportunity to discuss the constitutional status of the Scottish Parliament. The issue that arose here was the status of the Parliament vis-à-vis Westminster. According to the distinguished English constitutional writer A.V. Dicey, this doctrine is possessed of both a positive and a negative aspect. In a positive sense Parliament has the power to make or unmake any law, and in the negative sense no other body can make law.[98] But as we have seen, this doctrine was contested in the *MacCormick* case. The issue now is whether or not the idea of Scottish popular sovereignty will also be pressed into service in order partially to revive the seemingly obsolete historical Scottish constitutional tradition. This will remain uncertain until the UK Parliament legislates on a devolved matter without the consent of the Scottish Parliament. For now, this case at least offers some insight into judicial perceptions of the Scottish Parliament's status. Here Lord Rodger took the view that the Scottish Parliament is a creature of Westminster statute:

> As such, it is a body which, like any other statutory body, must work within the scope of those powers. If it does not do so, then in an appropriate case the court may be asked to intervene and will require to do so, in a manner permitted by the legislation. In principle, therefore, the Parliament like any other body set up by law is subject to the law and to the courts which exist to uphold that law.[99]

This seems to be a fairly straightforward reaffirmation of Dicean orthodoxy, whereby the Scottish Parliament is envisaged as just another creation of Westminster, to which it is beholden for its authority and by which that authority might be removed. Although the Lord President referred to the Scottish Parliament as a creature of statute like any other statutory body, he went on to note that it was entirely normal for a legislature to be subject to the law of the land and to the jurisdiction of the courts. Lord Prosser (also sitting on the court) agreed, stating that a limited parliament is an obvious feature of the rule of law: "a defined parliament is there to do not whatever it wants, but only what the law has empowered it to do."[100] This is followed by what seems like a reference to the anachronistic nature of the UK's traditional arrangements as Lord Prosser contrasts such a limited legislature with "the odd, and perhaps unsatisfactory, context of 'sovereign' or undefined powers."[101] Therefore, although confirming the limited nature of the Scottish Parliament's powers, Lord Prosser is suggesting that the notion of a limited parliament is a general principle that ought to apply to all legislatures. Lord Rodger also observed that the relationship between the Westminster Parliament and the courts was somewhat peculiar and that Westminster sovereignty was under attack from a different direction – that is, from the UK's membership in the European Communities.[102]

There is no suggestion that the *Scotland Act* makes further inroads into that sovereignty, but Lord Rodger does contextualize the Scottish Parliament in terms of Commonwealth legislatures that have made such inroads: "in many democracies throughout the Commonwealth, for example, even where the parliaments have been modelled in some respects on Westminster, they owe their existence and powers to statute and are in various ways subject to the law and to the courts which act to uphold the law. The Scottish Parliament has simply joined that wider family of parliaments."[103] It would be unwise to read too much into these comments, but they do offer a less than whole-hearted affirmation of Westminster sovereignty. Only in the event of a serious competence dispute between Edinburgh and Westminster (for example, the types of dispute that might arise should the Scottish National Party ever form a government in Scotland) will these rival constitutional stories be put to the test before not only the Scottish courts but also the Judicial Committee of the Privy Council, now the final word on competence disputes in terms of the *Scotland Act* 1998.

Concluding Remarks: Autonomy Disputes and the Judicial Safety Valve

The Supreme Court of Canada's decision in the *Secession Reference* offers many lessons in how courts can play a role in mediating diversity in multinational states with new levels of imagination and with reliance on unwritten constitutional norms as well as upon literal constitutional text. One initial lesson is to be found quite simply in the structure of the decision, where several things are immediately noticeable. The first is that it was unanimous. The Canadian Supreme Court generally endeavours to achieve unanimity in important constitutional cases, and it was especially important to make clear that the *Secession Reference* decision was a collective judgment of the whole court in circumstances where such radically new ground was being broken. Furthermore, previous important constitutional decisions have been rendered by one Justice with the concurrence of the others.[104] The *Secession Reference*, however, was rendered in the name of "THE COURT." Both of these features can be contrasted with the *Whaley* case in Scotland, where judgment was delivered by individual judges and which resulted in a split decision.[105] Another aspect of the *Secession Reference* decision's unanimity is that it was of course shared by English- and French-speaking judges. The issue of "national composition" of the bench is now an issue also in the UK through the Judicial Committee of the Privy Council, with observers paying close attention to the number of Scots judges involved in Privy Council decisions where "devolution issues" are raised.[106] A final structural point that can be made concerning the *Secession Reference* decision is that it seems to have been aimed at the citizens of Canada and not simply at the two governments or at legal experts.[107] This, then, is perhaps another example of the Supreme Court's attempt to draw on the democratic principle, with the implicit message that the constitution belongs to the people. As such, the symbol is perhaps one that nods toward popular sovereignty and in doing so reflects the substance of the decision itself, with its heavy reliance on democracy and on the legitimacy that democracy lends to constitutional structures and processes. The Supreme Court seems keen to ensure that citizens will have the chance to validate this decision *ex post facto* or at least to engage fully with it.

At the beginning of this paper it was suggested that the *Secession Reference* decision was important not only for the credibility of the Canadian constitution but also in terms of whether or not the Supreme Court could revive its own credibility in Quebec. In this respect the decision has met with considerable approval. Robert Young, for example, suggests that the first "and possibly most important" effect of the decision was that it "preserved the legitimacy of the Supreme Court itself. There was nothing in it that could be used to provoke a sense of humiliation or rejection in Quebec that could be directed against the court's authority."[108] Of course, there is still much work to be done. Turning to its future role, the Supreme Court observed that many of the issues that would surround negotiations are political, which is itself a recognition of the complexities and specific peculiarities that would attend any future negotiation process, with the Court surely mindful of the failed constitutional negotiations of the Meech Lake and Charlottetown years.[109] The Court is also aware that its constitutional role is not played out in a political vacuum and that ultimately there is a limited role for any court when the issue of secession "goes live," as it were. That is not to say that the Supreme Court has abdicated any possible future role for the judiciary in this area: "the nonjusticiability of political issues that lack a legal component does not deprive the surrounding constitutional framework of its binding status, nor does this mean that constitutional obligations could be breached without incurring serious legal repercussions."[110] This will become relevant in the event that Quebec once again embarks on the referendum process – that is, on the process of "initiating constitutional change," as the Court would have it. This could result in renewed tension if the Supreme Court again attempts to reassert the authority of the constitution and its own judicial *Kompetenz-Kompetenz* to provide the authentic rendition of constitutional meaning in terms of establishing a constitutional path to legitimate separation. For now, the *Secession Reference* represents closure on one stage of judicial deliberation on the secession issue, and as such it may be seen as a wake-up call to political actors in both Quebec and the rest of Canada to address the issue in a realistic manner and with an eye to the bigger picture. As Kenneth McRoberts puts it: "through the carefully constructed and balanced positions it did take, the court has transformed the terms of public debate over Quebec sovereignty, cutting through the posturing and pretence and focusing all sides on the central questions at hand. By restoring to its proper place the best of Canada's political tradition, the court provided a leadership that had been wanting among political and intellectual elites alike."[111]

In the UK much will also depend upon the capacity of judges to defuse political disputes and to prevent the courts from becoming an alternative for the playing out of political disagreements. As such it may also be anticipated that involvement of the courts will weaken the influence of simplistic political sloganeering on the issue of sovereignty, forcing all actors, including the electorate, to appreciate that what is involved in a modern, decentralized multinational democracy is a complex relationship wherein powers are shared between the centre and substate nations in often mutually beneficial ways, and where diversity needs to be mediated and negotiated through various institutional mechanisms. The greater role that the *Scotland Act* promises for the judiciary might in fact offer renewed legitimacy to the ongoing work of reshaping the Union by depoliticizing constitutional processes, provided an imaginative approach is adopted by judges similar to that taken by the Supreme Court of Canada in the *Quebec Secession Reference*. If the courts can achieve this, they may provide breathing space for the development of a more mature constitutional discourse and with it a more co-operative approach to constitutional coexistence than has hitherto prevailed.

Notes

1. Michael Keating has recently used the term "plurinational democracies," which he distinguishes in a nuanced way from "multinational democracies": "in order to express the plurality not merely of nations, but of conceptions of nationality itself" (2001, p. x). In this paper plurinational and multinational are used interchangeably.

2. *Reference re Secession of Quebec* [1998] 2 SCR 217 (hereafter the *Secession Reference*).

3. McRoberts (2001).

4. Dworkin (1996, p. 31).

5. As the international lawyer Martti Koskenniemi puts it, alluding to a difference between the politicized process of law creation and the possibility thereafter of finding some objective interpretation of what the law is: "As a matter of legislation, law is subjective, as a matter of adjudication, objective" (1991, p. 4).

6. Such a hard and fast distinction is of course not always achievable, and the questioning of law's credibility in subjective and objective ways often elide.

7. Harlow (2000), Monahan (1999).

8. Harlow (2000, p. 366). In the UK in recent years a number of prominent judges have argued that judges should be more aware of and engage more fully with the politically contextualized nature of adjudication. See, for example, Browne-Wilkinson (1992), Sedley (1995), Hope (1998), Bingham (2000).

9. John Marshall (1788) attrib.

10. Kymlicka (1995), Kymlicka (2001), Tamir (1993). See also Margalit and Raz (1990).

11. The Supreme Court has been criticized for what is perceived to be its "federalist" predisposition through which Quebec has been disadvantaged. Mandel (1999, p. 3). See also LaForest (1999).

12. *London Free Press*, September 2, 1995, cited by Young (1999, p. 106). On this issue see also Young (1999, p. 146).

13. This term used in the context of the European Union means literally "the competence of its competence"; in other words, the competence of a body to determine the limits, if any, of its own competence. This concept goes to the heart of the evolving relationship between the enduring sovereignty of member states and the new legal order of the European Union, which asserts its own supremacy in areas of EU competence. MacCormick (1999).

14. Section 52(1) of the *Constitution Act, 1982* provides that "[t]he Constitution of Canada is the supreme law of Canada, and any law that is inconsistent with the provisions of the Constitution is, to the extent of the inconsistency, of no force or effect."

15. Cited by Bayefsky (2000, p. 12).

16. *Bertrand c Bégin* (1995) RJQ 2500 (C.S.), translated as *Bertrand v Quebec* (1995), 127 DLR (4th) 408 (Que. SC) at 424-5.

17. Cited by Bayefsky (2000, p. 11). Notably, the federal government claimed that the purpose of its intervention was not to support the positions of either Messrs. Bertrand or Roopnarine Singh (who initiated an action similar to Bertrand's) but to challenge the Quebec position that these issues were nonjusticiable: The Hon. Allan Rock, House of Commons, *Debates*, May 3, 1996, vol. 134, no. 39, at p 2306.

18. A survey in the *Globe and Mail* published on February 21, 1998, suggested that a large majority of Quebecers felt that they should have the right to choose secession without the rules being set by the Supreme Court.

19. The term "substate nation" seems to apply at least to Scotland and Wales. The situation in Northern Ireland is more complex, with an Irish national minority that feels culturally and politically linked to the Irish state and another minority (which constitutes a majority in Northern Ireland) that sees itself as either British or specifically Northern Irish.

20. *Reference re Objection to a Resolution to Amend the Constitution of Canada* [1982] 2 SCR 793.

21. Oliver (2000, p. 75).

22. In the *Veto Reference* the Supreme Court confirmed the position taken in the *Patriation Reference* (*Reference re Amendment of the Constitution of Canada* [1981] 1 SCR 753), where it had decided that, by constitutional convention, fundamental constitutional change of this kind required the consent of a substantial number of Canada's 10 provinces. Despite Quebec's rejection of proposals then drawn up by the federal government and the other provinces, the Supreme Court felt able to confirm, on the basis of the "substantial number" rule, that these changes were valid.

23. Mandel (1999, p. 2).

24. Oliver (1999, p. 552).

25. *Reference re Objection to a Resolution to Amend the Constitution of Canada* [1982] 2 SCR 793 at 806.

26. *Secession Reference*, para. 32.

27. The preamble to the *Constitution Act*, 1867 stated that the new Dominion was to have "a Constitution similar in Principle to that of the United Kingdom." See also *Secession Reference*, para. 63.

28. In the *Senate Reference* (*Reference re Authority of Parliament in Relation to the Upper House* [1980] 2 SCR 54), the Supreme Court of Canada held that fundamental constitutional change had to be accomplished via the United Kingdom Parliament, since Westminster was the source of origin of Canada's essential constitutional texts. With regard to the *Patriation Reference*, Peter Oliver notes: "the Patriation Reference had confirmed that, as a matter of law, the United Kingdom Parliament's powers vis-à-vis Canada were undiminished" (2000, p. 69, n. 3). See also Oliver (1994). As the Supreme Court noted in the *Secession Reference*, this influence was, however, largely formulaic. At least since 1931 (*Statute of Westminster, 1931* [U.K.], 22 & 23 Geo. 5, c. 4) and perhaps since 1926 (the Balfour Declaration), "Canadian law alone governed in Canada, except where Canada expressly consented to the continued application of Imperial legislation...The proclamation of the Constitution Act, 1982 removed the last vestige of British authority over the Canadian Constitution" (*Secession Reference*, para. 46). Furthermore, the nature of the Canadian constitution has in the past 20 years changed dramatically. As a result of the adoption of the Canadian Charter of Rights and Freedoms, the Canadian system of government has been, in the words of the Supreme Court, "transformed to a significant extent from a system of parliamentary supremacy to one of constitutional supremacy" (*Secession Reference*, para. 72).

29. *Secession Reference*, para. 32, and para. 49 where the Supreme Court states "our Constitution is *primarily* a written one" [emphasis added].

30. As Gordon F. Gibson notes, "the court delivered a great deal more than it was asked to" (1999, p. 1).

31. McRoberts (1999, p. 2).

32. These questions were partly based upon issues set out by Mr. Justice Pidgeon in his decision. *Bertrand v Bégin* et al. (1996) 138 DLR (4th) 481 at 507-8.

33. Notably, the *amicus curiae* immediately questioned the Supreme Court's reference jurisdiction. Dodge (1999, p. 296).

34. *Patriation Reference*, p.874, cited by the Supreme Court in the *Secession Reference* at para. 32.

35. *Secession Reference*, para. 32.

36. Noticeably constitutionalism and the rule of law run together: "Simply put, the constitutionalism principle requires that all government action comply with the Constitution. The rule of law principle requires that all government action must comply with the law, including the Constitution" (*Secession Reference*, para. 72). On this basis, Kenneth McRoberts views the latter as the most important manifestation of the former (1999, p. 3).

37. *Secession Reference*, para. 49. The Court proceeded to discuss these principles and the ways in which they overlap.

38. *Secession Reference*, paras. 88 and 149.

39. *Secession Reference*, para. 84.

40. *Secession Reference*, para. 105. This is criticized by Mandel (1999, p. 1). Later in the paper we will return to the continuing uncertainty surrounding both the initiation and the process of any future negotiations.

41. Gibson (1999, p. 4).

42. Hogg (1999, p. 3).

43. There is even uncertainty as to who can participate in negotiations and what their respective rights and powers would be. See Joffe (1999, p. 3).

44. Hogg (1999, p. 3). John Whyte also queries the provenance of this duty and the Supreme Court's definition of "democracy" itself: "The court pulled the duty to negotiate out of rarefied air. There is nothing in the democratic principle that gives it a trumping effect over other more fundamental constitutional ideas. In fact, the court embraces an extremely simple or direct form of democratic expression over the multilayered understandings of democracy that are actually required to coordinate the democratic principle with constitutionalism" (1999, p. 3).

45. *Secession Reference*, para. 54.

46. Hogg (1999, p. 4).

47. *Secession Reference*, para. 59.

48. Greschner (1999, pp. 2-3).

49. The 1987 Meech Lake Accord was intended to lead to amendments to the constitution. The accord, which in the end failed to secure the ratification of all 10 provinces, described Quebec as a "distinct society" within Canada.

50. Le Clair (1999, p. 1).

51. "External" self-determination means, in effect, the right of a people to secede, as opposed to the weaker form of self-determination ("internal" self-determination), which is essentially an individual right to a representative form of government within one's existing state.

52. *Secession Reference*, para. 33.

53. *Secession Reference*, para. 78.

54. Tully (2001).

55. "The conduct of the parties in such negotiations would be governed by the same constitutional principles that give rise to the duty to negotiate: federalism, democracy, constitutionalism and the rule of law, and the protection of minorities" (*Secession Reference*, para 90). See also Newman (1999, p. 95).

56. Commentators like Newman would also argue that the written constitution comes first in terms of normative hierarchy, with unwritten principles coming into play in an ancillary way. For example, he cites with approval a decision rendered shortly after the *Secession Reference* in which a federal judge stated: "nothing in that case [the *Secession Reference*] supports the proposition that a court may ignore the express and unequivocal provisions of the *Constitution Act, 1967*." *Samson* et al. *v Attorney General of Canada et al.* (Fed. CT. T.D., docket T-1706-98), cited by Newman (1999, pp. 90-91). However, although the Supreme Court initially appears to reiterate the primacy of the written constitution (para. 53), this is qualified by the fact that the written constitution is not exhaustive, a fact that leaves the courts to fill gaps in the express terms of the constitutional text.

57. "No negotiations could be effective if their ultimate outcome, secession, is cast as an absolute legal entitlement to give effect to that secession in the Constitution" (*Secession Reference*, para. 91).

58. As Newman puts it: "The constitution, including its underlying principles...is relevant for sovereigntists...because it safeguards their legitimate interests, just as it does those of all Canadians" (1999, p. 86).

59. Newman (1999, p. 86).

60. Newman notes that central to the decision's "brilliance" was the Supreme Court's vision "to wed the value of constitutional legality with that of political legitimacy, and this on several levels" (1999, p. 84). In this context it is useful to consider James Tully's metaphor of a "mobius band," which he uses to describe the relationship between constitutional arrangements and democratic practices (2000).

61. Newman (1999, p. 86).

62. Tully is talking about the conjunction of two related concepts, which he nicely terms "constitutional democracy and democratic constitutionalism" (2000). In a perhaps similar way, the Supreme Court suggests that the four foundational principles to which it refers "function in symbiosis." None can be defined in isolation, "nor does any one principle trump or exclude the operation of any other" (*Secession Reference*, para. 49). See also McRoberts (1999, p. 3).

63. Franck (1995, p. 92).

64. *Secession Reference*, para. 75. Some liberal theorists have argued that a moral right of secession exists on precisely this kind of "contractual" basis – for example, Beran (1984), Beran (1987), Philpott (1995).

65. *Secession Reference*, para. 76.

66. *Secession Reference*, para. 76.

67. *Secession Reference*, para. 77.

68. *Secession Reference*, para. 78.

69. *Secession Reference*, para. 86.

70. Hogg (1999, p. 3).

71. José Woehrling argues that the amending formula would become relatively unimportant in such a situation (1999, pp. 2-3).

72. *Secession Reference*, para. 91.

73. *Secession Reference*, para. 92.

74. *Secession Reference*, para. 92.

75. *Secession Reference*, para. 88.

76. An example of how the principle of democracy can be invoked to *resist* secession was presented by Abraham Lincoln in defending the federal government's role in the American Civil War. "The central idea pervading the struggle," he said, "is the necessity...of proving that popular government is not an absurdity." McPherson (1991, p. 10).

77. *Secession Reference*, para. 66.

78. *Secession Reference*, para. 85.

79. Hogg (1999, p. 3).

80. As was noted above, Peter Hogg has asked this question in relation to the principles of both democracy and federalism. It would seem that the point being made here about the right to democracy being a mutual one would apply in similar ways to the principle of federalism.

81. *Secession Reference*, para. 86.

82. *Secession Reference*, para. 92.

83. Even the federal government, following the decision, stated: "[T]here is no major political party that suggests that a province be held in Canada against the clearly expressed will of its population...We realize that our Canadian identity is too precious to be based upon anything other than voluntary adhesion." Stéphane Dion, Minister of Intergovernmental Affairs, before the House Legislative Committee on the Clarity Bill (which he sponsored), Federal Government Press Release, February 16, 2000.

84. *Secession Reference*, para. 93.

85. *Secession Reference*, para. 103.

86. It is now open to any province to seek secession in this way, since the Supreme Court of Canada did not go so far as to say that this right of self-determination derived from Quebec's status as a nation or a "people" (see *Secession Reference*, para. 125, where the Court concludes that it is not necessary to explore whether the Quebec population constitutes a "people" in terms of international law); the constitution's commitment to the symmetry of Canadian federalism arguably precluded the Court from taking such a radical leap even if it had sought to do so. It can be argued that this new duty to negotiate the secession of a province was not the intention of the founders of the constitution in 1867 (Hogg, 1999, p. 4), and there is certainly precedent for constituent units being held within both Canada and Australia against their will. Peter Hogg points out that attempts to secede by Nova Scotia in 1868 and Western Australia in 1934 were successfully resisted (1997, p. 136). The most dramatic example is of course the American experience, where constitutional crisis and civil war led to the now generally accepted doctrine of the federal union as indivisible. *Texas v White* 74 U.S. (7 Wall.) 700 (1869).

87. This idea is encapsulated nicely in the title of Jean Le Clair's article "A Ruling in Search of a Nation" (1999).

88. The *Secession Reference* arose precisely because strong forces within a particular political community (Quebec) contested its cultural and constitutional involvement in a larger political community (Canada). A broadening of the

Canadian constitutional imagination as evidenced by the Supreme Court in the *Secession Reference* offers a path to resolve this question through negotiation. However, procedural avenues involving participation and discussion, in order to be effective, must not lose sight of the fact that the issue involved is one in which a particular political community, although engaging in this process, feels itself distinct from the other participants (the dominant culture as it were), and is negotiating in order to secure both recognition of that distinctiveness and political autonomy in order to foster that distinctiveness.

89. At a more prosaic level there are also considerable ambiguities within the act. Michael Ancram MP argued during its parliamentary process that the Scotland Bill was "littered" with "areas of potential conflict between Edinburgh and Westminster." H.C. Deb., Vol. 304, col. 41, January 12, 1998.

90. Himsworth (2001).

91. *MacCormick v Lord Advocate* [1953] Session Cases 396.

92. *MacCormick v Lord Advocate supra*, at 411.

93. *Gibson v Lord Advocate* [1975] Scots Law Times 134. Attempts to raise this issue before the courts occur from time to time. See Walker and Himsworth (1991).

94. *Pringle, Petitioner* [1991] Scots Law Times 330 and *Murray v Rogers* [1992] Scots Law Times 221. See also Munro (1999, pp. 137-42). However, for the alternative view that the Acts of Union retain special legal significance see Smith (1957), Mitchell (1964), MacCormick (1978).

95. Published on November 30, 1995.

96. This was signed by every Scottish Labour MP at the time with the exception of Tam Dalyell. Although advocating the modern notion of popular sovereignty, "Scotland's Claim, Scotland's Right" also noted Scotland's differing constitutional tradition: "This concept of sovereignty [the Westminster model] has always been unacceptable to the Scottish constitutional tradition of limited government or popular sovereignty." See also MacCormick (2000, pp. 729-30). An interesting parallel in terms of constitutional origins can be made here with Canada. The Supreme Court, in discussing confederation in the *Secession Reference* decision, seemed keen to distance Canada's constitutional origins from UK parliamentary sovereignty and to turn instead to some notion of popular will: "Confederation was an initiative of elected representatives of the people then living in the colonies scattered across part of what is now Canada. It was not initiated by Imperial *fiat*" (*Secession Reference*, para. 35). The Supreme Court also observed that the Canadian constitution has been "transformed to a significant extent from a system of Parliamentary supremacy to one of constitutional supremacy" (*Secession Reference*, para. 72). This would seem to encapsulate the aspirations for the UK constitution of many of those involved in the Scottish Constitutional Convention.

97. *Whaley v Lord Watson of Invergowrie* [2000] Session Cases 340.

98. Dicey (1927, p. 38).

99. *Whaley v Lord Watson of Invergowrie* [2000] at 348.

100. *Whaley v Lord Watson of Invergowrie* [2000] at 358.

101. *Whaley v Lord Watson of Invergowrie* [2000] at 358.

102. Lord Rodger, *Whaley v Lord Watson of Invergowrie* [2000] at 349.

103. *Whaley v Lord Watson of Invergowrie* [2000] at 358. One might ask whether there are parallels in terms of tone between this remark and the Canadian Supreme Court's comments in *Secession Reference*, para. 35 (with the obvious proviso that the latter was discussing an independent state, whereas the Scottish Parliament merely has devolved powers).

104. Newman (1999, p. 83, n. 31) provides a helpful list of these cases.

105. Although not a particularly high-profile case, there is no reason to expect a different approach in the event that major issues do arise before either the Court of Session or the Privy Council.

106. In Scotland, since devolution, the issues of judicial independence and impartiality have also been very much in vogue.

107. Newman (1999, p. 84, n. 32) citing comments to this effect made by Justice John Major.

108. Young (1999, p. 147). See also Newman (1999, p. 82).

109. The Charlottetown Accord of 1992 was another failed attempt to secure constitutional changes which would better accommodate Quebec within the Canadian federation.

110. *Secession Reference*, paras. 102 and 105: "In accordance with the usual rule of prudence in constitutional cases, we refrain from pronouncing on the applicability of any particular constitutional procedure to effect secession unless and until sufficiently clear facts exist to squarely raise an issue for judicial determination." As Peter Oliver puts it: "The Court was clearly reluctant to leave the negotiation of secession entirely to the political process. Had it done so Quebec would have been left with nothing more than the democratic legitimacy of its claim and an increased sense of grievance at its inequitable treatment by Canadian lawmakers. The Court was aware, however, that in setting out a legal obligation to negotiate it risked wading too deeply into political waters. This seems to explain the mixing of law and convention, legal and political" (2000, pp. 89-90).

111. McRoberts (1999, p. 4). See also Drache and Monahan (1999, p. 7): "Although the court was not expected to solve all of our problems, it has created a measure of common ground in the debate over the country's future. It is in this space where debate and dialogue can occur between sovereigntists and federalists, which is, in the end, no mean accomplishment." See also Newman (1999, pp. 87, 99).

Bibliography

Bayefsky, Anne F. "Introduction," in *Self-Determination in International Law: Quebec and Lessons Learned*, ed. Anne Bayefsky. The Hague: Kluwer Law International, 2000.

Beran, Harry. "A Liberal Theory of Secession." *Political Studies*, Vol. 32 (1984): 21-31.

———. *The Consent Theory of Political Obligation*. London: Croom Helm, 1987.

Bingham, Thomas Henry. *The Business of Judging: Selected Essays and Speeches*. Oxford: Oxford University Press, 2000.

Browne-Wilkinson, Lord. "The Infiltration of a Bill of Rights." *Public Law* (1992): 397-410.

Dicey, Albert Venn. *Introduction to the Study of the Law of the Constitution*, 8th ed. London: Macmillan, 1927.

Dodge, William. "Succeeding in Seceding: Internationalizing the Quebec Secession Reference under NAFTA." *Texas International Law Journal*, Vol. 34 (1999): 287-326.

Drache, Daniel, and Patrick J. Monahan. "In Search of Plan A." *Canada Watch*, Vol. 7 (1999). (References are to the Web version of the journal and to page numbers on this downloaded version: http://www.robarts.yorku.ca/canadawatch/vol_7_1-2/default.htm Accessed August 5, 2002.)

Dworkin, Ronald. *Freedom's Law: The Moral Reading of the American Constitution*. Cambridge, MA: Harvard University Press, 1996.

Franck, Thomas. *Fairness in International Law and Institutions*. Oxford: Oxford University Press, 1995.

Gibson, Gordon F. "A Court for All Seasons." *Canada Watch*, Vol. 7 (1999). (References are to the Web version of the journal and to page numbers on this downloaded version: http://www.robarts.yorku.ca/canadawatch/vol_7_1-2/default.htm Accessed August 5, 2002.)

Greschner, Donna. "What Can Small Provinces Do?" *Canada Watch*, Vol. 7 (1999). (References are to the Web version of the journal and to page numbers on this downloaded version: http://www.robarts.yorku.ca/canadawatch/vol_7_1-2/default.htm Accessed August 5, 2002.)

Harlow, Carol. "Disposing of Dicey: From Legal Autonomy to Constitutional Discourse." *Political Studies*, Vol. 48 (2000): 356-69.

Himsworth, Chris. "Rights Versus Devolution," in *Sceptical Essays on Human Rights*, ed. Tom Campbell, Keith Ewing and Adam Tomkins. Oxford: Oxford University Press, 2001.

Hogg, Peter. *Constitutional Law of Canada*, 4th ed. Toronto: Carswell, 1997.

———. "The Duty to Negotiate." *Canada Watch*, Vol. 7 (1999). (References are to the Web version of the journal and to page numbers on this downloaded version: http://www.robarts.yorku.ca/canadawatch/vol_7_1-2/default.htm Accessed August 5, 2002.)

Hope, Lord of Craighead. "Devolution and Human Rights." *European Human Rights Law Review*, Vol. 3 (1998): 367-79.

Joffe, Paul. "Quebec's Sovereignty Project and Aboriginal Rights." *Canada Watch*, Vol. 7 (1999). (References are to the Web version of the journal and to page numbers on this downloaded version: http://www.robarts.yorku.ca/canadawatch/vol_7_1-2/default.htm Accessed August 5, 2002.)

Keating, Michael. *Plurinational Democracy: Stateless Nations in a Post-Sovereignty Era.* Oxford: Oxford University Press, 2001.

Koskenniemi, Martti. "Theory: Implications for the Practitioner," in *Theory and International Law,* ed. British Institute of International and Comparative Law. London: BIICL, 1991.

Kymlicka, Will. *Multicultural Citizenship: A Liberal Theory of Minority Rights.* Oxford: Clarendon Press, 1995.

———. *Politics in the Vernacular.* Oxford: Oxford University Press, 2001.

LaForest, Guy. "The Judiciary Committee of the Privy Council." *Canada Watch,* Vol. 7 (1999). (References are to the Web version of the journal and to page numbers on this downloaded version: http://www.robarts.yorku.ca/canadawatch/vol_7_1-2/default.htm Accessed August 5, 2002.)

Le Clair, Jean. "A Ruling in Search of a Nation." *Canada Watch,* Vol. 7 (1999). (References are to the web version of the journal and to page numbers on this downloaded version: http://www.robarts.yorku.ca/canadawatch/vol_7_1-2/default.htm Accessed August 5, 2002.)

MacCormick, Neil. "Does the United Kingdom Have a Constitution?" *Northern Ireland Legal Quarterly,* Vol. 29 (1978): 1-20.

———. *Questioning Sovereignty Law, State and Nation in the European Commonwealth.* Oxford: Oxford University Press, 1999.

———. "Is There a Constitutional Path to Scottish Independence?" *Parliamentary Affairs,* Vol. 53 (2000): 721-36.

Mandel, Michael. "A Solomonic Judgment?" *Canada Watch,* Vol. 7 (1999). (References are to the Web version of the journal and to page numbers on this downloaded version: http://www.robarts.yorku.ca/canadawatch/vol_7_1-2/default.htm Accessed August 5, 2002.)

Margalit, Avishai, and Joseph Raz. "National Self-Determination." *Journal of Philosophy,* Vol. 87 (1990): 439-61.

McPherson, James M. "A War That Never Goes Away." in *The Civil War: The Best of American Heritage,* ed. Stephen W. Sears. Boston: Houghton Mifflin, 1991.

McRoberts, Kenneth. "In the Best Canadian Tradition." *Canada Watch,* Vol. 7 (1999). (References are to the Web version of the journal and to page numbers on this downloaded version: http://www.robarts.yorku.ca/canadawatch/vol_7_1-2/default.htm Accessed August 5, 2002.)

———. "Canada and the Multinational State." *Canadian Journal of Political Science,* Vol. 34 (2001): 683-714.

Mitchell, John David Bawden. *Constitutional Law.* Edinburgh: W. Green, 1964.

Monahan, Patrick J. "The Supreme Court's 1998 Constitutional Cases: The Debate over Judicial Activism Heats Up." *Canada Watch,* Vol. 7 (1999). (References are to the Web version of the journal and to page numbers on this downloaded version: http://www.robarts.yorku.ca/canadawatch/vol_7_1-2/default.htm Accessed August 5, 2002.)

Munro, Colin. *Studies in Constitutional Law,* 2nd ed. London: Butterworths, 1999.

Newman, Warren J. *The Quebec Secession Reference: The Rule of Law and the Position of the Attorney General of Canada.* Toronto: York University Press, 1999.

Oliver, Peter. "The 1982 Patriation of the Constitution of Canada: Reflections on Continuity and Change." *Revue Juridique Thémis,* Vol. 28 (1994): 875-913.

———. "Canada, Quebec and Constitutional Amendment." *University of Toronto Law Journal,* Vol. 49 (1999): 519-610.

———. "Canada's Two Solitudes: Constitutional and International Law in *Reference re Secession of Quebec,*" in *Accommodating National Identity: New Approaches in International and Domestic Law,* ed. Stephen Tierney. The Hague: Kluwer Law International, 2000.

Philpott, Daniel. "In Defence of Self-Determination." *Ethics,* Vol. 105 (1995): 352-85.

Sedley, Sir Stephen. "Human Rights: A 21st Century Agenda." *Public Law,* (1995): 386-400.

Smith, T.B. "The Union of 1707 as Fundamental Law." *Public Law* (1957): 99-121.

Tamir, Yael. *Liberal Nationalism.* Princeton: Princeton University Press, 1993.

Tully, James. *Constitutionalism in an Age of Diversity.* Cambridge: Cambridge University Press, 1995.

———. "The Unfreedom of the Moderns in Comparison to Their Ideals of Constitutionalism and Democracy." *Exeter Colloquium on Constitutionalism, Democracy and Citizenship: Current Debates,* November 24-25, 2000. http://les1.man.ac.uk/conweb/ papers/conweb6-2000.pdf. Accessed August 5, 2002.

———. "Introduction," in *Multicultural Democracies,* ed. Alain-G. Gagnon and James Tully. Cambridge: Cambridge University Press, 2001.

Walker, Neil, and Chris Himsworth. "The Poll Tax and Fundamental Law." *Juridical Review,* Vol. 36 (1991): 45-78.

Walters, Mark. "Nationalism and the Pathology of Legal Systems: Considering the Quebec *Secession Reference* and Its Lessons for the United Kingdom." *Modern Law Review,* Vol. 62 (1999): 371-96.

Whyte, John D. "Constitutionalism and Nation." *Canada Watch,* Vol. 7 (1999). (References are to the Web version of the journal and to page numbers on this downloaded version: http://www.robarts.yorku.ca/canadawatch/vol_7_1-2/default.htm Accessed August 5, 2002.)

Woehrling, José. "Unexpected Consequences of Constitutional First Principles." *Canada Watch,* Vol. 7 (1999). (References are to the Web version of the journal and to page numbers on this downloaded version: http://www.robarts.yorku.ca/canadawatch/vol_7_1-2/default.htm Accessed August 5, 2002.)

Young, Robert A. *The Struggle for Quebec: From Referendum to Referendum?* Montreal and Kingston: McGill-Queen's University Press, 1999.

10

questioning constitutional democracy in Canada: from the Canadian Supreme Court reference on Quebec secession to the *Clarity Act*

François Rocher and Nadia Verrelli

Accommodating diversity at a political level implies that the state, first, formally recognizes the diversity and, second and arguably more importantly, secures political avenues for the expression of this diversity. Does the federal government's latest quest to deal with the demand of the Quebec people to have its diversity accommodated both politically and constitutionally embody these two ideals? This is the question we address in this paper by examining the political significance of the *Bill to Give Effect to the Requirement for Clarity as Set Out in the opinion of the Supreme Court of Canada in the Secession Reference*, also referred to as the *Clarity Act* or Bill C-20. More specifically, we focus on the degree to which C-20 embodies the redefinition of constitutional democracy that was pronounced in the 1998 *Reference re Secession of Quebec*, or the *Secession Reference*. In its opinion, the Supreme Court conceptualized constitutional democracy as "a complex set of practices in which the irreducible conflicts over the recognition of diversity and the requirements of unity are conciliated over time."[1] Implicit in this reconceptualization are the principles of freedom and justice – two fundamental principles on which the Canadian political order was founded. Does the *Clarity Act* reflect this reconceptualization? That is, to what extent does C-20 reinforce the legitimacy of the Canadian political order?

In the first section of this paper, we examine the Supreme Court's opinion in the *Secession Reference*, exploring the theoretical questions raised by the Court. We then analyze the *Clarity Act* and the issues raised by this federal initiative.

Both the *Secession Reference* and the federal government's response to it in the form of C-20 are examined in terms of the principles of constitutional democracy. In the last section, we look at the debates the *Secession Reference* and C-20 precipitated within the media and amongst academics. More specifically, we examine which issues, and what aspects of these issues, were prioritized in Quebec and in the rest of Canada. The *Clarity Act*, part of the federal government's "Plan B" in dealing with the Quebec crisis, was supposed to, first and foremost, clarify the issues regarding the possible secession of Quebec and, second, enable the political accommodation of diversity. It accomplished neither objective; in fact, it further blurred the issues and, in a very real sense, has the potential to silence the democratic will of the Quebec people.

The Concept of Constitutional Democracy

In 1995, the government of Quebec held a referendum offering Quebecers the option of sovereignty while maintaining a partnership with the rest of Canada. The referendum question was the following: "Do you agree that Quebec should become sovereign, after having made a formal offer to Canada for a new economic and political partnership, within the scope of the bill respecting the future of Quebec and of the agreement signed on June 12, 1995?"A narrow majority of 50.6 percent voted against this option. In September 1996 the federal government, responding to the plethora of criticisms vis-à-vis the strategy it undertook during the referendum campaign, referred three questions to the Supreme Court of Canada regarding the constitutional ability of the province of Quebec to unilaterally secede from Canada: 1) Does the Quebec government, under the constitution, have the right to secede unilaterally? 2) Under international law, does it have this right? Further, does Quebec have the right to self-determination that will enable it to proceed with a unilateral secession? 3) If there is a conflict between domestic and international law, which of the two takes precedence?

On August 28, 1998, the Supreme Court rendered its opinion. On the first question, that of whether or not Quebec could, under the Canadian constitution, proceed with a unilateral secession, the Court responded that it could not. On the second question, the Court answered that since Quebec cannot be regarded as "being oppressed" within the Canadian political framework, the Government of Quebec does not have the right, under international law, to proceed with a unilateral secession. Since domestic law and international law do not conflict, there was no need to answer the third question.

Within the Court's detailed opinion, which surpassed simple and straightforward answers, three points, fraught with consequences, must be singled out. First, the Court indicated that the secession project is legitimate if it is supported by the people through a "clear" referendum. According to the judges, "the referendum result, if it is to be taken as an expression of the democratic will, must be free of ambiguity both in terms of the question asked and in terms of the support it achieves."[2] The Court went on to add that the democratic legitimacy of the secessionist project denoted a constitutional obligation to negotiate on the rest of the country insofar as "the continued existence and operation of the Canadian constitutional order cannot remain indifferent to the clear expression of a clear majority of Quebecers that they no longer wish to remain in Canada."[3] These negotiations, which would inevitably be difficult and whose results would obviously be uncertain, should take into account the interests of all the parties concerned (the governments of Canada and of Quebec and the other provinces, and other participants). Further, they should touch upon complex questions, which according to the Court may include economic interests, national debt, rights of linguistic minorities and the rights of Aboriginal peoples. However, the Court did not come to any conclusion concerning the substance of these negotiations. Finally, the Court, not wanting to decide the substantive issues, left the intricacies of the debate in the hands of the political players. In the Court's view, the process should be evaluated by the political actors who "would have the information and expertise to make the appropriate judgment as to the point at which, and circumstances in which, those ambiguities are resolved one way or the other."[4] It is the voters who, in the final analysis, are best able to evaluate the different positions of those who partake in the negotiation process.

Overall, the opinion rendered in the *Secession Reference*, particularly the obligation to negotiate, is based on four fundamental principles: federalism, democracy, constitutionalism and the rule of law, and the protection of minorities; all four are equally important, as no one principle takes precedence over another. According to the Court these principles must clarify the comprehension of the constitutional text. Although they are not explicitly written in the constitution, "the principles dictate major elements of the architecture of the Constitution itself and are as such its lifeblood."[5]

Underpinning these fundamental principles is the notion of constitutional democracy, which the Court conceptualized in both a procedural and a substantive manner. Referring to the decision in the *OPSEU v Ontario* case, it defined the concept as "the basic structure of our Constitution, as established by the Constitution Act, 1867, [which] contemplates the existence of certain political institutions, including freely elected legislative bodies at the federal and provincial levels."[6] Representative democracy is therefore stressed. In this view, a political system is contingent upon the principle of majority rule. It is linked to, among other things, the objective of governmental autonomy so that a sovereign people can exert their right of autonomy via the democratic process. It is in these relatively simple and traditional terms that the Court understands the democratic principle: "Historically, this Court has interpreted democracy to mean the process of representative and responsible government and the right of citizens to participate in the political process as voters."[7]

The Court's understanding of the democratic principle, however, surpasses this formal framework of representative and responsible government. It broadened its initial definition to include a less tangible dimension: democracy is also perceived as a process of deliberation, discussion, debate, expression of opinions, compromises and negotiations. In this sense, which is particularly important in the context of the *Secession Reference*, "no one has a monopoly on truth, and our system is predicated on the faith that in the marketplace of ideas, the best solutions to public problems will rise to the top. Inevitably, there will be dissenting voices. A democratic system of government committed to considering those dissenting voices, and seeking to acknowledge and address those voices in laws by which all in the community must live."[8] It is the integrity of this approach of substantive democracy that gives rise to the obligation to engage in constitutional negotiations in order to take into account the democratic expression of a province seeking a constitutional change.

This definition of constitutional democracy is supplemented by the principles of constitutionalism and the rule of law. The former requires that all government actions conform to the constitution of Canada. The latter "vouchsafes to the citizens and residents of a country a stable, predictable and ordered society in which to conduct their affairs. It provides a shield for individuals from arbitrary state action."[9] In short, the principle of popular sovereignty alone cannot be invoked to justify changes that are inherently constitutional; secession is one example of such a change. Political representatives must act within the constitutional framework. However, this is not a limitation; changes can be made to the constitution if they are so desired by an enhanced majority.

The Court's conceptualization of constitutional democracy conforms to the tradition that it itself established. Post-Charter court decisions have rested on an interpretation of democracy that emphasizes the primacy of individual rights, free from encroachment by the state.[10] However, these individual freedoms, fundamental to democracy, may be limited in the name of defending underprivileged groups and more particularly in the name of multiculturalism and tolerance values. This dimension underpins the Court's assertion that parliamentary supremacy has been replaced by constitutional supremacy.

In the end, however, democracy, which is expressed through the will of the people (particularly via a referendum) and more generally through the election of representatives, cannot trump the rule of law. Justly, the Court stated that a system of government cannot be based solely on popular sovereignty and must also have democratic legitimacy. However, the interaction between the rule of law and the democratic principle is treated on a hierarchical basis in which the first is privileged. This is hardly surprising when considering the subject matter of the *Reference*, the constitutionality of a *unilateral* secession, which would bring into question the integrity of the state and the viability of the constitution. However, the mandate of the Court is to protect both, and by doing this, it ensures its raison d'être. In short, the support of the principle of the rule of law is hardly surprising if one understands that the reasoning of the Court aims at reinforcing the old machinery of which it is one of the significant wheels.[11]

The Supreme Court's views on the principle of constitutional democracy enable us to consider the ways in which the Canadian political system guarantees the full autonomy and the full liberty of its various components. For James Tully,

> The answer is that a multinational society will be free and self-determining just insofar as the constitutional rules or recognition and association are open to challenge and amendment by the members. If they are not opened, they constitute a structure of domination, the members are not self-determining, and the society is un-free. Freedom *versus* domination is thus the emerging focus of politics in multinational societies at the dawn of the new millennium.[12]

According to Tully, the *Reference*, which stresses that the members of a constitutional democracy have the right to initiate political and constitutional changes and that the other parties have the constitutional obligation to negotiate these changes, recognizes that the Canadian constitution is not a straitjacket. In other words, Quebec's right of self-determination is entirely recognized.[13] However, political reality requires that the general principles translate into a real capacity for change. The right of self-determination and the obligation to negotiate need to be exercised through institutional mechanisms and, particularly, through the procedures giving them effect. Tully specifies that "if a constitutional democracy does not embody this right and duty in its political and constitutional practices, and so allow struggles for and against recognition to be played freely, it is a closed structure of domination and confined with regard to self-determination."[14]

For Tully, the *Reference* is revolutionary in that it reorients the traditional understanding of constitutional democracy from an "end-state" perspective to an "activity-oriented" one.[15] The articulation of the four fundamental principles identified by the Court would constitute a response to the justification of the sovereignty of Quebec, being that the federal regime is blocked. Further, it would give a new justification for continuing democratic activity that permits the reconciliation of diversity and unity within Canada.

This enthusiastic reading of the *Reference*, however, must be put into perspective in light of the multiple inaccuracies, silences and ambiguities evident in the Court's opinion. After the publication of the *Reference*, commentators and politicians focused mainly on two dimensions of the opinion: one, the requirement for "clarity" imposed by the Court on both the referendum question put to the people and the majority obtained ("a clear majority on a clear question," to reiterate the expression of the Court) and, two, the constitutional obligation to negotiate.

Common sense cannot oppose the requirement of clarity. The Court, however, did not specify what it meant by "clarity" other than to indicate that "the referendum result, if it is to be taken as an expression of the democratic will, must be free of ambiguity both in terms of the question asked and in terms of the support it achieves."[16] Rendering the matter even less precise, the Court stated that it was up to the political actors to judge the clarity of the question and of the majority and, in essence, to judge the legitimacy of both. The reasoning of the Court thus presents two conflicting concepts, clarity on the one hand and confusion or ambiguity on the other. It is not surprising that the Court failed to define what constitutes a clear question or even the conditions to meet or establish this "clarity," as it is impossible to do so. To call into question the notion of "clarity," the cornerstone of the prescriptive dimension of the *Reference*, does not mean that we are in favour of ambiguity, nor that we are calling for its elimination.

Ambiguity can be important and, to a certain extent, desirable. Can Erk and Alain-G. Gagnon accurately point out that "in federal systems with deep disagreements over the nature of the political commununity, there might be no common ground to establish a consensus. Consequently, quests for legalistic precision can only aggravate the conflict. Efforts to clarify legally the federal arrangement are therefore unlikely to ensure the stability of multinational federations."[17] Constitutional ambiguity therefore may be "a way to keep the federation going." The nature of a complex society like Canada is ambiguity; to remove it by demanding clarity is to undermine the Canadian federation.

Our support for both the notions of ambiguity and clarity may seem schizophrenic. Such is not the case. We do not aim to make a case for either; our point is simply that the Court put forth a false dichotomy. Moreover, it implicitly made a political judgment about past referenda and disputed the legitimacy of the past and present strategies of the Quebec government, an opening that the federal government was quick to exploit.

Democracy implies a continuous process of deliberation, dialogue, discussion and debate. Terms are not defined with unequivocal certainty, as the comprehension of these terms functions in the context in which they are used. Moreover, is "clear" that which is easy to understand or clarify? Is it apparent or obvious? In addition, political resolutions invariably bring forth multiple ramifications when dealing with complex questions. Effort is required not only on the part of the political actors to ensure that their point of view is well understood but also on the part of citizens to understand what is involved in the proposed resolutions. In this sense, a situation may be simultaneously complex and intelligible, provided that effort is made in that direction. To impose an obligation of clarity is to say that all members of a political community share the same point of view; this is both unrealistic and impossible, not to mention undesirable. Essentially, the Court, by requiring that the political actors determine if the conditions of clarity are respected, granted one party *un droit de regard* over the other (in this circumstance, the rest of Canada over the Quebec approach); one can also argue that a veto over the citizens' interpretation or perception of the resolution was also granted. Seeing that the political debate imposes, by its very nature, continuous discussion, it involves tensions while emanating the sense that the terms used act in everyone's interests; one cannot expect that there exists only one understanding of the words, notions and terms.

This is not to say that the political arena is full of confusion, but as the Court emphasizes, "no one has a monopoly on truth, and our system is predicated on the faith that in the marketplace of ideas, the best solutions to public problems will rise to the top."[18] The obligation of clarity seems to contradict this statement.

It can also be argued that this obligation defines democracy in apolitical terms. On the one hand, democracy ought to be considered as a marketplace of open deliberations, where ideas and notions are not necessarily perceived in a uniform manner. Political debates are essentially ambiguous; the meaning of the terms used may be interpreted differently depending on the audience, places, context, and the moment of their use. On the other hand, the imposition of this obligation of clarity, good in and of itself as no one favours confusion or ambiguity, is inspired by a Manichean vision of politics. The political approach essentially involves actors who put forth objectives and orientations that contain some form of ambiguity, thus allowing for several interpretations. The events surrounding the renewed constitution eloquently show that contradictory interpretations of the government's intentions were made. From 1987 to 1992, the notion of "distinct society," for example, however clear for some, seemed vague to others. Nonetheless, this did not prevent the federal government of the time from holding a referendum on this very complex constitutional proposal in the Charlottetown Accord. It would have been very difficult to meet the obligation of clarity as set out by the Court if the political actors had had to agree on the meaning of the term.

Furthermore, the Court is far from clear on what it means by a "clear majority." Without being explicit, it called into question the principle universally accepted (by all constitutional democracies) of 50 percent plus one; this principle ensures that a majority is obtained if the 50 percent plus one threshold is crossed. The Court indicated that it used "clear majority" in the qualitative sense, without clarifying what it meant by that.

Without a doubt, the most astonishing element of the *Secession Reference* is the obligation to negotiate. All parties concerned must take this seriously. Moreover, they must proceed to negotiate in good faith. However, beyond this general injunction, many elements remain particularly vague. First, the good faith of the political actors is subjected to the recognition of all parties involved. Further, this good faith does not necessarily lead to the realization of an agreement if the interests of both parties are irreducible. One could be tempted to judge good faith according to the accepted compromises; however, it is not always possible to obtain the latter even if the negotiations are being conducted in good faith. In the event that negotiations break down, it would be up to the international community to judge the legitimacy of a unilateral secession insofar as there exists, ultimately, no legal recourse to prevent it.

If, on the other hand, the Government of Quebec succeeds in asking an "acceptable" referendum question and obtaining an "acceptable" majority (judged by the rest of Canada), the question of which formal constitutional amending formula ought to be used to ensure its legal secession must still be answered. Nowhere in the *Reference* is there the question of which rules ought to preside over the negotiations. The Court was satisfied with re-emphasizing that "the negotiation process ...would require the reconciliation of various rights and obligations by the representatives of two legitimate majorities, namely, the clear majority of the population of Quebec, and the clear majority of Canada as a whole, whatever that may be. There can be no suggestion that either of these majorities 'trumps' the other."[19] Beyond this, the Court was silent. Consequently, there is no doubt that the results of the negotiations would be subject to the current constitutional amending formula. Taking into account the nature of the sovereignty issue, the unanimous consent of the provinces and the consent of the federal government would have to be obtained. If, for one reason or another, a province refused to ratify the proposed amendments, we could ask ourselves how a majority – in this case Canada outside Quebec – could avoid not only having the upper hand but also using that upper hand to the detriment of Quebec's constitutional agenda.

One could think, like the constitutionalist Peter Hogg, that "the vague principles of democracy and federalism, which were relied upon by the Court, hardly seem sufficient to require a federal government to negotiate the dismemberment of the country that it was elected to protect."[20] Furthermore, the multiple shady and inaccurate areas of the *Secession Reference* left a margin of interpretation sufficiently large enough to enable the negation of the very principles the Court identified as the heart of the Canadian constitutional regime. Jacques-Yvan Morin draws upon this point:

> The Supreme Court, with an eye on international law and opinion, has legitimized the *objectives* pursued by a substantial part of the Quebec people, but has failed to set out the *means* by which the principles upon which it has based its arguments can be carried out peaceably and with the greatest chance of mutual success. Can one speak of a "balanced" judgment? For Quebec, there is the satisfaction of being right in the field of principles; for Ottawa, a victory in the decisive elements that are the instruments of *realpolitik*.[21]

In this context, it is not surprising, as Tully points out, that political observers have focused on the second part of the *Reference*, which concentrates on the political dimensions of the document, rather than on the principles that informed the Court's opinion. It *is* surprising that political observers did not underline the contradictions between the broad and generous principles of the first half of the *Reference* in light of its real implications. Instead, the federal government, acting rather quickly, adopted in June 2000 Bill C-20, the *Clarity Act*, in order to give effect to the requirements of clarity as set out in the *Secession Reference*.

The *Clarity Act* (C-20): Principles in Practice

The *Clarity Act* is an important step in the process of redefining and reconstituting the borders of the political community. The Canadian government wanted to define a political community that included or even subordinated Quebec. The National Assembly, on the other hand, sought to reaffirm the right of the Quebec people to define their own political future without external interference. We need to acknowledge that though these two positions are fundamentally incompatible, both are legitimate and coherent within their own perspective. On a strictly political level, we must also acknowledge that the Quebec government faces difficulties that, if not insurmountable, problematize a discourse that excludes the sentiments of many Quebecers regarding their place in Canada.

The title of the federal bill wonderfully captures the nature of the political debate and the political rhetoric that fuels it. The bill deals with the issue of clarity. It opposes any strategy that would, in the eyes of the federal government, be ambiguous or cause uncertainty. In other words, it deals with, at least seemingly, the codification of virtue. However, no one was ever made the spokesperson for "confusion" in the sovereignist camp. It is impossible to be insensitive to how words are used. Thus, by portraying opponents of the bill as being opposed to the very notion of clarity, the federal government actually contributes to the belittling of its own law, to the point of embarrassment.

With regard to political propaganda, the federal government undoubtedly remains well ahead. To oppose the federal law with considerations of the fundamental rights of Quebecers leads us into a debate where one refuses to speak the language of the other. This permits federal spokespeople to sell the idea that the *Clarity Act* enables the National Assembly to pose any question it wants at the time of a referendum. However, it also enables them to add that "la Chambre des communes…a le devoir d'évaluer par elle-même si la question et la majorité indiquent un appui clair en faveur de la sécession avant de conclure que le gouvernement du Canada est tenu d'entreprendre de négocier la rupture du Canada."[22]

The central problem rests in the fact that the Canadian government, or, more specifically, the governing party, becomes the sole judge of what constitutes a "clear" question and a "clear" majority. With regard to the clarity of a referendum question, section 1(4) of C-20 specifies that a question will not be admissible if it is:

- a referendum question that merely focuses on a mandate to negotiate without soliciting a direct expression of the will of the population of that province on whether the province should cease to be part of Canada; or
- a referendum question that envisages other possibilities in addition to the secession of the province from Canada, such as economic or political arrangements with Canada, that obscure a direct expression of the will of the population of that province on whether the province should cease to be part of Canada.

Moreover, when judging the clarity of the question, the Canadian government assumes the right to consider not only the advice of the National Assembly as a whole but all other opinions it deems relevant.

The federal government adopts an even more restrictive approach when evaluating the clarity of the majority. Without setting a threshold, which it ought to have done, the federal government simply states that an absolute majority would not suffice[23]; it goes on to outline the three elements that ought to be considered when judging a clear majority: 1) the size of the majority of valid votes cast in favour of the secessionist option; 2) the percentage of eligible voters voting in the referendum; and 3) any other matters or circumstances it considers to be relevant. Again, as when judging the clarity of the question, the Canadian Parliament reserves the right to take into account whatever opinion it deems relevant.

Finally, the *Clarity Act* states that the secession of a province requires a constitutional amendment, which in turn requires the participation of all 10 provinces. It therefore becomes clear that this prerequisite translates into the need to obtain unanimity of the provinces when amending the constitution. Given that many elements of the current constitutional configuration would have to be modified if Quebec were no longer a part of Canada, it remains highly likely that the secession of Quebec requires an amendment to the constitution; this amendment, due to its fundamental nature, begs unanimity of the provinces.

It is important to stress that these provisions define the circumstances that the federal government would agree to engage in if negotiations with Quebec on the issue of secession were to arise. In other words, the *Clarity Act* outlines how the federal government interpreted the Supreme Court's opinion in the *Secession Reference*. The validity of this interpretation is doubtful in light of the four fundamental principles outlined by the Court, especially those of federalism and democracy.

It is necessary to recall the Court's conceptualization of democracy. On various occasions, it stressed that democracy means much more than simply majority rules. Beyond the necessary percentage required for the results of a referendum to be accepted, democracy demands a firm and unambiguous will of the political actors to discuss, debate and deliberate; simply put, it requires a continuous process of discussion and evolution. The Court proceeded to specify the framework in which these discussions should be held: "[t]he negotiations that followed such a vote would address the potential act of secession as well as its possible terms should in fact secession proceed."[24]

Nowhere in the *Reference* does the Supreme Court authorize or defend the idea that Parliament ought to unilaterally determine the conditions of the negotiation process[25]; that has to be determined by all the political actors after a referendum on sovereignty has been conducted. In fact, to proceed in this manner contradicts the democratic principle that demands that all political actors negotiate in good faith. However, if one thing surfaces from the *Clarity Act*, it is the unilateral strategy of the federal government; it grants itself the duty to reject the referendum question if it judges that question to be unclear. In passing such a judgment, the federal government dismisses the expressed will of the National Assembly and the debates that have taken place in Quebec. In other words, it is up to Quebec and Quebec alone to define the wording of the question. If this seems ambiguous to its people or its representatives, they will have the opportunity to express this view in the Quebec public arena. It is in the light of these debates that the federal government could then give its opinion on how it understands clarity. This, however, does not necessarily authorize the federal government to judge *ex cathedra* before having considered the political debate that has taken place within the Quebec political arena. To proceed differently simply amounts to short-circuiting the spirit of the *Reference*, which invites the political actor to evaluate the measure in which the referendum result constitutes a "rejection of the clearly expressed will of the Quebec people against the existing constitutional order."[26]

The intentions of the federal government are frankly political in nature. It aims primarily to reassert before Quebec and the rest of Canada Parliament's legitimacy when intervening in the referendum process, before the National Assembly has the opportunity to hold a referendum and, for that matter, even before it adopts the wording of the referendum question.

The political legitimacy of the federal government vis-à-vis the *Clarity Act* rests on a fragile, if not nonexistent, "legal basis." It cannot, under the Canadian Constitution, interfere with the legislative process of the National Assembly. This would revive the power of disallowance, which the Court has recognized as a power that has fallen into disuse; further, this power runs contrary to the federal principle. The intentions of the federal government, therefore, rest elsewhere, and are only political in nature. The *Clarity Act* does nothing but authorize Parliament to free itself from the obligation to negotiate the terms of secession. It is a question of politically destabilizing the sovereignty strategy on the one hand, while insisting on the difficulties of the endeavour, and, on the other hand, diffusing the message that Quebecers are not the only ones who play a role in this debate.

But this project is even more ambitious; it also deals with letting Quebecers know that the Canadian Parliament is the guarantor of their desire to remain Canadian citizens. It is for this reason that the federal government claims that its actions are legitimate. For two years, the minister of intergovernmental affairs, Stéphane Dion, justified the approach inscribed in the *Clarity Act* by arguing that "le gouvernement du Canada est lui aussi l'un des gouvernements des Québécois. Après la sécession, il ne le serait plus. Il a donc envers nous le devoir de ne pas se retirer du territoire sans avoir l'assurance que c'est tres clairement ce que nous voulons: que le Canada se retire du Québec."[27]

As we will see below, one understands why C-20 enjoyed vast approval from the rest of Canada when we consider Dion's justification. The reactions of Canadians outside Quebec to the tabling of the bill were different from those prevailing among both the sovereigntists and the federalists within Quebec.

Two aspects are worth noting. First, from the creation of the sovereignty-association movement up until 1995, the idea of a political and economic association with Canada was always linked to the sovereignty idea, although different forms were adopted depending on the time and the political players. This idea was at the heart of the referendum question in 1980, whereas in 1995 the condition that partnership with Canada was to be negotiated was proposed. For Quebecers, sovereigntists or not, this dimension has always existed and seems, to us, understood. In the rest of Canada it was different. The idea of partnership was and is always perceived as a ploy to increase the number of votes in favour of sovereignty. In fact, Pierre Trudeau went as far as to say, "si vous frappez à la porte de la souveraineté-association, il n'y a pas de négociations possibles." In a similar fashion, Jean Chrétien denounced the ambiguous character of the 1995 question for not speaking of sovereignty or separation alone. Overall, the eager reception of Bill C-20 in English Canada reinforces the perception of sovereignists as schemers.

Second, and most aggravating to Canadians outside Quebec, is the perception held by the rest of Canada that Quebec's approach is unilateral. Quebec sovereignty would modify the Canadian political regime without Canada having its say on the matter; it would have to accept a decision it did not participate in. Taking this into account, one can understand why English Canada would welcome the particular conditions imposed by the bill. From their standpoint, Canadians outside Quebec believe that the approach advanced by the federal legislation is just, as it re-establishes a balance that in their eyes was lacking. The federal government and the rest of Canada had to reconcile the aspect of the *Secession Reference* that established Parliament's constitutional obligation to negotiate the terms of sovereignty. The government had to find a way to release itself from this obligation while still complying with the terms of the *Reference*. The Court's insistence on the necessity of obtaining "a clear expression of a clear majority of the Quebecers that they no longer wish to remain in Canada"[28] provided the desired justification.

Beyond the fact that C-20 interprets the Court's opinion in its own fashion, the bill does not amount to much except that the federal government alleviated some of English Canada's fears regarding the sovereignty project. A referendum question posed to the people of Quebec cannot include a reference to the notions of association or partnership. Furthermore, Parliament reserves the right to judge the size of the majority needed and the other circumstances that it deems relevant (which, let us acknowledge, were not very clear).

The enthusiastic reception of C-20 in the rest of Canada demonstrates that, by passing the bill, Canada perceived that it had secured its future. The bill strengthened the widely held impression that if a referendum question dealt strictly with sovereignty, the sovereignist project would never succeed. If it did not succeed, the rest of Canada could always contest the majority obtained. In other words, through the *Clarity Act*, the federal government managed to ensure that Quebec would never meet all the conditions needed to legally secede from Canada.

In short, English Canada's support for the *Clarity Act* is based on the following elements:

- the bill strengthens the idea that the secession of Quebec will deeply upset and irreversibly damage the Canadian political order; thus it is just and equitable that the citizens of Quebec and its representatives are not the only ones entitled to be involved with the matter at hand;
- it establishes an explicit procedure concerning, one, the legitimacy of a referendum on the secession and, two, the obligations of the Canadian Parliament if a majority votes in favour of secession;
- it confirms the principle of the rule of law after a referendum and identifies the process that the political actors must conform to;
- it enlightens Quebec voters and the Canadian people as to what would happen after a vote in favour of secession;
- it conforms to the principle of democracy under which it is possible to require, in certain cases, an enhanced or qualified majority;
- it obliges the Quebec government and the Government of Canada to take into consideration the rights of the majority.

That being said, one could argue that if the bill is perceived as being legitimate in the rest of Canada, it invalidates, by the same token, Quebec's right to decide on not only the need to consult its population but also the methods that would be followed on the road to redefining its political future. Arguing otherwise would amount to reinforcing a "structure of domination" incompatible with the fundamental principles of liberty and justice that are at the heart of the compromises that characterize the multinational political space.

Taking this into account, let us now look more closely at both the enthusiastic response to the *Clarity Act* and its reception in Quebec. More specifically, how were the debates regarding C-20 played out in the media and in the academic circles of English Canada and Quebec?

C-20 Debated and Debatable

"Despite, or perhaps because of the importance of the bill" [the *Clarity Act*], its passage was rushed through the House of Commons; in fact, the "Liberals held only nine days of committee hearings."[29] As a result of this arguably intentionally hasty process, many of the issues discussed above were left untouched; subsequently, it was left to the media and academics to address and question the fundamentals of the *Clarity Act*. The issues raised within these circles ranged from the prerogatives of the federal government to pass such a legislation to the inclusion of minorities, both ethnic and linguistic, and other nongovernmental groups at the negotiating tables, to determining the required majority needed to initiate negotiations on secession.

For the purposes of this chapter, the issues raised in the media and by academics will be discussed in three broad categories. In the first category, we focus on the language used to describe the *Clarity Act* vis-à-vis the *Secession Reference;* this leads into the debate on whether or not the act is in keeping with the spirit of the *Secession Reference.* This debate subsequently leads to the conflicting and often controversial views of the raison d'être of the *Clarity Act:* is it deceptive in nature or does it in fact clarify the issues raised in the *Secession Reference?*

On a different note, but connected to the reasoning behind the act, is the second issue, which deals with the act's constitutionality. Within this discussion, two main debates emerged: one, the infringement upon matters that are strictly provincial in nature versus the prerogative of the federal government to take action upon such a matter; and two, the infringement upon the collective rights of Quebecers to determine their political future versus the enhancement of the individual rights of all Canadians.

The third category concentrates upon the issue of a clear majority: should the federal government require an enhanced majority? If so, does this requirement offend the well-established democratic principle of the equality of voters?

Two items must be noted before we proceed. First, these three issues are not mutually exclusive; they interact with and stem from one another. Second, and more importantly, underlying these first three issues is the question of who decides. In other words, what did the Supreme Court mean when it spoke of political actors?

A major assumption underpinning these debates and, for that matter, the act itself, is the way in which "political actors" is defined. As we pointed out above, it is not clear in the *Secession Reference* what the Justices had in mind when speaking of political actors. More specifically, when the Supreme Court stated that it is up to the political actors to determine what a clear majority on a clear question entails, it was and is not obvious that they referred to the federal government and the federal government alone. In fact, it can be inferred that, in using political actors in the plural form, the Supreme Court was speaking of more than one body. Furthermore, it is not clear that political actors are elected politicians or government institutions alone; they can very well include nongovernmental organizations. The federal government, however, in drafting and passing C-20, interpreted political actors as the House of Commons, as it is the House that is charged with the responsibility for determining, first, whether or not the question and the majority are clear, and, second, whether or not Canada will enter into negotiations with Quebec.

Those within the media and academic circles who did not question the role the federal government assigned itself shared this interpretation. Various academics and media personnel argued that the federal government was within its constitutional prerogative to enact the *Clarity Act*. Peter Hogg, at the Senate Committee hearings on Bill C-20, went so far as to state that "in the absence of this bill, it seems to me that there would be no choice but the Government of Canada, meaning the executive, the federal cabinet, who would have to make that choice [deciding whether or not the question is clear]."[30] Patrick Monahan, echoing Hogg, stated that the "political actors are charged with the responsibility to define a clear question and a clear majority; thus, the federal government is forced to take action through legislation."[31]

Roger Gibbins, in contrast, has voiced concern over this matter. He expressed his support "for the principle that the Canadian political community, as a whole, should play an active role in setting the conditions for any future sovereignty referendum in Quebec, and in responding to the outcome of any such referendum."[32] The government alone should not play this role, for two reasons: first, "the people should be directly involved because they have little faith that the government can adequately represent regional interests; [and second], provincial governments must be directly involved and not simply play an advisory role."[33]

Others, including Claude Ryan and those who argue that the act might be damaging to the democratic rights of Quebecers, indirectly conceded that "political actors" means much more than just the federal government. The loudest objection to this underpinning assumption of the act was expressed by the National Assembly, through its adoption and passage of Bill 99. This bill strongly affirms "that only the Quebec people, acting through its own political institutions, has the right to decide the nature scope and mode of exercise if its right to self-determination, and that no other parliament or government may reduce the powers, authority, sovereignty or legitimacy of the National Assembly."

The Debates

In exploring the debates played out in the media and among academics,[34] we were surprised to note that, at least in the media, these debates did not take place between the "federalists" of Canada outside Quebec and the separatists of Quebec. The discussion and critiques within the media vis-à-vis the *Clarity Act* involved hard-core federalists who felt that the federal government ought to take a strong stand against Quebec separatism and citizens of both English and

French Canada who were concerned not only with the collective rights of Quebec but also with how the *Clarity Act* challenged our traditional understanding of democracy and federalism.

Further, it was the media and the academics of French Canada who in their critique of the *Clarity Act* rejected to some degree the old notion of constitutional democracy. (It must be noted that this rejection was not outright, as their arguments against the act were mainly rooted in the collective rights of the Quebec people to live in a just federal state.) As a result, we see the debate in the French-Canadian media and among French-Canadian academics rooted more in the age-old discussion of what constitutes a just state and less on how the system can be more free and flexible. That is to say, the debate was shaped around the notion of what Tully describes as the end-state view of democracy, where the ultimate goal is that the system be just.[35]

The Raison d'Être of the *Clarity Act*

Among the various commentaries on the *Clarity Act*, there were differences in the language used to describe the act vis-à-vis the *Secession Reference*. For instance, Nahlah Ayed began his commentary by stating that "bill C-20 is *based* on a 1998 Supreme Court of Canada decision in which the Court outlined broad criteria for the secession of a province from Canada."[36] He went on to assert that "the bill says that without a clear question and a clear expression of will from the citizens of a province, there can be no negotiations with the federal government on a secession from Canada."[37] He understood this as a positive thing, based on the opinion expressed by the Supreme Court.

Similarly, Graham Fraser, writing for the *Toronto Star*, stated that "the clarity bill was introduced last fall after the Supreme Court advised the government as requested on Quebec secession."[38] Don Macpherson of the *Montreal Gazette* described it as a bill that "*elaborates* upon last year's Supreme Court decision on secession" [emphasis added].[39] In fairness to Macpherson, he did argue that Bill C-20 and Bill 99 were both futile; however, he saw C-20 as more legitimate, being based, unlike Bill 99, on the Supreme Court decision.

Monahan stated that "[C-20] is a reasonable attempt to *express* the principles identified by the S.C.C." [emphasis added].[40] He stressed that such a bill was necessary as secession of a province is irreversible.

Unlike the four above, Claude Bariteau, a professor of anthropology at Université Laval, began his commentary in *Le Soleil* by stating that the bill was *inspired* by the court ruling: "Inspired by the Supreme Court decision in the Secession Reference, Bill C-20 would consist of, according to some, setting up a framework embedding the secessionist process so as to avoid Canada being rendered devoid"[translation].[41] He proceeded to argue that the bill was "a project, strongly supported by federalists, aimed at opposing the accession of the Québécois to sovereignty" [translation].[42]

Such subtle differences in language are important: firm language such as "based on" or "expresses" locates the legitimacy of the federal government's actions within the Supreme Court decision, whereas words like "inspired" raise doubt as to this legitimacy. Noting this difference of language is a useful starting point in examining the debate on whether or not the *Clarity Act* was in the spirit of the *Secession Reference*. Those who used "firm" language argued that it was, and vice versa. From this debate emerges the discussion of the *real* reasons behind the federal government's action.

This debate took place mainly amongst academics. However, it was not split along the traditional French/English linguistic lines, where the French Canadians, or Quebecers, denounced the act simply because it was a federal initiative and the English Canadians supported it because it curtailed the secessionists' agenda. Instead, it was between those who endorsed a strictly legal or procedural approach to Quebec's goal of secession by setting out *the rules of the game* and those who sought to explore the deeper issues of giving effect to the *duty to negotiate* or a return to "Plan A," in which an attempt is made to accommodate Quebec.

At the Senate Committee hearings, Patrice Garant recognized that certain aspects of the act might not be in the spirit of the *Secession Reference*:

[I]mplicitly, this involvement [that of the 30-day period] could be considered as an attempt to influence the Quebec voters. So it would represent a type of involvement by a federal body in the relationship between a provincial legislature and its electorate, which leads us to question whether clause 1 is truly in keeping with at least the spirit of federalism and democracy which are two of the basic principles in the 1998 reference.[43]

He maintained, however, that overall the bill was in keeping with the spirit of the Supreme Court reference: "It certainly does not go against it, even though the Supreme Court did not state that it would like to see a statute prescribing the criteria for determining whether or not a question is clear."[44]

Monahan, firmer in his opinions, supported the enactment of the bill; he affirmed that the federal government had to introduce legislation in order to clarify and give effect to the Supreme Court ruling.[45] He argued that the bill

is a reflection of the Supreme Court's own instruction that the political actors give "concrete form to the discharge of their constitutional obligations." With the Court's having imposed on the government of Canada an obligation to negotiate secession if certain conditions are met, it is clearly appropriate and necessary for Ottawa to set out the criteria on which that judgment is to be based. Assuming that the government's criteria are a good faith attempt to give concrete form to the principles identified by the Court, which is the case with the *Clarity Act*, no objection to the legislation can be convincing.[46]

As we can see, therefore, Monahan accepted the purpose of the act to be simply the federal government's attempt to clarify the issues raised by the Court. Moreover, he accepted the purpose of the bill as it is described in its preamble: "the preamble to the bill states that its purpose is merely to clarify the circumstances under which the government of Canada would enter into secession negotiations and that it does not restrict the right of a provincial government to consult its population through a referendum on a question of the province's own choosing."[47]

The sentiment that the act was necessary and was in the spirit of the Supreme Court ruling was echoed by other academics, including Hogg and Pinard. Hogg firmly stated at the Senate Committee hearings that Bill C-20 was consistent with the Supreme Court ruling.[48] Pinard, reiterating this opinion, argued that the *Clarity Act* was needed in order to clarify the issues. He pointed out that there was confusion over the terms "sovereignty," "independence" and "partnership"; Quebecers did not understand what distinguishes these terms from each other or whether or not they were distinguishable, a confusion that worked in the favour of the Parti Québécois.[49] According to Pinard, "in any democracy, in any bureaucratic system, people who are not well informed will vote for the wrong option...There are ways to make things very clear and afterwards, democracy is served."[50]

Scott Reid, a reporter for the *National Post*, on the other hand, argued that a more proper name for the *Clarity Act* would have been Obscurity Act, as it failed to clarify any issue: "The strategy seems to have been adopted in order to permit Ottawa to claim it is complying with the Supreme Court's injunction to negotiate in good faith while ensuring negotiations would be endless, confused, and carry on until the separatists finally give up in exhaustion." Reid argued that the "so-called goal of the bill is to clear up the issues that the Supreme Court left to the political actors to work out – the *Clarity Act* does not provide us with such clarity. The *Clarity Act* simply employs delay tactics, without giving effect to the Supreme Court ruling."[51]

Others went beyond the argument that the bill failed to provide clarity; according to this group of critics, the act was a bullying tactic of the federal government, used to intimidate Quebecers. Further, it was seen as an attempt by the federal government to side-step its duty to negotiate.

Stéphan Larouche of *Le Devoir* saw the purpose of the act as a way for the federal government to withdraw from its obligation to negotiate: "Forging ahead with Bill C-20, the federal minister, Stéphane Dion, shows his and his government's will to withdraw themselves from the duty to negotiate, as set out by the Supreme Court, following the clearly expressed will of the Quebec people to attain sovereignty" [translation].[52] The *Clarity Act* indicated that the federal government wanted to withdraw from the obligation and the duty to negotiate, as every section leads to the federal government not to negotiate:

> [T]he federal government clearly demonstrates that the reference ruling embarrassed it and that it is ready to avoid the constitutional obligation to negotiate, imposed on it by the Supreme Court.
>
> Let us be clear. The raison d'être of C-20, as is set out by the federal government, has no other goal, but to withdraw itself from the duty to negotiate and to keep Quebec, against its will, in the rigidity of the Canadian federation. Whether one is a sovereignist or a federalist, we need to take note of these shameful tactics. [translation][53]

Guy Lachapelle argued at the Senate Committee hearing that the *Clarity Act* did not comply with the *Secession Reference*; in fact, it was a roundabout way for the federal government to try to get out of its obligation to negotiate: "Bill C-20 is a way for the federal government to withdraw itself from the duty to negotiate upon a referendum victory on sovereignty" [translation].[54]

According to Henri Brun, writing in *Le Devoir*, the real reason for the adoption of the *Clarity Act* was to prevent the National Assembly from holding yet another referendum on secession: "The federal government prepares itself to adopt the *Clarity Act* for one and only one reason: because, according to Canada, it has an effective way to prevent the Quebecers, once again, from having an occasion to express their desire to choose their political future" [translation]. He saw the act as an intimidation tool for the federal government to reach its goal (identified as what he perceived to be the raison d'être of the act): "Through intimidation, it makes Quebecers believe that it will always be impossible to bring the federal government to the negotiation table, or, if one prefers, it makes them believe that the federal government can do as it wishes despite the democratically expressed will of Quebecers" [translation].[55] The act was not in the spirit of the Supreme Court's ruling; in actuality, it inhibited what the Supreme Court Justices tried to do:

> To attain this discounted result, the *Clarity Act* deploys means which have nothing to do with the opinion of the Supreme Court, and which, in fact, completely contrasts with the spirit of the Court's opinion.

But what is important to underline is that while advancing all these artificial and arbitrary conditions, in order to get them to the negotiation table, the federal government claims to uphold the spirit of the Secession ruling. The Court, creating the obligation to negotiate, wanted, above all, to favour freedom of thought so as to ensure the exercise of a truly democratic choice. The *Clarity Act* does the complete opposite; it looks to inhibit that which the Supreme Court wanted to reassure. [translation][56]

Daniel Turp, one of the act's most vocal critics, reiterated this sentiment: "Even though the Court stressed the obligation to negotiate, C-20 shows that its focus is not on the obligation to negotiate, but rather on the obligation not to negotiate."[57] This is clear, according to Turp, in the very wording of the act; for example, section 1(6) stresses that the Government of Canada *shall not* enter into negotiations:

> There is a striking contrast between the language used by the Supreme Court and that used by the Government of Canada in relation to the obligation to negotiate. Whereas the Court presents the obligation to negotiate as a constitutional and binding obligation stemming from the democratic will of the people of Quebec, the government of Canada has drafted the *Clarity Act* in a way that suggests that it wants to dodge the obligation to negotiate.[58]

The Constitutionality of the Act

The two strongest and loudest voices in the debate about the act's constitutionality were those of Turp and Dion. Dion argued that "the bill protects the rights and interests of all Canadians from undemocratic attacks on federalism...Every Canadian will have the guarantee that the government of Canada will never enter into negotiations on the separation of a province unless the population of that province has clearly expressed its will to cease to be part of Canada."[59] According to Turp, "the bill is so undemocratic that it would even allow this House to make a judgment on the clarity of the question during the course of the referendum campaign...*would* that not be a totally unacceptable interference in democratic process?"[60]

Further, does the *Clarity Act* stifle the collective rights and goals of the Quebec people, or is it constitutional and within the federal government's prerogative to authorize?

Turp looked at the *Clarity Act* in terms of the federal principle, which has a "prominent role and the status of a cardinal rule of constitutional interpretation as seen through the Secession rule."[61] The Court, according to Turp, was guided by the federal principle when ruling on the legality of the secession of a province, "but Jean Chrétien's federal government has certainly not abided by this principle in bringing forward a *Clarity Act*. On the contrary, the *Clarity Act* tends to circumvent the federal principle."[62] The *Clarity Act* gives the federal government extraordinary powers, powers that offend the federal principle and breach the principle of obligation to negotiate.

Turp argued that the *Clarity Act* "subordinates Quebec, and for that matter all Canadian provinces, to a central authority and confers on the Parliament of Canada new powers that are inconsistent with the federal principle."[63] These "new" powers of Parliament are analogous to the powers of disallowance, which have long been deemed inconsistent with the federal principle: "The architect of Plan B, my colleague Stéphane Dion, may continue to argue that the National Assembly of Quebec can draft the question it wants and put it to a referendum: the reality is that the Clarity bill grants the House of Commons power to overrule any such question."[64]

Bariteau reiterated this when he argued that "Adopted, this law will legalize the subordination of the Quebec people" [translation].[65] Brun, echoing Bariteau, argued that the intention of the bill was to restrict the rights of the Quebec people: "...a law that has no other objective but to impede the most fundamental collective right: the liberty to express one's choice for his/her political future" [translation].[66]

Further, Brun argued that the bill was unconstitutional in that it was an attempt by the federal government to indirectly withdraw from the constitutional duty to negotiate: "In attempting to place this notion of clarity in a perfectly abstract judicial framework, the federal government, in reality, is acting completely unconstitutionally; it simply does not have the power to indirectly relieve the federal government from its Constitutional obligation to negotiate" [translation].[67]

Lachapelle reiterated the perception that the collective rights of the Quebec people were being infringed upon by arguing that "Bill C-20 is an attack on the democratic freedoms and values of Canadians and Quebecers. It is also a denial of the constitutional principles that guided the birth of Canada and the relations between Quebec, the federal government and the provinces of Canada." He went to state that "in our view, Bill C-20 is unconstitutional, not to mention that it works towards the domination of an executive type of federalism."[68]

Ryan also viewed the constitutionality of the *Clarity Act* as questionable in terms of federalism and democracy, as it "contains elements that are plainly unacceptable, not only to sovereignists, but also to many federalist Quebecers." The unconstitutional nature of the act rested in section 1, the very essence of the *Clarity Act*; it represents "an undesirable intrusion of the federal Parliament into a process that must unfold within Quebec." More specifically, the act recognizes the federal principle by acknowledging that each province has the right to consult its people via a referendum on an issue, but "it contradicts this recognition by a provision in the clarity bill that confers on the federal Parliament direct power of intervention in the referendum process at a stage when, by its own admission, this process lies within the jurisdiction of the Quebec National Assembly."[69] In addition, the federal government is intruding, at the very least indirectly, on the drafting of the question when it indicates the criteria that Parliament ought to use when judging the clarity of the question.

The view that the *Clarity Act* was both unconstitutional and an infringement upon the rights of the Quebec people was held not only by academics but also by the media in both English and French Canada: About 150 academics, unionists and activists signed an Open Letter in support of the Democratic Rights of self-determination for Quebec, which called the bill undemocratic and authoritarian because "it gives the federal government alone the power to determine the clarity of the question and to determine what constitutes a clear majority."[70]

A coalition of nongovernmental organizations in Quebec, including all major Quebec labour federations, teachers' unions, the writers' union and a federation of patriotic organizations, took out an advertisement in the *New York Times* entitled "Shame on Ottawa." In it, the coalition argued that "if adopted, the bill would negate the right of the people of the Quebec to freely decide their own future and make Canada into a prison of nations."[71]

In contrast, others held that the act was constitutional and did not infringe upon the rights of the Quebec people: "Bill C-20 doesn't deny Quebeckers the right to self-determination. It merely states that the federal government will not negotiate terms of separation if the question asked in a referendum is not clear, and unless a clear majority expresses such a preference. The House of Commons will judge if the question is clear."[72]

Monahan and Hogg both argued that the *Clarity Act* was constitutional under the Peace, Order and Good Government (POGG) clause. Hogg argued that the federal government under POGG had the constitutional authority to pass Bill C-20, "both in respect of entering negotiations for secession and in respect of proposing a constitutional amendment; those being the two things that Bill C-20 does."[73] Monahan agreed, and added that the federal government under section 44 of the *Constitution Act* of 1982 had the authority to pass this legislation. Under section 44 the federal government can unilaterally amend the constitution on issues that are strictly within the federal jurisdiction.[74] As Monahan argues, Bill C-20 places obligations and restrictions only on the House of Commons and the federal government itself. Further, it is only proper that the federal government assigns the role of determining the clarity of the question to Parliament, as this is the only body that is elected by all Canadians.

Pinard also argued that the bill was within the prerogative of the federal government: "the federal government is within its rights to impose conditions on the negotiations of a secession, as there are 'two parties' to every negotiation" [translation].[75]

Garant, though he argued that the 30-day period was an infringement on provincial powers, felt that the bill was not an exercise of the power of disallowance. He conceded, however, that "some might even say that the constitutionality is doubtful and that Parliament has found a clever way to interfere in our area of provincial legislative jurisdiction."[76]

Paul Jackson, a reporter for the *Calgary Sun*, was clear on his opinion on both the act and the reaction of Quebec to the act:

> Ever since (the introduction of bill C-20), separatists have been going ballistic – blood spurting out of their ears due to high blood pressure attacks and such like – insisting somehow their sovereign rights have been abrogated.
>
> What Dion really did was enhance the rights of all Canadians – including Quebecers – by preventing the separatists from stealing a slab of our nation using the methods of some fly-by-night snake of a salesman.[77]

In short, Jackson saw the actions of the federal government as positive in that the government took the matter into its own hands and gave very little role to a provincial government; ultimately Quebec separatists are enemies that need to be dealt with: "At the end of the day – or perhaps the start of a new era – the members of the House of Commons and Supreme Court will decide if the question was proper and the majority sufficient – then set the rules for a negotiated withdrawal from Canada."[78]

Enhanced Majority?

Another point of contention within the media and amongst academics is the requirement for an enhanced majority: by "clear majority," did the Supreme Court mean that more than 50 percent plus one is required? Further, if more than 50 percent plus one is required, would this offend the democratic principles we ascribe to, mainly the equality of voters?

According to both Monahan and Garant, the federal government should require more than 50 percent plus one; furthermore, it would be consistent with the Supreme Court decision to require an enhanced majority. Monahan stated: "Parliament should be able to say that a bare majority of 50 per cent plus 1 of those casting ballots does not constitute a clear majority, which would give effect to the view of the Supreme Court of Canada. The Supreme Court stated repeatedly in its judgment that a bare majority, a 'mere majority' rule, or something to that effect, is not in accordance with our constitutional tradition."[79] Garant felt that "[t]he spirit of the Supreme Court's judgment seemed to indicate that a higher bar should be set than a simple or absolute majority (50 per cent plus one) as is contained in bill 99."[80]

Lachapelle, on the other hand, argued that, based on the democratic principle of the equality of voters, 50 percent plus one should suffice. According to Lachapelle, when speaking of a "clear majority," the Supreme Court did not necessarily mean a qualified majority: "the rule of *fair play* is also a basic rule of any democratic exercise; to question it is to undermine a society. This principle should in fact be inscribed in Bill C-20."[81]

Larouche argued that the *Clarity Act* read into the Supreme Court decision by invoking the inequality of voters. This ignores, first, the sentiments of the Quebec sovereigntists and federalists that 50 percent plus one is sufficient; second, that this bar was understood as acceptable in the past two referenda; and, finally, that there is a clear precedent in Canadian constitutional history in the case of Newfoundland:

> While there is no mention, in the Supreme Court's opinion, of what a clear majority entails, section 2 of C-20 tries to consecrate the inequality of voters by granting more weight to the no vote than to the vote favouring Quebec sovereignty.
>
> Mainly sovereignists, but also Quebec federalists, argue that a clear majority remains that which has always been in our democratic system, 50 percent plus one. Granted, there have been no precise rules on the required percentage of a referendum, but the 50 percent bar was the one accepted by all actors, sovereignists and federalists alike, in the past two Quebec referenda. In addition, there is a clear precedent in Canadian history: Newfoundland, in 1949, joined Confederation with 52 percent support [translation].[82]

Chantal Hébert, in the *Hamilton Spectator*, pointed out the irony of the federal government requiring an enhanced majority: "The irony is that, under Dion's plan, Canada would engage in secession talks on the basis of a much weaker democratic mandate that Quebec's...Such a blank cheque approach by Ottawa to work out the break up of the country hardly offers Canadians the comfort they were told Bill C-20 could provide them."[83]

The unfortunate reality, however, is that the bill focuses not on how to reconcile unity through diversity but on how to "deal" with Quebec by rendering its constitutional aspirations nearly impossible. As Hébert points out, "knowing that the federalists only carried previous referendums by solemnly promising changes to Quebecers, does bill C-20 not amount to sending future federalist champions into the fray with an instruction manual to deal with failure rather than with tools to achieve success?"[84]

Conclusion

The problem with the *Clarity Act* and the analysis that followed is our relentless focus on the wording of the question in future referenda. This ignores the roots of the problem, that of linguistic duality and the diversity of Canada. As Ryan argued, since the *Secession Reference*, the public has been concerned with two issues, clarity of the question and the meaning of "clear majority"; the *Clarity Act* reinforces these two issues.[85] This narrow focus allows us to miss and, more importantly, ignore (which of course is harmful in itself) the crux of the conflict between Quebec and the rest of Canada. Instead, we should focus on more important questions: Why does a sovereigntist movement exist in Quebec? Why has this movement been so significant over the past quarter century? What is the best strategy to counter the idea of Quebec sovereignty? Rather than forcing Canadians, especially Quebecers, to choose between federalists and sovereigntists, the federal government, with the rest of the country, ought to engage in the endeavour of combining the two and not kill the possibility of reconciling unity through diversity.

Furthermore, the media, political observers and the federal government have focused on the second part of the *Secession Reference* and have failed to recognize the inherent contradictions of the Court's opinion – the conflict between constitutional democracy and the requirement of clarity. The former entails open and continuous debate, whereas the latter enforces one fixed definition of clarity. In the case of the *Clarity Act*, that one definition is the federal government's. The *Clarity Act*, in limiting what can be asked in a referendum on sovereignty, displaced the decision of defining clarity not only from the people of Quebec but also from the people of Canada as a whole. Under the act, the federal government alone has the power to define clarity. The Court, by presenting a very formalized definition of constitutional democracy through its demand for clarity, which is in and of itself ambiguous, enabled the subsequent action of the federal government. Democracy implies the existance of many debates, the purpose of which are to convince both the opposing party and the rest of the polis of one's point of view. This is the soul of democracy. By the Court's requiring one notion of clarity and by the federal government's assigning itself the role of spokesperson for defining or, better yet, setting the parameters of this notion, debate is ended and democracy, even as the Court defined it, is stifled.

35

Notes

1. Tully (2000).

2. Supreme Court of Canada, *Reference re Secession of Quebec* (hereafter *Secession Reference*), para. 87.

3. *Secession Reference,* para. 92; see also para. 104.

4. *Secession Reference*, para. 100.

5. *Secession Reference*, para. 51.

6. *Secession Reference*, para. 62.

7. *Secession Reference*, para. 65.

8. *Secession Reference*, para. 68.

9. *Secession Reference*, para. 70.

10. Lajoie et al. (1994, pp. 336-44).

11. Lajoie (2000, p. 37).

12. Tully (2001, p. 6).

13. Tully (2000).

14. Tully (2001, p. 7).

15. Tully (2000, p. 5).

16. *Secession Reference*, para. 88.

17. Gagnon and Erk (2002, p. 325).

18. *Secession Reference*, para. 68.

19. *Secession Reference*, para. 93.

20. Hogg (1999, p. 34).

21. Morin (1999, p. 5).

22. Dion (1999).

23. The preamble of the *Clarity Act* states: "Whereas the Supreme Court of Canada has stated that democracy means more than simple majority rule, that a clear majority in favour of secession would be required to create an obligation to negotiate secession, and that a qualitative evaluation is required to determine whether a clear majority in favour of secession exists in the circumstances."

24. *Secession Reference*, para. 151.

25. However, the preamble to the *Clarity Act* does state: "Whereas, in light of the finding by the Supreme Court of Canada that it would be for elected representatives to determine what constitutes a clear question and what constitutes a clear majority in a referendum held in a province on secession, the House of Commons, as the only political institution elected to represent all Canadians, has an important role in identifying what constitutes a clear question and a clear majority sufficient for the Government of Canada to enter into negotiations in relation to the secession of a province from Canada."

26. *Secession Reference*, para. 188.

27. Dion (1997).

28. *Secession Reference*, para. 151.

29. Rebick (2000, p. 5).

30. Hogg (2000).

31. Monahan (2000b).

32. Gibbins (2000).

33. Gibbins (2000).

34. In choosing which academics and reporters to study and analyze, we selected those who best articulated their position. In addition, we tried to capture the debate occurring all over the country by looking at media commentary from different parts of the country. Furthermore, in looking at the comments of academics, we tended to lean toward those who are well known in the field of constitutional politics.

35. Tully (2000, p. 4).

36. Ayed (2000). Emphasis added.

37. Ayed (2000).

38. Fraser (2000).

39. Macpherson (2000).

40. Monahan (2000b, p. 8).

41. Bariteau (2000).

42. Bariteau (2000).

43. Garant (2000).

44. Garant (2000).

45. Monahan (2000b, p. 9).

46. Monahan (2000b, p. 23).

47. Monahan (2000b, p. 20).

48. Hogg (2000).

49. Pinard (2000).

50. Pinard (2000).

51. Reid (2000).

52. Larouche (2000).

53. Larouche (2000).

54. Lachapelle (2000).

55. Brun (2000).

56. Brun (2000).

57. Turp (2000).

58. Turp (2000).

59. Turp (2000).

60. Ayed (2000).

61. Turp (2000).

62. Turp (2000).

63. Turp (2000).

64. Turp (2000).

65. Bariteau (2000).

66. Brun (2000).

67. Brun (2000).

68. Lachapelle (2000).

69. Ryan (2000, p. 27).

70. Rebick (2000).

71. Newswire (2000).

72. Kilgour (2000, p. 6).

73. Hogg (1999).

74. Monahan (2000a).

75. Pinard (2000).

76. Pinard (2000).

77. Jackson (2000).

78. Jackson (2000).

79. Monahan (2000b).

80. Garant (2000).

81. Lachapelle (2000).

82. Larouche (2000).

83. Hébert (2000).

84. Hébert (2000).

85. Ryan (2000, p. 29).

Bibliography

Ayed, N. "Clarity bill passes despite stalling tactics." Canadian Press [Ottawa], March 15, 2000. http://cgi.canoe.ca/CNEWSReferendum0003/mar15_clarity.html (accessed June 19, 2001).

Bariteau, C. "Pour les Québécois, être Canadiens implique la soumission aux diktats de la Chambre des communes." *Le Soleil* [Montreal]. February 9, 2000. http://www.vigile.net/00-2/20-bariteau.html (accessed June 19, 2001).

Brun, H. "Le gouvernement du Québec devrait contester par renvoi la constitutionnalité de la loi." *Le Devoir* [Montreal]. February 23, 2000. http://www.vigile.net/00-2/20-brun.html

Dion, S. "Au-delà du plan A et du plan B : les deux débats sur l'unité canadienne." Notes for a speech by the Hon. Stéphane Dion, President of the Privy Council and Minister of Intergovernmental Affairs, to the Montreal Press Club, December 3, 1997.

———. *Notes pour une allocution de l'honorable Stéphane Dion, Président du Conseil privé et ministre des Affaires intergouvernementales, lors du débat en deuxième lecture du projet de loi C-20*, House of Commons, December 14, 1999.

Fraser, G. "Senate stars attack 'clarity' bill." *Toronto Star.* June 29, 2000. http://king.thestar.com/thestar/editorial/canpol/20000629NEW07_NA-UNITY.html (June19, 2001).

Gagnon, Alain-G., and Can Erk. "Legitimacy, Effectiveness, and Federalism: On the Benefits of Ambiguity," in *Canadian Federalism: Performance, Effectiveness, and Legitimacy,* ed. H. Bakvis and G. Skogstad. Don Mills, ON: Oxford University Press, 2002.

Garant, P. "Opinion on C-20." *Proceedings of the Special Committee on Bill C-20.* Ottawa, May 29, 2000.

Gibbins, R. "Opinion on C-20." *Proceedings of the Special Committee on Bill C-20.* Ottawa, June 1, 2000.

Hébert, C. "Senate Tears into Clarity Bill." *Hamilton Spectator,* May 31, 2000. http://www.hamiltonspectator.com/hebert/237398.html (accessed June 21, 2001).

Hogg, P.W. "The Duty to Negotiate." *Canada Watch,* Vol. 7, nos. 1-2 (January-February 1999): 1, 33-34.

———. "Opinion on C-20." *Proceedings of the Special Committee on Bill C-20.* Ottawa, June 5, 2000.

Jackson, P. "Turning the tables on separatists requires absolutely certain rules." *Calgary Sun.* March 9, 2000. http://www.vigile.net/00-3/dion-calgary.html (accessed June 19, 2001).

Lachapelle, G. "Opinion on C-20." *Proceedings of the Special Committee on Bill C-20.* Ottawa, June 5, 2000.

Kilgour, D. "Clarity Bill aims to thwart separatists." 2000. http://www.david-kilgour.com/news/spring00/clarity.html (accessed June 21, 2001).

Lajoie, A. "La primauté du droit et la légitimité démocratique comme enjeux du Renvoi sur la sécession du Québec." *Politique et Sociétés,* Vol. 19, nos. 2-3 (2000): 31-42.

Lajoie, A., R. Robin, S. Grammond, H. Quillinan, L. Rolland, S. Perrault and A. Chitrit. *Osgoode Hall Journal,* Vol. 32, no. 2 (1994): 295-391.

Larouche, S. "C-20 ou [la volonté] de se soustraire à l'avis de la Cour suprême." *Le Devoir* [Montreal], August 22, 2000. http://www.vigile.net/00-8/c-20-larouche.html (accessed June 20, 2001).

Macpherson, D., "The anti-clarity bill." *The Gazette* [Montreal]. 2000. http://Canada-acsus.plattsburgh.edu/cannews/gaz121699D.html (accessed June 20, 2001).

Monahan, P. "Doing the Rules: An Assessment of the Federal Clarity Act in Light of the Quebec Secession Reference." *C.D. Howe Institute Commentary*, no. 135, February 2000a. http://www.cdhowe.org/pdf/monahan-2.pdf (accessed June 20, 2001).

———. "Opinion on C-20." *Proceedings of the Special Committee on Bill C-20.* Ottawa, May 29, 2000b.

Morin, J.-Y. "A Balanced Judgment?" *Canada Watch*, Vol. 7, nos. 1-2 (January-February 1999): 3, 5.

Newswire. "Quebec groups blast Ottawa's so called referendum 'clarity' bill in full-page ad in today's New York Times." *Newswire* [Montreal]. December 20, 1999. http://www1.newswire.ca/releases/december1999/20/c5439.html (accessed June 21, 2001).

Pinard, M. "Opinion on C-20." *Proceedings of the Special Committee on Bill C-20.* Ottawa, June 5, 2000.

Rebick, J. "Clarity bill is anything but." *CBC viewpoints* [Toronto], March 17, 2000. http://cbc.ca/news/viewpoint/columns/rebick/rebick000317.html (accessed June 21, 2001).

Reid, S. "Bill C-20's Byzantine negotiating procedures leave debt, borders and other such issues up in the air." *National Post* [Toronto], February 22, 2000. http://www.vigile.net/00-2/20-scott.html (accessed June 21, 2001).

Ryan, Claude. "Consequences of the Quebec Secession Reference: The Clarity Bill and Beyond." *C.D. Howe Institute Commentary*, no. 139, April 2000. http://www.cdhowe.org/ pdf/ryan.pdf (accessed June 19, 2001).

Supreme Court of Canada. *Reference re Secession of Quebec*, 2 SCR 217, 1998. http://www.lexum.umontreal.ca/csc-scc/en/pub/1998/vol2/html/1998scr2_0217.html (accessed June 21, 2001).

Tully, James. *The Unattained Yet Attainable Democracy: Canada and Quebec Face the New Century.* Montreal: Programme d'études sur le Québec de l'Université McGill, 2000.

———. "Introduction," in *Multinational Democracies*, ed. Alain-G. Gagnon and James Tully. Cambridge: Cambridge University Press, 2001.

Turp, D. "The Clarity Act and the Quebec Secession Reference: Shooting Down the Lodestar of Canadian Federalism." Speech before the Law Society of Upper Canada: Special Lectures 2000: Constitutional and Administrative Law. Osgoode Hall, Toronto, June 9, 2000.

Young, H. "Ottawa cherche à se soustraire d'une négociation". Canadian Press [Ottawa]. http://www.vigile.net/00-6/20-lachapelle.html (accessed June 20, 2000).

part III
diversity under stress

11

"transnationalism" or "renationalization"? the politics of cultural identity in the European Union

Peter A. Kraus

The European Union can be conceived of as a multinational polity of a new kind. So far, however, the advances achieved in integrating sectoral policies and extending fields of political regulation across European states have hardly been matched by parallel processes that ought to be giving the European Union a higher degree of politico-cultural cohesion. For this reason, recent analyses of the problems experienced when the strengthening of Europe's political dimension is at stake have often pointed to the weak cultural foundations available for constructing a European "state." From such a perspective, cultural heterogeneity, embedded in a system of entrenched nation-states, is seen as a major force inhibiting the formation and articulation of a common political will among Europeans. According to this view, the legacy of European nationalism appears as the main obstacle on the way toward the making of a proper European *demos*.

Put in a nutshell, nationalism is a principle that links political integration to a shared cultural identity. In this respect, it may well be significant that institutional attempts at creating a European identity "from above," by trying to find some common cultural denominators, have been largely unsuccessful. In some respects, one could even maintain that the Europeanization of policies and politics has been fuelling the reaffirmation of national identities all over Europe. This paper will try to assess the institutional impact of the multinational factor in the EU. It argues that the politics of cultural identity at the European level are strongly marked by the contradictions underlying the EU's institutional development. On the one hand, the principle of intergovernmentalism stresses the role of nation-states and tends to reinforce the weight of national cultures, understood as the cultures of nation-states, in the context of European decision-making. The corresponding political identity would not reflect much more than the pooling of the legitimizing resources provided by different state nationalisms. Yet, on the other hand, Europeanization does contribute to the erosion of traditional forms of national sovereignty. Thus, "transnationalism" offers possibilities for articulating cultural identities below and beyond the nation-state, contributing to some extent to the "denationalization" of political cultures in Europe. One may conclude that, until now, the institutional logics governing European integration have led not to the disappearance of nationalism but rather to a differentiation of the discourses connecting political and cultural identities, to a "reframing" of nationalism according to the varying imperatives and goals of the actors involved.

"Thin" Nationalism and the Modern Democratic Polity

Let me take a "thin" concept of nationalism as a point of departure. By using the term "thin," I simply want to make clear that the main focus of the argument put forward here is not on nationalism as a political ideology based on an elaborate catalogue of "thick" normative assumptions.[1] The following observations refer, rather, to nationalism as an organizing principle of modern societies. In this "thin" sense, nationalism is an omnipresent and indeed a "banal"[2] phenomenon that permeates our everyday lives and structures our cognitive approach to politics. A "thin" view of nationalism will tend to be normatively agnostic and sceptical of dichotomies as crude as that built on the stubbornly popular opposition of "ethnic" versus "civic" national affiliations. To speak of thin nationalism simply means to acknowledge the strong links that have been established between processes of political integration and cultural standardization in modern times. From the corresponding perspective, nationalism has been cultural politics *avant la lettre*. According to the definition given by Jordan and Weedon, the realm of cultural politics covers the agenda raised by the following questions: "Whose culture shall be the official one and whose shall be subordinated? What culture shall be regarded as worthy of display and which shall be hidden? Whose history shall be remembered and whose forgotten? What images of social life shall be projected and which shall be marginalized? What voices shall be heard and which silenced? Who is representing whom and on what basis?"[3]

If we place all these issues in a historical context, it becomes evident that in most cases the normal way of dealing with them has been some kind of nationalism. This seems especially true if we consider the relationship between cultural identity and political representation. Implicitly or explicitly, some type of cultural affinity has typically served as the foundation of political unity in modern, differentiated societies.

In the name of the nation, culture is politicized while politics are simultaneously culturalized. Nationalism's rationale is that sharing a culture is the fundament for building a polity and that integrating a polity requires a common culture. As Gellner succinctly put it: "Nationalism is a political principle which maintains that similarity of culture is the basic social bond."[4] For those who adhere to a thick nationalism, this is a normative claim, and its validity is supposed to be universal and perennial. In the notorious language of the extreme versions of thick nationalism, the "basic social bond" takes quite a literal meaning: "*über alles*," "*todo por la patria*," "right or wrong, my country." From the contrasting angle of thin nationalism, the connection of culture and politics has normatively neutral or ambiguous qualities, to say the least, but nonetheless reflects a blunt sociological reality, the relevance of which may vary with the historical and political context. Thus, the weight of the national bond becomes a contingent factor and does not correspond to any prior normative commitments.

In any case, taking nationalism seriously requires that we understand the prominent role cultural identity plays as the template for processes of political communication in modern societies. To a large extent, the integrated spaces of communication in which we are used to acting as citizens are created and reproduced by political institutions. In the course of its political institutionalization, a cultural identity gets a reified or structural character that "governs" the interactions of the members of a political community. Yet in spite of its structural aspects, the communicative spaces generated by an encompassing cultural identity do not delineate a closed system of meaning. Sharing a culture does not imply that there is a substantial consensus on shared values. To communicate includes the option of articulating dissent. A culture structures areas of common knowledge, but it does not rule out conflict over the content and interpretation of this knowledge.[5] Cultural identities do not simply display prefabricated answers to normatively relevant questions; they offer a changing repertoire of orientations for coming to grips with such questions. Nevertheless, the cultural repertoire has an almost "taken for granted" dimension. It comprehends the "basics" that the members of a political community learn while being socialized into this community. Precisely because of their "taken for grantedness," these basics play a crucial role in reproducing a political order. They are the source of the "diffuse support"[6] required if social conflicts are to be institutionalized in a democratic way.

Nationalism is born out of the intertwining of cultural and political integration in modern societies. With the emergence of national forms of rule, the cultural homogeneity of a polity became an important functional and legitimizing principle.[7] The functional aspect results from the increased need for regulating processes of social communication in modern states, as compared to traditional forms of political organization. Industrialism and bureaucracy are well-known motors of cultural standardization. The legitimizing aspect of culture is even more important in the context discussed here: in the overlapping areas of cultural reproduction and the democratic exercise of power, cultural identity becomes "national" identity. On the path of political modernization, the extension of citizenship rights was based upon the definition of a cultural profile common to all citizens. In contrast with instruments of authoritarian control, democratic institutions are contingent upon high levels of political loyalty and trust within the population. In the process of formation of democracies at the level of nation-states, cultural homogeneity was considered a precondition for political differentiation and the control of the conflict potentials it generates. The concept of democratic sovereignty presupposes the existence of a collective identity sustaining the polity that is conceived of as sovereign. From the viewpoint of democratic theory, however, the problem with this identity is that it can hardly be postulated to be the outcome of democratic decision-making. As democracies do not come into being in a historical void, and as there is no democracy before democracy, the roots of a sovereign people's identity are inextricably interwoven with a pre-democratic past. Hence, the collective subject in whose name a democracy is established – the *demos*, democracy's "we" – enters the democratic scene without democratic credentials.

This has been called the paradox of sovereignty.[8] The paradox of sovereignty represents one of the major blind spots in democratic theory. But the paradox does not only involve a great theoretical challenge: its practical impact is obvious as well, especially in those democracies in which the identity of the nation as the embodiment of popular sovereignty is an issue of political dispute. The paradox is also perceivable in the ongoing debate on the foundations available for creating a European democracy.

In the period of nation-state formation, cultural identity served as the frame that held the members of a political community together. It was the cement stabilizing the civic consensus that was considered necessary in order to guarantee the continuity and smoothness of the democratic process. Yet this cement was not simply "out there," offering a quasiorganic proof of common belonging. Nor were shared cultural attachments a by-product of voluntary negotiations leading to a civic contract. Normally, they were shaped by the policies of states claiming to be guided by democratic intentions while simultaneously trying to turn their population into a culturally homogeneous people. It seems questionable that there is any real historical case showing that the identity of the sovereign people was constituted as the spontaneous manifestation of a collective will articulated "from below." In many situations, a "top-down" dynamics of institutional strategies devoted to fostering a specific set of cultural patterns was arguably a much more important factor in "people-making" than popular mobilization itself. It should be added that, from the angle adopted here, the concepts of culture and cultural identity are used in a way that is deliberately rather selective, at least if compared to those approaches worked out in social anthropology and related disciplines. For the purposes of my argument, culture is understood as a set of highly institutionalized collective practices, and institutionalization means basically political institutionalization. In this context, the most significant aspects of culture tend to be the most obvious. Examples of this kind of institutionalized cultural identity include the public representation of national symbols (as in monuments and museums and on street names or banknotes), educational curricula, patterns of religious identification or secular creeds protected by the state as well as official languages.

As Robert Dahl cogently indicates, there can be no democratic decision-making if there is no unit that allows the rightful application of democratic procedures.[9] The rightfulness of the unit itself, however, cannot be determined just by making use of procedures that are derived from democratic criteria. Cultural identity has been so relevant for processes of democratic integration because it is an apparently "pre-political" and unquestionable resource for democratic politics; as such, it cannot easily be called into question. Where a democracy lacks the "natural" support of a shared cultural identity, political conflicts threaten to tear apart the civic community, evoking the spectre of secession. Yet the contribution cultural identity has typically made to circumvent the paradox of sovereignty is not politically innocent. The cultural elements at work when a democratic polity is constructed tend not to have a neutral origin, but are manifestations of cultural hegemony. Inasmuch as this is the case, they bear an aspect of domination that makes them politically contestable. Thus, the paradox of sovereignty reappears as the dilemma of cultural identity.

European Integration and Nationalism

After the Second World War, the desire to transcend the negative historical record of nationalism in twentieth-century continental Europe was one of the major driving forces of European unification, at least if we look at the political declarations of some of the foremost founding fathers of the EC/EU. The ideas of putting an end to a period of nationalistic barbarities, of overcoming ancestral Franco-German rivalries and of making Germany an integral part of a European peace system were important elements in the discourse of those who advocated a federated Europe. At the same time, however, integration was never supposed to question the continuity of the nation-states involved. According to a statement made in 1964 by one of the main architects of the nascent EC/EU, the former foreign minister of France Robert Schuman, the "European states are a historical reality; it is psychologically impossible to eradicate them."[10] To return to the categories introduced previously, on the one hand, the EC/EU constitutes an ambitious political attempt at overcoming thick nationalism, or at least radically containing its effects; on the other hand, one may argue that thin nationalism has been structurally built into Europe's institutional setting from the very beginning of the integration process and that it continues to be an important aspect of European politics. Broadly speaking, the process of constructing nation-states in Europe was hostile to diversity. For state-building elites, diversity was essentially an obstacle to political integration. Typically, the mainstream version of state theories reflecting the European tradition postulates that a state should have a uniform identity, a single source of sovereignty and a unitary conception of citizens' rights and obligations, thus presupposing societies that are culturally homogeneous.[11] Nonetheless, the record that reflects, especially, the experiences of the larger territorial states in western Europe cannot be generalized without qualifications. To assume that there was one standard model for the organization of rule by the nation-state in Europe would be misleading. If we look more closely at the degree of congruence between cultural and political integration patterns, the paths of state formation reveal considerable differences. In particular, those European polities that were the successors of the larger absolutist states did try to link the goals of territorial integration and cultural homogeneity when they applied the principle of sovereignty within their domain of rule. But although in some cases the efforts put into creating culturally uniform units were quite far reaching, the success story of the homogeneous European nation-state remains to a great extent a myth, if the long-term results are taken into account. Thus, establishing a monopoly of centralized political control in the realms of language and culture turned out to be almost impossible in those countries that had experienced only a limited "nationalization" of particular collective identities before they entered the period of democratic mass politics. In such cases, the institutional negation of cultural pluralism by the state would arouse the protest of mobilized ethno-linguistic groups.[12]

The paths of state building in Europe led to different levels of cultural homogenization and linguistic standardization. In the making of the European state system, the political principle *cuius regio, eius religio* and its regular concomitant *cuius regio, eius lingua* often became contested issues. Hence, the interplay of language and the political sphere in west European nation-states is characterized by a remarkable degree of variation. At present, the range of constellations to be found in the field of language policy, for example, stretches from an official monolingualism that by and large corresponds to the sociolinguistic reality of a country to the generalized multilingualism of public institutions. In the early modern period, city states and city leagues articulated possible alternatives to the institutional hegemony of the sovereign territorial state.[13] In the end, these alternatives were marginalized on the contingent path of political modernization. Yet remnants of the political model they had embodied survived in areas where functional and territorial domains of rule were being subdivided according to the logics of subsidiarity. Within the territory of the European city belt that reaches from Hanse-Germany to the contemporary Benelux countries and from upper Italy to Catalonia, the attempts to stabilize the hegemony of a single political centre over a clear-cut domain of rule that were typical of the age of absolutism met substantial resistance. That a diversity-sensitive federalism has for a long time been an important political factor in city-state Europe does not seem to be a coincidence.

At the same time, however, we must not forget that state building and war making were closely interrelated processes in the history of west European nation-states, including city-belt Europe.[14] The typical units of the emerging European state system were formed in a context of conflict, which often enough found final expression in open military clashes with neighbouring units. Cultural uniformity within a given unit was meant to increase the loyalty of the population toward "its" state, a state eager to protect or to expand a territorial sovereignty permanently threatened by the existence of other sovereign states. European integration, to the contrary, received a significant initial impulse from an explicit supranational agreement on breaking with a centuries-old legacy of interstate rivalries over regional geopolitical hegemony. This did not mean, however, that the states joining the EC/EU were eager to give up their sovereign authority for the sake of Europe. The "pooling" of sovereignty and the co-ordination of policies were, rather, meant to define a new frame for articulating national interests (and identities). In this respect, it is no wonder that the institutional evolution of the EC/EU's own domains of governance offered only some traces of an open and visible exercise of political power. A defining characteristic of the *méthode Monnet* was the effort to hide political decision-making behind inconspicuous technocratic routines.[15] Political authority was successively shifted to the European level with great discretion, so that the growing scope of integrated policies appeared to be an almost unintended effect of routine bureaucratic operations. This corresponded to the logic of the famous maxim that *petits pas* is the best strategy to adopt if one wants to bring about *grands effets*.

European integration by now goes well beyond the establishment of a common market. The political implications of Union membership are an issue that dominates the political agenda in all states that have joined or plan to join the EU. The EU constitutes a political system in its own right; it has evolved into a polity *sui generis*, as we are now used to saying. Even the most orthodox intergovernmentalist would be reluctant to classify the EU as "just another international organization." The Union is a multi-layered and contradictory institutional field, marked by the thorny cohabitation of the two opposed principles of supranationalism and intergovernmentalism.[16] In its institutional setting, the member states do delegate significant portions of the competences they formerly held in a sovereign way to the transnational level. In the European system of multi-level governance,[17] the logics of political decision-making vary substantially in different policy areas. Thus, for the moment, the EU offers an institutional image that is far less coherent than the ideal concept we have of the modern state. It is hardly a surprise that the interplay of the competing political forces underlying the EU's institutional development reverberates in the politics of cultural identity in Europe. In the present constellation, the nation-states tend to take all precautions against any tendency that might provide the EU with state-like powers, as far as the connection of political and cultural identities is concerned. Whenever it is at work, intergovernmentalism puts all emphasis on the importance of the member states' national cultures in the European context. In contrast, European transnationalism may encourage the articulation of cultural identities below and beyond the nation-state level and contribute to a new political configuration of identity options.

In an EU facing the challenges of eastern enlargement, debates on whether Europe needs a proper constitution in order to be able to tackle urgent institutional reforms and meet democratic standards are intensifying. The tension between thin nationalism and transnationalism is a significant feature of these debates. At one end, discussions are dominated by some version of what has been frequently called the "no *demos*" thesis. In political terms, the most articulate exponent of the thesis is French "sovereigntism." The basic postulate of the "no *demos*" approach to Europe is that plans to constitutionalize the EU are premature, as there is no European *demos* that could give a democratic Euro-polity the necessary socio-cultural base. One of the principal spokesmen of the sovereigntist currents in France, Jean-Pierre Chevènement, has stressed on different occasions that democratic debate cannot and must not be stretched beyond the institutional frame of the nation and the national public sphere.[18] As we know, Chevènement, as a French republican nationalist, tends to conflate the normative and sociological dimensions of the concept of the nation. But the capability of the EU to become a fully fledged democracy is also questioned in accounts of the "no *demos*" thesis that are normatively less biased.[19] In all approaches, however, the crucial problem remains, for the time being, that democracy is bound to be national, since patterns of legitimation transcending national boundaries remain weak. It is typically in this context that culture comes in: the differentiation of cultural identities and the heterogeneity of political loyalties it entails are seen as a critical barrier against all constitutional attempts at founding a democratic European polity that could rely on the common political attachments of Europeans.

In academic circles, the main opponents of the "no *demos*" view have been the exponents of late Frankfurt-inspired post-nationalism.[20] Yet in the world of day-to-day European politics, the proposals put forward by the advocates of a European constitution have tended to be much more moderate than the positions of post-nationalist intellectuals. The catchphrase in recent political discussions is the "federation of nation-states." The formula introduced by Jacques Delors is becoming an obligatory point of reference in a series of official statements dealing with the constitutional issue.[21] In spite of the growing popularity of the concept, it is difficult not to feel somewhat confused by its striking ambivalence. We may even ask ourselves if we are not confronting a plain oxymoron: the fusion of nation and state aims at creating an institutional realm emanating from an undivided and indivisible source of sovereignty. In contrast to this, a federation can only come into being if there is some division of sovereignty between different institutional levels of decision-making. Seen in this light, plans to build a federation of nation-states come pretty close to an attempt at finding a square transnational form for the intergovernmental circle.

The EU can be conceived not only as a polity of a new kind: it can also be seen to represent a new form of multinational polity. Its novelty would reside in the creation of a multinational order that lacks a hegemonic internal force and that has a culturally open or "undetermined" constitutional structure. Against this background, it is no coincidence that, as was said earlier, analyses of the problems experienced when the strengthening of Europe's political dimension is at stake often point at the weak cultural foundations available for constructing a European "state." From such a perspective, cultural heterogeneity, embedded in a system of entrenched nation-states, is seen as a major force inhibiting the formation and articulation of a common political will among Europeans. Thus, the legacy of European nationalism appears as a main obstacle on the way toward the making of a European *demos*. What makes the present situation in Europe so interesting is the circumstance that normative presuppositions become inextricably intermingled with the sociological realities of democratic politics. For the first time in the history of modern constitutionalism, the paradox of sovereignty is experienced by a mass public as a social and political reality. The safeguards still available in most of the history of European nation-building have become porous. Without a fixed realm, without a shared past, without an unchallenged cultural identity and without a common language, the foundations of the political unity of the EU look shaky. In view of the precariousness of the cultural resources sustaining political rule, the emperor has never been as naked as he appears to be in the headquarters of the European institutions in Brussels.

European Identity

The EC/EU may claim to have been actively engaged in "identity politics" well before it became a subject of major concern for the humanities and the social sciences. In the domain of European institutions, the career of the identity concept dates back to the early 1970s. More precisely, it began in December 1973, at an EC summit held in Copenhagen, when a "Declaration on European Identity" was adopted. The declaration listed the principles of representative democracy, of the rule of law, of social justice and of respect for human rights as the fundamental elements of the European identity and emphasized the will of the – at that moment, nine – member states to preserve the rich variety of their national cultures. At the same time, European identity was envisioned as something dynamic, both as a starting point and as a product of an open political process. The European "discovery" of the identity concept reflected the crises experienced in a changing world order at the beginning of the 1970s. The political attempt at launching the idea of a European identity in that context may well be interpreted as evidence of the weak bases of the common identity the integration process had generated so far.[22]

The main ingredients of the European identity discourse have remained surprisingly constant since 1973. On the one hand, a set of common political values establishes the framework for unity. On the other hand, cultural diversity retains a central normative status. Thus, the Millennium Declaration adopted by the European Council in Helsinki in December 1999, more than 25 years after Copenhagen, reads as follows:

> The European Union is based on democracy and the rule of law. The Union's citizens are bound together by common values such as freedom, tolerance, equality, solidarity and cultural diversity.
>
> The European Union is a unique venture, with no model in history. Only together, through the Union, can we and our countries meet tomorrow's challenges.[23]

From Copenhagen to Helsinki, the EC/EU's official approach to the question of cultural identity has been extremely cautious. At present, the recurrent pledge to respect and protect the diversity of cultures has almost developed into a ritual. Obviously, culture is a highly sensitive matter in European politics. It continues to be a competence primarily held by the member states, which are eager to take care of their "identity affairs." Nonetheless, since 1973 the cultural dimension has attained a more and more prominent role in the efforts officially undertaken in order to define Europe's identity, as a look at treaties, declarations and related documents shows. The evidence is particularly striking when we study the political dynamics in the period leading from the EC to the EU.

In the preamble of the Treaty on European Union signed in Maastricht in 1992, the member states manifest their desire "to deepen the solidarity between their peoples while respecting their history, their culture and their traditions." The announcement of a Common Foreign and Security Policy is linked to the intention of "reinforcing European identity and its independence."

Article 6 indicates:

1. The Union is founded on the principles of liberty, democracy, respect for human rights and fundamental freedoms, and the rule of law, principles which are common to the Member States...
3. The Union shall respect the national identities of its Member States.[24]

The Treaties of Maastricht and Amsterdam (1997) included an amendment of the treaty establishing the European Communities that was signed in Rome in 1957. The modified version of the Treaty of Rome contains a specific title (XII) for culture. As its Article 151 affirms:

1. The Community shall contribute to the flowering of the cultures of the Member States, while respecting their national and regional diversity and at the same time bringing the common cultural heritage to the fore.
2. Action by the Community shall be aimed at encouraging cooperation between Member States and, if necessary, supporting and supplementing their action in the following areas:
   - improvement of the knowledge and dissemination of the culture and history of the European peoples;
   - conservation and safeguarding of cultural heritage of European significance;
   - non-commercial cultural exchanges;
   - artistic and literary creation, including in the audiovisual sector...
4. The Community shall take cultural aspects into account in its action under other provisions of this Treaty, in particular in order to respect and to promote the diversity of its cultures.[25]

All in all, Maastricht and Amsterdam bolstered a tendency that was already present in the Copenhagen Declaration of 1973: the goals of establishing "an ever closer union" based on common values and preserving the diversity of cultures – a diversity that essentially has to be seen as a diversity of the cultures of nation-states – are set next to each other, without major efforts placed on reconciling their potentially conflicting logics. The Charter of Fundamental Rights of the European Union, solemnly proclaimed by the European Parliament, the Council and the Commission in Nice in December 2000, may be read as a text summarizing developments after Copenhagen. The following paragraphs are taken from the Charter's preamble:

> The peoples of Europe, in creating an ever closer union among them, are resolved to share a peaceful future based on common values. "Conscious of its spiritual and moral heritage, the Union is founded on the indivisible, universal values of human dignity, freedom, equality and solidarity; it is based on the principles of democracy and the rule of law. It places the individual at the heart of its activities, by establishing the citizenship of the Union and by creating an area of freedom, security and justice.
>
> The Union contributes to the preservation and to the development of these common values while respecting the diversity of the cultures and traditions of the peoples of Europe as well as the national identities of the Member States and the organisation of their public authorities at national, regional and local levels; it seeks to promote balanced and sustainable development and ensures free movement of persons, goods, services and capital, and the freedom of establishment.

Article 22 of the Charter of Rights consists of one short sentence that puts additional stress on the political significance of cultural diversity in the EU: "The Union shall respect cultural, religious and linguistic diversity."[26]

While trying to consolidate Europe as an "identity project," official European actors have not been limiting their efforts to the level of basic treaties and official declarations. This is especially true for the Commission under Delors during the Maastricht period and its aftermath. The institutional outcomes must not be underestimated. They comprise such measures as the introduction of Union citizenship, the proliferation of official European symbols in all realms of social life and the adoption of several important European programs devoted to education and culture. To say that attempts at identity-building from above have been a main concern of the EC/EU in the last two decades is hardly an exaggeration. Yet, it seems that these attempts have only had limited success in resolving the contradictions built into the European project. With few exceptions, as far as the mass public is concerned, identification with "Europeanness" lags well behind national and regional attachments. In some cases, there are even clear symptoms that the growing visibility of a "Europeanization" of everyday politics is provoking an increase in anti-European sentiments.[27] At any rate, European identity does not necessarily imply the formation of a harmonious link between different levels of political and cultural loyalties. It should not be complacently taken for an efficient tranquilizer, to be prescribed whenever European politics begin to follow a dynamic that brings them close to the territory of cultural politics. Often enough, instead of concealing the tensions between different identity options, the medication ends up revealing them. Fortunately, as we may be tempted to say, the new clothes of European identity do not cover enough of the emperor's body to make it look "natural."

Between Transnationalism and Renationalization

The French Revolution was a crucial starting point for the spread of nationalism. The fusion of the state and "the people" in the name of the nation, constituting a political community conceived of as sovereign and indivisible, must be regarded as a decisive turning point in modern European history. During the period of the Napoleonic wars, nationalism became a powerful instrument of political mobilization on a continental scale for the first time. Even traditional dynastic powers began to rely on the national principle in order to underscore their political legitimacy. The national pathos that had paved the way for the victories of the French armies was seen as a model to be imitated. If one wanted to prevail against the French, France had to be fought making use of the very same weapons that had made France's triumphal campaigns possible.[28] In the German lands, for instance, the wars against the French armies were considered to be liberation wars. The battle between Napoleon's troops and the joint forces recruited by Austria, Prussia, Sweden and Russia at Leipzig in 1813 came to be known as the "battle of the nations."[29] If we understand this battle as a protracted struggle between nation-states over hegemony in Europe, it did not come to a real end until the 1950s, when a stable peace settlement was reached, at least for the western half of the continent, a settlement that the east began to join after 1989. To what extent can this settlement be properly described as the beginning of a new transnational European order? I will sketch out a tentative answer to this question in two steps, looking at both the *inter*state and the *intra*state levels that regulate institutional approaches to diversity in the European Union.

The Interstate Level

Almost 200 years after Leipzig, another political event that might be called a "battle of the nations" occupied the centre of Europe's political stage: the EU summit at Nice in December 2000. To speak of a "battle of the nations" in the context of the Nice conference certainly requires some important qualifications. But allow me to briefly recapitulate the events first. The central purpose of Nice was to pave the way for far-reaching institutional reform, reform that is unavoidable if the EU is to be able to manage the challenges associated with its eastern enlargement. Moreover, the pressures toward realizing major institutional changes were thought to offer a unique opportunity for achieving higher levels of transparency and efficiency in the processes of European decision-making. At least, this was the declared goal of the numerous voices claiming that the widening and the deepening of the EU were in no way incompatible, but even mutually reinforcing political objectives.[30] Hence, in more general terms, the main tasks of the meeting consisted of discussing Europe's "finality," the general interests uniting all Europeans and perhaps even defining such a thing as the European "common good." In this respect, hardly any commentator would not describe the results of the Nice conference as utterly disappointing. The "all-European" perspective was virtually lost in an arena of tough intergovernmental bargaining. In the course of the prolonged and difficult negotiations, the representatives of the member states seemed to focus almost exclusively on their respective national interests. The strategy of *sauve qui peut* began to erode the effects of the traditional European *on s'arrange et puis on voit*. Even old cleavages typical of the European system of nation-states in a foregone period were apparently re-emerging. As a well-informed inside observer put it: "For the historically minded, a shadow of the continent's troublesome past which was characterized by endless struggles about dominance became visible for a moment."[31]

In press reports covering the Nice summit, analogies to war-like situations were frequently used: commenting upon the re-weighing of power and the modifications affecting the use of qualified majority voting (QMV) in the EU, newspapers spoke of an intense and open confrontation between France and Germany as well as of a clash of the smaller and the larger countries. In the end, there was much speculation about the winners and losers at Nice and about the forces giving proper support to the tiny compromises reached at the conference. In any case, it was evident that the main players in Europe's institutional setting were still the nation-states. This became especially visible in the discussions concerning the redistribution of voting power in the Council. The new procedure adopted requires that decisions made under QMV meet three conditions: they must be supported by a qualified majority of weighted votes, count on a majority of member states and, finally, represent a demographic majority of 62 percent of the EU's population. All in all, the weight of intergovernmentalism in Europe's semi-constitutional structure means that stateness receives a high premium in terms of political representation: in a European Union with

27 member states, Germany, with a population of approximately 82 million (17 percent of the total), gets 29 votes in the Council (8.4 percent); for Luxembourg, the corresponding figures are 429,000 (0.09 percent) and 4 (1.16 percent). Thus, when it comes to assigning voting powers in Europe's political system, the principle of equality of states clearly predominates against the principle of equality of citizens. This is also true in the context of the European Parliament: here, for example, a British parliamentarian represents roughly 823,000 citizens, whereas in the Irish case the ratio is 312,000 citizens per MEP.

I will not go into any further detail here. Of course, I am aware that formal procedures do not necessarily reflect factual political weight. Nevertheless, it seems fairly obvious that the nation-states are not about to stop being the basic political units in the EU. Hence, political interests continue to be principally framed as national interests, in the sense of the interests of nation-states. In spite of the institutional discourses and institutional structures created around "other" Europes, such as the Europe of the citizens, the Europe of the regions or the Europe of organized interests represented in the Economic and Social Committee, the European Union has been built as a union of nation-states. Its institutional structure is permeated by thin nationalism. The commitment to protect cultural identities that are institutionally framed as the national identities of the member states is not simply an exercise in rhetoric; it is well embedded in the Union's semi-constitutional architecture. Hence, my guess is that the EU is far away from superseding nationalism (at least in its "thin" versions). Rather, it is fostering its re-articulation in a new political setting. The institutional logics of the EU imply a more or less continuous reproduction of national structures. In the context of EU politics, this means basically that political interests are legitimized on the grounds of entrenched cultural identities, as long as these identities are those of nation-states.

The Intrastate Level

As was observed in an earlier section of this paper, variations between institutional approaches to dealing with linguistic and cultural diversity in western Europe are still remarkably high, even if the trend toward creating homogeneous nation-states was the historically dominant pattern. Against this background, a significant development deserves to be mentioned: during the last two decades, the protection of linguistic and national minorities within nation-states has progressively become a matter regulated by an emerging European human rights regime. The promotion of human rights has traditionally been one of the main tasks of the Council of Europe. Since eastern European states began joining the Council after 1989, its human rights policies gained additional relevance. The Council's corresponding initiatives received the unconditional and active support of EU institutions. In the 1990s, the Council devoted a good part of its activities to defining a set of minimal standards concerning the protection of minorities.[32] By doing so, it established a close connection between questions of cultural recognition and human rights, as could be seen in the Convention for the Protection of National Minorities introduced in 1995. The Council had already made a first paradigmatic breakthrough in terms of setting cultural rights standards in 1992, with the elaboration of the European Charter of Regional or Minority Languages. For the time being, the Charter may be taken as the principal outcome in terms of establishing a catalogue of norms for dealing with linguistic diversity in Europe.

The preamble to the Charter emphasizes the principles of democracy and cultural diversity within the framework of the national sovereignty and territorial integrity of the Council of Europe's member states. Moreover, it states that the protection of minority languages should not be detrimental to the official languages of these states. Part I of the Charter (Articles 1 through 6) defines regional or minority languages as those languages that are "traditionally used within a given territory of a State by nationals of that State who form a group numerically smaller than the rest of the State's population."[33] Dialects of an official language or the languages of migrants are not taken into account. The languages to be considered are not specified. The Charter includes a catalogue of concrete obligations to be met by the signatory states, but it does not provide the subjects of language rights with the possibility of lodging a formal complaint should the catalogue not be applied. A committee composed of experts is set up as the controlling organ. Thus, in spite of its legally binding character, the Charter is still a very flexible instrument. Part II (Article 7) lists common objectives and principles to be followed by all the parties signing the treaty. The states are expected to recognize regional or minority languages "as an expression of cultural wealth." They have to make sure that these languages are not subject to any discriminatory measures. According to the "à la carte" structure of the Charter, the parties have to undergo a minimum of obligations picked out of the inventory given in Part III (Articles 8 through 14). More concretely, the states signing the Charter must choose and implement at least 35 out of 68 indicated options. At least three of these 35 options have to relate respectively to the areas delineated in Article 8 ("education") and in Article 12 ("cultural activities and facilities"). At least one measure must be chosen from Article 9 ("judicial authorities"), Article 10 ("administrative authorities and public services"), Article 11 ("media") and Article 13 ("economic and social life"). The options picked refer exclusively to the language or languages determined by a signatory state.

The Charter's main guidelines had already been worked out before 1989. Accordingly, the priorities set in the document reflected mainly the western

European situation. Nonetheless, the Charter gained much additional relevance after the collapse of communist rule and the intensification of minority problems it entailed. Voices assessing the contribution that the legal text makes to the protection of minorities are frequently sceptical. Blumenwitz argues that the document will have little practical impact due to the high number of conditional clauses it contains; according to his view, the Charter will serve as a proper framework for minority protection only in those states that have already been following a generous approach when dealing with minority issues.[34] A somewhat more optimistic view is offered by Tomuschat, who argues that if all Council of Europe members made an effort to implement the Charter's program extensively, virtually no demand made by a linguistic minority would be left unsatisfied.[35] All in all, one may interpret the Charter as a European treaty that explicitly works against all kinds of state activities aiming at the repression or assimilation of minorities.

Toward the end of 2002, the Charter had been ratified and had entered into force in 17 member states of the Council of Europe. Amongst these, we find eight EU members, namely Austria, Denmark, Finland, Germany, the Netherlands, Spain, Sweden and the UK.[36] In spite of its deliberately moderate tone and the flexibility of its provisions that leaves much space for maintaining nation-state prerogatives, the treaty raised serious reservations in several European states, both outside and within the EU. A look at the French example seems particularly instructive in this context. In France, the Charter became a subject of long and severe political controversies. France signed the document in May 1999. The socialist prime minister, Lionel Jospin, had been one of the main advocates of this symbolically important declaration of political intent. The signature had been preceded by a protracted period of preparations and consultations, devoted to making sure that the articles adopted from the Charter would be compatible with the constitution of the French Republic. When putting together its specific catalogue of measures in the area of language policy, the French executive remained very cautious, signing only 39 of the 68 articles, thus hardly going beyond the juridically strictly required minimum level of 35. In particularly "sensitive" domains, such as justice and administration, the self-imposed concessions had a rather restricted character. Consequently, from the point of view of regionalist forces, the reforms to be expected were disappointingly small. For some Gaullists, as well as for the guardians of republican orthodoxy gathered around the figure of Jean-Pierre Chevènement, however, the changes were an unacceptable expression of "a communitarian view of society."[37]

Although France did finally sign the Charter, this step was not followed by ratification. Jacques Chirac, acting as the president of the Republic, appealed to the *Conseil constitutionnel* immediately after the signature in order to receive an assessment of the treaty's conformity with the French constitution. In June

1999, the *Conseil* determined that the contents of the Charter violated the constitution. According to the view adopted by the judicial body, the document's preamble is not compatible with the constitutional principles affirming the indivisibility of the Republic, equality before the law and the unity of the French people. Thus, the treaty's entry into force would require a modification of the constitution. Since 1999, the process of ratifying the Charter in France has remained stalled.

Even when touched upon in such careful ways as is done in the Charter, the issue of language pluralism does apparently affect core areas of the French republican creed. Article 2 of the constitution was changed only in 1992. The article now reads: "The language of the Republic is French." By introducing this statement, France became the only EU member state to explicitly affirm a single official language without mentioning other languages that are present on its territory.[38] For those calling for a straightforward defence of the republican tradition, the Charter – as well as the whole sample of documents elaborated by the Council of Europe in order to deal with minority problems and to address questions of local and regional autonomy – represents a frontal attack against the spirit of the French constitution. They suspect that the Council covers the activities of "national-regionalist lobbies." From the corresponding angle, the Charter for Regional or Minority Languages, opened for signature in 1992, plainly manifests its "ethnicist and communitarianist inspiration" and challenges sacrosanct postulates of French constitutionalism.[39] Notwithstanding the constitutional vicissitudes the Charter had to face in France, one has to keep in mind that major political obstacles to adopting the treaty had initially been removed even in the French case.

At the level of the European Union's member states, France may well be located at one end of a fairly broad political spectrum reflecting varying institutional approaches to the management of cultural diversity. For countries like Finland or Spain, ratifying and applying the Charter did not entail any substantial difficulties, as they had previously made far-reaching concessions in the area of cultural and linguistic rights for reasons of their domestic political situation. Seen in this light, the Charter can be interpreted as an expression of a minimal European consensus on regulating former nation-state prerogatives in the field of institutional identity politics. It has to be noted that EU institutions have been actively involved in formulating this consensus. The Committee of the Regions, for instance, called on the member states to ratify the treaty in an own-initiative opinion adopted on June 13, 2001.[40] From the very opening of the signature process, the Charter also received the continuous and consistent support of the European Parliament. In February 1994, the European chamber passed the Killilea Resolution, which urges all member states to work toward a quick ratification of the treaty, by a majority of 321 votes to 1 and six abstentions.[41] Viewed against this background, the Charter seems to be more than an instrument of international law, designed to avoid minority conflicts in a traditional sense. As it contains a serious effort to define common European standards for managing linguistic diversity in a manner that corresponds to a deeper understanding of human rights, the document also holds considerable interest for members of larger language communities. In this respect, it can be legitimately seen as a milestone with a meaning that certainly goes far beyond the "spirit of Nice."

Conclusion

What happened during the conference of the European Council held in Nice in December 2000 can hardly be depicted in terms of a collective departure from the national principle for the sake of, say, a European republic based on post-national principles. However, one must be careful not to slope too much into the opposite direction, stretching historical analogies in an excessive fashion. The qualitative differences between what happened at Leipzig in 1813 and the events that took place in Nice two centuries later are simply overwhelming. The transnational reality of the EC/EU has definitely contributed to an unprecedented taming of west European nationalisms. Think of what the political articulation of the disputes between Germans and French would have looked like only five decades ago. Think of the efforts made by a vast majority of European leaders in order to keep a low profile when national interests are pursued. Think of the symbolic importance of the Charter of Fundamental Rights, which will be difficult for any member state to ignore, even if it lacks a treaty-like status. In this respect, Europe does come close to a civic community built upon a set of shared values yet respectful of diversity. It may never become a "state," but it seems to have at least some critical potential for institutionalizing the process of a permanent dialogue in which all the parties are prepared to take the role of the other and put into practice a "reflexive identity management." Thus, the tension between nationalism and transnationalism could keep its politically productive momentum.

In the long run, however, the momentum of democratic procedures will be lost unless European polity-building proceeds in a direction that allows for the negotiation of diversity and "multinationalism" in ways that are much more proactive than the strategies followed until now. I conclude with a sceptical remark concerning a paradox the politics of cultural identity in the EU seem to be generating. As was pointed out before, in matters of culture, respect for the national identities of the member states is the highest priority of the policies set up by the European Union. The Union's institutions seem overwhelmed by the challenge of finding a balance between the protection of diversity and the development of a common political framework for Europeans.

Institutional inertia, however, will not provide for proper defence against the dynamics of "negative" integration. Due to the lack of explicit political deliberation and regulation, matters of collective concern end up becoming the object of "invisible" market forces. Culture should not be regarded as a domain that is immune to this kind of tendency. The way the language issue is dealt with in the realm of European institutions is a good case in point: the option for non-decision-making in the field of language policy is not a support for cultural pluralism; it will end up producing very specific and selective results.[42] Instead of breeding an interplay of identities that is free of domination, negative integration in the field of culture will lead to standardization without a political debate. In order to counteract this trend, the EU would have to be prepared to (re)constitute itself as a polity that takes nationalism and its diverse forms seriously, but that also aims at overcoming the institutional rigidities of the nation-state model in the realm of culture. When we look at the past and present of the European continent, it becomes obvious that this is not a modest purpose.

Notes

1. For recent attempts at defending nationalism as a normative standard see Tamir (1993) and Miller (1995).

2. See Billig's *Banal Nationalism* (1995).

3. Jordan and Weedon (1995, p. 4).

4. Gellner (1997, p. 3).

5. Cf. Eder (1999, p. 149).

6. Easton (1965).

7. Gellner (1983).

8. An early assessment of the paradox can be found in the work of Rousseau ([1762]1998, pp. 87-89). For more recent approaches to the issue see Connolly (1993, pp. 51-52) and Tully (2000, pp. 475-76).

9. Dahl (1989, p. 207).

10. Quoted in Moravcsik (1998, p. 86).

11. Parekh (1997, p. 192).

12. This can be shown following Stein Rokkan's seminal interpretation of the processes of nation-state building in modern Europe; see Rokkan (1975) and Rokkan and Urwin (1983).

13. Spruyt (1994).

14. Tilly (1990).

15. Featherstone (1994).

16. The respective weight of these principles has been the subject of academic dispute since the beginning of the integration process. Haas (1958) can be considered a classic representative of the "functionalist" supranational view. For a recent approach to the EU written from the perspective of "neo-realist" intergovernmentalism see Moravcsik (1998). See Schmitter (1996) for a compact overview.

17. Hooghe and Marks (1998).

18. See Chevènement's declarations in the German weekly *Die Zeit*, no. 26, 2000.

19. Cf. the case made by the German constitutional lawyer Dieter Grimm (1995).

20. The obligatory reference is the work of Jürgen Habermas; see, especially, Habermas (1998).

21. See the interview with Delors published in *Le Monde*, January 19, 2001. Since that date, the concept has been picked up by a number of high-ranking European politicians such as Joschka Fischer, Lionel Jospin and Johannes Rau.

22. Stråth (2000, p. 403).

23. Helsinki European Council, Millennium Declaration, Bulletin EU 12-1999, Annexes to the Presidency conclusions (2/7), Annex I (http://europa.eu.int/abc/doc/off/bull/en/9912/p000030.htm).

24. Treaty on European Union (signed in Maastricht on February 7, 1992), consolidated version incorporating the changes made by the Treaty of Amsterdam amending the Treaty on European Union, the Treaties establishing the European Communities and certain related acts, signed at Amsterdam on October 2, 1997 (European Union 1999, pp. 11-68).

25. Treaty establishing the European Community (signed in Rome on March 25, 1957), consolidated version incorporating the changes made by the Treaty of Amsterdam amending the Treaty on European Union, the Treaties establishing the European Communities and certain related acts, signed at Amsterdam on October 2, 1997 (European Union 1999, pp. 69-354).

26. Charter of Fundamental Rights of the European Union, in: Official Journal of the European Communities, 18.12.200, C 364/1-C 364/22. The Charter has sometimes been portrayed as an embryonic sketch of a European constitution; however, it is not a legally binding document.

27. At least, this is the impression one gets when studying the results of recent Eurobarometer surveys. According to the findings of Eurobarometer 54, published in April 2001 by the European Commission, the Union citizens conceiving of themselves as predominantly European are still a small minority. The overall identification with Europe does not seem to have been increasing during the last decade. Apparently, support for the membership has even declined in some key member states, such as the FRG.

28. Schulze (1999, p. 190).

29. The German term, *Völkerschlacht*, has somewhat bolder connotations.

30. For instance, this message was one of the central components of the famous speech delivered by German Minister of Foreign Affairs Joschka Fischer at Berlin's Humboldt University in May 2000; see Fischer (2000).

31. Neunreither (2001, p. 191).

32. Aarnio (1995).

33. European Charter for Regional or Minority Languages, quoted after the version published on the Web site of the Council of Europe: http://conventions.coe.int/Treaty/en/Treaties/Html/148.htm.

34. Blumenwitz (1996, p. 185).

35. Tomuschat (1996, p. 102).

36. Status as of September 23, 2002; source: Council of Europe, Treaty Office. (http://conventions. coe.int).

37. Cf. the article "La France signe la Charte européenne des langues régionales," published in *Le Monde*, May 8, 1999.

38. Birnbaum (1998, p. 355).

39. Here, I am paraphrasing an assessment given by Anne-Marie Le Pourhiet (2001, pp. 213-14), a public lawyer at the University of Rennes.

40. Bulletin EU 6-2001, 1.4.19 (http://europa. eu.int/abc/doc/off/bull/en/200106/p104019.htm).

41. Grin (2000, p. 17).

42. Kraus (2000).

Bibliography

Aarnio, Eero J. "Minority Rights in the Council of Europe: Current Developments," in *Universal Minority Rights*, ed. Alan Phillips and Allan Rosas. Turku: Åbo Akademis tryckeri, 1995.

Billig, Michael. *Banal Nationalism*. London: Sage, 1995.

Birnbaum, Pierre. *La France imaginée*. Paris: Fayard, 1998.

Blumenwitz, Dieter. "Das Recht auf Gebrauch der Minderheitensprache. Gegenwärtiger Stand und Entwicklungstendenzen im europäischen Völkerrecht," in *Unterdrückte Sprachen: Sprachverbote und das Recht auf Gebrauch der Minderheitensprachen*, ed. Karin Bott-Bodenhausen. Frankfurt a.M.: Peter Lang, 1996.

Connolly, William E. "Democracy and Territoriality," in *Reimagining the Nation*, ed. Marjorie Ringrose and Adam J. Lerner. Buckingham: Open University Press, 1993.

Dahl, Robert A. *Democracy and Its Critics*. New Haven: Yale University Press, 1989.

Easton, David. *A Systems Analysis of Political Life*. New York: Wiley, 1965.

Eder, Klaus. "Integration durch Kultur? Das Paradox der Suche nach einer europäischen Identität," in *Kultur. Identität. Europa. Über die Schwierigkeiten und Möglichkeiten einer Konstruktion*, ed. Reinhold Viehoff and Rien T. Segers. Frankfurt a.M.: Suhrkamp, 1999.

European Union. *Selected Instruments Taken from the Treaties*. Book I, Volume I. Luxembourg: Office for Official Publications of the European Communities, 1999.

Featherstone, Kevin. "Jean Monnet and the 'Democratic Deficit' in the European Union." *Journal of Common Market Studies*, Vol. 32 (1994): 149-70.

Fischer, Joschka. "Vom Staatenverbund zur Föderation: Gedanken über die Finalität der europäischen Integration (Rede in der Humboldt-Universität in Berlin am 12. Mai 2000)," in *What Kind of Constitution for What Kind of Polity? Responses to Joschka Fischer*, ed. Christian Joerges, Yves Mény and J.H.H. Weiler. Florence: Robert Schuman Centre for Advanced Studies/European University Institute, 2000.

Gellner, Ernest. *Nations and Nationalism*. London: Blackwell, 1983.

————. *Nationalism*. London: Weidenfeld & Nicolson, 1997.

Grimm, Dieter. "Does Europe Need a Constitution?" *European Law Journal*, Vol. 1, no. 3 (1995): 282-302.

Grin, François. *Evaluating Policy-Measures for Minority Languages in Europe: Towards Effective, Cost-Effective and Democratic Implementation* (ECMI Report # 6). Flensburg: European Centre for Minority Issues, 2000.

Haas, Ernst B. *The Uniting of Europe: Political, Social and Economical Forces 1950-1957*. London: Stevens & Sons, 1958.

Habermas, Jürgen. *Die postnationale Konstellation*. Frankfurt a.M.: Suhrkamp, 1998.

Hooghe, Liesbet, and Gary Marks. "Contending Models of Governance in the European Union," in *Europe's Ambiguous Unity*, ed. Alan W. Cafruny and Carl Lankowski. Boulder: Lynne Rienner, 1998.

Jordan, Glenn, and Chris Weedon. *Cultural Politics: Class, Gender, Race and the Postmodern World*. Oxford: Blackwell, 1995.

Kraus, Peter A. "Political Unity and Linguistic Diversity in Europe." *Archives Européennes de Sociologie*, Vol. 41, no. 1 (2000): 137-62.

Le Pourhiet, Anne-Marie. "Langue(s) et Constitution(s)." *Raisons politiques*, Vol. 2 (2001): 207-15 .

Miller, David. *On Nationality*. Oxford: Clarendon Press, 1995.

Moravcsik, Andrew. *The Choice for Europe: Social Purpose and State Power from Messina to Maastricht*. Ithaca: Cornell University Press, 1998.

Neunreither, Karlheinz. "The European Union in Nice: A Minimalist Approach to a Historic Challenge." *Government and Opposition*, Vol. 36, no. 2 (2001): 184-208.

Parekh, Bhikhu. "Cultural Diversity and the Modern State," in *Dynamics of State Formation: India and Europe Compared*, eds. Martin Doornbos and Sudipta Kaviraj. New Delhi: Sage, 1997.

Rokkan, Stein. "Dimensions of State-Formation and Nation-Building: A Possible Paradigm for Research on Variations within Europe," in *The Formation of National States in Western Europe*, ed. Charles Tilly. Princeton: Princeton University Press, 1975.

Rokkan, Stein, and Derek W. Urwin. *Economy, Territory, Identity: Politics of West European Peripheries*. London: Sage, 1983.

Rousseau, Jean-Jacques. *Du contrat social. Édition originale commentée par Voltaire* (1762). Paris: Le Serpent à Plumes, 1998.

Schmitter, Philippe C. "Examining the Present Euro-Polity with the Help of Past Theories," in *Governance in the European Union*, ed. Gary Marks, Fritz W. Scharpf, Philippe C. Schmitter and Wolfgang Streeck. London: Sage, 1996.

Schulze, Hagen. *Staat und Nation in der europäischen Geschichte*. München: Beck, 1999.

Shore, Chris. *Building Europe: The Cultural Politics of European Integration*. London: Routledge, 2000.

Spruyt, Hendrik. *The Sovereign State and Its Competitors*. Princeton: Princeton University Press, 1994.

Stråth, Bo. "Multiple Europes: Integration, Identity and Demarcation to the Other," in *Europe and the Other and Europe as the Other*, ed. Bo Stråth. Brussels: P.I.E.-Peter Lang, 2000.

Tamir, Yael. *Liberal Nationalism*. Princeton: Princeton University Press, 1993.

Tilly, Charles. *Coercion, Capital, and European States, AD 990-1990*. Oxford: Blackwell, 1990.

Tomuschat, Christian. "Menschenrechte und Minderheitenschutz," in *Neues europäisches Völkerrecht nach dem Ende des Ost-West-Konfliktes?* ed. Hanspeter Neuhold and Bruno Simma. Baden-Baden: Nomos, 1996.

Tully, James. "Struggles over Recognition and Distribution." *Constellations*, Vol. 7, no. 4 (2000): 469-82.

12

paradiplomacy: a nation-building strategy? a reference to the Basque Country

André Lecours and Luis Moreno

One of the less commonly discussed features of multinational societies is the effort of their distinctive segments to become active internationally. This is most noticeable in Canada, where Quebec has developed considerable international contacts since the 1960s and where Aboriginal populations have taken their claims to international forums. It has more recently become a striking characteristic of the Belgian political system as the Flemish and Walloon governments have, since the formal federalization of 1993, developed their own foreign policy and conducted their own international relations. In Spain, Catalonia and the Basque Country have been developing, according to the provisions of their Statutes of Autonomy, a significant international presence. These developments have been associated with similar outcomes in other decentralized countries such as Australia, Germany and the United States and treated under the wider rubric of paradiplomacy, that is, the foreign policy/international relations of regional governments. There is nothing inherently flawed in considering the international activity of Quebec, Flanders or Catalonia in relation to that of Queensland, Baden-Württemburg and California, nor is it necessarily problematic to view all of those cases as instances of paradiplomacy. However, the tendency of paradiplomacy theorists to view federalism as the most important explanatory variable for the international activity of regions produces an incomplete, even inadequate understanding of the phenomenon. Indeed, this position fails to recognize and account for the qualitative difference between this outcome in multinational states and in nation-states. It marginalizes the importance of nationalism in explaining the breadth, scope and intensity of a region's international activity in the former and its absence, or lesser prominence, in the latter. Consequently, paradiplomacy, at least in its most developed form, needs to be reconceptualized through a theoretical linkage with substate nationalism.

This chapter shows how nationalism logically leads regional governments to seek international agency. The first section argues that paradiplomacy is a likely consequence of the existence of a strong nationalist movement because it provides opportunities for identity/nation-building, political-territorial mobilization and the promotion of regional interests. This does not mean that substate nationalism is a necessary condition for paradiplomacy, or that the intensity of a region's international activity is a straightforward function of the strength of a nationalist movement. Domestic and international structural contexts play an important role in conditioning the consequences of nationalism for regions operating internationally, and also in determining the likelihood of paradiplomatic activity in the absence of nationalism. The second section therefore suggests that regional autonomy, constitutional frameworks and the national foreign policy agenda are the crucial elements of this domestic context, while political and/or economic continental regimes and the behaviour of foreign states and regions represent key elements of the international environment shaping paradiplomacy. The third section examines the case of the Basque Country. It begins by discussing Basque nationalism and then shows how it is at the core of historical as well as contemporary Basque paradiplomacy. In addition to linking nationalism in the Basque Country to paradiplomacy, this section highlights the importance of such institutional elements as the European Union, the French *pays basque*, the Basque Centres, the Autonomous Communities (*Comunidades Autónomas*) system and the Spanish foreign policy agenda in explaining and shaping Basque international relations.

Nationalism and the International Agency of Regions

Territorial forms of politics in advanced industrialized societies are undergoing a fundamental change with respect to their relationship with the "external." Domestic elements such as cultural diversity, institutional configurations, national and regional patterns of economic development and elite behaviour are still central to the study of regionalism and nationalism, but international processes, most importantly globalization and the construction of continental regimes, can no longer be marginalized. How can the international realm be integrated into a discussion of territorial politics? There are two angles. The first, and most straightforward, is to include variables such as global economic/technological change and supranational integration into an *explanation* for the presence and nature of nationalist/regionalist movements in Western societies. This angle of analysis has been the most popular as scholars are increasingly recognizing the importance of establishing causal relationships between external variables and domestic outcomes. It generally leads to suggestions that contemporary territorial politics are transformed by the international context, and are therefore qualitatively different from earlier regionalist and nationalist movements. A second, less visible and less discussed, type of linkage between territorial politics and the "external" involves domestic territorial units projecting themselves onto the international scene and, consequently, becoming international actors. In other words, another perspective on integrating international processes into territorial politics is to consider the latter an explanatory variable for one particular international process, namely the international relations of regions.

A regional government operating beyond national borders is not a new phenomenon. Many southern US states developed an international presence as early as the late 1950s to stimulate export and attract foreign investment, while their northern counterparts followed in the mid-1970s, for similar reasons. Quebec became internationally active in the wake of the 1960s Quiet Revolution; other Canadian provinces, most importantly Ontario and Alberta, did the same, albeit in a much more limited fashion, in the 1970s. The first Basque government (1936-39) sent delegations abroad and had contacts with foreign governments, diplomats and other interlocutors in the context of the Spanish Civil War. Nevertheless, the international activity of regional governments, often called paradiplomacy, has acquired new prominence in the 1990s. In all of the previously mentioned cases and others such as Australian states, the scope and intensity of paradiplomacy has greatly increased in the last few years. Regions open offices and conduct "trade missions" abroad, become involved in regional/international organizations, participate in regional/international conferences, establish bilateral relationships with states and other regions, and so on. This new prominence is the result of both domestic and international change: domestically, crucial processes include a surge in territorial politics and institutional transformations toward decentralization, while internationally they correspond with economic globalization and the construction of supranational institutions. Of foremost importance is the fact that these processes feed off each other to put pressure on central states and empower regions.

Recent literature on paradiplomacy has broadened the empirical scope of existing studies and raised new questions about the meaning of regional governments acting internationally. However, one key proposition about paradiplomacy has persisted: federalism constitutes its most important theoretical determinant.

This linkage probably derives from the fact that scholars of federalism were the first to write on paradiplomacy, and that international relations specialists who have also taken interest in the topic tend to focus on the role of constituent units in the foreign policy making of federal states. While there is most certainly a connection between federalism and paradiplomacy, the idea that the former can essentially explain the latter is questionable. Constituent units of federal (or decentralized) states may conduct paradiplomacy, but not all regions of a state develop international personalities. Furthermore, those regional governments that have been most active internationally (Quebec, Flanders, Wallonia, Catalonia and the Basque Country) share one common feature: nationalism.

Empirical evidence shows that regions that have been most successful in becoming international agents are penetrated by strong nationalist movements. Indeed, nationalism involves three processes that can be logically and functionally related to paradiplomacy. The first is identity construction and consolidation. Nationalism is a form of identity politics. It involves establishing boundaries between groups by providing objective markers such as language with subjective meaning. Identities are constructed and consolidated through a variety of mechanisms whose importance varies from one situation to another: cultural change, institutional development, socio-economic transformations or political context/competition. However, above and beyond these structural variables, the articulation and therefore the construction of the identities underlying nationalism is ultimately the product of discursive practices. Creating and shaping national identities necessitates "speaking the nation," that is, promoting the idea of a national community. These claims have the most impact when put forward by political leaders since, in the context of liberal democracies, they combine popular legitimacy with policy-making powers.

The development of a region's international presence constitutes for nationalist leaders an additional opportunity to build and consolidate a national identity. Indeed, the discourse of international relations is one of nations and, considering that states and nations are systematically conflated, so is the practice of international relations. In other words, the very definition of international agents, at least with respect to territorial-institutional units, entails nationhood. From this perspective, the development of an international agency on the part of a regional government is full of symbolic meaning, and it is therefore an attractive strategic option for nationalist leaders. Some forms of paradiplomacy are more significant than others with respect to identity construction and consolidation; namely, those involving (albeit implicitly) recognition by one or more sovereign states of the legitimacy of a region as an international actor. Bilateral relationships with states, as the closest thing to traditional diplomacy, are particularly important symbolically. So is participation in regional and international organizations/conferences. The relevance for identities of these acts of paradiplomacy is not limited to the acts themselves; equally important is the fact that these highly visible paradiplomatic activities give nationalist leaders the opportunity to play to their domestic audience. They provide a scene from which nationhood can be proclaimed most forcefully, as a foreign, regional or even international focus offers legitimacy and discursive/communication opportunities. In short, through paradiplomacy, regions can both behave as nations and present themselves as such.

The second process of nationalism is the definition and articulation of regional/group interests. Indeed, the development of subjective communities associated with the erection of boundaries between groups involves not only identities but also a specific conception of the common good, or at least the identification of certain elements that should be promoted and/or defended. In turn, the regional/group interest definition is linked to and becomes an integral part of the collective identity. There are generally two dimensions to this definition. The first is centred on culture. In building and shaping identities, nationalist movements emphasize and politicize cultural distinctiveness; consequently, they tend to define the "national interest" primarily in terms of cultural protection/preservation. The second dimension is more clearly ideological. The emergence of nationalist movements tends to be associated with and supported by ideologically specific political forces. This has been the case in Flanders, where the Flemish Movement is strongly associated with Christian Democracy, and in Quebec, where nationalism is closely associated with trade unions and left-leaning organizations. As a result of these linkages, nationalist movements and the regions they seek to represent, although never monolithic, often have an ideological personality.

Processes of interest definition and articulation are highly intelligible in international politics. After all, traditional foreign policy is fundamentally about the definition, defence and promotion of a (state) national interest. This is why the interest component of paradiplomacy is the most straightforward and visible; indeed, regional governments operating on the international scene adopt statelike discourses, that is, they express preferences in the context of a national interest framework. These preferences may be ideological in nature and therefore lead regional governments to take a stand on such issues as free trade or the social nature of the European Union. In such cases, the issues put forward by paradiplomacy may be understood in terms of the domestic dynamics surrounding nationalism. Paradiplomacy preferences may also follow the cultural aspect of interest definition. In fact, cultural defence and promotion tend to be the most important issues of paradiplomacy, because they are central to its underlying force, nationalism. Paradiplomacy extends the domestic struggles of nationalist movements for cultural preservation into international politics. The Quebec government, for example, expresses concerns over the linguistic nature and consequences of such international processes as globalization and the liberalization of trade, a preoccupation stemming from its domestic struggle for the prominence of French in Quebec society. Culture therefore shapes the foreign-policy agenda of regional governments, including targeted interlocutors. Flanders' paradiplomacy focuses on countries such as the Netherlands, Surinam and South Africa, where there is a cultural kinship.

The third process of nationalism is political-territorial mobilization. Nationalism is a form of politics, and is therefore fundamentally about power. The development of nationalist movements is the product of power struggles between and within groups. It primarily involves competing political elites claiming to speak on behalf of communities, that is, presenting themselves as their "true" and legitimate voice. In liberal democracies, where political legitimacy ultimately emanates from civil society, nationalist leaders seek popular support in the form of political mobilization to substantiate their various claims (representation, policy, institutional arrangements and so on). The peculiar feature of nationalism compared with other forms of politics is that mobilization has to have a territorial basis; indeed, nationalist leaders need to structure mobilization in a way that transcends social cleavages and emphasizes a commonness linked to territory. Political-territorial mobilization, although generally sporadic and fluctuating in intensity, is necessarily a feature of nationalism because it underlies claims both for power and for policy/institutional change. The power of nationalist leaders rests on the prominence, even the hegemony, of nationalism as a form of politics. In turn, this state of affairs is itself conditional on popular support, as is the ability of these leaders to bring about policy and institutional change corresponding with their specific claims, usually formal recognition/distinct status, autonomy, federalization or independence.

Political-territorial mobilization as a process of nationalism may be logically related to regional governments looking to develop international agency. The peculiarity of paradiplomacy as a form of international expression is its highly conflictual domestic dynamic. Paradiplomacy does not merely feature conflict over the definition of foreign policy objectives as is the case for traditional (state) diplomacy; it also involves struggles over the very expression of foreign policy. States rarely welcome the idea of regions "going abroad"; in fact, they tend to oppose it vigorously. Some regional political forces may adopt a similar attitude. Consequently, paradiplomatic activity, particularly in its most visible forms (regional-international conferences, bilateral relationships with states, and so on), present nationalist leaders with opportunities to stimulate political-territorial mobilization because it pits the region against the centre, and sometimes regional nationalist forces against non-nationalist ones. Since foreign policy is one of the last reserved domains of the state, paradiplomacy represents, in the context of domestic politics, a statement about power. It can therefore be understood not only as the emergence of new actors on the international scene, but also as the most recent dimension of historical territorial conflicts whose most prominent and acute manifestation is nationalism and nationalist mobilization.

Paradiplomacy is closely linked to political-territorial mobilization, not only because it represents an additional variable in political conflicts and power struggles that tends to provide opportunities for stimulating this process, but more specifically because it can serve as a tool for achieving domestic policy objectives. The development of a strong international personality gives regional leaders a prestige that can be used as leverage in negotiations on constitutional and institutional change. In fact, a region that is very active internationally projects notions of distinctiveness and autonomy in a way that may lower the degree of contention surrounding certain regional claims and demands. In the special cases where the institutional change sought by a regional government is independence, international activity becomes a functional necessity. Secessionist forces need to establish an international network and present their project to foreign states in the hope of obtaining formal recognition following a declaration of independence.

Paradiplomacy and Opportunity Structures

Nationalism is the single most important variable conditioning paradiplomacy. Regions where there are strong nationalist movements are much more likely to develop an international presence than are regions where there is no such movement. Also, the paradiplomacy of the former is generally more intense and extensive than that of the latter. However, structural contexts – both domestic and international – also play an important role in determining the likelihood of regions becoming international actors, because they provide opportunities for action while imposing constraints. These contexts also shape paradiplomacy agendas because they dictate the types of opportunity available to regional governments.

Three elements of the domestic structural context are particularly important in conditioning the international agency of regions. The first is the level of autonomy enjoyed by a regional government. As previously mentioned, the literature on paradiplomacy has typically considered the linkage between federalism and the international activity of regions to be most important. While we have argued that nationalism is the critical variable, the structure of the territorial power distribution also needs to be considered. Federations, and some other decentralized systems such as Spain's Autonomous Communities (*Comunidades Autónomas*) and devolution in the United Kingdom, create regional agents. This agency is in turn susceptible to developing an international dimension, and the greater the regional autonomy the better the opportunity for paradiplomatic activity. This means that the active paradiplomacy of Quebec and Flanders, while primarily explained by nationalism, is also shaped by the decentralized structures of their respective federations. Similarly, the weaker international presence of American and Mexican states, while primarily the result of the absence of nationalist movements, is partially attributable to those countries' more centralized federalism.

The constitutional framework accompanying these institutional arrangements is the second element of the domestic structural context that shapes paradiplomacy. Typically, constitutions are not conducive to regions operating in the international arena; they tend to make international affairs the reserved domain of the central state. Some constitutional frameworks are particularly austere in this respect and, consequently, make paradiplomatic activity quite difficult. Mexico's constitution, for example, explicitly forbids regions to sign agreements with foreign powers. The federal government's stranglehold on international relations stemming from a 1917 provision was further reinforced in 1988, when the constitution was modified to give the president power over foreign policy rather than the narrower "diplomatic negotiations." At the other end of the spectrum are the (rare) constitutions that explicitly give regional governments power over some aspects of international affairs. These constitutional frameworks remove a crucial obstacle for regions to access the international sphere and, as a result, make paradiplomacy more likely to occur. The 1993 reform of the Belgian constitution, which included the transfer of power over international affairs to the constituent units, triggered a flurry of international activity from governments in Flanders, Wallonia and the French-speaking community.

Finally, the focus of a national foreign policy, and of international affairs more generally, also conditions the opportunities for paradiplomacy. In a context where strategic and military issues are emphasized, regions have little to say since defence policy remains the exclusive prerogative of central states. There is more room for regions to find their way onto the international scene (if cultural and economic issues are more prominent), as regional governments often have, by virtue of the domestic distribution of power, an initial interest and some degree of empowerment with respect to these matters. It is no coincidence that paradiplomacy has become more important since the end of the Cold War; indeed, the breakdown of the conceptual categories of "high" and "low" politics has rendered national foreign policy agendas less hierarchical and therefore more likely to attract the attention of regions.

It is interesting to note that these three sets of domestic opportunity structures, which complement nationalist movements, in analyzing the origins and nature of paradiplomacy tend to be most favourable when such movements actually exist. In other words, the domestic structural context cannot always be neatly separated from nationalism. Extensive regional autonomy is often, although not always, the product of nationalism. Constitutions that give regions powers over international affairs are likely to have their roots in nationalist conflicts, as is the case in Belgium. Culture as a foreign-policy issue may be important to various types of states, but it is particularly important to multinational ones, which tend to be naturally sensitive to cultural differences.

The international agency of regional governments in the West is also shaped by at least two sets of international structures. The first is continental regimes. In Europe, the EU represents a political regime that provides regions with the opportunities and impetus to act beyond national borders. It does so in at least three ways. First, at the broadest level, the EU has fundamentally changed the nature of the Western European state by capturing some of its sovereignty. In so doing, it has changed the view of the state by political actors from one of a coherent, monolithic unit serving as the only possible linkage between inside and outside to one of a perforated entity. It has also invited previously domestic actors such as regional governments to take advantage of the new openings to access the international scene. Second, EU policies such as structural adjustment programs that make regions their central units build regional governments as potential international actors by establishing a conceptual and political link with the "outside." Third, the EU, through the Committee of Regions, offers immediate channels through which regional governments can become international actors. Despite its political weakness, the Committee presents some regions with a concrete opportunity to operate beyond national borders, while drawing others that might not have had the means or motivation to actively seek an international role. In other words, the EU can be seen not merely as an opportunity structure, but indeed as a force behind the very international agency of some Western European regional governments.

Of course, the EU is also an economic regime. As such, it shapes the relationship between regions and the "outside," as do less developed free trade structures like those existing in North America. Continental economic integration and the larger process of globalization have diminished the capacity of states to structure their domestic economies, including and perhaps most importantly their ability to tackle issues of territorial economic inequalities and discrepancies. Consequently, the phenomenon of states losing power to market forces is a particularly significant development for regions. In response to this weakened leadership of central states in governing the economy, many regional governments have taken it upon themselves to actively attract foreign investment and promote exports. These are core objectives of most if not all paradiplomacies, and they involve some international network/action: offices abroad, trade missions and so on. Economic integration and trade liberalization – because they come with a set of norms and rules – also involve challenges to forms of socio-political and cultural organizations that may be specific to some regions. Consequently, some regional governments (Quebec, for example) have viewed the development of an international voice as a necessary condition for dealing effectively with these processes.

The second set of international structures shaping paradiplomacy is the state system. Regional governments are generally excluded from formal bilateral and multilateral relationships. In fact, traditional diplomacy has been built around the sovereign state, and the rules and procedures that structure it have further reinforced the hegemonic role of states as actors in international politics. However, states are increasingly willing to have bilateral relations with regional governments. Flanders, for example, has signed co-operation agreements with Canada, the United States, South Africa, Russia and Japan. Some states have in fact developed particularly significant relationships with foreign regions. France, for example, treats the Quebec premier very much like a head of state and deals with the province in a fashion approximating its traditional bilateral relations. These opportunities for regional governments to enter into formal relationships with states give them new legitimacy and enhance their international personality. Finally, bilateralism in paradiplomacy is not limited to state-region relations; in fact, the bulk of paradiplomatic activity occurs between regional governments, that is, in the form of interregional and transborder/transnational relationships. The Four Motors of Europe – an organization composed of the regions of Rhône-Alpes, Lombardy, Catalonia and Baden-Württemberg that seek closer economic, social and cultural co-operation – is a well-documented instance of this type of paradiplomacy. Bilateral relationships between regions trigger a dynamic process that is central in developing the international activity of regions: indeed, because these relationships are not contingent on foreign states recognizing regions as international actors, they offer great potential for the autonomous development of regional governments' international legitimacy, an outcome that in turn fosters these same transnational relationships.

Basque Nationalism

The Basque Country is geographically situated at the western end of the Pyrenees and covers territory in Spain and France. The most populated area of the Basque Country is in Spain, which is a compound state incorporating various degrees of internal ethno-territorial plurality.

The modern political unification of Spain took place by means of a dynastic union under the Catholic Kings in 1469 (Isabella of Castile and Ferdinand of Aragon). However, its constituent territories (crowns, kingdoms, principalities, dominions and provinces) maintained their autonomous existence. The incorporation of these territories into the Hispanic monarchy was achieved at an early stage of the European Modern Age, centuries before the processes of national homogenization were carried out by other European monarchies.

Prior to the union of the Catholic Kings, the Castilian princes had brought about – through conquests and royal marriages – the unification of Leon and Castile (1230) as well as the incorporation of the Basque provinces of Guipuzcoa (1200), Alava (1332) and Biscay (1379). According to Salvador de Madariaga,[1] the three Basque provinces were not constituent units of the Basque Country. That was a modern political creation. But all three provinces took good care of their *fueros*, or local rights and traditions, before and after they joined the Castilian Crown: "They would not recognized Lord or King without the prior and solemn pledge for honouring their *fueros*."[2]

During the nineteenth century, many territories of Spain, particularly those with strong historical identities and traditions of self-government, perceived liberal centralism as unnatural and stifling. This provoked these regions to demand the restitution of their *fueros*, or ancient rights to autonomy. Navarre, the Basque provinces and Catalonia were most vehement in contesting attempts at centralist reform. The circumstances ensured that the rebel Carlists were able to benefit from the peripheral hostility toward government in Madrid.

After the Carlist defeats in the civil wars of 1833-40, 1846-48 and 1872-75, the Basque Nationalist Party (*Partido Nacionalista Vasco–Euzko Alderdi Jetzalea*, PNV-EAJ) was founded in 1895 by an early Carlist, Sabino de Arana Goiri. In its early stages, Arana developed his nationalist proposals for the province of Biscay, not the whole of the Basque Country, with the label of *bizkaitarrismo*. In 1893 his *Bizcaya por su independencia* (Independence for Biscay) was published. At the beginning of the twentieth century, the PNV-EAJ was less successful in contesting elections and in obtaining class-wide support than the Catalanist *Lliga*, partly because of its religious emphasis and its ethnocentric claims. Early Basque nationalism stressed traditional community values that were opposed to bourgeois industrial society, the effects of which involved a considerable influx into the Basque Country of migrants from the rest of Spain.

Primitive Basque essentialism of a racist nature was the ideological basis of early Basque nationalism, which combined with powerful populist elements and ethno-religious exclusivism to produce a discourse quite distinct from that of Catalan nationalism. This latter ideology was more intellectual, less folkloric and less secessionist. It possibly provoked greater resistance than Basque nationalism because it offered an alternative view of Spain, whereas the Basque frequently turned its back on Spain. Both nationalisms, however, can be seen as political manifestations of a vigorous and prosperous periphery, in contrast with the inept and parasitical centralism of the Spanish state to which it was subordinated.

In spite of its short existence, the Second Republic (1931-39) contributed considerably to the resolution of ethno-territorial conflicts in Spain. The most notable improvement was the constitutional design of the state following a regionalized model, situated somewhere between a unitary and a federal state. This led to statutes of autonomy for Catalonia, the Basque Country and Galicia.

Three days after the proclamation of the Second Republic in 1931, an assembly of Basque mayors gathered by José Antonio Aguirre, leader of the Basque Nationalist Party, claimed their right to autonomy within a Spanish federal republic by the legendary Oak of Gernika. Months later, another assembly of mayors met in the city of Estella (Lizarra) and passed the proposal for a statute of autonomy, ratified also by the Navarran local councils and the Carlist representatives. Nevertheless, the proposal's passage through the Spanish Parliament was thornier than was the Catalan Statute.

A new statute project for the Basque Country was prepared in 1932, but it was rejected by the Navarran local councils. By the end of the following year, the project did not include Navarre and was supported in a referendum by 47 percent of Alavese and almost 90 percent of Biscayans and Guipuzcoans. The proposal was put forward in the Spanish Parliament in December of 1933, but two years later it had still not been passed. After the left-wing victory of the Popular Front in the February 1936 elections, the members of Parliament for the Basque Country presented the proposal, approved by referendum in October 1933, to Parliament once again. By the beginning of the Civil War, the Parliamentary Commission had practically completed its approval. On October 1, 1936, the Basque Statute of Autonomy was passed, with similar rights and powers to those of Catalonia.

After the Civil War, the country fell firmly into the hands of a deeply centrist, reactionary coalition, which even had imperialist pretensions. The dictatorship did not truly end until General Franco died in 1975. Paradoxically, Franco's dictatorship provided an atmosphere that was conducive to the regionalism, autonomism and nationalism of today (although strictly speaking separatism and federalism have older roots). There was substantial consensus among the forces opposing Francoism, an indication of the capacity of substate nationalism to overcome ideological and political divisions.

In the Basque Country, the secessionist guerrilla group ETA found considerable popular support, and, as a result of the oppressive political environment, became intertwined with the democratic movement. In 1973, ETA assassinated Admiral Carrero Blanco, Franco's prime minister and heir apparent. Those who advocated political violence against the Franco dictatorship at that time were not regarded without sympathy by many sectors of the population, and not only in the Basque Country. With the advent of liberal democracy, many of these people would eventually distance themselves from ETA, largely because of the intensification of its campaign. The military nucleus of ETA continued to insist that the militants of the Basque national liberation movement were the only victims of police torturers and of the representatives of Centrist oppression.

The 1978 democratic Constitution was made possible by a wide agreement among Conservatives, Centrists, Nationalists, Socialists and Communists for the implementation of the federalizing *Estado de las Autonomías*. This agreement took the form of an unwritten pledge to extend the political dialogue and consociationalism into the future. This open model of asymmetrical federalization did not presuppose the ways and means by which the different "historical nationalities" (Basque Country, Catalonia, Galicia) and regions could finally be articulated.

Since 1978, Spain has witnessed a profound decentralization and devolution of power to the regions. Spanish meso-governments have full control over all aspects of the *ab novo* programs produced by their political initiative, including the budgets. Table 1 shows the territorial reallocation of public spending in the last 20 years. There has been an impressive expansion of regional expenditure. Despite requests by local authorities and municipalities to have a greater share of the Spanish total public expenditure, the increase has been little more than 3 percent, whereas regional spending has climbed 30 percentage points.

The exercise of home rule implies setting budgetary priorities for all policies and services to be complied with statutorily. Certainly the Basque Country and Navarre, with a system of fiscal quasi-independence, have been able to fund their policies more generously. The *concierto* financial system allows them to collect all main taxes, including income tax, corporate taxes and VAT, and also, since 1997, the "special taxes" (on petrol, tobacco and spirits). Thus, the Basque and Navarran institutions collect practically all taxes and transfer an agreed-upon quota to the Spanish central treasury. These transfers represent compensation for Spanish common expenditures and cover the costs of running the state administrative bodies. Consequently, the per capita level of public expenditure in the Basque Country is much higher than the Spanish mean. Compared with the autonomous public spending in Catalonia, the Basque per capita expenditure is 1.8 times higher. (According to 1995 data, mean nonfinancial per capita spending carried out by Catalonia and Galicia was 1,373 euros, compared with 2,508 euros in the Basque Country.)

During this period of generalized home rule (1978-2000), the situation in the Basque Country has been highly conditioned by political violence, in particular the intensification by ETA of its terrorist strategy. A third of all assassinations by ETA occurred during the critical period of transition to democracy (1978-80). A second wave of terrorism coincided with the formation of a nationalist/non-nationalist PNV-EAJ and PSE-PSOE coalition government. This followed the spiral

Table 1

Territorial Distribution of Public Expenditures in Spain (%)

	1981[1]	1984	1987	1990	1992	1997	2000[2]
Central	87.3	75.6	72.6	66.2	63.0	59.5	54.0
Regional	3.0	12.2	14.6	20.5	23.2	26.9	33.0
Local	9.7	12.1	12.8	13.3	13.8	13.6	13.0

[1] Beginning of the process of devolution.
[2] Government's estimates.
Source: Spanish Ministry of Public Administrations (1997).

of action-repression-action first deployed by ETA during the late Franco period, which aimed at consolidating a counterstate and counter-society – comprising a significant proportion of the population operating with its own laws and code of conduct. In reaction to this strategy of violence, during the period 1988-98 all the major democratic parties operating in the Basque Country concluded the *Pacto de Ajuria Enea*. This was a Basque democratic interparty platform to co-ordinate their policies against terrorism in a quest for consociational solutions to achieve peace. This Pact reflected the societal reaction against ETA's terrorism.

On September 12, 1998, the Basque nationalist parties (*Partido Nacionalista Vasco*, *Herri Batasuna* [later to become *Euskal Herritarrok*, or EH], and *Eusko Alkartasuna*, EA, together with the Basque branch of the Spanish coalition of United Left [IU]) signed the *Pacto de Lizarra* (Estella), claiming to be inspired by the 1998 Good Friday Agreement in Northern Ireland. The Basque wings of neither of the main Spanish political parties (PP and PSE/EE-PSOE) participated in this forum. The main claim of the Pact was to negotiate political sovereignty, territoriality and self-determination with the Spanish central government. It was signed five days before ETA declared a truce. Since then the signing of the *Pacto de Lizarra*, dialogue and negotiations among the Basque political forces have proven difficult. In the meantime, the 1998 Basque elections, held on October 25, 1998, resulted in a political stalemate. The ceasefire declared by the Basque terrorists in September 1998 was unilaterally revoked 14 months later. This presented a new set of political challenges for the political parties and the citizenry at large. ETA intensified its campaign of terrorism, in which representatives of the non-nationalist parties, PP and PSE/EE, were killed. These events have dramatically polarized the political situation in the Basque Country.

The strategy of sectarian terrorism deployed by ETA can be seen as a prolonged attempt to break the mould of Basque dual identity. This dual identity is a societal feature characteristic not only of the Basque Country, but also of Spain as a whole, with its plural ethno-territorial makeup. It is an important factor that explains to a large extent the respective degrees of internal consent and dissent in decentralized Spain.

Here, as in other multinational states, the quest for home rule by nationalist movements corresponds with the manifestation of this duality in people's self-identification: the more the primordial regional (ethno-territorial) identity prevails, at the expense of an identification with the modern state, the greater will be the demands for political autonomy. Conversely, the more developed the national (state) identification is, the less likely it is that ethno-territorial conflicts will occur. At the other extreme, the complete absence of one of the two elements of a dual identity would lead to deep socio-political divisions. If this were the case, the demand would be for outright sovereignty and independence instead of for self-government. In other words, when citizens in a substate community identify themselves exclusively, the institutional manifestation of their identification will tend also to be exclusive.

The results of the Basque elections held on May 13, 2001, reflected a polarization of voters' nationalist and non-nationalist preferences into two blocs of similar electoral weight. In no previous Basque elections have the blocs been as close to each other in electoral support. In 1998, nationalist parties (PNV-EAJ, *Eusko Alkartasuna* and *Euskal Herritarrok*) collected fewer votes (54.5 percent) as compared with the 1994 elections (56.3 percent). In 2001, votes cast for the nationalist parties decreased to 53.2 percent of the total, whereas the non-nationalists obtained 46.8 percent of the vote. These percentages translated into 40 nationalist and 35 non-nationalist seats. Less than 90,000 votes separated the two blocs (the total votes cast was approximately 1.4 million). The trend indicates a narrowing in the difference between the popularity of the two blocs. One possible interpretation of this electoral shift is that the Basque electorate sought to avoid a clear victory of one camp over the other. According to this interpretation, electoral polarization served the purpose of preventing political imposition of the victorious over the defeated.

Overall, the most significant result of the 2001 Basque elections was the decline of EH, the coalition sponsored by ETA. This follows a rejection by a majority of Basques of ETA's strategy of terrorism to achieve its political goals. EH representation in the Basque Parliament of Vitoria-Gasteiz decreased by 50 percent (from 14 seats in 1998 to 7 seats in 2001). The popular vote for EH dropped dramatically, from 17.8 percent in 1998 to 10 percent in 2001. There was an almost linear transfer of votes from EH to the coalition formed by PNV and EA. This can be interpreted as a political statement by those who identify themselves as nationalists but do not want a Basque nation built on assassinations and extortion, against the sectarian killings by ETA. Clearly, a large majority of Basques want to avoid a societal fracture that could lead to civil confrontation.[3]

The clear victory of the PNV-EA coalition can be interpreted as not only support for a coalition of democratic nationalist parties but also a reaction against the Spanish media campaign that portrayed PNV and EA as demons, or as being the same as ETA. The aggressive PP campaign in the Basque Country, where it hoped to win the election after the signing of a Pact for the Liberties with the PSOE, also contributed to an electoral backlash. As has often been the case in Spain since the transition to democracy, nationalists in the three historical nationalities (Basque Country, Catalonia and Galicia) have gained support in elections by portraying themselves as "victims" of political attacks by the central state. This discourse, which gives cohesion to nationalist parties, paints 'Madrid' as the external adversary and illustrates how nationalism has proven to be a powerful instrument to achieve electoral success.

There are various possible scenarios for the future of the Basque country. There is no doubt that political uncertainty will remain highly conditioned by ETA's terrorism. After 2001 the level of tension between the two blocs (nationalist and non-nationalist) did not decline. The Spanish premier, José María Aznar (PP), has made it clear that there is no place for self-determination outside the constitutional procedures established to reform the Basque Statute of Autonomy and the provisions of the 1978 Spanish Constitution. The *Lehendakari* (president) of the Basque government made a proposal before the Basque Parliament on September 27, 2002, for a Pact for Cohabitation (*Pacto para la Convivencia*). This is based on free association and cosovereignty between the Basque Country and Spain, and does not imply outright independence or secession.

A sizable number of nationalist voters stated that they do not want the Basque Country to secede from the rest of Spain (see table 2). At the same time they want the Basque Country to have a high degree of political autonomy – namely, self-determination – that would preserve its political distinctiveness within a democratic Spain, and they want a European Union where meso-communities have a greater say in public affairs. Only one-fifth, approximately, of PNV voters were in favour of full independence for the Basque Country.

Table 2

Preferences for the Territorial Organization of the Basque Country
(% of Voters)

	Basque Country	PNV	EA	HB
Centralized	6	5	1	-
Autonomy as at present	34	33	21	2
More autonomy	22	35	42	9
Independence	19	18	21	83
Don't know	19	8	15	5

Source: Spanish *Centro de Investigaciones Sociológicas* and Pallarés et al. (1997, table 10).

Xabier Arzallus, leader of the PNV, believes that just 51 percent of "yes" votes in a referendum for independence would be enough to secede from Spain. In this situation the PNV would expect its supporters to vote in favour of independence. However, the same day this statement was made to the media, Iñaki Anasagasti, leader of the PNV parliamentary group in the Spanish Parliament in Madrid, expressed a contrary view by saying that "it would be politically absurd to propose an independent Basque Country in a united Europe."[4] These differing viewpoints reflect the ambivalent stance of the PNV with respect to this delicate issue. A clear position in either direction would unequivocally alienate sections of PNV voters.

The Basque Country, Paradiplomacy and the European Union

Throughout the twentieth century, the international dimension of the Basque Nationalist Party (PNV-EAJ), as the main political representative of the nationalist movement in the Basque Country, has acquired paramount importance. Already at the time of the interparty negotiations over the wording of the Statute of Autonomy during the Second Republic (1931-39), the thorniest issue was the Basque nationalists' demand to establish independent and bilateral relations between the Basque Country and the Roman Catholic Church. Many Basque nationalists, fervent Catholics, resented the anticlerical republican climate. They proposed an independent Concordat between the Basque Country and the Vatican. At the end of 1931, the central government had decided to suspend 12 Basque newspapers because they were encouraging a popular uprising against civil authorities so that "the interests of the Catholic religion could be defended."[5]

After the *coup d'état* by General Franco in 1936 and the subsequent outbreak of the Civil War, the Basque Statute of Autonomy was approved on October 1, 1936, with similar rights and powers to that of Catalonia. Representatives of all Republican parties were present at the ceremony to appoint José Antonio Aguirre as *lehendakari*, or president, of the Basque autonomous government. At the same time, Manuel Irujo, representative of the PNV-EAJ, became a member of the Spanish central government. Later on, during the Civil War, "Basque governmental officials behave as if they were running an independent state. Furthermore, they maintained secret bilateral contacts not only with Britain and the Vatican, but also with fascist Italy so that a separate armistice could be worked out [for the Basque Country]... However, after Franco took control of the territories in the northern coast of Spain, the Basque leaders moved to Barcelona were they continued to participate in the Republican government and to support the Republican Army [during the rest of the Civil War]."[6]

During the long Francoist dictatorship the Basque autonomous government in exile was very active. It took every opportunity to denounce to international bodies the lack of liberties in the Basque Country. These activities were given a priority and served the "domestic" purpose of keeping the Basque government in exile as the institutional reference of an active opposition to Franco's regime. The PNV, as one of the founding parties of the Christian-Democrat International, received support mainly from "brother" parties in Europe and Latin America. Let us remember that it was only in the late 1990s and after its confrontation with the Spanish *Partido Popular* (PP, also a Christian-Democrat party) that the PNV abandoned the European Popular Party and similar Christian-Democrat international organizations.

As previously mentioned, regions where there are strong nationalist movements are much more likely to develop an international presence than regions where no such movement exists. With the ratification in 1980 of the Basque Statute of Autonomy, early Basque governments (mostly coalitions between nationalists and socialists) put active involvement in European affairs high on their agenda. In fact, some of the Spanish historical nationalities decided to establish representative offices – quasi-embassies – in Brussels to monitor European decisions affecting them and to promote their interests in relation to their devolved powers and autonomous competencies. The Spanish government contested the establishment of such delegations in Brussels in the Spanish Constitutional Court. However, in 1994, the highest tribunal in Spain supported the prerogative of the Basque government to set up its office of representation in Brussels. By virtue of this decision (165/94) the rights of the other Spanish Autonomous Communities to do the same later on were recognized.

The first process of nationalism, providing cohesion to territorial identities, has made international participation a cornerstone of meso-level political activism. In Spain all the regionalisms and home rule movements, not only the powerful Basque and Catalan nationalisms, have clearly expressed their European vocations. They all share the desire of the Spaniards to become full European citizens after a long and sordid dictatorship. They have been able to develop a new cosmopolitan activism that combines, on the one hand, an active opposition to the centralized model of the nation-state and, on the other, a mobilization of substate identities coupled with active supranational participation.

In order to illustrate how this and the other processes of nationalism are linked to Basque paradiplomacy, references to the 2001 electoral programs of the Basque parties – in particular those of the PNV/EA nationalist winning coalition and EH – will be made. The PNV/EA coalition put forward a general statement for a federal Europe promoting the notion of a Peoples' Europe and stressing the idea of a institutional aggregate in which nation-states and stateless nations would be secured a say in the running of their own affairs.[7] In this context, the EU serves as an external opportunity structure for the nationalist coalition to project, both discursively and politically/institutionally, the idea of the Basque nation outside Spain. By conceptually associating the Basque Country with EU member states, it further blurs the distinction between region and state, thereby bolstering the potential for the Basque identity to be considered national. This approach involves, for the main nationalist coalition, two specific objectives with respect to its European policy: 1) to secure the direct participation of the Basque government in EU institutions, and in particular in their own exclusive areas of competence (e.g., fiscal and tax matters), and 2) to safeguard the principle of territorial subsidiarity in the EU, which means that decisions are to be taken transnationally only if the local, regional or national level cannot perform better. In other words, the preferred locus for decision-making is the one closest to the citizen.

A peculiarity of the Basque case with respect to the process of identity construction is that the Basque nation is conceptualized, at least following the more nationalist interpretation, as encompassing not only the Spanish provinces of Araba, Gipuzkoa and Biscay, as well as Navarre, but also the French districts of Labourd (Lapurdi), Soule (Zuberoa) and Lower Navarre (Behenafarroa, or Nafarroa Beherea) in the *département* of the Atlantic Pyrenees. In this context, the supranationalism of the EU allows for the articulation of a Basque identity that is not limited to Spanish territories, which is politically more credible – albeit still problematic – than if Basque parties were confronted with a "traditional" international border. This does not mean, however, that Basque nationalist forces are satisfied with the current European order. The program of the radical EH puts the emphasis on the lack of sovereignty of stateless nations in Europe and the impossibility for them to participate in decision-making: "we are in the hands of Madrid and Paris."[8]

With respect to the second process of nationalism, the definition and articulation of regional/group interests, the main trigger for Basque involvement in international affairs has no doubt been culture. The very nature of the Basque language, whose origins are simply unknown, has contributed to feeding the Basque mythology of uniqueness. In this area, the unity of the Basque Country is based upon those lands (*Euskal Herria*) where *Euskera* (the Basque language) is spoken. Consequently, culture and the Basque diaspora are of great importance to the PNV/EA coalition. There are around 130 *Euskal Etxeak* (Basque centres) in the world, which are seen as channels for spreading the Basque culture internationally. These centres – the product of Basque nationalism – are an element of the international structural context that favours and facilitates the Basque Country government's international activity. For the PNV/EA coalition, these structures serve to promote Basque institutional interests in the countries where Basque Centres are located. For *Euskal Herritarrok* (EH), a priority is to create an Institute of Culture for International Relations, with the aim of promoting its ideas by participating in international meetings "where Euskal Herria is recognized as a nation."[9]

With respect to the third process of political-territorial mobilization, the international dimension is particularly crucial because the Basque nationalist movement seeks recognition of a right, that of self-determination, which finds all its meaning in the international arena. Indeed, after the 2001 Basque elections, the PNV-EA coalition made self-determination a priority to achieve peace. Self-determination is closely linked with the so-called Basque realm of political decision-making, or the "we-decide approach." In Basque paradiplomacy the linkage between self-determination and the international arena serves to support Basque claims with the Spanish state of the Basque Country's inherent right to self-determination through international agency, a key aspect of nationhood.

In the Basque case, self-determination has an inherent international dimension, since it involves all of *Euskal Herria*, thus extending over parts of two member states of the European Union, Spain and France. EH considers the constitutional arrangements in Spain and France (autonomism and Jacobinism) "incompatible with Basque democracy because their existence imply [sic] our national disappearance. The toughest negation suffered by the Basque nation is its territorial division..."[10] For the PNV-EAJ coalition, a strategic goal is to allow a federation between the

Basque Country and Navarre in Spain, and to "guarantee the liberty to establish any mode of association and/or co-operation with Iparralde"[11] (i.e., the French territories of Lapurdi, Zuberoa and Nafarroa Beherea).

As pointed out earlier, the power of nationalist leaders rests on the prominence of nationalism as a form of politics and the leaders' ability to bring about policy and institutional change. In our case study, the claims for self-determination do not prejudge what institutionalized form will be achieved by *Euskal Herria*. The PNV is employing a degree of calculated ambivalence on this delicate issue. Basque self-determination cannot be equated with the constitution of a fully independent nation-state that would incorporate territories of both Spain and France. Instead, transfrontier co-operation is regarded as the means to secure "direct representation before EU institutions..."[12]

Basque paradiplomacy aims to achieve formal recognition by the EU of its capacity for self-government and self-determination on those matters on which the subsidiarity principle allows for autonomous governmental policies. In this context, the considerable autonomy enjoyed by the Basque Country within Spain puts the region in a favourable position to be active in the EU and beyond. This domestic autonomy is likely to keep increasing, the two other historical nationalities (particularly Catalonia), as well as some of the other regions, are attempting to outdo each other in their territorial claims, which will intensify the pressure on the Spanish state. Of course, Basque autonomy falls short of what could be considered full sovereignty in some areas, namely fiscal and tax matters. This has made possible the implementation of new policies with far-reaching consequences, not only for the Basque Country, but also for Spain as a whole. For example, the implementation in 1988 of a minimum income guarantee program to combat poverty and social exclusion provoked a "demonstration effect" in the rest of the Spanish Autonomous Communities. At present all these regional programs are important constituents of the Spanish welfare "safety net."

The Spanish constitution appears to leave little room for involvement of regions in international affairs, since it stipulates that the central state has exclusive jurisdiction over international relations (article 149). However, Autonomous Communities do have power over matters such as research and the promotion of culture (article 148), which are increasingly acquiring an international dimension. These powers are confirmed in the Statute of Autonomy of the Basque Country (Title I, article 10).

As a feature of the domestic institutional context, the Spanish constitutional framework also allows for a horizontal consultation process and, eventually, codetermination on matters affecting both central and regional governments (such as the EU). The efficacy of the conferences is related not to the generalization of the policy-making process but to the exchange of information as mechanism of "institutional courtesy." Indeed, sectoral conferences have often served to outline the parties' respective positions. In line with the vocational European approach shown by all the Spanish regions, the Sectoral Conference for European Affairs has so far been the most effective of all 24 conferences as a forum for multilateral discussion and for preparing further decisions. Interestingly, the Basque government has been reluctant in some cases to fully participate in these horizontal consultations and has preferred to follow its own course of action, which is congruent with an original feature of Basque nationalism, its particularism and preference for bilateral relationships with the Spanish central state and/or European institutions.

In the past decade Spanish foreign policy has favoured the international agency of Autonomous Communities since its thrust has become the Europeanization process, which increasingly involves regions. This focus on Europe by the Spanish state has coincided with less attention being given to strategic and military matters in the context of a post-Cold War, economics-oriented global order and, in Western Europe, a period of relatively stable economic growth characterized by the absence of war. Since this period of peace and stability is likely to last, despite some authors' pessimistic predictions (trade conflicts between world regions, religious fundamentalism, xenophobia and so on), Spain's Autonomous Communities will profit from a political/foreign policy agenda that is generally friendly to regional governments.

Finally, one issue that is usually overlooked but that has proven to be of the utmost importance for paradiplomacy and external relations in Spain is the links and party allegiances between regional and central governments. When regional and central level executives are on good terms, the central state will take into account the position and interests of regional governments, even when the matter concerns areas of its exclusive jurisdiction. This domestic dimension of EU decision-making, however, has been scarcely analyzed, and further research is needed.

Conclusion

Among recent developments in the politics of Western states and international relations, the phenomenon of regional governments seeking to develop international agency has generally been marginal and unremarkable. This is hardly surprising since the past 15 years have been marked by ethnic conflicts, civil wars, trade liberalization, the restructuring of welfare states and other major developments. However, paradiplomacy is bound to have far-reaching consequences for multinational states, as it affects their domestic politics and the very nature of internal-external linkages.

Paradiplomacy encourages nationalism because it presents opportunities for political-territorial mobilization and the promotion of regional-specific interests. Once a regional government takes an interest in developing its own international personality, foreign affairs are likely to become an additional source of conflict in the multinational state. On the surface, these central-regional disputes might appear to be about the division of power and differing foreign policy objectives; in reality, they are fundamentally about identity and political legitimacy. This makes paradiplomacy a form of territorial conflict that is more difficult to manage in multinational states than in traditional nation-states. Regions where there is a nationalist movement engage in paradiplomatic activities, even if their foreign policy agenda is very similar to that of the central state, thus rendering any compromise over the content of foreign policy almost meaningless. By the same token, central states, in addition to seeking to preserve their traditional role, associate exclusivity in international affairs with the expression of a coherent national identity. This suggests that a division of international affairs whereby each level of government is empowered to act internationally in areas of domestic jurisdiction would be an unworkable solution for most states. It did occur in Belgium, but only because nationalism there comes from the Flemings who, because they represent a numerical majority, control central institutions and drive constitutional-institutional reforms.

As a result of paradiplomacy, multinational societies are at the forefront of a new mode of internal-external linkage. Traditionally, the state served as the most important if not the only connection with the international realm; through foreign policy, it aggregated domestic interests and preferences and expressed them to other international actors, usually states. This mechanism is still significant, but now it coexists with other forms of domestic-international linkages. Examples of these are the social, religious and cultural movements that increasingly target international processes such as globalization, and take organizational forms that do not recognize national borders. These movements are transnational; they involve individuals, groups and associations establishing connections – often through new technologies – with similar actors in other countries, without going through the state. Paradiplomacy is another type of internal-external connection that shares characteristics with traditional state foreign policy and transnationalism, without being one or the other. Indeed, it involves statelike units projecting themselves onto the international scene without the help and often against the will of the central state. Regional governments as international actors have the fluidity of transnational movements, yet they are intelligible to the traditional state because of their territorial-institutional nature. Some multinational states thus wield a special and potentially very effective international agency that connects domestic and international politics. The manner in which they do this needs to be explored further.

Notes

1. Madariaga (1979).

2. Pi i Margall (1977, p. 251).

3. Jaúregui (1996).

4. *El País*, Dec. 14, 1999.

5. Madariaga (1979, p. 331)

6. Olábarri Gortázar (1985, p. 135)

7. Partido Nacionalista Vasco – Euzko Alderdi Jetzalea (2001).

8. Euskal Herritarrok (2001).

9. Euskal Herritarrok (2001).

10. Euskal Herritarrok (2001).

11. Partido Nacionalista Vasco (2001).

12. Partido Nacionalista Vasco – Euzko Alderdi Jetzalea (2001).

Bibliography

Aldecoa, Francisco, and Michael, Keating, eds. *Paradiplomacy in Action: The Foreign Relations of Subnational Governments*. London: Frank Cass, 1999.

Bélanger, Louis. "La diplomatie culturelle des provinces canadiennes." *Études internationales*, Vol. 25, no. 3 (September 1994): 421-52.

Bernier, Ivan, and Jean-Philippe Thérien. "Le comportement international du Québec, de l'Ontario et de l'Alberta dans le domaine économique." *Études internationales*, Vol. 25, no. 3 (September 1994): 453-86.

Bourne, Angela. "Centre and Periphery in the European Union." Paper presented at the ECPR Workshop No. 4, Grenoble, April 2001.

Chomsky, Noam. *World Orders, Old and New*. London: Pluto, 1994.

Courchene, Thomas, and Colin R. Telmer. *From Heartland to North American Region State*. Toronto: Centre for Public Management, University of Toronto, 1998.

Durazo-Hermann, Julián. "L'activité internationale des régions. Une perspective mexicaine." *Études internationales*, Vol. 31, no. 3 (September 2000): 475-87.

Euskal Herritarrok. "Acuerdo Nacional para la Soberanía." http://www.euskal-herritarrok.org Accessed May 8, 2001.

Grau i Creus, Mireia. "Spain: The Incomplete Federalism," in *Federalism and Political Performance*, ed. Ute Wachendorfer-Schmidt. London: Routledge, 2000, pp. 58-77.

Hocking, Brian, ed. *Foreign Relations and Federal States*. London: Leicester University Press, 1993.

Hooghe, Liesbet, and Gary Marks. "'Europe with the Regions': Channels of Regional Representation in the European Union." *Publius*, Vol. 26, no. 1 (winter 1996): 73-91.

Jaúregui, Gurutz. *Entre la tragedia y la esperanza: Vasconia ante el nuevo milenio*. Barcelona: Ariel, 1996.

———. *Los nacionalismos y la Unión Europea*. Barcelona: Ariel, 1997.

Keating, Michael. *The New Regionalism in Western Europe: Territorial Restructuring and Political Change*. Cheltenham: Edward Elgar, 1998.

Kincaid, John. "The International Competence of US States and Their Local Governments," in *Paradiplomacy in Action: The Foreign Relations of Subnational Governments*, ed. Francisco Aldecoa and Michael Keating. London: Frank Cass, 1999, pp. 111-33.

Lecours, André. "Ethnonationalism in the West: A Theoretical Exploration." *Nationalism and Ethnic Politics*, Vol. 6, no. 1 (spring 2000): 103-24.

Letamendía, Francisco. "On Nationalisms in Situations of Conflict (Reflections from the Basque Case)," in *Nationalism in Europe: Past and Present*, ed. Justo G. Beramendi, Ramón Maiz and Xosé M. Nuñez. Santiago: Universidad de Santiago de Compostela, Vol. 2 (1994): 247-75.

Llera, Francisco José. "Basque Polarization: Between Autonomy and Independence," in *Identity and Territorial Autonomy in Plural Societies*, ed. William Safran and Ramón Máiz. London: Frank Cass, 101-120.

Loughlin, John. *Subnational Democracy in the European Union: Challenges and Opportunities*. Oxford: Oxford University Press, 2001.

Madariaga, Salvador de. *España: Ensayo de Historia Contemporánea*, 14th ed. Madrid: Espasa-Calpe, 1979.

Massart-Piérard, Françoise. "Politique des relations extérieures et identité politique: la stratégie des entités fédérées de la Belgique." *Études internationales*, Vol. 30, no. 4 (December 1999): 701-27.

Michelmann, Hans J., and Panayotis Soldatos, eds. *Federalism and International Relations: The Role of Subnational Units.* Oxford: Clarendon Press, 1990.

MAP. *Estudio sobre reparto del gasto público en 1997 entre los distintos niveles de administración.* Madrid: Ministerio de Administraciones Públicas, 1997.

Moreno, Luis. *Decentralisation in Britain and Spain: The Cases of Scotland and Catalonia.* Ph.D. thesis, University of Edinburgh, 1986.

———. "Local and Global: Mesogovernments and Territorial Identities." *Nationalism and Ethnic Politics*, Vols. 3/4 (autumn/winter 1999): 61-75.

———. *The Federalization of Spain.* London: Frank Cass, 2001.

Moreno, Luis, and Ana Arriba. *Welfare and Decentralization in Spain.* EUI Working Paper EUF No. 99/8. Florence: European University Institute, 1999.

Olábarri Gortázar, Ignacio. "Un conflicto entre nacionalismos: La 'cuestión regional' en España, 1808-1939," in *La España de las Autonomías*, ed. Fernando Fernández Rodríguez. Madrid: Instituto de Estudios de Administración Local, 1985, pp. 71-143.

Palard, Jacques, ed. "Les relations internationales des régions d'Europe." *Études internationales*, Vol. 30, no. 4 (special issue, December 1999).

Pallarés, Francesc, José Ramón Montero and Francisco José Llera. "Non State-Wide Parties in Spain: An Attitudinal Study of Nationalism and Regionalism." *Publius: The Journal of Federalism*, Vol. 27 (fall 1997): 135-69.

Partido Nacionalista Vasco. "Acuerdo de Bases Políticas y Programáticas para la Colaboración entre EAJ-PNV y EA durante la legislatura 2001-2005." http://www.eaj-pnv.com Accessed May 8, 2001.

Partido Nacionalista Vasco–Euzko Alderdi Jetzalea. "Programa Electoral. Elecciones al Parlamento Vasco 2001." http://www.eaj-pnv.com Accessed May 8, 2001.

Pi i Margall, Francesc. *Las nacionalidades* (4th edition; first published 1876). Madrid: Librería de los Sucesores de Hernando, 1977.

Ravenhill, John. "Federal-State Relations in Australian External Affairs: A New Co-operative Era?" In *Paradiplomacy in Action: The Foreign Relations of Subnational Governments*, ed. Francisco Aldecoa and Michael Keating. London: Frank Cass, 1999, pp. 134-52.

Solé Tura, Jordi. *Nacionalidades y nacionalismos en España. Autonomías, federalismo, autodeterminación.* Madrid: Alianza, 1985.

Ugalde Zubiri, Alexander. "The International Relations of Basque Nationalism and the First Basque Autonomous Governments," in *Paradiplomacy in Action: The Foreign Relations of Subnational Governments*, ed. Francisco Aldecoa and Michael Keating. London: Frank Cass, 1999, pp. 170-84.

13

undermining federalism and feeding minority nationalism: the impact of majority nationalism in Canada

Alain-G. Gagnon

There is a prevailing view, fed by some intellectuals and by spokespersons of the dominant political forces in Canada, that minority nationalism acts chiefly as a threat to political stability and endangers democratic practices. Authors such as Eric Hobsbawm, Hudson Meadwell and Minister Stéphane Dion can easily be associated with this line of thought. To counterbalance this position, authors such as Michael Keating, Rainer Bauböck and James Tully, as well as former Parti Québécois political adviser Jean-François Lisée, have shown that minority nationalism can be both socially and politically constructive in terms of legitimacy and representation. I explore how majority nationalism constitutes a major impediment to political changes in Canada and contributes to the mobilization of minority nationalist forces as they respond to the push and pull of the dominant political order.

So far, the tendency has been to explore "state-seeking" nationalisms and to overlook the "nationalizing practices," to use Rogers Brubaker's perceptive phrase, of dominant groups in established states.[1] To translate this into the Canadian context, one sees the federal government initiating a variety of measures, stretching from the imposition of a Canadian Charter of Rights and Freedoms to pension benefits, innovation funds, flag distribution and millennium chairs in education, in an attempt to superimpose a pan-Canadian sense of nationhood and to present substate nationhood simply as folkloric expression, when not actually subversive.

The proposition I wish to examine is that, with the patriation of the Canadian Constitution in 1981, the proposed Charlottetown Accord in 1992 and the Calgary Declaration in 1997, followed three years later by the *Clarity Act*, Quebec has viewed its policies as being dominated and, most times, even set by majority nationalist political forces, contributing to making that member state an unsatisfied partner in a less and less federal political system. Indeed, I argue that the Canadian federal system continues to shed some of its founding elements through the denial of federal practices in several policy fields.

I will examine three policy fields. I will look at, first, the Social Union Framework Agreement, since it addresses intergovernmental dynamics in the social policy field; second, the continuing force of a pan-Canadian Charter of Rights and Freedoms through which central judicial institutions undermine the representative capacity of Quebec's National Assembly and seriously alter the relationship between citizens and governments across Canada; and, third, the gradually constrained role of Quebec in international relations.

Theoretical Considerations

Building on some of my earlier work on the influence of political ideas, I will analyze majority/minority nationalism as an independent variable and as a key factor that informs policy outcomes. Nationalism is many things to many people, but it also refers to what Michel Foucault calls a "discursive formation" or, to quote Craig Calhoun, "a way of speaking that shapes our consciousness, but also is problematic enough that it keeps generating more issues and questions, keeps propelling us into further talk, keeps producing debates over how to think about it."[2] The term "hegemony" reverberates here.

After analyzing English, French, Russian, German and American nationalisms, Liah Greenfeld concludes her seminal study, *Nationalism: Five Roads to Modernity*, by stating: "The role of vanity – or desire for status – in social transformation has been largely underestimated, and greed or will to power are commonly regarded as its mainsprings. In all five cases…the emergence of nationalism was related to a preoccupation with status. The English aristocracy sought to justify it; the French and the Russian nobility – to protect it; the German intellectuals – to achieve it. Even for the materialistic Americans, taxation without representation was an insult to their pride, more than an injury to their economic interests. They fought – and became a nation – over respect due to them, rather than anything else."[3] Status-seeking and greed have also been the name of the game in Canada, as this analysis illustrates.

In the Canadian context, both Jane Jenson and Sylvia Bashevkin,[4] among others, have stressed the "universe of political discourse," claiming that looking exclusively at state-society relations may mean missing the whole picture. A longitudinal view of policy outcomes from either a state- or a society-centric model, though relevant, is in itself insufficient as one needs to investigate the domain of ideas concurrently. Policy legacies matter, particularly in a federal state such as Canada where majority/minority nationalisms generate competing political discourses.[5]

Bashevkin considers that pan-Canadianism – what I depict as a majority nationalist discourse – is characterized by a left of centre world view dependent on the ascendant role of the federal government. She describes this nationalist world view as "the organised pursuit of a more independent and distinctive Canadian in-group on the North American continent through the introduction by the federal government of specific cultural, trade and investment policies that would limit US out-group influences."[6] Although the federal government has gradually abandoned its left-of-centre approach in favour of downsizing and open international trade, the outcome remains similar. One sees on a daily basis manifestations of majority nationalism in Canada in which images of a state without territorial differentiation in world events, imposition of "national standards," as well as citizen and private-sector soft involvement in governance underpin the dominant political discourse and help to weaken the ability of the Quebec state to implement its own policies over its own territory.

Pan-Canadianism, as Bashevkin conceives it, rests on preconceived political discourses. Majority nationalism can also be evaluated through an analysis of spending power and fiscal control, as well through the degree of respect shown for the contractual arrangements establishing power-sharing in a federal regime.[7] This is especially salient considering that discussions dealing with power-sharing are essentially left to intergovernmental negotiations that leave Quebec with little room to manoeuvre. Let me point out that with the defeat of the Conservatives and the election of Jean Chrétien's Liberals in Ottawa in 1993, intergovernmental negotiations have largely become a thing of the past and are no longer viewed by the federal governing party as a legitimate place for discussion, as it wants to keeps negotiations out of public scrutiny. The Charter has exacerbated this trend further. The aim of achieving equal outcomes for citizens anywhere in the territory of Canada in the name of a universal set of rights has resulted in the inevitable homogenization of policies across the country and displaced the realm of political conflict from negotiations between federally and provincially elected representatives to centrally appointed judges. As a consequence, provincial premiers' conferences have largely become non-events.[8]

In addition, it is often argued that international commercial entanglements have reduced state capacity and, by extension, sovereignty. This leads the federal government to strip provinces of their ability to shape domestic policy. Several of the weaker provinces have no bone to pick with this new trend, but Alberta, Ontario and Quebec, all stronger provinces, have over the years frequently expressed their concerns and frustrations. Provinces are told that they now have a greater advocacy role and administrative capacity. However, since they have simultaneously been stripped of their capacity to shape policy, this supposed lever of empowerment is rendered hollow. As a result, member states of the Canadian federation, Quebec included, are lumped together with other advocacy groups in any given policy field, notwithstanding the formal division of powers. In this condition, whatever sovereignty remains as a result of a globalizing world belongs to the central government. This discourse rests on some vague conception of provincial participation in the policy process, and terms such as "collaboration," "partnership"[9] and "unity" turn out to be empty and serve only to reinforce the central government. As a result, the intent of collaboration, as framed by majority nationalists in Canada, refers to the construction of a single national identity irrespective of differences.

In Brubaker's terms, one is confronted with a nationalizing state that acts on behalf and at the behest of a "'core nation' whose language, culture, demographic position, economic welfare, and political hegemony must be protected and promoted by the state. The key elements here are 1) the sense of 'ownership' of the state by a particular ethnocultural nation that is conceived as distinct from the citizenry or permanent resident population as a whole, and 2) the 'remedial' or 'compensatory' project of using state power to promote the core nation's specific...interests."[10]

Quebec's competing minority nationalism, which is represented across the board by all the political parties in Quebec's National Assembly and single-handedly by the Bloc Québécois in Ottawa, has little recourse in attempting to translate Quebec's political claims into public policies and for obtaining recognition for Quebec's specificity. Facing a nationalizing state, these political parties are left fighting what seem to be rearguard battles, whereas majority nationalists, rejecting original contracted federal arrangements, are able to couch their project in terms of national unity. Let us proceed to a cursory examination of three policy fields that have produced some important conflicts between Quebec and the central government that intensified following the Liberals' return to power after having occupied the seats of the Opposition for a decade.

Public Policies: Social Union, the Constitutional Entrenchment of the Charter of Rights and Freedoms, and International Relations

The following examination of recent federal policies in fields as diverse as social policy, the constitutional entrenchment of the Charter of Rights and Freedoms and international relations will show the extent to which Brubaker's depiction of nationalizing states in eastern and central Europe applies equally to Canada.[11]

Social Union

The case offered by the social union reveals a major attempt to transform a policy field from above without any respect for the division of powers. In other words, the imposition of Canada's social union by the federal government is viewed as an "instrument of statecraft."[12]

The notion of a social union in Canada entered public discourse in the aftermath of the failed Meech Lake Accord (1987-90), just at the time of the constitutional discussions surrounding the federal proposals of September 1991. The concept had initially been imagined by Ottawa as an element of nation-building, then as a way for the member states of the federation to fully assume their responsibilities in this policy field and make concerted claims to the federal government through intergovernmental negotiations. Ultimately, following the push and pull of federal-provincial relations, the social union turned out to be simply the expression of a majority nationalist project without regard for the formal division of powers. The "power of the purse" was to cast a shadow over formal constitutional arrangements.

Everything ensues from the recognition of federal spending power, because only member states that recognize this power have access to federal generosity. It is no longer an option for the provinces to exercise their right to opt out with full compensation unless the precise conditions set by Ottawa are met. The central government, that is, reserves the right to contribute to provincial budgets on the condition that provinces, first, endeavour to attain the Canada-wide objectives in health care, post-secondary education, social assistance and social services – all sectors of exclusive provincial jurisdiction – and, second, agree to faithfully respect the accountability framework sanctioned by Ottawa and the provinces with the exception of Quebec.[13] As we are reminded by Will Kymlicka,

> If language rights and standards in social programs should be national [read pan-Canadian] in scope, this means that decisions must now be made at the federal rather than the provincial level. And this, in turn, means that decisions will be made in a forum where English-speaking Canadians form an overwhelming majority...
>
> In short, the idea that Canadians form a single nation from sea to sea, and that the federal government should define and promote this common nationhood, increases the mobility and political power of English-speaking Canadians.[14]

Developing this interpretation, Alain Noël argues that the only avenue left to Quebec is to mark its disagreement as a footnote to imposed federal programs.[15] This spells the end of a federalism that is couched in terms of real collaboration among member states and, more pointedly, between the member states and the central government.

In addition, the central government, through the Social Union Framework Agreement, has decreed that it can now launch new initiatives, provided it gives provincial and territorial governments a minimum of three months' notice, via direct transfers to individuals and organizations involved in health care, post-secondary education, social assistance and social services. This is one of the most questionable changes involving power-sharing in Canada, and is a trans-formation that neglects the multinational nature of the country, over which the central government wants to superimpose a mononational federalism. The sit-uation can be depicted as one in which Ottawa continues to dispose of norma-tive considerations at the roots of federalism and imposes a domineering vision without much concern for the national communities involved.

"Change by other means" has become the key objective in Ottawa as it launches a series of initiatives that amount to nothing less than constitutional modifications.[16] Those changes are encompassing and structuring, and they create precedents that will have to be taken into account in federal-provincial affairs. However, it is left to Quebec to demonstrate to its partners in the feder-ation that the federal principle is being trampled over once again. This might one day backfire on Ottawa, as Jennifer Smith reminds us:

> [T]he tradition and the [federal] principle remain benchmarks by which to evaluate the state of federalism in the country. These benchmarks can serve to de-legitimise non-constitutional, anti-federal change...
>
> The federal principle is a critical component of democracy in large states. This is why it ought not to be jettisoned easily, however "tradi-tional" it might appear. Certainly it ought not to be jettisoned in a series of developments that mount up to informal constitutional change. The more important the principle, the greater the need for formal processes of change.[17]

The examination of social policy confirms the central government's desire to intervene, notwithstanding the Canadian Constitution, in an effort to impose its centralist vision. This is done under the cover of collaborative federalism, a euphemism coined in the 1960s to paper over expressions of a domineering federalism.

The Entrenchment of the Charter of Rights and Freedoms

Perhaps the most overt nationalizing act committed by the federal government was the constitutional entrenchment of a pan-Canadian Charter of Rights and

Freedoms as the key element of repatriation in 1982. The entrenchment of rights represented a radical break from the Canadian constitutional and legal order[18] and challenged the supremacy of legislatures in both provincial and federal jurisdictions. Indeed, the adoption of a Charter within a constitution to which Quebec did not consent represents not only a modification of power-sharing in Canada but a fundamental redefinition of federal practice and the most overt nation-building initiative by the federal government to date.

The Charter of Rights and Freedoms was the brainchild of Pierre Elliott Trudeau, and along with multiculturalism and bilingualism it represented the final piece of the puzzle in instilling universal bases of identity across Canada. For Trudeau, the juridical nation, in which each citizen enjoys a measure of individual rights, represented the institutional expression of a "just society" – one based on reason as opposed to the "parochial" and "emotive" regional identities upon which Canada was constructed.[19] This was perhaps the most blatant attack on the policy-making capacity of the Quebec legislature, as the individual rights regime created by the Charter does not comply with Quebec's interpretation of federalism. James Tully aptly describes the effects of majority nationalism implicit in the adoption of the Charter:

> When the Quebec Assembly seeks to preserve and enhance Quebec's character as a modern, predominantly French-speaking society, it finds that its traditional sovereignty in this area is capped by a Charter in terms of which all its legislation must be phrased and justified, but from which any recognition of Quebec's distinct character has been completely excluded. The effect of the Charter is thus to assimilate Quebec to a pan-Canadian national culture, exactly what the 1867 constitution, according to Lord Watson, was established to prevent. Hence, from this perspective, the Charter is "imperial" in the precise sense of the term that has always been used to justify independence.[20]

Rights are prepolitical goods, and the government charged with defining them is the winner in any political dispute in a federal system. According to Guy Laforest, the federalist shortcoming of a nation built on a Charter of Rights lies to some extent in the fact that contrary to the Quebec nation, whose expression was bolstered and somewhat modernized by the provincial government during the Quiet Revolution, the English-Canadian nation was very much a creation of the central state, dating back to Confederation.[21] The central state in this sense has always represented the Canadian nation – Canadian identity, or majority nationalist expression, runs through the federal government.[22] The Charter can thus be interpreted as a direct response to the growing influence of the Quebec state in defining and promoting the Quebec nation. Through a rights regime, the federal government defined what level of allegiance would be accepted by citizens of Canada.

According to Peter Russell, the unifying and nation-building aspects of the Charter are threefold.[23] First, the Charter is a unifying symbol in that its audience, through a set of rights and a discourse of shared values, is Canadians from coast to coast. This symbolic function is fundamental in defining Canadian citizenship and identity. Second, the Charter promotes national standards; as such, it homogenizes policies to conform to a set of rights that cannot be touched by the National Assembly in Quebec. Language policy is an obvious example. Finally, the judicialization of the Canadian political system meant that issues ceased to be regionally defined and addressed by provincial representatives and instead took on a nonterritorial and "national" character. This point is further strengthened by the fact that the Canadian judicial system is hierarchical, and the Supreme Court's jurisprudence is binding on all other courts. Laforest supports this point when arguing that "[t]he 1982 Charter shifted the ground of conflict, drawing it out of provincial confines and inserting it in a pan-Canadian legal and political arena, where the Supreme Court, which is under the jurisdiction of the central state, is the court of final appeal."[24] Moreover, Laforest contends that, while standardizing certain social practices, the Charter also contributes to the convergence of common law and Quebec's civil code, a central tenet of Quebec's distinct status in Canada.

As a corollary to its nation-building functions, the Charter's impact also undermined federalism as a legitimating principle of the country. Federalism is inherently built upon regional or territorial demarcations, and the Charter shifts the arena of political conflict in favour of minority identities without territorial bases. The principle of "two majorities," which has been supported by most political and social actors in Quebec, was diluted to include nonterritorial groups and individuals operating within the Canadian national community. In short, majority nationalism has rendered the other a minority through the Charter. Quebec, now a province like the others under this system, is constrained in terms of the extent to which it can promote a set of community values and priorities that are different from other jurisdictions.

Janet Hiebert has undertaken the task of empirically examining whether the Charter's interpretation and application has indeed undermined the territorial pluralism of Canadian federalism or whether it has allowed for provincial diversity in policy-making.[25] Without detailing the particular court cases she highlights, it is sufficient to note her conclusions that Charter decisions have, for the most part, been interpreted in a manner consistent with federal diversity. In this sense, the Supreme Court's sensitivity to provincial concerns is claimed to serve as a buffer against the centralizing tendencies of the Charter. While not going so far as to argue that the Charter has had no impact on diversity in policy-making among provinces, Hiebert does contend that there are no empirical reasons to support the idea that Charter jurisprudence has resulted in a uniform interpretation of rights that disregards regional differences. However, one key qualification is offered:

> The Charter poses the greatest constraint on provincial autonomy when legislation is in direct conflict with a protected right that is specific in its definition...However, the majority of protected rights are stated in vague and abstract terms. Therefore the constraint on Quebec's capacity to determine school language instruction policy should not serve as the basis for a general proposition that the pursuit of cultural objectives or community values by provinces will inevitably be vetoed by the Charter.[26]

The basis of such decisions is that the "reasonableness" clause provided by section 1 of the Charter is interpreted specifically in a federalism context. Limits on a rights regime, in other words, are precisely what make the Charter compatible with federalism. In this view, a given policy initiative is given sufficient leverage to trump individual rights if the values to be promoted are consistent with a free and democratic society. The onus is on governments to justify their objectives, and this is wholly compatible with the principle of provincial diversity. While section 33, the override clause, would more directly allow for provincial diversity, its perceived illegitimacy in an increasingly "Chartered" political culture has meant that provincial governments are unlikely to employ it.

Hiebert's study, while important for its empirical contributions to the debate surrounding the Charter's compatibility with federalism, does not fundamentally challenge the contention that the Charter is a nonfederal document and represents a rupture with Canadian constitutional practice. First, as Hiebert admits, the jurisprudence with regard to provincial diversity is rather limited. This is not simply a statistical question. It may very well be the case that the Charter's impact is felt prior to such matters going to the courts, as state managers succeed in complying with the Charter at the stage of formulating policy. The homogenizing tendencies of the Charter cannot, in this sense, be determined by looking at jurisprudence alone. Otherwise stated, the process of homogenization may take place ahead of litigation, and a more accurate measure of the homogenizing effects of the Charter may emerge by looking at the policy process itself. As such, by merely looking at a limited body of jurisprudence, Hiebert can make the claim that the Charter is not biased in favour of the central government, when all along the strongest homogenizing/

centralizing effects of the Charter are occurring as policy-makers attempt to avoid litigation in the first place. Hiebert's analysis may rest on a methodological approach that serves to obscure the effects of the Charter rather than to clarify them.

Second, even if we accept that provinces enjoy leverage through section 1 of the Charter, they are still required to demonstrate their intentions and justify their actions to a central institution. The effects of majority nationalism may be subtle, but a central institution is still acting as an arbitrator in areas of exclusive provincial jurisdiction. The logic here is similar to the one that nourishes the popularity of the *Clarity Act*. Do what you please but we (a central, pan-Canadian institution) have the final say!

Third, as Knopff and Morton argue, the federal government is in a win-win situation. If provinces lose an appeal, the result is the loss of provincial diversity and the maintenance of uniform boundaries for provincial policy initiatives. If the federal government loses an appeal, the result is that a central institution won – a central judiciary interpreting a central Charter of Rights – and the policy-making forum is still country-wide. For the federal government, a lost appeal is nothing more than a lost appeal, while for provinces, it severely limits their ability to experiment and adapt policies to the particular needs of their populations in their areas of jurisdiction. Moreover, every time the Supreme Court is called upon to rule on a Charter case it reinforces the sentiment that Canadians are bearers of nonterritorial rights, and the federal government adds to its arsenal of resources in future conflicts with the provinces.[27] This point is significant to the extent that federalism presupposes regional diversity and experimentation. Again, the Charter is a nonfederal document and the costs of losing an appeal are significantly greater for the provinces than they are for the federal government.

Finally, the Charter may be redundant if the claim is that section 1 promotes federal diversity. As Knopff and Morton argue, if diversity itself is enough of a test for reasonableness, this might render the Charter a practical nullity. If rights are vague and represent "targets" whose limits are open to interpretations that vary from state to state, then why shouldn't provinces be allowed to differ in their interpretation of fundamental rights? Indeed, Quebec enacted its own Charter of Human Rights and Freedoms prior to the entrenchment of the Canadian Charter. It has demonstrated a commitment, in line with most Western countries, to fundamental human rights. Why, then, should its own legislature not be responsible for upholding the rights of its citizens in its fields of jurisdiction? The answer lies precisely in the intent of nation-building by the federal government, acting as the caretaker not only of citizens across the country but of the perceived vagaries of provincial governments and Quebec in particular.

International Relations

The issue at stake in the field of international relations is not the role of the Quebec state in external affairs as such, since in this domain Quebec's stances generally correspond to those of Canada with respect to refugees, peace missions, NORAD, NATO, the fight against terrorism and the like. What is at stake is the possibility for Quebec to expand its internal responsibilities at the international level. So far, this has tended to be done through paradiplomacy, as both Panayotis Soldatos and Daniel Latouche[28] have remarked, and has involved nonstate actors and less frequently state actors.[29]

The position adopted by the Quebec government is that of the Gérin-Lajoie doctrine. Put simply, the argument is that it is possible for a member state of the federation to expand its provincial responsibilities (culture, education, language, health, etc.) outward.[30] This has led to some important conflicts with the federal government in the area of la Francophonie over the years, especially under prime ministers Trudeau and Chrétien because, for them, Canada's foreign policy could not be shared with any member state of the Canadian federation. Federal attitudes were somewhat modified during the tenure of Brian Mulroney from 1984 to 1993. For example, during a visit of Laurent Fabius in November 1984, two months after Mulroney's Progressive Conservatives defeated the Liberals, the new prime minister declared:

> The Government of Canada intends to fully exercise its constitutional responsibilities with regards to international relations. However, we consider it normal and desirable that the Government of Quebec maintains relations with France, justified by Quebec's cultural identity. We recognize the legitimacy of direct and privileged relations between Paris and Quebec, as long as they respect and deal with areas that do not clash with federal jurisdictions.[31]

With respect to the United States, however, even under the Conservatives the federal government has been keen to keep Quebec representatives at bay as much as possible. A letter dated April 18, 1988, that was sent to a Quebec senior civil servant reads: "The Canadian Government considers it an obligation that Canada assures active, diligent, and homogeneous representation in Washington and with respect to American federal organizations. In this context, it is essential that the unique character with which we will mark our presence in Washington not be altered in any way."[32]

Since the changing of the guard in Ottawa in 1993, the governing Liberals have been quick to defend their original position of a single foreign policy, denying member states any role in international relations even when social, cultural or educational affairs are being discussed. Quebec has been affected the most by this since it is the member state that has tended to exercise its jurisdictions in those domains most significantly over the years.

Following the 1995 referendum, Ottawa launched a series of new initiatives with the intention of further limiting Quebec's presence in international fora. Inspired by what has been described as "Plan B," Ottawa has elaborated *a politics of containment* with the firm intention of removing Quebec spokespersons from the public eye. Many examples can be provided, among which is the invitation issued in 1998 to Louise Beaudoin, the Quebec minister of culture and communications, by Sheila Copps, the federal minister responsible for Heritage Canada, to participate in an international conference on cultural diversity but with no right of intervention.[33]

This politics of containment was also forcefully enacted during the FTAA Summit in April 2001, when neither the Quebec premier nor any ministers from the Quebec government were allowed to make public speeches or representations of any significance before the 34 heads of government meeting in Quebec's national capital.[34]

A Plea for an Expanded, Multiperspective Approach

At the symposium that led to the publication of *Multinational Democracies*, authors pioneered their way into a multiperspective and critical analysis of multicultural and multinational democratic societies. The fields of comparative politics and political philosophy were combined to shed new light on power relationships and issues of governance. I feel this constitutes a major step toward capturing the essence of politics. Following my own study of Canadian public policies, I feel another literature ought to be brought into the equation.

The nonconstitutional and centralist thrust of policy-making in Canada can best be viewed through the introduction of studies of international relations into traditional models of comparative politics. More specifically, Robert Keohane's arguments concerning Hegemonic Stability Theory (HST) in the absence of clearly delineated constitutional safeguards may go a long way toward capturing the incentives and motivations to co-operate or collaborate in a federal system that is increasingly defined by the edicts of a central hegemon.

In other words, Canadian federalism can be likened to a self-help system, or a situation of anarchy, in which states have no alternative to opting out of specific Canada-wide policies other than an outright declaration of sovereignty. If collaboration implies a disregard for constitutional mechanisms as the reference for intergovernmental relations, as illustrated above, then the principle of "harmony of interests," which supposedly underpins the will to co-operate in the first place, is held in place not by mutual agreement and consent by all parties but by a majority force that defines those interests and imposes them on weaker partners. In a true state of collaboration, states may defect as long as their interests are no longer maintained by the co-operative venture. In the present Canadian federal system, this is not an option due to institutional obstacles.

Collaboration in Canada resembles HST to the extent that the central government sets the parameters for co-operation through incentives and penalties. Collaboration in such a federation resembles co-operation through hegemonic stability in international relations, which, in Keohane's words, "relies on a dominant power making rules and providing incentives for others to conform with those rules."[35] Collaboration and compromise, by definition, require a system in which negotiating parties are allowed to co-ordinate and compromise. However, as Alain Noël argues, "When the promotion of a common interest is automatically obtained and does not demand mutual adjustments, coordination or negotiations, there is no need to collaborate."[36] The fiat of majority nationalism in Canada defines policy interests, not the negotiating members. Co-operation is a political game, while preconceived and unquestionable assertions of harmony from a central power are not. In the context of intergovernmental negotiations, collaboration often emerges because Quebec's consent is deemed unimportant and is simply disregarded. Indeed, the final draft of SUFA was basically the one written by federal civil servants.

One manifestation of majority nationalism in the present situation is that many provinces want less to develop their own programs than to be heard in the planning of pan-Canadian policies, without questioning their pan-Canadian nature. Provincial governments are of the view that citizens trust Ottawa on these questions. As such, we are confronted with a situation where provincial governments are competing for "exposure" to their citizens in the same pool of jurisdictions, with the distinction that they are addressing an overlapping electorate (as opposed to sovereign states, which have to worry about the effects of co-operation on clearly demarcated electorates). This distinction is important because it provides a stronger incentive for the central government to act as a hegemon and gives it a perceived legitimacy to do so among a majority of Canadians. Theories of hegemonic leadership are thus not solely based on power, as is the case in international relations, but are based on a majoritarian fiat that is more difficult to challenge since "opting out" is not readily available as it is in the anarchic setting of interstate relations. This line of argument is informative in terms of the future of federal practices in Canada. How does a state challenge a hegemon when it is viewed as a legitimate proposition in most of the country and is supported by nine other states? Is co-operation (or "collaboration") possible where there is not necessarily a harmony of interests to begin with, as is assumed in theories of co-operation at the international level?

Conclusion

Our three cases demonstrate that Quebec's capacity to shape both international policies and domestic politics is being more and more constrained, and even reduced, in the name of the "national interest." Ottawa, acting as the single embodiment of Canadian identity, argues that it has the mandate to do so. In short, this is the ultimate expression of majoritarian nationalism that federal politicians intend to impose on all.

In successive attempts to circumvent the provinces, Ottawa has decided to initiate a series of reforms through citizen engagement and third-party consultation. Based on this model, the central government makes the argument that it is the only government that can speak on behalf of all Canadians whatever the policy field and, by extension, whatever jurisdiction that policy field falls under. As a result, collaboration and partnership are merely words used to cover over a situation where the provinces, and in particular Quebec, should not expect any constitutional discussion because that implies confrontation and competition, and this is not, they are told by federal politicians, "what Canadians want." End of discussion.

This trend led political philosopher Will Kymlicka, while reflecting on the emerging role of the federal government in the area of new reproductive technologies (NRTs), to identify a major shortcoming:

> The problem, of course, is that (true) federalism puts serious limits on the extent to which English Canadians can act on this national identity. The only way for English Canadians to act collectively in an area like NRTs is to undermine the federal principles which have made it possible for Quebeckers to act collectively. In other words, the impasse in Quebec-Canada relationships is not simply that Quebeckers have developed a strong sense of political identity, that is straining the bonds of federalism. The problem is also that Canadians outside Quebec have developed a strong sense of pan-Canadian political identity that strains the boundaries of federalism...If we are to unravel the paradoxes of Quebec's national identity, we need to look more honestly at the development of English Canada's political identity.[37]

It seems highly relevant to refer here to a central point made by the Supreme Court of Canada in its reference case with respect to the secession of Quebec. The Supreme Court states in section 66:

> The relationship between democracy and federalism means, for example, that in Canada there may be different and equally legitimate majorities in

different provinces and territories and at the federal level. No one majority is more or less "legitimate" than the others as an expression of democratic opinion...A federal system of government enables different provinces to pursue policies responsive to the particular concerns and interests of people in that province.

What is one to make out of this context? Simply that Canada continues to strengthen its majoritarian nationalist position through denying federal practices, while accusations of destabilizing the country continue to be made against spokespersons of the Quebec state without any shame. To return to Brubaker, nationalizing practices have never been as healthy in Canada, and this will continue to undermine Quebec's trust in federal institutions that are, more and more, anything but federal.

Notes

The research assistance of Raffaele Iacovino (McGill University) is gratefully acknowledged.

1. Brubaker (1996, p. 9).

2. Calhoun (1997, p. 3).

3. Greenfeld (1992, p. 488).

4. Jenson (1993), Bashevkin (1991).

5. Swinton and Rogerson (1988).

6. Bashevkin (1991, p. 157).

7. Guy Laforest denounces imperial practices prevailing in Canada (1995b).

8. Simeon and Papillon (forthcoming).

9. Smith (2002, pp. 40-58), Noël (2000).

10. Brubaker (1996, pp. 103-104).

11. This study could easily be extended to other areas such as labour mobility and manpower training, financial aid to students, and post-secondary education, as well as to child benefits and innovation measures.

12. See Gagnon and Iacovino (forthcoming) for an application of this concept.

13. I develop this point in Gagnon (2000, pp. 129-54).

14. Kymlicka (1998, pp. 30-31).

15. Noël (2000). See also Burelle (1999).

16. Smith (2002, pp. 40-58).

17. Smith (2002, p. 55-56).

18. See the Report of the Commission on the Constitutional and Political Future of Quebec (1991, p. 34) for more on this interpretation.

19. For more on Trudeau's use of judicial nationalism as a bulwark against Quebec nationalism, see Oliver (1991).

20. Tully (1995, p. 8).

21. Laforest (1995a).

22. For more on the role of the federal government in shaping the Canadian nation, see Resnick (1989).

23. Russell (1983).

24. Laforest (1995a, pp. 134-35).

25. Hiebert (1996).

26. Hiebert (1996, p. 137).

27. Knopff and Morton (1985, p. 149).

28. Soldatos (1988, pp. 109-23), Latouche (1988, pp. 29-42).

29. Thérien, Bélanger and Gosselin (1993, pp. 259-78).

30. Balthazar (2002).

31. Bastien (1999, p. 262). See also *Le Devoir* (Montreal), November 8, 1984.

32. Cited in Bastien (1999), correspondance de F.M. Filleul à Julien Aubert, le 18 avril 1988, Archives du ministère des Relations internationales du Québec.

33. With respect to the diplomatic considerations of "Plan B," see Turp (2000, pp. 109-45).

34. The politics of containment was also intended for academic circles. In 1997 high-ranking officials in Ottawa made several attempts to call upon Canadian embassies to stop the establishment of the International Association for Québec Studies. After an uncertain start, during which federal officials made many accusations of antipatriotism against the founders, the association has rallied scholars from all disciplines as well as from many parts of the world and now counts more than 800 members and maintains direct contact with over 2,000 Quebecists worldwide.

35. Keohane (1984, p. 183).

36. Noël (2000, p. 4).

37. Kymlicka (1995, p. 15).

Bibliography

Balthazar, Louis. "Les Relations internationales du Québec," in *Québec: État et Société*, ed. Alain-G. Gagnon. 2nd edition. Montreal: Québec Amérique, 2002.

Bashevkin, Sylvia. *True Patriot Love: The Politics of Canadian Nationalism*. Toronto: Oxford University Press, 1991.

Bastien, Frédéric. *Relations particulières*. Paris: Boréal, 1999.

Brubaker, Rogers. *Nationalism Reframed: Nationhood and the National Question in the New Europe*. Cambridge: Cambridge University Press, 1996.

Burelle, André. "Mise en tutelle des provinces." *Le Devoir* [Montreal], February 15, 1999.

Calhoun, Craig. *Nationalism*. Minneapolis: University of Minnesota Press, 1997.

Commission on the Constitutional and Political Future of Quebec. *The Constitutional and Political Future of Quebec*. Quebec: The Commission, 1991.

Gagnon, Alain-G. "Working in Partnership for Canadians," in *The Canadian Social Union Without Quebec: Eight Critical Analyses*, ed. Alain-G. Gagnon and Hugh Segal. Montreal: Institute for Research on Public Policy, 2000.

Gagnon, Alain-G., and Raffaele Iacovino. "Refusing to Divorce Function from Territory: The Strengthening of Regional Responsiveness and Democracy in Canada," in *The Changing Nature of Democracy and Federalism in Canada*, ed. Paul Thomas and David Stewart. Winnipeg: University of Manitoba Press, forthcoming.

Greenfeld, Liah. *Nationalism: Five Roads to Modernity*. Cambridge: Harvard University Press, 1992.

Hiebert, Janet L. *Limiting Rights: The Dilemma of Judicial Review*. Montreal and Kingston: McGill-Queen's University Press, 1996.

Jenson, Jane. "Naming Nations: Making Nationalist Claims in Canadian Public Discourse." *Canadian Journal of Sociology and Anthropology*, Vol. 30, no 3 (1993).

Keohane, Robert O. *After Hegemony: Cooperation and Discord in the World Political Economy*. Princeton: Princeton University Press, 1984.

Knopff, Rainer, and F.L. Morton. "Nation-Building and the Canadian Charter of Rights and Freedoms," in *Constitutionalism, Citizenship and Society in Canada*, Alan Cairns and Cynthia Williams, research co-ordinators. Toronto: University of Toronto Press, 1985.

Kymlicka, Will. "The Paradox of Liberal Nationalism." *Literary Review of Canada*, November 1995.

———. "Multinational Federalism in Canada: Rethinking the Partnership," in *Beyond the Impasse, Toward Reconciliation*, ed. Roger Gibbins and Guy Laforest. Montreal: Institute for Research on Public Policy, 1998.

Laforest, Guy. *Trudeau and the End of a Canadian Dream*. Montreal and Kingston: McGill-Queen's University Press, 1995a.

———. "Souveraineté et humanisme." *Le Devoir* [Montreal], May 12, 1995b.

Latouche, Daniel. "State Building and Foreign Policy at the Subnational Level," in *Perforated Sovereignties and International Relations: Trans-Sovereign Contacts of Subnational Governments*, ed. Ivo D. Duchacek, Daniel Latouche and Garth Stevenson. Westport, CT: Greenwood Press, 1988.

Noël, Alain. "Without Quebec: Collaborative Federalism With a Footnote." *Policy Matters*, Vol. 1, no. 2 (March 2000): 1-26.

Oliver, Michael."Laurendeau et Trudeau: leurs opinions sur le Canada," in *L'engagement intellectuel: mélanges en l'honneur de Léon Dion*, ed. Raymond Hudon and Réjean Pelletier. Sainte-Foy, QC: Presses de l'Université Laval, 1991.

Papillon, Martin, and Richard Simeon. "The Weakest Link? First Ministers' Conferences in Canadian Intergovernmental Relations," in *Canada: The State of the Federation, 2001-2002. Canadian Political Institutions: Pressures, Constraints and Adaptations,* ed. Harvey Lazar and Hamish Telford. Kingston: Queen's Institute of Intergovernmental Relations, forthcoming.

Resnick, Philip. *Letters to a Québécois Friend.* Montreal and Kingston: McGill-Queen's University Press, 1989.

Russell, Peter. "The Political Purposes of the Charter of Rights and Freedoms." *Canadian Bar Review,* Vol. 61 (1983): 1-33.

Smith, Jennifer. "Informal Constitutional Development: Change by Other Means," in *Canadian Federalism: Performance, Effectiveness, and Legitimacy,* ed. Herman Bakvis and Grace Skogstad. Don Mills, ON: Oxford University Press, 2002.

Soldatos, Panayotis. "Les relations internationales du Québec: la marque d'un déterminisme économique," in *L'année politique au Québec, 1987-1988,* ed. Denis Monière. Montreal: Québec Amérique, 1988.

Swinton, Katherine E., and Carol J. Rogerson, eds. *Competing Constitutional Visions.* Toronto: Carswell, 1988.

Thérien, Jean-Philippe, Louis Bélanger and Guy Gosselin. "Quebec: An Expanding Foreign Policy," in *Quebec: State and Society,* ed. Alain-G. Gagnon. 2nd edition. Scarborough: Nelson Canada, 1993.

Tully, James. "Let's Talk: The Quebec Referendum and the Future of Canada." The Austin and Hempel Lectures, Dalhousie University and the University of Prince Edward Island, March 23 and 27, 1995.

Turp, Daniel. *La nation bâillonnée. Le plan B ou l'offensive d'Ottawa contre le Québec.* Montreal: VLB éditeur, 2000.

14

nationalism's third way? comparing the emergence of citizenship regimes in Quebec and Scotland

Martin Papillon and Luc Turgeon

The politics of minority nations suggest that, while it is popular today to talk of "postnational," "transnational" or "multilevel" citizenship as an emerging alternative to the traditional model of nation-state membership,[1] the relationship between consolidation of national communities and control over what we will define as the "citizenship regime" remains powerful today. It is through the articulation of specific citizenship regimes that the boundaries of political communities are defined and distinct national identities emerge or are strengthened. This is why the redefinition of citizenship is the object of contemporary nationalist struggles at least as much as the redefinition of constitutional arrangements.

A question remains, however: to what extent can the citizenship regime associated with a sovereign state be fragmented or redefined "from within" by small nations? Even highly autonomous local states or provinces, such as Quebec, do not have full control over formal citizenship. This does not mean, however, that they have no control over the specific conditions, practices and norms of membership.

Our objective in this chapter is to explore how nationalist movements in minority nations have successfully sought to develop specific citizenship regimes from within. For small nations that are often faced with internal divisions and resistance from central governments, the consolidation of such regimes can be seen as a "third way" between secession and reform of the central institutions. Without ruling out constitutional changes, the articulation of regimes from within has allowed minority nations to resist nation-building efforts by central governments and to de facto consolidate their own boundaries.

We will compare the emergence and consolidation of what we suggest is an explicit citizenship regime in Quebec with the situation in Scotland, another small nation where nationalist discourse has gained prominence in recent decades.[2] The case of Scotland is interesting because of the explicit distinction made by Scottish nationalists and many in the UK between nationhood and citizenship. Despite the absence of an explicit discourse on Scottish citizenship, we suggest here that much of the discourse over autonomy and devolution in Scotland is in fact about greater control over an increasingly distinct citizenship regime.

We will first discuss how the two small nations have historically developed their own citizenship regime in reaction to nation-building efforts by the central government. We argue that the development of citizenship regimes from within is an unintended and certainly counterintuitive result of the growth of the welfare state. The welfare state is generally understood as a centralizing and universalizing mechanism that contributed to the strengthening of British and Canadian citizenship regimes. We suggest it also reinforced the relationship between citizens in the minority nations and their respective autonomous state (or bureaucracy in the Scottish case), thus creating a space for competing regimes to emerge.

Second, we will explore how this story of competing regimes has unravelled in the recent period of welfare state retrenchment and globalization. We will suggest that in both cases, retrenchment, combined with a process of fragmentation of the relationship between nations, citizenship and the state "from above," has opened new routes for the strengthening of distinct citizenship regimes "from within." This process is resulting in highly distinct articulations of citizenship in Quebec and Scotland. While in Quebec the construction of a distinct citizenship model is increasingly defined in opposition to the federal regime, in Scotland the notion of multilevel citizenship is much more prominent. This double process may well create something much closer to a regime in which orders of government share the attributes of citizenship rather than compete for the creation of distinct and separate regimes as seems to be the case in Quebec.

As such, what we offer in this chapter is both a confirmation and a cautionary note to advocates of "postnational" citizenship regimes. While there is indeed a redefining of citizenship taking place, it is not a one-way transformation. Citizenship is still closely associated with the production and consolidation of boundaries of political communities. Nation-building still takes place today, and the strengthening of the link between the nation and the attributes of citizenship (what we define as the citizenship regime) is still the core of political battles in multination states.

Defining Citizenship Regimes

In its modern expression, citizenship formally defines the boundaries and conditions of membership in a political community. As T.H. Marshall pointed out in his famous essay on the question, it is through citizenship rights that social differentiation resulting from the market economy is transcended to create a common bond among individuals.[3] Citizenship is thus more than status. It is an institution defining a two-level relationship, first, between the state and individuals, and second, between the members of a political community themselves. It is through citizenship-related policies that the state interacts with the different groups, classes and actors of society to produce a sense of common purpose and status. As such, while citizenship, state and nationality cannot be reduced to each other, they are intimately connected in the history of modern nation-states.[4]

Far from a static concept, citizenship is also an historically defined institution that varies according to social and economic forces. It is thus subject to power relations and challenges by political actors. For the state, it is an important political tool for regulating the nature of the relationship between the state, markets and communities. For political actors, it is also a powerful tool for making claims against established norms and institutions and for greater recognition, inclusion and political rights. In other words, citizenship is a central aspect of modern political struggles and its definition may well vary considerably not only from one place to another, but also across time within the same political community.[5]

To make sense of this dynamic relationship between the state, political actors and the structural conditions of the time, the concept of regime is a useful one. Jane Jenson has developed the idea of citizenship regime, first with Susan Phillips, as a tool to explain contemporary shifts in policy- and claims-making in Canada.[6] The idea of a regime underlines the institutional dimension of citizenship, its normative content and its nature as a contested arena subject to political struggles and transformations.

A citizenship regime has three dimensions.[7] First, through formal recognition of particular rights (civic, political, social and cultural, as well as individual and collective) it establishes the *conditions of inclusion and exclusion* of a political community. In doing so, it identifies those entitled to full citizenship status and those who only, in effect, hold second-class status. Second, a citizenship regime prescribes the *democratic rules of the game* for a polity such as the institutional mechanisms giving access to the state, legislatures and courts and the modes of participation in civic life and public debates. Third, and most important for the present study, through the recognition of formal status to individuals as well as its use of cultural and historical references to qualify the community, a citizenship regime also contributes to the *definition of the national community.* It is through the exercise of – or claims for – citizenship rights and democratic practices that the borders of belonging and collective identities are defined.

By articulating the rules and practices of membership, the modes of access to the state and the boundaries of belonging, a citizenship regime sets *the social, cultural and geographical borders of the political community*, giving meaning to the frontiers between states. While all three dimensions are found in modern regimes, the specific content (in terms of rights, for example) as well as its symbolic representation among citizens vary considerably from one polity to another.[8]

This is precisely why citizenship regimes were long considered to be the exclusive apparel of sovereign nation-states. It is the citizenship regime, much more than cultural difference, that distinguishes one modern state from the others and provides legitimacy to political boundaries. In a sense, political identities are constructed through the differentiation process between citizenship regimes, and Andersons's famous "imagined communities"[9] emerge mostly in comparison with other regimes.

This relationship assumed its greatest significance in the twentieth century, with the consolidation of the welfare state. Postwar citizenship regimes in liberal democratic states varied but they shared a common assumption about the relationship between universal rights, social integration and political membership. As David Miller and others have suggested, redistributive measures associated with universal citizenship and the welfare state both necessitate *and* reinforce the sense of solidarity associated with national identity.[10] As the welfare state expanded, the notion of a national community was considerably strengthened. Universal social programs necessitated a strong sense of community in order for redistributive mechanisms to be effective.

In a multinational state where a significant minority is contesting the definition of the boundaries of the political community, the construction of a unified citizenship regime has obviously been particularly challenging. The orthodoxy of modernity led to an understanding of citizenship as an exclusive form of political membership, leaving little room for small nations to develop and reproduce themselves within broader political units. Minority nationalisms were thus considered pockets of resistance to the great march of modernity.[11] But as we will now discuss, the definition of unified citizenship regimes through welfare polices was not a one-way process in multinational states such as Canada and Britain. The nation-building process triggered a countermovement, and control over various dimensions of the citizenship regime became an object of contention.

This historical process illustrates how control over the citizenship regime is central to minority nationalists challenging the central state nation-building process and also how it is in fact quite possible for small nations to develop their own regime despite the central state's resistance.

Historical Roots of the Distinct Regimes in Quebec and Scotland

The roots of distinct citizenship regimes in both societies can be traced back to the rise and the long-term consequences of the welfare state. Paradoxically, therefore, these distinct regimes find their roots in the development of a new form of socio-economic regulation whose objective was, for its promoters, to centralize decision-making, strengthen national unity and create a universal set of rights that would apply to all citizens, in particular new social rights.

This centralizing process was in large part successful. In both Canada and the UK, a new national identity was slowly formed that came to replace the old identity, which was associated, in both cases, with a loyalty to the Empire. Viable bureaucratic systems were put in place and developed programs, such as the health care system, that were beneficial to a large number of Canadian and British citizens. These societies, which had grown following the second industrial revolution in a highly fragmented and unequal manner, became more egalitarian and unitary. Indeed, most citizens took pride in the ability of their country to provide better life opportunities for those who were not lucky enough to be born into a privileged environment. As previously discussed, the expansion of citizenship rights was closely associated with access to state institutions and contributed to creating a much more integrated political identity. Because of the strength of a political party that was supposed to transcend identity differences (the Labour Party) and the unitary nature of the political system, this project was more successful, as we will see, in securing unity in Britain than in Canada.

Yet, in both cases the way the welfare state was administered and managed opened the door to the development of semi-autonomous welfare regimes in Quebec and Scotland, leading to a fragmentation in the central citizenship regime in the 1980s and 1990s as this same welfare state was partly dismantled. There was, to use the language of neo-institutionalism, a policy feedback to the development of the welfare state that had unintended consequences once the politics of retrenchment replaced the politics of expansion.[12] Moreover, these two new citizenship regimes were reinforced by two different events: the creation of two distinct linguistic regimes in Canada in the 1970s and the emergence and growing importance for the UK of the European Union, particularly in the 1990s.

Scotland's Own Version of British Citizenship

The British welfare state emerged mostly following World War Two and the rise to power of the Labour Party. Despite the central role of the Labour Party in pushing for welfare and economic reform, in subsequent years the Conservative Party also played an important role in consolidating and developing them. In fact, throughout the Western world the logic of the welfare state became a policy paradigm; that is, a set of central economic and social principles were accepted as legitimate by all the main political actors.[13] In Britain, this new Keynesian paradigm in social issues was viewed through the commitment to 1) a universal system of social insurance whose objective was to protect citizens from contingencies of life such as old age, unemployment and work-related incidents and 2) expanding public services in the health (NHS), housing and education sectors.[14] In Britain, not only did these new programs have a socioeconomic function related to the postwar settlement, they also played a symbolic role for a new Britishness that would replace the unifying appeal once provided by the British Empire.[15]

The welfare state was nonetheless largely administered locally. In Scotland, the Scottish Office (created in 1885 and moved to Edinburgh in 1939), which was mainly composed of Scottish technocrats, came to play an major role in the implementation and management of the welfare state, particularly in areas where Scots had largely been autonomous since the Treaty of Union of 1707, such as education and law. In these policy domains, and in others where it was less autonomous such as housing, child law, roads and regional economic development, Scotland developed policies that, while compatible with the general principles adopted in Westminster, were also distinct in scope and content. In a controversial book, Lindsay Paterson argues that Scottish autonomy was de facto similar to many small nations in federal systems, and that we could even speak of a "Scottish state."[16] In a similar way, James Kellas developed the idea of a distinct "Scottish political system."[17]

Whether we agree or not with Paterson and Kellas' claim about the degree of autonomy of Scotland, the fact remains that the Scottish Office had a considerable impact on the provision of social policies in Scotland. First, it demonstrated to the people that there was potentially a distinct Scottish way of providing social policies. Second, in order to compensate for Scottish civil society's lack of access to the bureaucratic decision-making process, the Scottish Office developed a neocorporatist model of consultation outside the formal boundaries of the state. These practices reinforced the link between the semi-autonomous bureaucracy and the existing Scottish civil society. It thus consolidated its legitimacy and strengthened the position of actors (the new middle class) whose interest and identity were deeply rooted in this specific institutional and social framework.

This relative autonomy did not immediately lead to the creation of a distinct citizenship regime, however. While the British welfare state generated a strong British identity, it did not directly challenge the Scottish sense of distinctiveness.

There was room in the British model of welfare rights for the expression of Scottish difference. The British citizenship regime was certainly centralizing, but it was nonetheless rooted in the history of the Union. It was possible to be a British citizen, benefiting from membership in one of the most advanced industrialized societies, and simultaneously a Scottish national with a specific relationship to the state through the Scottish Office. As such, the British citizenship regime remained ambiguous as to the boundaries of political communities. While fuzzy boundaries were acceptable as the welfare state was consolidated, this uncertain model proved to be rather weak once the welfare-state regime began to unravel.

It is generally accepted that the growing differentiation Scottish citizens felt with the rest of the country can in part be linked to the rise to power of Margaret Thatcher and subsequent attempts to dismantle the welfare state.[18] The rise of Thatcher was important for Scotland in many ways. First, following the logic of her agenda for a thinner but more effective state, she tried to circumscribe the power of the Scottish Office to act autonomously. In doing so, she contributed to the alienation of the citizenry from this institution and led to a major questioning of the technocratic management of Scottish affairs. This is a process common to most advanced industrial states,[19] but reactions to the contradictions of the welfare state took a decisively nationalist colour in Scotland. As we noted, the welfare state was associated with a distinct network of community organizations that came to define the "Scottish way," and retrenchment was perceived as a direct attack on Scottish identity and strong civil society. Moreover, the dramatic restructuring was associated with the governing party, the Conservative Party, which had very limited support and hence legitimacy in Scotland.

In a very stimulating book written from an anthropological perspective, Jonathan Hearn demonstrates how the new middle class, which was largely a product of the welfare state, occupied a central place in the new movement for a Scottish parliament.[20] What is interesting about Hearn's study is not so much the association between the middle class and nationalism (which has often been argued), but rather how the conjunction of Thatcher's government policies and the presence of a more militant middle class led to a growing discourse on Scotland's unique historical values.

Scots had for a long time viewed themselves as distinct because of their history of independence prior to the Union of 1707, their different blend of Protestantism, and their rich civil society that draws on their distinct university and legal systems. Yet, for two hundred years they shared similar interests and values with the rest of England concerning the Empire and in the welfare state. What was unique about the 1980s, one could argue, is the development of a new discourse on Scottish identity explicitly associated with the rise of a distinct conception of citizenship rights and state-society relations. Hearn demonstrates how the discursive scheme in Scottish civil society emphasized the egalitarian nature of Scotland and the presentation of Scots as a covenanted people, governed by a social contract.[21] In that perspective, despite the fact that retrenchment policies had an impact on all the citizens of Britain, it was presented more specifically as an attack on the foundations of Scotland, its distinct historical traditions and its conceptions of rights and institutions. In other words, it was an attack on its distinct citizenship regime.

The actions of the Thatcher government in Scotland triggered an important debate on democracy within the Union, and most importantly on the democratic deficit, since Scotland was governed by a party that had limited support from the population. More democratic autonomy, then, it was argued, would guarantee better protection for the Scottish social citizenship regime, which was by then seen as increasingly distinct from Britain's. Calls for a Scottish parliament, where such debate could take place, became the focal point of a revived movement for greater autonomy (home rule) among the middle class. The debate on social policy, as argued by Lindsay Paterson, revived the memory of a time when Scots were more autonomous within the Union:

> When the Conservative government then began to move away from consultation, from permitting Scottish distinctiveness and from the coherent approach to social policy that Scottish social democracy had adopted as its own, a memory of its successes became a leitmotiv of the campaign for home rule. Hence the theme of limited sovereignty, of consultation, of coherent government that runs through the Claim of Rights of 1988, the report of the Constitutional Convention in 1995, the UK government's white paper that was endorsed in the referendum of 1997, and the report of the Consultative Steering Group which established the standing orders and working practices of the Parliament we now have.[22]

This new discourse explicitly associates claims for greater control over social policies (rights), democratic autonomy (access) and a distinct identity rooted in a common history (belonging). A different understanding of citizenship was thus slowly emerging in Scotland from the 1980s on. It was associated not only with a possible set of distinct social policies, but also with the possibility of a new political ethos that would favour the growing participation of all citizens. The latter was particularly evident in the demands, before the referendum, by women's groups for an electoral system that would ensure a more proportionate gender representation. As Alice Brown notes:

The renewed demands for a Scottish Parliament were fuelled by the frustration of being governed by a Party (Conservative) that the majority of the Scottish electorate did not support, leading to claims of a "democratic deficit." This engendered a wide-ranging debate about the nature of democracy, participation and representation. Women in Scotland claimed a "double democratic deficit" on the grounds that they were excluded as Scots and as women. Gender equality thus became an intrinsic part of the broader campaign for reform toward a democratic, accountable and representative Scottish Parliament in the 1990s.[23]

The 1997 referendum on the re-establishment of a parliament in Edinburgh concretized the emerging parallel citizenship regime in Scotland. The Parliament created within the UK a different system of access to political institutions and reinforced the legitimacy of claims of its multinational character. As we will see, however, it is still uncertain how exactly the Scottish citizenship regime will be articulated and structured in the British and European contexts.

The Establishment of a Counter-Regime in Quebec

The development of the welfare state in Canada has had a different impact on the unity of the country. In fact, it is widely acknowledged that, since most social policies come under provincial jurisdiction, it led not only to a period of nation-building, but also to a period of "province-building," as the provinces were expanding their bureaucracies and becoming more involved in the daily lives of their citizens.[24] The federal government clearly had a central role in defining the principles of the welfare state and in ensuring its pan-Canadian expansion through transfer payments and equalization programs, but it had limited direct contact with citizens. Federal visibility was mainly through the development of national cultural institutions (the Canadian Broadcasting Corporation, and the National Film Board and various research councils) and in those areas where it had used its spending power such as old age pensions, unemployment insurance and family allowance.

In Quebec, the development of the welfare state encouraged the rise of nationalism and the transformation of Quebec's identity in many different ways. In the first phase of its development by the federal government, the welfare state was deeply opposed by Quebec's Conservative prime minister, Maurice Duplessis, who viewed it as an encroachment on the province's autonomy in the field of social policy. Partisan of a *laissez-faire* approach to socio-economic issues, Duplessis mounted a vigorous campaign against federal intrusions in the social realm, which he viewed as a threat to Quebec's tradition of church and private management of social problems.[25] Another reason the welfare state failed to play a nation-building role was that Ottawa's bureaucracy was largely inaccessible to the rising new French-speaking middle class that was graduating from the social sciences. With little chance of finding employment in Ottawa, most of them started to become active in organizations that fought against the Duplessis regime's reluctance to adopt a set of comprehensive social policies. They were joined by a rising tide of protest in existing institutions of civil society, which were increasingly calling on the Quebec government to play a leading role as the "national government" of Quebecers.[26]

Some of these reforms, which were demanded by a new middle class and a substantial part of Quebec civil society, were first put in place by the Lesage government, which came to power in 1960. Under the motto "Masters in our own house," the Liberal Party developed a series of institutional reforms and implemented new social policies. Benefiting from the Pearson-led federal government's willingness to provide more autonomy to Quebec, the province opted out of various social programs (in particular the pension plan) in order to establish what Keith Banting calls a unique "comprehensive provincial welfare state,"[27] which, in turn, reinforced Quebec's distinctiveness in Canada. Among the elements of its distinctiveness have been the development of the Caisse de dépôt et placement du Quebec, which invests the revenue from the pension plan scheme in Quebec businesses, and the network of CLSCs, the local community health care system. Jane Jenson presents the development of Quebec's distinct citizenship regime from the 1960s on in the following way:

> Since 1960, political forces within Québec, both federalist and sovereignist, have shared a commitment to the modernization of the society, to the construction of a state capable of promoting a transcendence of traditional economic, social and cultural forms, and more importantly to building a protected space for the French language. Since the Liberals of Jean Lesage first swept the Union Nationale from office, this has been a collectivist project – *a projet de société* [emphasis in original].[28]

These differences in Quebec and Canada regarding the orientation of the welfare state have widened in the last decade as neoliberal governments in other provinces (such as in Ontario and Alberta) have aggressively challenged the social consensus of the postwar era. Although the Quebec government has also reduced its social investments, it has not done so at the same rate as the federal government and most other provinces. It created new programs in the 1990s, such as a drug insurance plan and a popular public child care system, while maintaining the most accessible post-secondary education system in Canada. According to some analysts, the strong support for Quebec secession in the 1995 referendum can be explained by these growing distinctions in what Alain-G. Gagnon and Guy Lachapelle present as two distinct societal projects.[29]

It would be a mistake, however, to present the current movement in Quebec simply as one of diverging social policies.[30] The difference in welfare-state projects created a much more significant fracture in the constitutive elements of the citizenship regime. As we discussed earlier, there is an intimate link between the articulation of the relationship between the state and citizens in terms of rights and access mechanisms and the definition of boundaries of belonging. The initial development of the welfare state in Canada and its impact on the development of a stronger provincial government also had a major impact in transforming Quebecers' identity, which in turn led to a response by the federal government that only reinforced the gap between Quebec and the rest of the country.

First, the development of the Quebec welfare state led to the transformation of the traditional identity of French-speakers in the Quebec territory from French-Canadian to Quebecer, grounding their identity in a specific geographic location and in a specific state.[31] Second, the rise of this distinct identity and the nationalist movements that came with it encouraged a counter-reaction by the federal government, and in particular by the prime minister, Pierre Trudeau. Trudeau believed that the proper reaction to the rise of Quebec nationalists and their demand for recognition of a special status and of bicultural and bilingual Canada was to develop a new Canadian identity based on equality of individuals and languages (as opposed to communities and cultures).[32]

Trudeau's strategy resulted in the policy of official bilingualism in 1969, the policy of multiculturalism in 1971, and the constitutional Charter of Rights and Freedoms in 1982. During the same period, the Quebec government adopted competing policies that expressed clear opposition to Trudeau's view of the country and reinforced the uniqueness of Quebec: the Charter of the French language in 1977, which declared Quebec officially a French-speaking political entity, the adoption of a Quebec Charter of Rights and, later, the development of a new model of integration for immigrants called interculturalism which, while very similar to Canadian multiculturalism, explicitly defined the French language as the element of convergence in Quebec.[33] Following an administrative agreement with the federal government, Quebec is also responsible for the selection of immigrants other than political refugees. The government thus has significant leverage in defining who is to become a member of the political community (selection) and under what conditions (integration policies).[34]

Comparing Quebec and Scotland

What can we learn from this comparative history? First, in both Canada and the UK the citizenship regime was never fully centralized in the period of consolidation of the welfare state. The provincial state in Quebec and the local bureaucracy in Scotland maintained a considerable degree of autonomy in the articulation of the regime, leaving room for development of a particular relationship between rights, access and belonging. The centralizing forces of welfare nation-building were thus counterbalanced by a strengthening of the relationship between civil society and the local state in both Scotland and Quebec, thus creating the basic conditions for the development of distinct citizenship regimes.

Second, that welfare-state retrenchment played a central role in reinforcing both regimes from within by opening the debate about the nature and boundaries of communities of solidarity and regimes of access to the state. Competing definitions of solidarity and community emerged in Scotland and Quebec as a consequence of welfare retrenchment. In both cases, nationalists took advantage of this opening in the definition of the regime to reassert their claims for greater autonomy or, in the case of Quebec, sovereignty.

We can also point to important differences between the two cases. In Quebec, the notion of two competing regimes emerged early on. As a province, its institutional autonomy was much greater than Scotland's. After all, citizenship regimes in federal states are naturally fragmented. Quebec already controlled its own elements of the pan-Canadian regime. What distinguishes Quebec from other provinces, however, is the extent to which the federal government's definition of the pan-Canadian regime during the postwar period was rejected. Part of the explanation, as we saw, lies in the attempt by the federal government to define the pan-Canadian regime as a national project defining the political community in exclusive terms, leaving little place for the separation of citizenship and nationality (as was perhaps more the case in Britain). Quebec nationalists responded with their own articulation of a citizenship regime, defining the boundaries of the political community within Quebec rather than as a federal society. Two competing national projects, supported by two competing citizenship regimes, thus emerged.

In Scotland, it is only with welfare retrenchment that an obviously differentiated regime, or, rather, the rhetoric of something like a differentiated regime, emerged. The explanation obviously lies partly in the limited nature of Scottish political autonomy. But as we saw, there was room in Britain for the articulation of a distinct regime corresponding to and reinforcing Scottish identity. The administration of the welfare state through the Scottish Office led to the creation of a distinctly Scottish policy-making network, thus reinforcing the autonomy of civil society rather then limiting it. In the period of retrenchment, this autonomous regime emerged as a clear alternative to Thatcherism around which citizens could mobilize. These differences continue to influence the nature of the debate about citizenship in Scotland and Quebec.

Competitive or Fragmented Regimes?
Contemporary Struggles for Citizenship in Quebec and Scotland

Fundamental changes in the structure of state-society relations in Canada and the UK opened the door to a more explicit renegotiation of the citizenship regime in the late twentieth century. Immigration, increased mobility, and the emergence of an international human rights regime and supranational institutions such as the EU, and to a lesser extent NAFTA, also challenged the exclusive relationship between state sovereignty and citizenship regimes as established by the orthodoxy of the nation-state. The idea of exclusive membership was thus increasingly hard to sustain in the late twentieth century. The result is growing opportunities for small nations to gain control over citizenship regimes, or at least renegotiate them in part to reinforce the boundaries of their political community.

As we saw, welfare-state retrenchment also dramatically altered the relationship between the state as a guarantor of rights and the citizens as members of a community bound by notions of solidarity and equity. This triggered a need to redefine the nature of the bounds of citizenship. In both Canada and the UK, the last decade has been characterized by explicit attempts by the state to promote and strengthen citizenship. Talk about social cohesion, citizenship education and community-building is common in both the Blair and Chrétien governments' policy books. As we will see, this resulted in a more open confrontation with emerging regimes in Quebec and Scotland, leading to explicit debates about the definition of identities and the boundaries of community.

In the following pages, we will discuss how small nations such as Quebec and Scotland have consolidated their distinct citizenship regime in the last decade. Welfare retrenchment, then differentiation, resulted, we suggest, in a more explicit debate around political identities and institutions in the recent period.

The Consolidation of a Competitive Regime in Postreferendum Quebec

In the aftermath of the close results of the 1995 referendum, it rapidly became apparent that if separation was not an option for a significant proportion of Quebec voters, the current federal regime was clearly not drawing much more support. Facing a divided electorate and with limited possibilities for significant institutional reforms,[35] both the federal government and the nationalist government in Quebec embarked on a political battle for control of the citizenship regime.

In an attempt to consolidate the idea of a pan-Canadian community, the federal government sought to increase its visibility in Quebec and revived the idea of Canada as a country defined by its social programs and conception of inclusive citizenship. This led, among other things, to the negotiation of an agreement with all the provinces except Quebec on the constitutive elements of the social union. The Social Union Framework Agreement was seen as an alternative to constitutional negotiations in order to renew the relationship between the federal government and the provinces. As Alain Noël notes, SUFA recognizes a role for the federal government in areas of social policy constitutionally defined as provincial jurisdictions.[36] It was openly defined by federal politicians as an attempt to strengthen pan-Canadian social citizenship. The relationship between social policies and identity was made explicit by the minister of justice, Anne McLellan, when she declared: "the notion of social union captures our solidarity with one another, our understanding that we are stronger together."[37]

The Quebec government did not sign the agreement. It was dismissed as "another attempt by the federal government to build a unitary national state at the expense of provincial autonomy" and "another coup by the federal government to isolate Quebec." [translation][38] While the Parti Québécois was attacking federal attempts to rebuild the pan-Canadian citizenship regime through centralization of social policies, however, it was also involved in its own version of citizenship-building. As we discussed earlier, social policies occupied a central place in the consolidation of a distinct regime in Quebec from the 1960s onward. In the aftermath of the referendum, it took a somewhat different path.

After the vote, it became evident that the PQ's societal project had been rejected overwhelmingly by the nonfrancophone minorities, especially in the multicultural city of Montreal. While the French-speaking majority voted 60 percent in favour of the PQ's sovereignty-partnership proposal, the English-speaking and recent-immigrant populations, with some exceptions, rejected the proposal massively. Aboriginal peoples also campaigned actively against sovereignty, some openly questioning the legitimacy of the referendum process.[39] Moreover, Quebec's business class, now dominated by francophones, was fairly vocal against the nationalist project, citing economic uncertainty. This led the premier and leader of the "Yes" forces, Jacques Parizeau, to declare, in his speech on the evening of the referendum, that the country was lost "because of money and ethnic votes." Parizeau resigned the following day, leaving a daunting heritage for his successor. Gaining support from the financial sector and cultural minorities became the priority of the new leader, Lucien Bouchard.

The nationalist leadership rapidly came to the conclusion that independence would be impossible without fiscal balance, a strong economy and the support of nonfrancophones in this increasingly diverse society. A rearticulation of the citizenship regime was thus necessary. First, the need to define Quebec's political community in more inclusive terms, by breaking the association between Québécois and *francophone de souche* (old-stock francophones), triggered a debate about the nature of the relationship between national identity, political membership and cultural heritage. One of the most tangible results of the close vote in 1995 was thus profound introspection about the meaning, relevance and history of Québécois identity, the values defining this community and their articulation in consensual policies.

Second, business groups and foreign investment firms found a sympathetic ear in the person of the new premier. Quebec entered its own period of welfare retrenchment.[40] This obviously had a deep impact on the capacity of nationalist forces to define their project in social terms. In Quebec, as elsewhere in Canada, claims for equity and inclusion became central to the new politics. Faced with a more proactive federal government whose fiscal situation was much stronger, the Quebec government needed to remobilize its citizens and consolidate its citizenship regime.

As with Scotland, a strong relationship between the state and civil society characterizes the citizenship regime in Quebec.[41] The economic model in Quebec has often been defined as neocorporatist, and unions are more powerful in Quebec than anywhere else in North America.[42] For better or for worse, civil society organizations have historically benefited from both financial support and access to the decision-making process more in Quebec than elsewhere in Canada.[43] Soon after its election in 1994, the PQ launched an important initiative to revitalize what in Quebec is called *le secteur communautaire* (the third sector), a network of community groups, social movements and nonprofit organizations that form the core of civil society. In 1995, a few months before the referendum, a secretariat was created to co-ordinate government action and define a new policy regarding consultation and funding for nongovernmental organizations.[44]

The government capitalized on its relationship with the *secteur communautaire* after the referendum. A series of forums or summits was organized to discuss some key dimensions of the citizenship regime with unions, the business council, community-based organizations, student associations, the well-organized women's movement and many other representatives of civil society. The government sought to include the sector in the renegotiation of the citizenship regime that was to take place in the following years.

Among other things, the 1996 "Sommet socio-économique" discussed the challenges of economic restructuring in Quebec. The objective was to reach a consensus on the priorities for economic and social development. In exchange for tacit support for the government's objective of a zero deficit by the year 2000, civil society organizations obtained a series of government commitments regarding child poverty, education, health and other issues. The summit discussed the terms of the new "social contract" between the state and civil society in an era of restructuring, consolidating the link so essential for legitimization of a citizenship regime.

Following the postreferendum debate on identity, the integration and participation of cultural minorities also attracted government attention. The challenge was to create the conditions for the emergence of a common identity among all Quebecers, where French is a constitutive element but where one did not draw categorical distinctions based on language. As we have seen, Quebec early on developed its own model of integration for immigrants. The policy was explicitly framed in citizenship terms with the return to power of the nationalist Parti Québécois in 1994. The government then created the Ministère des Relations avec les citoyens et de l'Immigration (MRCI). The mandate of the new department was to develop and strengthen the cohesion among "Québécois d'origines diverses" by linking them to "common civic elements" defined as the building blocks of Quebec's political community.[45]

In September 2000, the government held a National Forum on Citizenship and Integration, where different actors in civil society were asked to comment on a working document for a new policy on citizenship and integration in Quebec. The working document stressed the historical importance of Quebec citizenship, which originates in the political institutions predating the Canadian federation.[46] It stated that "Quebec citizenship is based upon shared references. Those references are obviously cultural and identity-based. But they are, more importantly, of a political order...as expressed through the State, laws and institutions" [translation].[47] The core of the document was a proposal that membership in the political community should be based on a "civic contract," which includes a shared commitment to, among other things, common democratic institutions and values, social justice, respect for minorities and the use of French as a common public language. It was thus an explicit attempt at defining the conditions of membership in the political community.

What is striking about the document, and indeed about most documents related to citizenship produced in the same period by organizations close to the nationalist project,[48] is the complete absence of references to the Canadian federation, except to define it as an obstacle to the establishment of an inclusive citizenship regime in Quebec. In the forum's working document, Canadian citizenship is associated with the French concept of "nationalité" and defined as a formal status, as opposed to a more substantive Quebec citizenship: "nationality refers to the international domain. It constitutes the link, in relation to third countries, between a person and a state" [translation].[49] The lack of distinction between nationality and citizenship in Canada creates confusion and conflicts of legitimacy, according to the document, suggesting that the only substantial – and legitimate – citizenship regime is the one built around Quebec's political institutions.

Many representatives of civic groups present at the forum were critical of the document, suggesting it was tainted by its political bias in favour of the governing party's sovereignist agenda. The definition of Quebec citizenship, one representative of a Montreal-based community centre for immigrants argued, should not be defined in opposition to Canadian citizenship but as a specific component of it.[50] The document was also criticized by community groups for its overwhelming focus on cohesion and integration as the main functions of citizenship, thus giving priority to "the nation over social and economic inclusion and participation" [translation].[51]

This episode was followed by a similar debate a year later. As we discussed earlier, Quebec developed its own linguistic regime in the 1970s in response to the federal government's bilingualism policy. Quebec's language policies were challenged in court and many of its most controversial dispositions struck down under both the Quebec and the Canadian charters of rights. The linguistic legislation nonetheless became a pillar of Quebec's distinct citizenship regime. In response to growing concerns from its militant base regarding the state of French in multilingual and multicultural Montreal, the PQ government put together another forum, the Commission des États généraux sur la langue française, to evaluate the state of French in Quebec 20 years after the adoption of the Charter of the French Language. The commission released its report in August 2001. It suggested the cornerstone of a renewed linguistic policy in Quebec should be the creation of a formal Quebec citizenship around which a "new linguistic consensus" could be built.[52]

Again, the report stressed the function of citizenship as "an explicit recognition of national belonging" [translation].[53] Further, "it aims to reflect the ties between Quebecers and the shared institutions and heritage that constitute the foundations of the Quebec nation" [translation].[54] Not surprisingly, the report, at least this specific aspect of it, was roundly rejected by representatives of the English-speaking minority and by a number of federalists for its assumption that membership in Quebec's political community can be defined outside the Canadian context.[55]

There is no space here to report on the full spectrum of the debates surrounding the renegotiation of Quebec's citizenship regime in recent years. But the few examples above demonstrate the extent to which the PQ has attempted to redefine the boundaries of the political community in association with the key sectors of Quebec's civil society. The message, it seems, is that the Quebec state has a much closer relationship with society and thus a much stronger citizenship regime than does the federal government. The two documents produced by government-appointed commissions also illustrate how identities are being negotiated. Citizenship replaced "la nation" in the discursive landscape. As we have seen, this realignment, which emerged as a response to the need to build a more inclusive political community, is framed mostly in opposition to the alternative citizenship regime as it currently exists in Canada. The Canadian regime is seen at best as a complementary regime, at worst as a competing one.

More recently, a distinct citizenship model has also been associated with a debate over the quality of democracy in Quebec and a possible reform of democratic institutions. Changing the electoral system to adopt some degree of proportional representation, the election of the prime minister, and a more systematic use of referenda, including citizen-initiated referenda, are among the ideas circulating in government circles as part of an attempt to "revitalize the link between the citizens and their democratic institutions."[56] In the absence of any significant institutional change in the federal arrangement with Canada, a reform of democratic institutions, says the minister responsible, is the only way to revitalize Quebec's political community and strengthen it in the face of increasing pressure from global forces.

This use of the vocabulary of citizenship is obviously part of a much more global phenomenon. Today, questions of citizenship related to education, social programs, immigration and democratic participation are debated throughout the world. We thus have to be careful in concluding from this discourse that what is taking place is specific to Quebec. What does distinguish the discussion surrounding citizenship in Quebec, however, is the extent to which the regime is defined as a renewed partnership between the *provincial state* and civil society. This renewed partnership is being defined in opposition to, not as a complement of, the federal regime.

Postdevolution Scotland: Toward a Fragmented Citizenship Regime?

During the 1997 referendum campaign in Scotland, the Scottish parliament was seen by nationalists of various tendencies as a way for the Scottish civil society to regain access to and control over the articulation of its relationship with the state. Scots were to regain control over the citizenship regime, as expressed in distinct social policies, a sense of a distinct national identity with different values and distinct democratic institutions that would encourage participation by citizens in public affairs. These institutions in particular were viewed as providing the opportunity to introduce a "new politics" that would be more inclusive of citizens from different political orientations. As Ailsa Henderson argues, "the arrival of devolution, then, not only provided an opportunity to produce policies that are more representative but to create institutions that exuded a different working culture."[57]

It is probably too early to evaluate the effect of devolution on the definition of citizenship in Scotland. In fact, Scots have so far shown limited enthusiasm for the Scottish Parliament and are generally sceptical of its ability to introduce a new type of politics.[58] Some analysts have even gone as far as to argue that devolution may have in fact increased the elitist character of Scottish public life.[59] Still, our objective here is not so much to come up with definitive conclusions on the workings of the Scottish Parliament, but rather to see whether Scotland may be following a path similar to Quebec's, by defining a citizenship regime in competition with the British model.

In contrast to the situation in Quebec, the term "Scottish citizenship," with some exceptions, does not seem to have entered the discursive space of Scottish politics. One exception is a policy document of the Scottish National Party (SNP) on the future of Scotland and the nature of citizenship in an independent Scotland.[60] The document, *Talking Independence,* stresses (in bold letters) that the SNP has an "an open and inclusive approach to citizenship" and that, in the eventuality of Scottish independence, "the automatic right of citizenship will be open to all those living in Scotland, all those born in Scotland, and all those with a parent born in Scotland." The document also stresses that since Scotland's problem is emigration, not immigration, citizens "should therefore welcome the contribution of the new Scots who wish to make this country their home."[61] The second exception is the wide consultation on citizenship education, "Learning and Teaching Scotland," in which references to "citizenship in Scotland" are numerous while the notion of British citizenship is relatively absent. Finally, the Civic Forum[62] includes a number of citizenship-related initiatives, mostly related to issues of discrimination and ways of promoting equal opportunities in Scotland.

In Scotland, therefore, citizenship has not been a subject of debate as it has in Quebec. It has essentially been discussed by the SNP in the context of a postindependence citizenship and by different organizations of civil society around issues of rights, obligations, discrimination and citizenship education. Citizenship is thus viewed either as denoting membership in a sovereign nation-state or as type of behaviour. Citizenship as a form of belonging to a specific political community, as expressed in the Quebec case, has not so far occupied an important place in the discursive space of Scottish politics.

This absence of explicit debates on Scottish citizenship is somewhat paradoxical given the nature of nationalist discourse in Scotland. As we have seen, the re-establishment of a Scottish parliament was defined as a question of democratic access and control over the substance of the citizenship regime. Part of the explanation perhaps lies in the British government's insistence on the "one citizenship, many nations" motto. As Nicola McEwen argues, "the New Labour government has sought to emphasize the continued relevance of dual (i.e., Scottish and British) national identity among Scots with reference to the achievements of the postwar welfare state."[63]

Moreover, the Blair government's discourse, in face of the potential threat of the SNP, has been not so much to propose an alternative model of citizenship as to insist on the pursuit of this long tradition of respect for a different Scottish national identity. Britain has a long history of dealing with the fragmented and fuzzy nature of identities now celebrated by partisans of postnational citizenship. As Robin Cohen argues with regard to the development of the British identity:

> British identity shows a general pattern of fragmentation. Multiple axes of identification have meant that Irish, Scots, Welsh and English people, those from white, black and brown Commonwealth, Americans, English-Speakers, Europeans or even "aliens" have had their lives intersect one with another in overlapping and complex circles of identity-construction and rejection. The shape and edges of British Identity are thus historically changing, often vague and, to a degree, malleable – an aspect of British identity I have called "a fuzzy frontier."[64]

But this "fuzzy frontier" may well reach a point where it becomes too fuzzy for Scottish nationalists. It is hard to imagine that the consolidation of many aspects of the citizenship regime in more explicit Scottish terms will not be accompanied by a renegotiation of boundaries of identities and belonging, especially given the roots of the current institutional transformation. Let us not forget that the response in Scotland to the restructuring of the citizenship regime conduced by Thatcher in the 1980s was a realignment in identities toward a more Scottish-oriented regime of rights and democratic access.

Not only is a de facto Scottish regime emerging, but the British regime is becoming fragmented from above with the development of a European citizenship.[65] It is paradoxical that certain Scottish nationalists welcome the development and strengthening of European citizenship. They seem to acknowledge that citizenship can be tied to institutions and rights above the state level but hesitate to draw a parallel between this and developments within Scotland.[66]

It is hard to measure the impact of the EU on Scotland, but two elements are important in the continuous development of a distinct Scottish citizenship regime. First, as exemplified by the slogan of the SNP, "Independence in the European Union," the EU provides a new political arena into which Scots can bring their distinct voice. There is already evidence that the EU constitutes a distinct political space for Scotland, as exemplified by the participation of local authorities in the European Committee of Regions and the fact that most departments of the Scottish Executive have developed links with their European counterparts in the European Commission.[67] The Scottish Executive has also established an External Relations Division, which co-ordinates the Executive's involvement in European and external affairs.[68]

Second, the development of a European political community, especially the European Convention on Human Rights, has contributed to the development of a rights regime that in part transcends UK political institutions. This innovation of the postwar era has been given new life recently with the *Human Rights Act* of 1998, which incorporates the Convention into UK law. Interestingly, in its attempt to maintain the principle of parliamentary supremacy, Westminster has only allowed legislation in devolved areas to be struck down by the courts in light of the European Convention.[69] This has two consequences: it reminds everyone of the Scottish assembly's status as a creature of Westminster, but it also creates an interesting situation whereby Scottish (and Northern Irish) citizens may be able to seek redress from the Convention and not their fellow citizens of England.[70] The existence of the European political community provides Scots with a new regime of rights and potentially a new political arena where they can express their distinctiveness. Indeed, when asked in May 2000 which institution would be the most important in two decades' time, 37 percent of Scots identified the Scottish Parliament, 33 percent the European Union and 17 percent the UK Parliament.[71]

Finally, while there is no explicit debate on citizenship in Scotland, there are a number of elements of the citizenship regime that could be objects of political debates in the coming years. The *Scotland Act* of 1998 reserves primary legislative power for the Scottish Parliament in many important fields related to the welfare state. Despite current disappointment among Scottish citizens about the impact of the Parliament, there is no significant body of opinion that questions the legitimacy of the devolution arrangements.[72] Scotland is free to make its own laws and to change existing laws in the fields of health, education and training, local government, social work, housing, economic development and many other areas.[73] As such, all the elements of a more active debate on citizenship are present, in particular around social issues.

The current Scottish Executive is dominated by the Labour Party and remains closely aligned with the government of Tony Blair. The domination of the Labour Party in Scotland has certainly limited major policy divergence with the rest of Britain. In the eventuality of a change of government at either Holyrood or Westminster, however, roads may well part on priorities and approaches with regard to citizenship-related polices. Moreover, the adoption of some degree of proportionality with the *additional member system*, which makes any majority government less likely and coalitions necessary, means that the Scottish Executive must be much more attentive to shifting moods in Parliament. A government too closely connected to London may well lose some of its support in the Scottish Parliament, and among the population as well.

With regard to citizen and civil society participation in the affairs of the Parliament, there is still much confusion as to the exact role the Civic Forum will play and what modifications should be made to the committee system to make it more accessible and open. Yet, consultation is enshrined in the founding principles of the Parliament and the work of some committees has led to a distinct Scottish consensus. Indeed, the Scottish Parliament, following consultation with representatives of civil society, has already implemented policies and practices that tend to maintain and to a certain extent accentuate its distinct approach to social policy.

The most highly visible element has been the adoption of a distinctive system of tuition fees at the post-secondary level. Scottish students do not pay upfront tuition fees for higher education, whereas students in the rest of the UK do.[74] The field of education, in line with Scottish tradition, has witnessed many changes toward a system that is more liberal than that in the rest of the UK.[75] Other significant decisions unique to Scotland include an increase in teachers' salaries and, even more significantly from the standpoint of social citizenship, a commitment to introducing free long-term health services for the elderly.

Scotland seems to be in a transition period. It exhibits many characteristics of a differentiated regime, but there is no explicit debate on the boundaries and control of the citizenship regime as there is in Quebec. The regime emerging in Scotland seems to be composed of a number of overlapping rather than competing regimes (Scotland, UK, Europe) that provide citizens with different identities, opportunities for political participation and rights regime.

Conclusion

While academics studying the changing nature of citizenship often point to the transformations from above currently taking place in most industrialized societies, few point to equally important transformations from within. Citizenship is closely associated with the modern process of nation-building. The definition of political boundaries between communities has its roots in the emergence of specific citizenship regimes. This is why small nations such as Quebec and Scotland are involved in struggles for control of the citizenship regime. The definition of nation remains meaningless without the tools to define the relationship between the state and the political community.

In the mid-twentieth century, nation-building took the form of welfare regimes based on a shared definition of the rights of citizenship. Paradoxically, welfare-state regimes also strengthened small nations' sense of political distinctiveness. In both Canada and the UK, the citizenship regime was never fully centralized during the period of consolidation of the welfare state. The provincial state in Quebec and the local bureaucracy in Scotland maintained a high degree of autonomy in articulating the regime, leaving room for the creation of a particular relationship between rights, access and belonging. The centralizing forces of welfare nation-building were counterbalanced by a strengthening of the relationship between civil society and the local state in both Scotland and Quebec, creating the conditions for the development of distinct citizenship regimes.

In Quebec, a distinct citizenship regime was more explicitly defined. That was partly because of greater institutional autonomy, but it was also because the federal government imposed a citizenship model that did not allow for the expression of different conceptions of allegiance and belonging. Despite the federal nature of the Canadian state, there was to be only one regime of rights, access and belonging in Canada. This resulted, as we have seen, in the emergence of a competing regime in Quebec. In Scotland, the citizenship regime was, and still is, more implicit. The UK is historically defined as a multinational society, allowing greater space for the negotiation of identities within a unified regime. But a citizenship regime still emerged in Scotland through the relationship between the Scottish Office and civil society. It was, however, more of a complement to the larger British regime than a competing regime.

Welfare-state retrenchment played a central role in reinforcing both regimes "from within" by opening up the debate about the nature and boundaries of communities of solidarity and regimes of access to the state. Competing definitions of solidarity and community emerged in Scotland and Quebec as a consequence of welfare retrenchment. In both cases, nationalists took advantage of this opening of the definition of the regime to reassert their claims for greater autonomy or, in the case of Quebec, sovereignty.

In both Quebec and Scotland, the redefinition of the regime first took the form of a rearticulation of the relationship between the state and civil society in order to compensate for the weakening of the welfare state. In Scotland, this was realized through a new parliament with the stated objective of bringing politics closer to the Scottish people. In Quebec, it took the form of a series of forums aimed at redefining the conditions of membership in the political community. The definition of Quebec citizenship, its conditions and boundaries, emerged as an explicit issue on the political agenda in the postreferendum period. This citizenship regime was again defined in opposition to its federal counterpart and as a tool to consolidate solidarity and cohesion from within.

By contrast, no explicit discussion about citizenship emerged in postdevolution Scotland. It may be just a question of time, however, given the nature of powers devolved to the Scottish Parliament and the potential contradictions between what we defined as the latent Scottish regime and its UK parent. The main distinction between Scotland and Quebec is perhaps the greater possibilities for the former to develop as a true multilevel regime in which different aspects of citizenship are played out in different political spaces. The Scottish,

UK and European regimes may well evolve into complementary regimes, rather than competing ones as in the case of Canada and Quebec.

The current context opens possibilities for small nations to reassert their claims regarding citizenship. This takes various forms, as illustrated by the cases of Quebec and Scotland. The redefinition of the relationship between states, citizenship and political communities is thus not a one-way process toward a postnational or transnational model. Competing political forces are engaged in a struggle for control over the content of citizenship regimes. For competing states, it is a struggle for allegiance and legitimacy. In response to the fragmentation of the citizenship regime based on the welfare state, small nations have recreated their regimes on new grounds. In an era of fragmentation, after constitutional reforms that failed (Canada) and succeeded (Britain), building distinct citizenship regimes from within, where state and civil society are strongly embedded, may well be nationalism's third way between independence and assimilation, between renewed federalism and secession.

Notes

A version of this chapter was presented at the annual meeting of the Canadian Political Science Association, Toronto, May 2002. We would like to thank David Denver and Ailsa Henderson for their helpful suggestions. We would specially like to acknowledge the very insightful written comments on an earlier draft of this chapter provided by Nicola McEwen. Obviously, we are solely responsible for any omissions or factual mistakes.

1. See, for example, Soysal (1994) and Held (1996).

2. The process of differentiation between the Canadian and Quebec regimes was first explored by Jenson (1997). This chapter seeks to expand on this idea using Scotland as a comparative standpoint.

3. T.H. Marshall did not problematize cultural differences, but his argument can be extended to include such rights. See Marshall (1976).

4. Marshall's work is central here, and so is that of many others who inform us of the historical role of citizenship rights in the process of constructing modern nations. See Bendix (1964), Polanyi (1957), Gellner (1983) and, more recently, Miller (1999).

5. Jane Jenson has often made this point about the nature of citizenship as an object of contention. See Jenson (1997, p. 631).

6. For a detailed definition and discussion, see Jenson and Phillips (1996). A citizenship regime consists of the "institutional arrangements, rules and understandings that guide and shape concurrent policy decisions and expenditures of states, problem definitions by states and citizens, and claims-making by citizens." This definition is a modified version of the definition of a welfare-state regime developed by Gøsta Esping-Andersen (1990, p. 80). See Jenson (1997, p. 631).

7. On the three dimensions, see Jenson and Papillon (2000b) as well as Antje Wiener (1998).

8. On variations in the meaning of citizenship in different time and space, see Heater (1999).

9. Anderson (1991).

10. Miller (1995, p. 92); see also Keating (1996, p. 34).

11. For example, see Eric J. Hobsbawm's account of the recent wave of "ethnic group assertion" in the second edition of *Nations and Nationalism Since 1780* (1992, p. 168 and following).

12. For a review of the notion of policy feedback, see Pierson (1993).

13. See Hall (1989) on the Keynesian paradigm and its diffusion in the world.

14. Elisson and Pierson (1998, p. 2).

15. On the importance of the nation-building function of the British welfare state, see McEwen (2001a).

16. Paterson (1994).

17. Kellas (1989). For a critique of Kellas' perspective, see Midwinter et al. (1991).

18. For theoretically oriented and explicit accounts of the relationship between attempts to dismantle the welfare state and support for devolution, see McEwen (2001b, 2002).

19. Offe (1984).

20. Hearn (2000). On the different organizations in the 1980s and 1990s that militated in favour of a new Scottish parliament, see Mitchell (1996).

21. The main argument here is not so much that Scots have different values from the English on, for example, social issues, but rather that Thatcher's behaviour allowed for the development in the public sphere of a discourse stressing the imposed nature of the Conservative Party's action. For a critique of the myth of the progressive nature of Scottish society in relation to English society, see Miller et al. (1996).

22. Paterson (2000); see also McEwen (2002).

23. Brown et al. (2002, p. 72).

24. On province-building, see Cairns (1977).

25. On Duplessis' liberal ideology of *laisser-faire*, see Bourque et al. (1994).

26. On the role of civil society in the rise of the welfare state in Quebec, see Turgeon (1999). On the rise of a new Quebec educated middle class, see Behiels (1985).

27. Banting (1987, p. 74).

28. Jenson (1997, p. 639).

29. Gagnon and Lachapelle (1996).

30. In fact, recently, a political party proposing more neoliberal reforms, the Action démocratique du Québec (ADQ), has substantially increased in popularity.

31. On the relation between the welfare state and the transformation of Quebec's identity, see Southam (1989).

32. On Trudeau's view of Canada and Quebec, see McRoberts (1997).

33. For an analysis, see Gagnon and Iacovino (2001) and Labelle and Rocher (2001).

34. Not surprisingly, Quebec is the only province actively seeking immigrants from francophone countries.

35. Opening the constitutional Pandora's box was not seen as a politically wise option in federal circles. The conditions leading to the failure of the Meech Lake and Charlottetown accords a few years before were still very much present, as indicated by the popularity of the Reform Party's strong stand on Quebec during and after the referendum.

36. Noël (1998, p. 26).

37. McLellan (1998, p. 6).

38. Facal (1998, p. 6).

39. For a discussion of competing democratic claims on the part of Aboriginal peoples and Quebec, see Jenson and Papillon (2000a).

40. Welfare restructuring was already taking place in Quebec, but it is only with the Bouchard government that the zero-deficit target was reached through significant restructuring of social programs.

41. For an analysis, see Laforest and Phillips (2001).

42. See, for example, Montpetit (2002).

43. See Laforest and Phillips (2001, p. 57).

44. Laforest and Phillips (2001, p. 59).

45. The current mission statement of the MRCI reads "promouvoir et soutenir le plein exercice des droits et des responsabilités que confère la citoyenneté au Québec et de favoriser la solidarité au sein de la société québécoise." www.mrci.qc.ca

46. Ministere des Relations avec les citoyens et de l'Immigration (2001, p. 14).

47. Ministere des Relations avec les citoyens et de l'Immigration (2001, p. 12).

48. See, for example, the working document on citizenship and democracy prepared by the Bloc Québécois (1999).

49. Ministère des relations avec les citoyens et l'Immigration (2001, p. 14). It is interesting to note how the document employs the distinction between nationality and citizenship commonly used in France and awkwardly applies it to Canada, without pointing out the significant institutional and historical differences between these countries.

50. Based on anonymous interviews conducted during the Forum, September 22, 2000.

51. "Pas de consensus" (2000).

52. Commission des États généraux sur la situation et l'avenir de la langue française au Québec (2001, p. 14).

53. Commission des États généraux sur la situation et l'avenir de la langue française au Québec (2001, p. 14).

54. Commission des États généraux sur la situation et l'avenir de la langue française au Québec (2001, p. 21).

55. See Perrault (2001); see also the analysis by Proulx (2001).

56. Secrétariat aux Affaires intergouvernementales canadiennes (2002).

57. Henderson (2002, p. 8).

58. See Suridge (2002).

59. See Hassan and Warhurst (2001).

60. See Scottish National Party (2002).

61. Scottish National Party (2002).

62. The Civic Forum, composed of a number of Scottish organizations, attempts to bring them into a dialogue with Parliament. See its Web site at www.civicforum.org.uk

63. McEwen (2001a, pp. 96-97).

64. Cohen (1994, p. 35). On that issue, see also Colley (1992) and Turgeon and Gagnon (forthcoming 2003).

65. On the construction of the European citizenship regime, see Wiener (1998).

66. We thank Nicola McEwen for pointing this element out to us.

67. On the presence of Scotland in the EU, see Salmon (2001).

68. See the Web site of the Scottish Executive EU office at http://www.scotland.gov.uk/euoffice/default.asp

69. In cases of legislation enacted by Westminster, the court can make a "declaration of incompatibility," which sends the signal to Parliament that legislation is not "Convention-proof." For a useful presentation of the implications of the *Human Rights Act* of 1998, see (Harrington, 2000/2001).

70. On that topic, see Keating (2001b, chapter 5).

71. Reported in Paterson (2000).

72. See Bradbury and Mitchell (2002).

73. See Keating (2001a).

74. Instead of paying fees, Scottish students pay an endowment after graduating.

75. See Paterson (2000).

Bibliography

Anderson, Benedict. *Imagined Communities: Reflections on the Origins and Spread of Nationalism.* London: Verso, 1991.

Banting, Keith. *The Welfare State and Canadian Federalism,* 2nd ed. Montreal and Kingston: McGill-Queen's University Press, 1987.

Behiels, Michael. *Prelude to Québec's Quiet Revolution: Liberalism versus Neo-Nationalism.* Montreal: McGill-Queen's University Press, 1985.

Bendix, Reinhard. *Nation Building and Citizenship.* New York : John Wiley, 1964.

Bloc Québécois. *Chantier de reflexion sur la Citoyenneté et la democratie: c'est l'affaire de tour le monde.* Riviere-du-Loup, Conseil general du Bloc Québécois, April 1999.

Bourque, Gilles, Jules Duchastel and Jacques Beauchemin. *La société libérale duplessiste.* Montreal: Presses de l'Université de Montréal, 1994.

Bradbury, Jonathan, and James Mitchell. "Devolution and Territorial Politics: Stability, Uncertainty and Crisis." *Parliamentary Affairs,* Vol. 55 (2002): 299-316.

Brown, Alice, Tahyna Barnett Donaghy, Fiona Mackay and Elizabeth Meehan. "Women and Constitutional Change in Scotland and Northern Ireland." *Parliamentary Affairs,* Vol. 55 (2002): 71-84.

Cairns, Alan. "The Governments and Societies of Canadian Federalism." *Canadian Journal of Political Science,* Vol. 10, no. 4 (1977): 695-725.

Cohen, Robin. *Frontiers of Identity: The British and the Others.* London: Longman, 1994.

Colley, Linda. *Britons: Forging the Nation, 1707-1837.* New Haven: Yale University Press, 1992.

Commission des États généraux sur la situation et l'avenir de la langue française au Québec. *Le Français, une langue pour tout le monde.* Rapport final. Gouvernement du Québec, 2001.

Elisson, Nick, and Chris Pierson. *Development in British Social Policy.* London: Macmillan, 1998.

Esping-Andersen, Gøsta. *The Three Worlds of Welfare Capitalism.* Princeton: Princeton University Press, 1990.

Facal, Joseph. "Pourquoi le Québec a dit non à l'Union Sociale." *La Presse,* February 18, 1998.

Gagnon, Alain-G., and Raffaele Iacovino. "Framing Citizenship in an Age of Poliethnicity: The Québec Model of Interculturalism," in *The State of the Federation 2000/2001,* ed. Harvey Lazar and Hamish Telford. Kingston: Institute of Intergovernmental Relations, 2001.

Gagnon, Alain-G., and Guy Lachapelle. "Québec Confronts Canada: Two Competing Societal Projects Searching for Legitimacy." *Publius,* Vol. 26, no. 3 (1996): 177-91.

Gellner, Ernest. *Nations and Nationalism.* Oxford: Blackwell, 1983.

Hall, Peter A., ed. *The Political Power of Economic Ideas: Keynesianism across Nations.* Princeton: Princeton University Press, 1989.

Harrington, Joanna. "Rights Brought Home: The United Kingdom Adopts a 'Charter of Rights.'" *Constitutional Forum,* Vol. 11, no. 4 (summer 2000/2001): 105-11.

Hassan, Gerry, and Chris Warhurst. "New Scotland? Policy, Parties and Institutions." *Political Quarterly*, Vol. 72, no. 2 (April 2001): 213-26.

Hearn, Jonathan. *Claiming Scotland.* Edinburgh: Polygon, 2000.

Heater, Derek Benjamin. *What Is Citizenship?* Cambridge: Polity Press, 1999.

Held, David. "Democracy: From City-States to a Cosmopolitan Order?" in *Prospects for Democracy: North, South, East, West,* ed. David Held. Stanford, CA: Stanford University Press, 1996.

Henderson, Ailsa. "New Politics and the Rhetoric of Renewal." Presented at the annual meeting of the Canadian Political Science Association, Toronto, May 2002.

Hobsbawn, Eric J. *Nations and Nationalism Since 1780,* 2nd ed. Cambridge: Cambridge University Press, 1992.

Jenson, Jane. "Fated to Live in Interesting Times: Canada's Changing Citizenship Regime." *Canadian Journal of Political Science,* Vol. 30, no. 4 (1997): 624-44.

Jenson, Jane, and Martin Papillon. "Challenging the Citizenship Regime: James Bay Cree and Transnational Action." *Politics and Society,* Vol. 28, no. 2 (2000a): 245-64.

———. "The Changing Boundaries of Citizenship: A Review and Research Agenda." In *Modernizing Governance: A Preliminary Exploration.* Ottawa: Canadian Centre for Management Development, 2000b.

Jenson, Jane, and Susan D. Phillips. "Regime Shifts: New Citizenship Practices in Canada." *International Journal of Canadian Studies,* Vol. 14, no. 14 (fall 1996): 111-35.

Keating, Michael. *Nations against State.* London: Macmillan, 1996.

———. "Managing the Multinational State: Constitutional Settlements in the United Kingdom," in *The Dynamics of Decentralization,* ed. Trevor C. Salmon and Michael Keating. Kingston: School of Policy Studies, 2001a.

———. *Plurinational Democracy.* Oxford: Oxford University Press, 2001b.

Kellas, James. *The Scottish Political System,* 4th ed. Cambridge: Cambridge University Press, 1989.

Labelle, Micheline, and François Rocher. "People Who Live in a Glass House: Citizenship and National Identity in Canada and Québec." In *Scottish Affairs,* special issue, ed. John MacInnes and David McCrone. Edinburgh: Unit for the Study of Government, 2001.

Laforest, Rachel, and Susan Phillips. "Repenser les relations entre gouvernement et secteur bénévole: à la croisée des chemis au Canada et au Québec." *Politiques et Societés,* Vol. 20, no. 2 (2001): 37-68.

Marshall, T.H. *Class, Citizenship and Social Development.* Westport, CT: Greenwood Press, 1976.

McEwen, Nicola. "State Welfare Nationalism: The Territorial Impact of Welfare State Development in Scotland." *Regional and Federal Studies,* Vol. 12, no 1 (2002): 66-90.

———. "The Nation-Building Role of State Welfare in the United Kingdom and Canada." In *The Dynamics of Decentralization,* ed. Trevor C. Salmon and Michael Keating. Kingston: School of Policy Studies, 2001a.

———. "State Welfare Nationalism: The Territorial Impact of Welfare State Development in Scotland and Quebec." Unpublished Ph.D. thesis, University of Sheffield, 2001b.

McLellan, Anne. "Modernizing Canada's Social Union: A New Partnership among Governments and Citizens." *Policy Options* (November 1998): 6-8.

McRoberts, Kenneth. *Misconceiving Canada.* Toronto: Oxford University Press, 1997.

Midwinter, Arthur F., Michael Keating and James Mitchell. *Politics and Public Policy in Scotland.* Basingstoke: Macmillan, 1991.

Miller, David. *On Nationality.* Oxford: Oxford University Press, 1995.

Miller, David. *Principles of Social Justice.* Cambridge, MA: Harvard University Press, 1999.

Miller, William, Annis May Timpson and Michael Lessnoff. *Political Culture in Contemporary Britain: People and Politicians, Principles and Practice.* Oxford: Clarendon, 1996.

Ministère des Relations avec les citoyens et de l'Immigration. *La Citoyenneté Québécoise. Document de consultation pour le Forum national sur la citoyenneté et l'intégration.* Quebec: Gouvernement du Quebec, 2001.

Mitchell, James. *Strategies for Self-Government.* Edinburgh: Edinburgh University Press, 1996.

Montpetit, Éric. "Les réseaux néo-corporatistes québécois à l'épreuve du fédéralisme canadien et de l'internationalisation," in *Québec: État et Société,* ed. Alain-G. Gagnon. Montreal: Québec-Amérique, 2002.

Noël, Alain. "Les Trois union sociales." *Policy Options* (November 1998): 26-29.

Offe, Claus. *The Contradictions of the Welfare State.* Cambridge: Cambridge University Press, 1984.

"Pas de consensus sur la citoyenneté québecoise." *La Presse,* September 23, 2000, A3.

Paterson, Lindsay. *The Autonomy of Modern Scotland.* Edinburgh: Edinburgh University Press, 1994.

———. "Scottish Democracy and Scottish Utopias: The First Year of the Scottish Parliament." *Scottish Affairs,* no. 33 (autumn 2000). Available at *http://www.scottishaffairs.org/onlinepub/sa/paterson_sa33_aut00.html* Accessed May 5, 2002.

Perrault, Laura-Julie. "On se reverra en cour! Brent Tyler juge illégitime le rapport Larose." *La Presse,* August 22, 2001.

Pierson, Paul. "When Effect Becomes Cause: Policy Feedback and Political Change." *World Politics,* Vol. 45 (1993): 595-628.

Polanyi, Karl. *The Great Transformation: The Political and Economic Origins of Our Time.* Boston: Beacon Press, 1957.

Proulx, Jean-Pierre. "Le Rapport Larose s'accroche a un but plus grand que lui." *Le Devoir,* August 28, 2001, p. A5.

Salmon, Trevor. "Oxymorons: The Scottish Parliament, the European Union and International Relations?" in *The Dynamics of Decentralization,* ed. Trevor C. Salmon and Michael Keating. Kingston: School of Policy Studies, 2001.

Scottish National Party. "Talking Independence" (February 2002) http://www.eksnp.org/independence/ Accessed May 15, 2002.

Secrétariat aux Affaires intergouvernementales canadiennes, Gouvernement du Québec. "Le Ministre Charbonneau annonce la création d'un secrétariat à la réforme des institutions démocratiques," press release, March 21, 2002. *http://www.mce.gouv.qc.ca/e/html/e2122001.html* . Accessed May 12, 2002.

Southam, Peter. "Réactions québécoises à l'État-providence en émergence : perspectives historiques." *Service Social*, Vol. 38. no. 2-3 (1989): 161-78.

Soysal, Yasemin. *The Limits of Citizenship: Migrants and Postnational Membership in Europe*. Chicago: University of Chicago Press, 1994.

Suridge, Paula. "Society and Democracy: The New Scotland," in *New Scotland, New Society?* eds. John Curtice, David McCrone, Alison Park and Lindsay Paterson. Edinburgh: Polygon, 2002.

Turgeon, Luc. "La grande absente: la société civile au coeur de la Révolution tranquille." *Globe: Revue internationale d'études québécoises*, Vol. 2, no. 1(1999): 35-56.

Turgeon, Luc, and Alain-G. Gagnon, "Managing Diversity in 18th and 19th Century Canada: Quebec's Constitutional Development in Light of the Scottish Experience." *Journal of Commonwealth and Comparative Politics* (forthcoming, 2003).

Wiener, Antje. *"European" Citizenship Practice: Building Institutions of a Non-State*. Boulder, CO: Westview Press, 1998.

notes on contributors

Alain-G. Gagnon is professor of political science at the Université du Quebec à Montréal, where he holds the Canada Research Chair in Quebec and Canadian Studies. He is also the co-ordinator of the Research Group on Multinational Societies. His most recent publications include *Ties That Bind. Parties and Voters in Canada* (with James Bickerton and Patrick Smith, 1999). He has edited *The Canadian Social Union without Quebec* (with Hugh Segal, 2000); *Multinational Democracies* (with James Tully, 2001); and *Repères en mutation* (with Jocelyn Maclure, 2001).

Montserrat Guibernau is senior lecturer in politics at the Open University and visiting fellow at the London School of Economics. Her main publications include *Catalan Nationalism: Francoism, Transition and Democracy* (2002); *Nations without States* (1999); and *Nationalisms: The Nation-State and Nationalism in the Twentieth Century* (1996). She has edited *Governing European Diversity* (2001); *Nationalism: Debates and Dilemmas for a New Millennium* (2000); *Understanding Nationalism* (with John Hutchinson, 2001); and *The Ethnicity Reader: Nationalism, Multiculturalism and Migration* (with John Rex, 1997). At present she is researching the ESRC-funded project, Regional Identity and European Citizenship, and preparing a book, "National Identity and its Future." She has taught at the universities of Cambridge, Warwick and Barcelona.

Michael Keating is professor of regional studies at the European University Institute and professor of Scottish politics at the University of Aberdeen. He has published abundantly on the subjects of local and regional politics and on nationalism. He is the author of *Plurinational Democracy: Stateless Nations in a Post-Sovereignty Era* (2001); and *Nations Against the State: The New Politics of Nationalism in Quebec, Catalonia and Scotland* (2001).

Peter A. Kraus is with the *Institut für Socialwissenshaften* at the Humbold-Universität zu Berlin. He specializes in the areas of the European Union, cultural pluralism and linguistic diversity. His work has been published in the *Archives européennes de sociologie/European Journal of Sociology* and the *Journal of Commonwealth Market Studies.*

André Lecours is assistant professor at Concordia University, Montreal. His research focuses on nationalism, with a particular focus on Belgium, Spain, Canada and the United Kingdom. He is currently conducting research on nationalism in relation to paradiplomacy and social policy. His research also involves developing and applying a new institutionalist persepective to nationalism. His work has been published in *Nationalism and Ethnic Politics, National Identities, Space and Polity,* the *Canadian Journal of Political Science* and the *Journal of Multilingual and Multicultural Development.*

John Loughlin is professor of politics at Cardiff University, Wales. He has held, or holds, visiting professorships or fellowships at the Institut d'études politiques, Paris; the European University Institute, Florence; and other European universities. He founded and for 11 years was managing editor of *Regional and Federal Studies.* Among his recent books are *Subnational Democracy in the European Union,* co-edited with M. Keating and K. Deschouwer (2001); and *Culture, Institutions and Regional Development: A Comparative Analysis* (2003).

Roderick A. Macdonald is F.R. Scott Professor of Constitutional and Public Law at McGill University, Montreal, where he was dean of law (1984-89). He was co-director of the Community Law Program at the University of Windsor (1976-79), chaired the Task Force on Access to Justice for the Ministère de la justice du Québec (1989-1991), served as director of the Law and Society Program of the Canadian Institute for Advanced Research (1989-1994), and participated in the Ontario Civil Justice Review (1995). He was elected to the Royal Society of Canada in 1996. He was founding president of the Law Commission of Canada (1997-2000).

Jocelyn Maclure is post-doctoral fellow at the Center for Research in Ethics at Université de Montréal/Department of Political Science, University of Toronto. He is currently working on public reason and social integration under conditions of pluralism. He has published, among other things, *Quebec Identity: The Challenge of Pluralism* (McGill-Queen's University Press, 2003).

David McCrone is professor of sociology at the University of Edinburgh and director of that university's Institute of Governance. His recent books include *Understanding Scotland: The Sociology of a Nation* (2001); *New Scotland, New Society?* (2001); *New Scotland: New Politics?* (2000); and *The Sociology of Nationalism: Tomorrow's Ancestors* (1998). He was a member of the Expert Panel that devised procedures and standing orders for the Scottish Parliament and was advisor to its Procedures Committee, which reviewed the Parliament's founding principles.

Kenneth McRoberts is principal and dean of Glendon College, York University, Toronto. He is also professor of political science. His publications include *Quebec: Social Change and Political Crisis* (1993); *Misconceiving Canada: The Struggle for National Unity* (1997); and *Catalonia: Nation-Building without a State* (2001). He has edited *Beyond Quebec: Taking Stock of Canada* (1995) and *The Charlottetown Accord, the Referendum and the Future of Canada* (with Patrick J. Monahan, 1993).

Luis Moreno is senior research fellow with the Spanish National Research Council (CSIC) in Madrid. His main research interests are the welfare state and social policy, and territorial politics. Recent works in the area of territorial politics include *The Federalization of Spain* (2001); "Ethnoterritorial Concurrence in Multinational Societies: The Spanish *comunidades autónomas*," in Alain-G. Gagnon and James Tully (eds.), *Multinational Democracies* (2001); and "Local and Global: Mesogovernments and Territorial Identities," in *Nationalism and Ethnic Politics* (1999).

Martin Papillon is a Ph.D. candidate in political science at the University of Toronto and a research associate with the Canadian Policy Research Networks (CPRN). His current research focuses on the transformation of citizenship regimes in multinational societies. He is co-author of, among other works, "Challenging the Citizenship Regime: The James Bay Cree and Transnational Action," *Politics and Society* (2000); "Parallel or Embedded? Aboriginal Self-Government and the Changing Nature of Citizenship in Canada," in G. Kernerman and P. Resnick (eds.), *Rethinking Citizenship: Essays in Honour of Alan C. Cairns* (forthcoming); and "The Weakest Link? First Ministers' Conferences in Canadian Intergovernmental Relations," in H. Lazar and H. Telford (eds.), *Canada: The State of the Federation* (forthcoming).

Ferran Requejo is professor of political science at the Universitat Pompeu Fabra in Barcelona. Among his recent works are "Federalism and the Quality of Democracy in Plurinational Contexts: Present Shortcomings and Possible Improvements," in U. Amoretti and N. Bermeo (eds.), *Federalism, Unitarianism and Territorial Cleavages* (2002); "Federalism and National Groups," *International Social Sciences Journal* (2001); "Political Liberalism in Multinational States: The Legitimacy of Plural and Asymmetrical Federalism," in A. Gagnon and J. Tully (eds.), *Multinational Democracies* (2001); "National Pluralism and Federalism: Four Political Scenarios for Spanish Plurinational Democracy," *Perspectives on European Politics and Society* (2001); "Cultural Pluralism, Nationalism, and Federalism: A Revision of Democratic Citizenship in Plurinational States," *European Journal for Political Research* (1999); *Zoom Polític: democràcia, federalisme i nacionalisme des d'una Catalunya europea* (1998); and *Federalisme, per a què?* (1998). He has edited *Democracy and National Pluralism* (2001); *European Citizenship, Multiculturalism and the State* (with U. Preuss, 1998); and *Asimetría Federal y Estado Plurinacional. El debate de la diversidad en Canadá, Bélgica y España* (with E. Fossas, 1999).

François Rocher is professor of political science at Carleton University in Ottawa, where he is also director of the School of Canadian Studies. He served as president of the Société québécoise de science politique (2001-2002) and co-editor of the *Canadian Journal of Political Science* (1996-99). His research centres on Canadian federalism, citizenship, and inter-ethnic relations in Canada. He is a member of the Research Group on Plurinational Societies and the Centre for Research on Immigration, Ethnicity and Citizenship. He is the editor of *New Trends in Canadian Federalism* (with Miriam Smith, 1995), as well as *Bilan québécois du fédéralisme canadien* (1992).

Michel Seymour is professor in the department of philosophy at Université de Montréal. He is the author of *Le pari de la démesure* (2001), for which he won the 2001 Richard-Arès prize; *La nation en question* (1999); and *Pensée, langage et communauté* (1994). He has edited *États-nations, multinations et organisations supranationales* (2002); *Nationalité, citoyenneté et solidarité* (1999); and *Une nation peut-elle se donner la constitution de son choix?* (1995); and co-edited *Rethinking Nationalism* (with Jocelyne Couture and Kai Nielsen, 1996). He is currently preparing a collection of essays entitled *The Fate of the Nation State* (forthcoming, McGill-Queen's University Press).

Stephen Tierney is a lecturer in law at the University of Edinburgh. His main research interests are constitutional law and international law. He is a member of the editorial board of *European Public Law*, and is rapporteur to the Committee on Theory and International Law of the International Law Association (British branch). His publications include "Devolution Issues and s.2(1) of the Human Rights Act," *European Human Rights Law Review* (2000); "Convention Rights and the Scotland Act: Redefining Judicial Roles," *Public Law* (2001); "Constitutionalising the Role of the Judge: Scotland and the New Order," *Edinburgh Law Review* (2001); and "The Search for a New Normativity: Thomas Franck, Post-Modern Neo-Tribalism and the Law of Self-Determination," *European Journal of International Law* (forthcoming). He has edited *Accommodating National Identity: New Approaches in International and Domestic Law* (2000) and contributed to and edited a special double edition of the *International Journal of Minority and Group Rights* (1999).

Luc Turgeon is a doctoral candidate in the Department of Political Science at the University of Toronto. His research looks principally at the relations between the state and society in Canada and in Great Britain, public policy of economic development and theories of constitutionalism and federalism. He has published articles in *Globe, Revue internationale d'études québécoises*, the *Journal of Commonwealth and Comparative Politics* and *Le Devoir*, and has forthcoming chapters in books on Quebec politics, democratic consolidation and transnational democracy.

Nadia Verrelli is a doctoral candidate in the political science department at Carleton University, Ottawa, in the areas of Canadian federalism and Canadian constitutional politics. More specifically, she focuses upon the influence of the Supreme Court of Canada on the conceptualization and evolution of Canadian politics as well as Quebec politics and the dynamics of the separatist movement.

MEMBER OF SCABRINI MEDIA

Quebec, Canada
2003